North American Monsters

North American Monsters

A Contemporary Legend Casebook

Edited by
David J. Puglia

Utah State University Press
Logan

Published by Utah State University Press
An imprint of University Press of Colorado
245 Century Circle, Suite 202
Louisville, Colorado 80027

The University Press of Colorado is a proud member of
the Association of University Presses.

The University Press of Colorado is a cooperative publishing enterprise supported, in part, by
Adams State University, Colorado State University, Fort Lewis College, Metropolitan State University of Denver, Regis University, University of Alaska, University of Colorado, University of
Denver, University of Northern Colorado, University of Wyoming, Utah State University, and
Western Colorado University.

∞ This paper meets the requirements of the ANSI/NISO Z39.48–1992 (Permanence of Paper)

ISBN: 978-1-64642-159-6 (paperback)
ISBN: 978-1-64642-160-2 (ebook)
https://doi.org/10.7330/9781646421602

Library of Congress Cataloging-in-Publication Data

Names: Puglia, David, editor.
Title: North American monsters : a contemporary legend casebook / David J. Puglia.
Description: Logan : Utah State University Press, 2021. | Series: Contemporary legend casebook
series | Featured folklorists include James P. Leary, Lee Haring, Mark Breslerman, Loren
Coleman, Michael Taft, Charlie Seemann, Angus Kress Gillespie, Norine Dresser, Hans-W.
Ackermann, Jeanine Gauthier, John Ashton, Elizabeth Tucker, Alan L. Morrell, Andrew Peck,
Mercedes Elaina Torrez, David Clarke, Gail de Vos, Lisa Gabbert, Carl Lindahl, and Benjamin
Radford. | Includes bibliographical references and index.
Identifiers: LCCN 2021035723 (print) | LCCN 2021035724 (ebook) | ISBN 9781646421596
(paperback) | ISBN 9781646421602 (ebook)
Subjects: LCSH: Monsters—North America—Case studies. | Folklore—North America—Case
studies. | Legends—North America—Case studies. | Urban folklore—North America—Case
studies.
Classification: LCC GR825 .N67 2021 (print) | LCC GR825 (ebook) | DDC 001.94407—dc23
LC record available at https://lccn.loc.gov/2021035723
LC ebook record available at https://lccn.loc.gov/2021035724

Support for this project was provided by a PSC-CUNY Award, jointly funded by The Professional Staff Congress and The City University of New York.

Cover illustrations: hand-drawn chupacabra by Benjamin Radford (*front*); early drawing of Sharlie, public domain image (*back*).

To Dr. Simon J. Bronner,
mentor extraordinaire.

Contents

Foreword

Elizabeth Tucker

I'M DELIGHTED TO WRITE A FOREWORD FOR THIS wonderful book, the second in our series of contemporary legend casebooks. When all of us on the executive board of the International Society for Contemporary Legend Research started this new series, we hoped to appeal to three kinds of readers: folklore scholars, current or former university students, and people who love legends. Belonging to all three of these categories, I can say that David Puglia has succeeded extremely well in showing what monsters mean to us. As he states in his letter to young Virginia in "Are There Monsters?" "[North America] would be a dreary place with no monsters." Monster legends both frighten and excite us, reminding us that the world holds more than we can easily understand. What is lurking in the shadows of our well-lit homes at night? And what is hiding under our beds, growling softly as it waits for us to fall asleep? We cannot know for sure, so when monster legends come up, we listen closely.

North American monster legends evoke thoughts of an earlier era. Settlers who came to North America from Europe were acutely aware of the dangers that might befall them. Bringing old stories of ravening sea serpents, dragons, and other monsters with them, they looked nervously over their shoulders as they explored *terra incognita*. And although this land was new to them, it was well known to Indigenous people, who had told stories about monsters since their own arrival in North America. Legends about the cannibal windigos and other fearsome creatures became familiar to settlers and then citizens of the United States, who told the stories to their children. At summer camps throughout the United States, counselors tell monster stories that show the influence of both Indigenous and European legends.

Most of the monsters described in this book are male; so are most of the authors of the chapters. Only six of the authors, including me, are female. Why are monsters so closely connected with masculinity in America?

https://doi.org/10.7330/9781646421602.c000a

Looking back at Greek mythology, we find both male and female monsters, but some of the scariest ones are female. When I was a child, I was horrified by Medusa, the Gorgon with snakes on her head whose eyes turned people to stone. Scylla and Charybdis, the monstrous rock and whirlpool sisters who caused countless shipwrecks, were pretty bad too. When I got a little older and discovered the Anglo-Saxon epic *Beowulf*, I learned about Grendel, the male monster who savagely killed men as they caroused in Hrothgar's hall. Although Grendel was a terrifying monster, his mother, who burst out of a lake to avenge her dead son, was even worse. Some societies emphasize masculinity in their monster legends more than others do. It is interesting to consider why North America is one of the areas where this happens.

In *Manly Traditions: The Folk Roots of American Masculinities* (2005), Simon J. Bronner and his contributors examine displays, performances, expressions, and texts that are associated with manliness. W.F.H. Nicolaisen's study of legend characters in Bronner's book makes the point that most killers, assailants, and other criminals in contemporary American legends are male, but some female legend characters commit crimes to avenge their victimization by men (rather like Grendel's mother). Further insight into characterization of men in legends comes from Jeannie Banks Thomas, who coined the term "extreme guy" in 2007. Extreme guys are aggressive, destructive, violent men who don't care whom they harm as long as they can express their turbulent feelings. Thomas identifies the female counterpart of the extreme guy as the "deviant femme," who acts eccentric or crazy because of terrible things that have happened to her. The deviant femme may commit crimes, destroying property and killing people, but usually she does this in response to an assault or injury.

It is important to recognize the work of Elaine J. Lawless, whose analysis of domestic violence narratives identifies monstrous behavior. In "The Monster in the House: Legend Characteristics of the 'Cycles of Violence' Narrative Prototype" (2002), Lawless explains that legends express shared values and fears. While collecting women's narratives about relationship violence that they had suffered, Lawless found that typical narratives about domestic violence tend to become contemporary legends. In legends about victims of domestic violence, the central male character is a monster who first seems to be a kind husband, partner, or boyfriend but suddenly becomes a menacing assailant or rapist. The horror of his attack comes from the shock of this rapid role reversal. Instead of being outside the home, which should make family members feel safe, this monster appears inside, scaring everyone who sees him. Lawless explains that women gain power by telling their own domestic violence narratives and sharing legends related to their own experiences or those of friends and relatives. Although telling a story does not make the monster less monstrous, it gives the teller a greater sense of understanding and control.

In other contexts as well, images of monsters arise when people feel fearful and worried. During the COVID-19 pandemic, adults and children identified the novel coronavirus as a metaphorical monster. In his television news show on CNN, *Cuomo Prime Time*, Chris Cuomo called the virus a "beast," explaining, "The beast comes out at night." In a similar vein, some parents warned their young children that "Rona" would get them if they didn't behave. Since this virus was so scary, so hard to locate, and so hard to understand, it fit the profile of a fledgling legendary monster perfectly. This rapid characterization of the virus as a monster showed how meaningful and important such frightening figures are to us today.

Metaphorical monsters are significant, but literal monsters take center stage in this eloquently written casebook. Whether they are shambling out of a swamp, swimming in a lake, or running after horrified humans, monsters fascinate and mystify us. Curiosity makes us want to learn more about them, but self-preservation makes us hesitate to get too close. Although monsters may seem quaint and exciting, they do not make comfortable companions.

Reading the excellent chapters that David Puglia has put together here, I marvel at the range of monster figures and the diversity of local and regional legends. The prefaces of all of the chapters are extremely insightful and witty; I read them with monstrous enjoyment. I am sure that other readers will enjoy the chapters and their prefaces as much as I have.

REFERENCES CITED

Bronner, Simon J., ed. 2005. *Manly Traditions: The Folk Roots of American Masculinities.* Bloomington: Indiana University Press.

CNN. "Chris Cuomo on life with Covid-19: The beast comes out at night." *YouTube* video, 10 minutes. April 3, 2020. https://www.youtube.com/watch?v=E1Ph8pKHISI.

Lawless, Elaine J. 2002. "The Monster in the House: Legend Characteristics of the 'Cycles of Violence' Narrative Prototype." *Contemporary Legend*, new ser., 5: 24–49.

Nicolaisen, W.F.H. 2005. "Manly Characters in Contemporary Legends: A Preliminary Survey." In *Manly Traditions: The Folk Roots of American Masculinities*, ed. Simon J. Bronner, 247–60. Bloomington: Indiana University Press.

Thomas, Jeannie Banks. 2007. "Gender and Ghosts." In *Haunting Experiences: Ghosts in Contemporary Folklore*, ed. Diane E. Goldstein, Sylvia Ann Grider, and Jeannie Banks Thomas, 81–110. Logan: Utah State University Press.

Preface

AS GENRE LITERATURE, MONSTERS SELL WELL; AS POPULAR nonfiction, they also boast something of a following; as academic literature, there is a noticeable gap; in folklore studies, there's a surprising absence. This casebook is an attempt to mind that gap, and begin to mend it, by mining those analytical and folkloristic treatments of legendary North American monsters.

My first aim for this casebook is to exhibit folklorists who have performed exemplary collection and documentation of local monster legends, and my second is to demonstrate their sophisticated analysis of the same. Some chapters presented here focus primarily on fieldwork or archival results, and several potential chapters were eliminated because they lacked analysis or interpretation. As a multidisciplinary endeavor, the best folkloristic essays apply historical, sociological, anthropological, psychological, and other critical perspectives in an attempt to deepen understanding of monster legends and the people who tell them. While many "monster" books exist, the goal and benefit of a casebook is to simultaneously reveal multiple approaches and perspectives, in this case, rooted in fieldwork and documented sources. This collection is meant to be diverse. In author and perspective, approach and methodology, geography and setting, theme and argument, the essays presented here cover an exciting array of North American monsters, joined together by an interest in living communities and an ethnographic approach. For a variety of readers, then, this collection should be of some use and interest: a rationale for monster study, a description of monsters and creatures across North America, a discussion of methods and theories for research, and a compendium of model studies.

One of the difficulties of monster research is finding a suitable starting point. Academics are said to stand on the shoulders of giants, but where are these giants found? The pursuit of these scattered scholarly giants, I have realized, becomes its own variety of monster hunting. Proper folkloristic monster studies are more likely to be found in small folklore journals than in large ones, just as likely to be out of print as to be digitized, sometimes piled amid conference proceedings or published as one-offs in affiliated disciplines' journals. Such, one might surmise, indicates the respectability of monster studies, even among folklorists, a coterie not known for putting

https://doi.org/10.7330/9781646421602.c000b

on airs. Locating the best of this scholarship can be a bewildering and time-consuming task, made even more difficult given the near–cottage industry of fabulists and pseudo-scientists cranking out monster fluff every year. But folklorists should not seek to reinvent the proverbial wheel. Scholarship begins where others' has ended, and that end at the moment, while far from being conclusive, constitutes a sizeable head start. In one volume, students of legendry will now find a representative sampling of the best that has been collected, thought, and written about North American legendary monsters in the twentieth and twenty-first centuries.

This casebook is intended for several audiences and several purposes, all close to my heart, all developed out of personal experience. First are active students, scholars, and researchers, from wide-eyed freshmen with pending term papers to grizzled tenured professors contemplating new articles, who would like to pursue the study of legendary monsters and creatures themselves and require a model and guide. I was once one of those students, and discovering, acquiring, and sorting through this scattered scholarship required extensive time and energy that nearly grizzled me. By collecting this scholarship, by making model case studies widely available, by showing the trending themes over the last half century, and by articulating approaches and methodologies, it is my hope that other researchers can spend less time in haphazard backstudy and more time building a large corpus of legendary monster research. And while the present focus is the monster and the folklorist, as folklorists themselves borrow freely from a number of disciplines, those allied fields—anthropology, sociology, history, cultural geography, belief studies, regional studies—may find this volume of use for infusing courses or research with a folkloristic perspective.

Another audience I have envisioned is a range of college folklore instructors, from those wishing to make monsters the basis of an introductory course to those simply responding to the desires of students. It's a hazard of the sheer breadth of folkloristics that a specialist in folk art or folk music may find a classroom demanding attention to Bigfoot and the chupacabra, or perhaps a folklorist newly appointed in New Jersey cannot escape the wings of the Jersey Devil, even if she would like to. These instructors need ready resources to meet student demand, and for that contingent, I offer this casebook as a "greatest hits" on the subject. At the other end of the spectrum, for instructors intrigued by the prospect of a monster-laden folklore course, it is my experience that legendary monsters prove to be worthy teaching assistants, not just as an introduction to legend but as an accessible and entertaining introduction to folklore methods and theories generally. Monsters are an ideal starting point for teaching folklore in the classroom, readily connecting to students' own preconceptions of folklore, and once a basis is established, instructors can digress, using demonstrated theories and methods as entry points into other folklore genres.

Instructors, both folklorists and those from affiliated disciplines, who teach courses that do dwell on monsters and belief—from more general courses on folk narrative, folk belief, or the supernatural to courses specifically on monsters and the monstrous—know monsters prove effective and worthwhile in the classroom. Monsters sell themselves, and these instructors will not need any of my attempts at persuasion to incorporate more monsters into their courses. That would be preaching to the converted. What they do need is a respectable corpus of model ethnographic case studies, exemplars from the field and from the archive, scholarly monster research from a folkloric and ethnographic perspective covering methods, theories, themes, and variants that, collectively, offer students broad immersion in the subject. And, I hope, based on the geographic diversity presented here, this book will offer the opportunity to include not just legendary monsters but *nearby* monsters as well.

The final intended audience is the monster enthusiast and general reader. This passionate lot deserves respect, as they, from hobbyist hunters to investigative journalists, often don the mantle of monster study long before academics arrive. They also deserve admiration for remaining enthusiastic despite being forced to sort through drivel, fiction portrayed as fact, outrageous theories, dubious sources, and outright fabrications. The essays presented here are all eminently readable, and I suspect the rigorous research methods and cited sources will be a refreshing reprieve from more questionable research and presentation practices. And those readers not concerned with folklore theory, historical origin, symbolism, or psychological introspection can sit back and enjoy the creativity of the North American imagination on full display as it whispers and wonders, boasts and guffaws about the menacing and amusing monsters of the American landscape.

The casebook presents, in chronological order, extant legendary monster scholarship. It emphasizes existing literature because the purpose of this work is to offer, in a coherent, organized manner, the legendary North American monster research folklorists have undertaken to this point, as it stands at the end of the first quarter of the twenty-first century: the full arc from start to finish. Even the original contributions expand upon research initiated long before I commissioned them, as conference presentations, side projects, or book-length studies. The essays flow in chronological order, each standing on its own, but each also reflecting back on previous essays, directly or indirectly, and anticipating upcoming chapters.

The chapter prefaces are meant to reveal legend scholarship gradually, connecting one legend to the next, but also to act as a legend primer, so that while interested readers progress through the monsters of North America, they also progress through the major concepts of legend scholarship, starting with the most basic principles and then branching off down the twisting and divergent paths of legend study. Novices, by the end of the casebook, will have encountered best practices for initiating their own monster study. Readers may or may not find persuasive any of the various theoretical attempts to illuminate North American monsters in tradition, but at the very least, they will come to understand that monsters are much more than simple, scary creatures of the North American mind. Monsters have been and continue to be complex factors in the lives of all those who chance upon or live among them—in reality, in fiction, or in folklore. While not every legendary North American monster could be included here, tragically, many accounts have yet to be written. And there is where my sincerest hope for this casebook lies: that it will assist students of legendary monsters in embarking on their own research, of a monster presented here, of one not yet covered, or in other legendary pursuits. May this sampling spur the study of legendary monsters forward in the twenty-first century.

Acknowledgments

IT'S A TIRED CLICHÉ IN ACKNOWLEDGMENTS THAT BOOKS are a collective effort, but it is a cliché I must resort to. This casebook has quite literally been a group endeavor, from conception to compilation and from writing to production: one that began years before I appeared. Credit goes to Elizabeth Tucker, a constant beacon of support, for recommending that the International Society for Contemporary Legend Research (ISCLR) start a book series and to Diane Goldstein for recommending that the series be a casebook series. For green-lighting the project, my thanks go to the esteemed ISCLR casebook editorial board, made up of Elizabeth Tucker, Diane Goldstein, Bill Ellis, Lynne McNeill, John Laudun, Elissa Henken, and Jeffrey Tolbert. Acquisitions editor Rachael Levay, who oversees the casebook series for Utah State University Press, was enthusiastic from the jump, and director Darrin Pratt and assistant editor Kylie Haggen also provided valuable assistance, as did other staff members of Utah State University Press and the University Press of Colorado. Robin DuBlanc provided expert copyediting. An extra shout-out to Lynne McNeill for a sneak preview of her and Libby's *Legend Tripping* manuscript, which offered a blueprint, and to Alan Dundes, a folklore casebook connoisseur, whose stunning array of casebooks was a personal inspiration that I returned to time and again.

I extend my sincerest gratitude to the officers and employees of a host of scholarly societies, academic journals, and university presses, all of whom supported this research in one way or another over the past half century. The list includes Ellen McHale, Laurie Longfield, the New York Folklore Society, and *New York Folklore* (in its many title manifestations); Paul Jordan-Smith, the Western States Folklore Society, and *Western Folklore*; Stephen Williams, Brian Carroll, and Indiana University Press; Jon Kay, the Hoosier Folklore Society, *Indiana Folklore*, and *Midwestern Folklore*; Valerie Nair and the University of British Columbia Press; ISCLR, *Contemporary Legend*, its current editors Ian Brodie and Andrea Kitta, and its secretary Elissa Henken; Ivan Babanovski and the University of Wisconsin Press;

Angela Burton and the University of Illinois Press; and Ann Ferrell, Jessica Turner, the American Folklore Society, and the *Journal of American Folklore*. I'd also like to thank the many archives, repositories, and universities that keep endangered materials available, especially Open Folklore, Hathi Trust, Indiana University, the University of California, the University of Michigan, and the Utah State University Digital Repository.

Others assisted with timely answers to questions along the way: Robert Cochran at the Center for Arkansas and Regional Studies, Paulette Goldweber at Wiley-Blackwell, Joe McManis at the Lily Library at Indiana University, Christina Barr at Nevada Humanities, Steve Winick at the American Folklife Center, and Sheila Ashton, wife of the late John Ashton. I would like to thank Penn State Libraries for digging up many obscure research articles and CUNY Libraries for lending hard-to-find books. Funding for the project was provided by the CUNY Research Foundation, PSC CUNY, and the Bronx Community College Foundation, and Rolly Wiltshire, Freda Paterson, and the RF CUNY staff helped me realize that funding. I presented portions of this casebook at the Cryptozoology Conference in Monroe, New Jersey, at the Eastern American Association Conference in Summersdale, Pennsylvania, and at the Perspectives on Contemporary Legend Conference in Memphis, Tennessee, and I thank all panelists and audience members who patiently listened and offered comment and critique. I benefited especially from the words, ideas, and general brilliance of Eleanor Hasken and Paul Manning.

A tip of the hat to my lovely Bronx Community College colleagues for their collegiality, especially the once overlooked but never unappreciated Jillian Hess: romantic scholar, devoted teacher, and assessor extraordinaire. A firm slap on the back goes to Julia Rodas for assistance with the concept of "monstrous," recommending a talented indexer (Paula Durbin-Westby), and enhancing department life in general, and to Robert Beuka and Kathleen Urda for endless letter writing, tireless form signing, and lots of jovial support. For both academic and life support, I'd like to acknowledge Simon J. Bronner (my mentor), Libby Tucker (my stepmentor), my parents Shelley Jimeson and Ray Puglia (my lifelong mentors), and Mira Johnson (my spousal mentor). The book cover creature comes thanks to my buddy Benjamin Radford, who supplied the original chupacabra field sketch he drew based on the eyewitness testimony of Madelyne Tolentino. Daniel Pratt designed the cover. Artist and childhood friend Matt Long advised me on the internal images. Simon Bronner and Libby Tucker both read early drafts of the glossary: any pithy genius is theirs; all blunders are mine.

And, of course, I thank the contributors—nay, all monster research-ers, here and beyond, past, present, and future. Without the contributors, a casebook is nothing more than a good idea. In fact, I'm acutely aware that, while my name graces the cover, my words constitute only a mere third of the book. I corresponded directly with all living reprinted contributors, and all gave full-hearted endorsement to this casebook and the reprinting of their monster scholarship within. (The writer scared to share his work with others is a common trope—now consider the courage necessary to allow a new generation to appraise something you wrote while Richard Nixon was in office). So my sincere thanks go to James P. Leary, Lee Haring, Mark Breslerman, Loren Coleman, Michael Taft, Charlie Seemann, Angus Kress Gillespie, Norine Dresser, Hans-W. Ackermann, Jeanine Gauthier, John Ashton, Elizabeth Tucker, Alan L. Morrell, Andrew Peck, and Mercedes Elaina Torrez. And to the commissioned contributors, David Clarke, Gail de Vos, Lisa Gabbert, Carl Lindahl, and Benjamin Radford: you were a pleasure to work with, an inspiration to read, and a blessing to know. Other monster authors not featured in this volume, you deserve thanks as well—you are here in spirit, your words and ideas influencing these chapters, even if your essay was a little too long or your topic a wee bit too monster-adjacent to make it between these covers. And finally, I'd like to recog-nize readers and future researchers, who make such a collection a worthy endeavor: thank you.

Are There Monsters?

Dear Editor:

Some of my friends tell me there are no monsters. Please tell me the truth. Are there monsters in North America?

—Virginia

Yes, Virginia, there are monsters in North America. They exist as certainly as fear and anxiety and apprehension of the unknown exist. It would be a dreary place with no monsters—no Jersey Devil flying over the Pine Barrens, no Goatman trotting through the Maryland woods, no Sharlie gliding through Payton Lake. The cosmic horror that fills us with the dread of darkness would be all but extinguished.

Not believe in monsters? You might as well not believe in Satanic child sacrifices, the headlight initiation rites of gang members, or vanishing hitchhikers. You might pay a team of monster hunters to bring their night vision cameras and EMF meters, but even if they come up with nothing but grainy video and ambiguous noises, what would that prove? Nobody captures high-definition photographs of monsters, but that's no sign that there aren't monsters. The most real thing in the world is a creature that can send a tingle up your spine and sweat beading down your neck without you ever seeing it. Did you ever see the bogeyman hiding in your closet? Of course not, but that's no proof that he wasn't there. Nobody can conceive or imagine all the horrors that are unseen and unseeable in this world.

You may tear apart the accounts of a witness and speculate what's within—a fabulist, a prankster, an inebriate—but there is a mist saturating the outer fringes of our world that even the most rational human can never fully disperse. Legend inhales that mist and exhales the disquiet and unease of those peripheries.

Are monsters real? Ah, Virginia, in all this world there is nothing more real and abiding than the lurking terror of creatures who live outside the rules and boundaries of civilization. No monsters! They live now, and they live forever. A thousand years from now, Virginia, nay, ten times ten thousand years from now, they will continue to torment the human psyche.

Sincerely,
David J. Puglia
New York, New York

https://doi.org/10.7330/9781646421602.c000c

North American Monsters

Introduction

Legendary North American Monsters

David J. Puglia

NORTH AMERICANS LIVE AMONG LURKING LEGENDARY monsters who hide in thick forest groves, along dark country roads, beneath shimmering lakes—palpable but intangible, like wind rustling leaves. These monsters swim, slither, scamper, and soar across the continent, haunting peripheries, their legends preceding them. They bedevil a strange "New World," one where newcomers encountered unfamiliar inhabitants, peculiar flora, frightening fauna. In the Age of Discovery, explorers were primed to see monsters everywhere in the Americas. Christopher Columbus received reports of cannibals, Cyclopes, singled-breasted Amazon warriors, and dog-headed humanoids; Ferdinand Magellan found naked giants singing and dancing in Patagonia.[1] Indeed, some scholars argue that colonizers saw the native inhabitants as monsters themselves, or at the very least subhuman, a belief that permitted their subjugation and the conquest of their land.[2] Europeans also crossed paths with unfamiliar species, like opossums (which conquistador Vicente Yáñez Pinzón deemed a "strange Monster") and manatees (which Columbus mistook for mermaids "not so beautiful as they are painted, though to some extent they have the form of a human face").[3] As pioneers penetrated into still more distant lands, legends of monsters flourished: yeahohs in the Appalachians, thunderbirds along the Mississippi, sea serpents off the coasts. In later years, more reports emerged: the Jersey Devil gliding over the Pine Barrens, Champ knifing through Lake Champlain, Cropsey stalking the Catskill Mountains.

The study of monsters boasts a long history, dating at least as far back as Pliny the Elder (AD 23–79), who wrote in his *Natural History* of monsters populating faraway lands and the edges of civilization: monsters, it seems, as manifestations of ethnocentrism and xenophobia.[4] During the Enlightenment, scientists pursued "teratology," the study of monstrous births.[5] Throughout the twentieth century, scholars offered analyses of monsters embedded in literary and ethnographic case studies as part of larger inquiries into myth, folktale, and ritual.[6] In the late twentieth century,

https://doi.org/10.7330/9781646421602.c000d

the thematic field of "monster theory" or, alternatively, "monster studies" was born, a multidisciplinary venture similar to other thematic fields like American studies, women's studies, or gender studies, equally broad in mandate but more lightly institutionalized. Often cited as the genesis for the field is the 1996 edited collection *Monster Theory: Reading Culture*, a volume that editor Jeff Jerome Cohen himself later glossed as inquiry into "the cultural work that the monstrous accomplishes" (2013, 452).[7] While not the beginning of the study of monsters, it marked the dawn of an era of concerted and unified cross-disciplinary effort to understand monsters and the monstrous.

Monster studies' subject (that is, monsters) can be found almost everywhere—from ancient myth to science fiction—and almost anything could conceivably be viewed as a monster, from anarchists (Gabriel 2007) to failed subway systems (Cohen 2013, 464). Monsters are particularly prolific in world folklore. Folklorists' interest in monsters, in fact, predates the formal organization of monster studies and, for that matter, predates the formal organization of folkloristics, if we acknowledge the full body of narratives and motifs folklorists have traditionally monitored. Note, for example, how the *Motif-Index of Folk-Literature* (Thompson 1955–1958) elucidates with ease the traditionality of Yeti (or Abominable Snowman) lore by linking its core motifs to still older world lore. Bacil F. Kirtley, in his essay on the abominable snowman (1964), references several motifs from the *Motif-Index* that encompass the building blocks of that monster legend: F433.1, Spirit of snow; F436, Spirit of cold; F441.3, Wild man as wood spirit; F460, Mountain spirits; F521.1, Man covered with hair like an animal; F567 (type 502), Wild man; F567.1, Wild woman (77f). While not always rigorously analyzed, monsters have blipped on folklorists' metaphorical radar since the advent of their discipline.

These alluring legendary monsters, feared and beloved by the communities that host them, continue to attract the interest of folklorists, who see significance in such community-curated narrative belief traditions. Folkloristic studies of legendary American monsters based in ethnographic fieldwork, with the necessary attention to context, variants, and narrative performance, are still rare, but model studies do exist, and such case studies offer exemplary approaches to studying local legendary monsters. This casebook exhibits these methods by mining a dispersed vein of folklore journals and books and excavating a collection of essays that demonstrates notable legendary monster research and encourages future scholarly monster pursuits.[8] Avoiding North American ghosts and spirits, a more prolific subgenre, in favor of ostensibly living creatures strongly tied to particular geographic areas, this volume offers nineteen such gems, folkloristic case studies from the last half century of specific monsters in their native habitats.[9]

Despite teetering on the "triviality barrier" (Sutton-Smith 1970), monster matters have proven popular with a broad segment of society, and thus, necessarily, this volume's chapters feature a wide variety of scholars from a diversity of backgrounds, ranging from cryptozoologist Loren Coleman to skeptic Benjamin Radford, all bound by commitment to a folkloristic approach. Most contributors, however, are dyed-in-the-wool folklorists, interested in neither promoting nor debunking but rather in investigating, listening to, and reflecting on community-sustained monster narrative and belief. Within this folkloristic subset, there are assorted approaches, from archival to ethnographic and from historical to digital. My hope is that this casebook will reignite scholarly interest in the study of local legendary monsters and fan the flames of folkloristic monster legend research, theory, and method throughout the classroom, the academy, and the general public.

MONSTER STUDIES AND FOLKLORE STUDIES

The legendary monster is frightening yet fascinating. Most are familiar with monsters through novels, short stories, comic books, television, and film, monsters in media that lurk on distant islands, creep out of lagoons, ascend from the bottom of the sea. But monsters didn't originate in mass media. Literary and motion picture monsters are secondary, deriving from a long history of legends found across the globe. It's these traditional monster legends that provide the source for endless literary and film depictions of this particular representation of horror. And far from a static tradition or a historic anomaly, legendary monsters continue today to be invented, modified, and reconstituted in communities across the United States through the endlessly creative folklore processes of repetition, variation, and re-creation.

These monsters menace; they threaten wayward travelers, amorous lovers, and cherubic campers alike. But monsters also amuse; their accounts delight listeners around wooded campfires, in campus dormitories, and on dark country roads. Of course, monsters exist not only in legend but in myth, fairytale, literature, and film as well: in myth live Hydra, Cerberus, sphinxes, and Cyclopes; in folktale, dragons and ogres and the Big Bad Wolf; in literature, Frankenstein's monster, Grendel, and Cthulu; and in film, King Kong, Godzilla, and the Creature from the Black Lagoon. Legends inspire media monsters, and media monsters influence legends. But in this casebook, the authors scrutinize only the legendary variety: vampires and zombies, Slender Man and Bigfoot. And it's these monsters, folklorists argue, that are of the greatest importance because such legends require a committed community to sustain them, and for a group to expend such energy, its monsters must hold significant meaning. While legendary monsters are easily overlooked, folklorists contend that deciphering patterns of meaning in such folkloric texts offers a valuable window into raw, uncensored everyday life, into group values, and into contemporary worldviews.

One of the goals of this casebook, therefore, is to demonstrate how folkloristic and legendary monster studies approaches can benefit the larger umbrella discipline of monster studies, a field in which folklorists—and anthropologists, for that matter (Musharbash and Presterudstuen 2014, 2020)—feel underrepresented. At present, the bulk of academic scholarship devoted to monsters has tended to concentrate on literary and popular culture manifestations, offering scant attention to their folkloristic underpinnings. The present casebook is an attempt to redress that disparity. In response to this perceived imbalance, literary monsters such as Frankenstein's or Dracula will be mentioned only in passing; there are plenty of books and articles devoted to those novels alone. This collection of essays is specifically designed instead to treat traditional, not mass media, monsters, except in the few cases where authors examine how the media co-opt or spawn legendary monsters.[10]

In 2014, anthropologist Yasmine Musharbash detailed how anthropology and monster studies had yet to fully collaborate to one another's mutual benefit. In comparison to anthropological perspectives, she argued, much of monster studies appeared unnecessarily limited: its media-of-choice—novels, films, and television—and its subject matter preoccupied with zombies, vampires, and werewolves (2). Anthropologists, she promised, could offer monster studies examples from beyond the realm of popular media, from beyond the West, and from field sites where monsters are encountered in the "real world." In this ethnographic endeavor, folklorists can help.

While folklore and anthropology are separate fields with distinct missions, the two have shared an alliance from their inceptions, and folklorists can assist anthropologists in their mission to broaden the field of monster studies; monster studies, in return, will profit from a greater embrace of folkloristic inquiry. Folklorists offer to monster studies an intellectual heritage similar to anthropologists', that is, a concern with monsters as they are found in the field, in oral tradition, and as carried on and curated by communities. While anthropologists contribute by offering monsters beyond the West, folklorists offer the extreme opposite: not the unfamiliar but the familiar, not monsters from afar but monsters lurking in their own backyards. The monsters folklorists encounter aren't exotic creatures; many are hyperlocals. As it happens, in this casebook, several authors are so familiar with their monsters that their chapters begin by reflecting on and recounting verbatim the monster lore of their childhood.[11]

Folkloristic methods offer monster studies the means to demonstrate the ubiquity and diversity of monster tradition and how the monsters and the monstrous are conceived and perceived at the local level. A folkloristic approach allows for a nuanced, flexible, and sensitive understanding of monster traditions, conceptions that permit the meaning of monsters to change over time and space. Folklorists can expand, improve, and invigorate the already thriving thematic discipline of monster studies by offering ethnographic attention to monster tradition, by capturing and appreciating local understandings of monsters and the monstrous, and by providing careful, detailed attention to continuity and change in monsters and their relation to eras and to landscapes.

Monster studies, in return, offers folklorists the opportunity to think more deeply about definitions of monsters and characteristics of the monstrous, about how such categories are constructed, and about their social and political implications. Some folklorists' most rigorously fieldworked essays remain light on interpretation; monster studies can assist field-weary folklorists by demonstrating best practices in analysis and interpretation of these same diligently researched monster legends. The mere label of "monster studies" encourages grander theories and cross-cultural comparison of phenomena that might not otherwise be intellectually linked, and the comparison of which could prove profitable for all parties involved. As an interdisciplinary endeavor, folklorists and their monster studies partners both benefit from mutual engagement, as the chapters in this casebook hope to demonstrate.

MONSTER DEFINITIONS REAL AND IMAGINARY, BELIEVABLE AND UNBELIEVABLE

An introduction to a book on monsters should attempt to offer a definition of the term *monster,* but monsters are notoriously difficult to define. Many scholars are content to leave their monster definitions malleable; suggesting the exact nature of the monster is less important than the insights into culture that nightmarish, non-normative beings provide. I will attempt to offer my own tentative definition, but before I do so, I would like to divulge what's perhaps a monster studies dirty secret: most academic monster books skirt the issue, refusing to offer clear definitions or offering admittedly flimsy ones. Stephen T. Asma, for example, in *On Monsters*, writes honestly in his epilogue, "One will search in vain through this book to find a single compelling definition of monster. That's not because I forgot to include one, but because I don't think there is one" (2009, 281–82). Peter Dendle sees the term *monster* as inherently unstable, "partially semantic" (2013, 439), and suggests that "by definition it remains at the boundary of epistemological comfort, even as science progresses and taxonomies continue to shift and evolve" (440). W. Scott Poole in his *Monsters in America* also refuses to give a straightforward monster definition, instead warning the reader to "not expect neat definitions when it comes to a messy subject like monsters" (2011, xiv). Michael Dylan Foster prefers to leave his definition "open-ended" (2008, 2). And Jeffrey Andrew Weinstock theorizes monsters form "a loose and flexible epistemological category that allows us a space to define that which complicates or seems to resist definition" (2020, 5). Further complicating definitions, "monsters" make useful metaphors; those researchers who include metaphorical monsters chance inviting almost any phenomenon or concept that is large, scary, frightening, grotesque, or non-normative.

To fulfill its elementary mission, I believe this casebook needs to risk, at the very least, a tentative working "monster" definition. The challenge, then, is to offer something serviceable while simultaneously avoiding ensnarement in unsatisfactory criteria. For my own definitional attempt, I plan to do a bit of skirting and a dash of equivocating, prefaced at the outset with some navel gazing and hairsplitting, as I review how critics have crafted "monster" definitions and quibble with the criteria and their minute implications.

At this point in any scholarly monster book, as we attempt to come to a definition, it's common convention to pause and relate the etymological history of the word *monster*. The term consistently notes those beings that are considered strange or unnatural; "monster" comes to us from the Latin *monstrum*, stemming from the root *monere*, "to warn." Of particular interest to legend scholars is that this root, incidentally, dovetails with one prime function of contemporary legend, on the topic of monsters or otherwise, to *warn*, with urgency and immediacy, of lurking dangers.[12] In English, what we call monsters can also be referred to as beasts, fabulous beings, or bogeymen, and nuanced variants can be labeled ogres, giants, goblins, demons, mutants, or freaks, each possessing subtle shades of specificity. The *Oxford English Dictionary* offers little to narrow down the subject. It tells us that a monster is "a large, ugly, and frightening imaginary creature," "a thing of extraordinary or daunting size," or "a congenitally malformed or mutant animal or plant." It can also be used to refer to cruel adults or unruly children. Dictionary definitions are especially inapt for legendary monsters in North America. North American legendary monsters are plausible, not purely imaginary. They can be large, but needn't be. Some are scary, but many are comic. Some have religious roots, but most are secular, not sacred. And while they can be naughty, as Foster writes, monsters are "not necessarily defined by bad behavior" (2015, 136).

Indeed, one simple but effective dealing with monster definition is Foster's, who tentatively offers that a monster is a "weird or mysterious creature," but with the caveat that monsters are "more complicated and more interesting than these simple characteristics suggest" (2015, 5).[13] Anthropologist Marjorie M. Halpin was comfortable including "all beings or creatures which human beings have reported from their experience but which have not been catalogued as real by natural science" (1980, 5). Canadian folklorist Carole Carpenter, for one, preferred the term "extraordinary beings" to avoid the connotation of large and evil, features that many legendary monsters don't possess (1980, 107). Folklorist Richard M. Dorson constructed his own *American* legendary monster classification, which included six parts (1982, 12–14), briefly summarized:

1. They have a life in oral tradition (even if folklorists are left wanting for field-recorded texts).
2. They "inspire belief and conviction" but also "hilarity and tomfoolery."
3. They "endured for a considerable period of modern history."
4. They've become personalized, institutionalized, adopted by chambers of commerce, and have their own "charisma."
5. They are all mythical, fanciful, or "legendary"—they can't be captured, but possess their own "reality" by being part of community knowledge.
6. They have a comical side, which makes them "endearing."

Foster muses that perhaps the only way to define a monster is to list examples and to offer overviews of their general tendencies (2015, 8), and this approach has crossed the minds of many academics struggling with monster definitions. Dendle, for example, suggests researchers could attempt to study monsters by studying the word itself, and perhaps related words, searching over the centuries for the creatures those words have referred to (2013, 438–39). While such an endeavor may prove a Herculean task, one related practical approach would be to define monsters according to how authors use the term in one particular collection. That is, a

"monster" is the subject covered in a book on monsters. While such definitional equivocating is usually tongue-in-cheek, were it appropriate anywhere, a multi-authored casebook *might* be the venue. But even with this
possibility of a strictly limited notion of monster in mind, I will continue to
hold off on my definition for now while considering the criteria of real and
imaginary and believed and not believed.

REAL OR IMAGINARY?

One concerning tendency is defining monsters as inherently fictional,
imaginary, or nonexistent—impracticable criteria for *legendary* monsters,
or "cryptids," who are presumed (but not proven) to exist.[14] Considering
definitional features, Asa Simon Mittman, for example, writes in his introduction to *Monsters and the Monstrous*, "Monsters, of course, do not exist"
(2013, 4) and that a monster is "that which is horrible, but *does not actually
exist*" (5; his emphasis). Anthropologist David Gilmore in his *Monsters* study
"confine[s] usage to supernatural, mythical, or magical products of the
imagination," summarizing that "for our purposes the, monsters are *imaginary, not real*, embodiments of terror" (2003, 6; my emphasis). And devel-
opmental psychologist Jacqueline D. Woolley states directly, "Monsters, by
definition, are not real" (1999, 440).[15] Similarly, but with more nuance, the
preface to *Manlike Monsters on Trial* opens with the confirmation that "officially, scientifically, it [the manlike monster] does not exist" (Ames and
Halpin 1980, xiii).

But is this something of a No True Monster fallacy? While "fictional,"
"imaginary," or "nonexistent" might be central to some definitions, many
monster critics, especially those of a folkloric or anthropological persuasion, take issue with such ontological considerations as defining features
(e.g., see Dendle 2013, 440; Hufford 1977, 234; Goldstein, Grider, and
Thomas 2007, 14–17). Dendle asks us to consider a thought experiment:
"Even if a colossal, hitherto unknown species suddenly rose from the
oceans and began destroying coastal cities, it would only be called a 'monster'—it could only have the ineffable mystery of a monster—during the
crisis and its immediate aftermath. Over time, once it was categorized,
dissected, and integrated into contemporary taxonomies, it would simply
be regarded as an animal. We would still tell our children monsters don't
exist" (2013, 441). We can take Dendle's perceptive thought experiment
further, using a more plausible scenario, to demonstrate how, in at least
some instances, an unknown, frightening animal is phenomenologically the
same as a legendary monster.

You are stomping through the woods on a solo thru-hike. You will have no contact with the outside world for several days. You are charged by a ferocious creature you can't identify (in fact, a mangy, hairless bear), a beast you have never seen or encountered before. You escape, but for the next few days, out of contact with civilization, you feel the creature following you, you worry it's hot on your trail, and even though you cannot see it, you flee from it anyway. You offer dire warnings to passing hikers about your terrifying close encounter. And those wary hikers then pass along the warning to still more hikers.

For those hikers, what's the difference between a legendary monster and any other scary, unfamiliar animal?

If we are willing to accept a flexible definition of monsters that includes even the known (if rarely seen) animal world, there are plenty of fearsome-looking, possibly aggressive, potentially deadly "monsters" that, faced in the wild, would be little different than chancing upon a legendary monster. I use a mangy, hairless bear here (trust me—Google it), but I think a black mamba, a great white, or a man-of-war could all evoke a similar response. Dendle agrees that "probably nothing comes closer to a core notion of the 'monstrous' as an intimate and almost numinous sense of helplessness before the elemental and uncaring dangers of a savage world, such as unexpected animal attacks or instances of psychopathic violence. These are phenomenologically real" (Dendle 2013, 441). In this way, some monsters do exist; they are simply recategorized over time: monsters upon first contact, classified creatures thereafter. At the very least, monsters as an *experience* certainly exist.[16]

Elaborating on definitional slippage from an anthropological perspective, Musharbash writes that we can "capitalize on the elementary instability of the term monster which allows it to adjust to the ontology of it users" (2014, 5). In fact, contemporary usage of the term allows for both ontological and epistemological ground shifting. As Jeannie Banks Thomas reminds us, additional definitional difficulties lie in folklorists' distaste for universals, preferring instead to deal with emic understandings of those beings that particular groups choose to place in such cultural categories (2015, 18). A medievalist in addition to a monster specialist, Dendle observes how strange it is to include "fictional" as part of the definition of monsters, considering that such a designation isn't only questionable in our time, it also contradicts the term's usage in past eras (2013, 442). Dendle contends that one problem with attempting to define the monster is that the monster lives its life "at the boundary of epistemological comfort" (442) or, in other words, like monsters themselves, monster definitions elude us because they always creep just beyond our comfort zone.

Approaching monsters as experience rather than "real" or "imaginary" corresponds with the trajectory of folkloristics in the twenty-first century. Folklorists undertook a gradual journey over the twentieth century, resituating folkloristics from studying folklore as text to examining folklore as process, with an added emphasis on behavior and performance: from ballads to the singing of ballads, from superstition to invoking superstitions, from legends to telling legends. Monsters, too, are undergoing this theoretical shift, from monsters to "monsterizing" (Weinstock 2020, 39–44)— that is, in the phenomenological sense, monsters, too, are created in the telling. Monster studies has critiqued "monsters" as a taken for granted cultural category, one that demands more rigorous, analytic investigation. Critical approaches have resituated the monster from a natural, neutral, or static classification to one constructed of difference, from monster to monsterization. In this conception, monsters are not "found" but rather constructed through cultural processes of power relations and social differences, tools of resistance or domination, a politics of monsters. A creature, thereby, is not a monster in any eternal, essential, or universal sense. Rather, humans monsterize, casting some as monsters, some as not in perceptions shifting over time and space. Weinstock argues that the cornerstone of contemporary monster studies is this social construction of monsters to reflect anxiety and desire and "wittingly or not—to achieve particular sociopolitical objectives" (39). And here folklorists might take heed while also adding their disciplinary history and knowledge to this conversation.

The 1960s and 1970s reconceptualized folklore from static text to behavior, performance, and context, from constant to emergent.[17] So too can folkloristic conceptions of monsters move from text to process, from monsters to monsterization, formed and re-formed daily through continual social negotiation. In this formulation, scholars do best to avoid taking monsters for granted, instead systematically examining their construction, invention, and re-creation and investigating their continuity and change, their preservation and transformation. Folklorists can overcome the unnecessary definitional criterion of "imaginary" by exploring the "monsterizing" concept while at the same time continuing to emphasize the monsterization of literal monsters over metaphorical ones, ostensibly real monsters over overtly fictitious ones, and vernacular monsters over popular ones.

In response to "Are monsters real?" the necessary follow-up question is "What does the questioner mean by 'monster'?" Explorers who had never seen an opossum before, for example, labeled it a monster (see Eastman 1915; Parrish 1997). Explorers *monsterized* opossums, and they were then referred to as such by others. Opossums, we know, are real. The same is true for the *tanuki*, or the Japanese raccoon dog, which is both an animal (Nyctereutes procyonoides viverrinus) and a Japanese monster (see Foster 2015, 186–93). Tanukis, too, are real. Tanukis, too, are monsterized. Now if the questioner actually means "Do creatures that by definition don't really exist really exist?" then the answer is, of course, no. Monsters that are inherently imaginary can't exist. But if the question is "Do monsters exist?" then the answer is yes: monsters, at least some monsters, historically and circumstantially, do exist. I will attempt to avoid, therefore, any qualifications of real or imaginary in my impending legendary monster definition.

TO BELIEVE OR NOT TO BELIEVE?

A corollary to whether monsters exist is whether people *believe* in monsters. Indeed, one of the central and differentiating concepts for legendary monsters is belief. In attempts to define legend or superstition, for example, folklorist David Hufford emphasizes that, regardless of content, the overriding characteristic is that such materials are said to "be believed" (1977, 234). Such a definition, in regard to monsters at least, presents a conundrum. Mittman, for one, recognizes that "whether we believe or disbelieve the existence of a phenomenon is not what grants it social and cultural force" (2013, 6). Folklorists and legend scholars can be useful here by advancing more complex and nuanced perspectives to this aspect of the debate. Folklorists are the first to proclaim that the factuality of a monster legend isn't of greatest import; rather, possibility and plausibility are the key to *legendary* monsters. Possibility is what makes monsters *legendary*, as opposed to mere folktales. "Legendary monsters" are by definition possibly or plausibly real.

Older explanations were likely to be dismissive of belief, or what Hufford refers to as "What I know I *know*, what you know you only *believe*" (1982, 47–48). Folklorist Louis C. Jones, a respected and impressive collector of New York supernatural materials, for example, opens his preface to the new edition of *Things That Go Bump in the Night* assuring readers he is not a believer (1983, vi). French folklorist Michel Meurger attributes sightings to cultural reworkings of visionary experiences (1989). And Bacil F. Kirtley, in one of the earliest legendary monster articles published in *Western Folklore*, hypothesized informants do not deliberately lie, but rather "translated experiences which perhaps were baffling and disturbing, short-circuited from the empirically defined mental world of normative reality into the realm of myth" (1964, 87–88), concluding that even the most believable reports "are simply myths and emanate from persons who have made distorted

interpretations of their own experiences" (89). These explanations no longer satisfy folklorists, nor did they always in the past; famed British folklorist and anthropologist Andrew Lang complained that we are "bullied
by common-sense into accepting feeble rationalizations" (Lang 1894, 173,
cited in Bennett, 1999, 32).

Accordingly, a more nuanced understanding of "belief" is a contribution folklorists can proffer to monster studies. Where there is legend, there
is always some element of belief, as legend operates as "potential fact"
(Ellis 2003, 6). Musharbash (2014) notes how anthropologists (folklorists'
closest allies in belief endeavors) are no strangers to investigating belief in
culturally relative and emic terms. Or as another anthropologist, Michael
M. Ames, writes, "Anthropologists are more at ease dealing with the realm
of beliefs, with the cultural rather than the natural existence of anomalous
creatures" (1980, 303). Purely metaphoric readings ring hollow to field-
workers who see monsters "alive" in the field, stirring a community. Indeed,
the exploration of the nature of reality is another of legend's prime functions, and folklorists take legendary monsters and all supernatural beliefs
seriously, investigating them analytically as significant and plausible cultural
texts. It's this understanding of a monster's reality that folklorists can offer
to monster studies.

Legendary monsters differ from popular or literary monsters: legendary monsters must hold some possibility of existence and some vague communal agreement of physical description, topographic territory, and motive.
Left implicit, however, and according to Hufford equally important, is *who*
does the believing (e.g., see Hufford 1977). The scholars themselves who
hunt out such legends, capture them, and analyze them often don't *believe*
them. In truth, this stance is, at times, the fieldworker's default position. The
collector finds such legends interesting *because* the stories feel personally
unbelievable. Such preconceptions presume the collector is more in touch
with reality than the informant, and thus a legendary monster becomes
any reported creature that the informant "believes" exists that the collector "knows" does not. To counter this fallacy, Hufford encourages an
"experience-centered" approached to studying such belief traditions (e.g.,
see Hufford 1982). Such a phenomenological approach avoids a default
state of disbelief, focusing instead on the relationship between belief and
experience. An overriding thesis in Hufford's oeuvre is that consistent features in narrative belief reports prove many folk beliefs to be accurate,
rational, and reasonable accounts of actual experiences.[18]

But *nobody* believes in monsters anymore, right? *Wrong.* Scientific progress and technological advancement were supposed to kill off beliefs in

monsters, ghosts, and the supernatural, ushering in an era of rationality and enlightenment.[19] They didn't. British folklorist Karl Bell quips that such misconceptions have "proved almost as difficult to eradicate as those beliefs themselves" (2019, 1). Indeed, "alive and well" is the general consensus among folklorists studying the supernatural. Jeannie Banks Thomas (2015) contends that the supernatural now lives among technology and progress, and the two are fast friends and good allies. Diane Goldstein argues that, contrary to public perception, belief in the supernatural is so widespread it "might even be considered the norm" (2007, 66), and Barbara Walker sees the supernatural "comfortably incorporated into everyday life" (1995, 1). Gillian Bennett cautions that to think otherwise is to be "deceived by the official rationalist world view" (1999, 2). Dendle, reviewing the statistical literature, finds that "attempts to dismiss these [remaining] supernatural beliefs as eccentricities of the superstitious, the uneducated, or the provincial are not uniformly supported by data, and do not do justice to the scope and variety of beliefs in context" (2013, 441).

In fact, Dendle offers a compelling analysis of this quantitative data behind legendary monster belief. He unearths one surprising data collection from 2005; the Institute for Studies of Religion at Baylor University found that nearly *half* of respondents either agreed with or were "unsure" of whether "creatures such as Bigfoot and the Loch Ness monster will one day be discovered by science" (2013, 444). Nearly half! So while legendary monsters may be dismissed as comical, unbelievable, or preposterous publicly, a startling number of Americans seem less certain, especially when polled discreetly. While many scholars accept that monsters, at the very least, have *survived* the technological era, Dendle argues that monsters might thrive *because of* the technological era.[20] Others, too, raise techno-supernatural examples, such as Spiritualists embracing the telegraph (Luckhurst 2002b; Manning 2018) or paranormal hunters wielding electromagnetic field (EMF) meters and electronic voice phenomenon (EVP) recorders (Goldstein, Grider, and Thomas 2007, 3). Meurger suggests that stunning scientific discoveries over the last century probably make monsters and other supernatural possibilities *more plausible* to the human mind, not less (1989). And undergirding it all, digital communications technology, such as the Internet, smartphones, and social media, provide an ideal and novel forum for sharing experiences of monsters and the supernatural with like-minded people (McNeill and Tucker 2018, 28), in addition to the creation of new digital monsters (e.g., see Blank and McNeill 2018; Peck 2015, Tolbert 2013). Scientific and technological progress hasn't sounded the death knell for monsters; it has reared and nurtured them.

Alas, I promised I would attempt to offer a tentative, admittedly unsatisfactory but hopefully handy definition, while also doing plenty of evading and equivocating. Here I present my cautious attempt. I am fortunate, as I don't need (or mean) to attempt to define "monster," as some authors must, but only "legendary monster," a more limited subset. A legendary monster, for the purposes of this casebook and in my limited usage, is a strange, frightening, or unusual human or creature, real or imaginary, believed or not believed, that is, at the time of the telling, purported but not scientifically verified to exist in our world. In description, a legendary monster most often resembles a disfigured human, a gruesome beast, or some other uncanny hybrid of discrete cultural categories. Delineating common characteristics can be helpful in identifying those entities that humankind has referred to as "monsters," but we will never devise the perfect monster definition that encompasses all those extraordinary beings sometimes considered monsters while simultaneously excluding all those that don't pass muster. Indeed, because of the semantics at play, no two authors will entirely agree on what is and what is not a monster. As to its application in this casebook, it's important to acknowledge that in such a volume, especially one that highlights preexisting work, contributors will not necessarily agree on terms, nor should we expect them to. Rather, we can think of *monster* as a useful umbrella term to bring together a variety of ongoing and valuable thematic scholarship that may benefit from the joining.

LEGENDARY MONSTERS AND LOCAL MONSTER LEGENDS

As the focus of this casebook is legendary monsters, and my definition covers only legendary monsters, a necessary consideration is *when* a monster becomes *legendary*? Answering this question requires a definition of "legend." A contemporary legend is a plausible but unverifiable narrative that is repeatedly retold. The "contemporary" refers not to a requirement of novelty, but rather to a legend, in any era, speaking to contemporaneous needs and anxieties, as opposed to a historical legend set in the distant past covering the feats of extraordinary heroes and their role in world-changing events. In the performance of a contemporary legend, neither the teller nor the audience must necessarily "believe" the legend (belief being a slippery substance to nail down), but there must be *plausibility*; there must be a *possibility* of belief. But even this lone criterion can prove problematic. The monsters in H. P. Lovecraft's Cthulu Mythos are explicitly fiction, yet attract a community of belief (e.g., see Quinn 2010). On the other hand, animals found today in American zoos—gorillas, manatees, platypuses, Komodo dragons—were once legendary creatures, their horrors chronicled in medieval bestiaries (e.g., see Hassig 1995). A story told purely as entertainment is fiction; purely as news, it becomes "fact" (Oring 1990). Legendary monsters haunt the gray area between fact and fiction: stories told as true, not so fantastical as to be impossible (even if they invert scientific rationalism), not so believed as to go unquestioned.[21] A successful legend teller, intentionally or not, will carefully "map the story onto the landscape or social relations of the reader/listener's everyday lifeworld" (Stewart 1982, 35). In the field, when folklorists hear a story of a friend of a friend's ghastly encounter with a dreadful creature not too far from here, they know they are in *legendary* monster territory.

Folklore, a discipline with an affinity for meaningful repeated cultural practices, includes within its purview the study of *legendary* monsters. Legend forms one folklore genre, and the genre's devotees, known as legend scholars, research the legend gamut, from saints' legends to national legends. Over the last half century, there has been increased emphasis on studying "contemporary legends"—those living, emergent stories that warn, amuse, and speak to modern-day concerns and anxieties. The popular press sometimes calls these "urban myths"—a misnomer folklorists dislike—or "urban legends," the term used by renowned legend scholar Jan Brunvand (e.g., see 2003). Today's legend scholars prefer "contemporary legend," which includes traditional accounts of embarrassing missteps, comical accidents, and treacherous criminals. And monsters too. Legends abound: legends of gold mines, buried treasures, outlaws, saints, omens; legends that function as folk history; and legends that function as folk news. There are legends that reflect our hopes, our fears, our anxieties. There are grand legends that are performed in dramatic recountings, and there are covert legends that sneak into conversations barely noticed. The legend genre provides significant human insight because, in comparison to cautious, self-censoring official channels, legend reveals honest, graphic North American attitudes and convictions. Legend is perhaps best understood as the informal grapevine that supplements professional news reports. Rather than showing the world as always extraordinary, contemporary legends accentuate the extraordinary intruding on the ordinary or, as Bruvand writes, prove "that the prosaic contemporary scene is still capable of shocking occurrences" that happen to real, nearby people (2003, 12).

One paradoxical factor to ponder: legendary monsters are often *not* legendary in the secondary definitional sense of the word—that is, "legendary" as "remarkable enough to be famous" or "very well known." In reality, most legendary monsters know little fame beyond their local confines, nor do they seek it. Folklorists writing on the topic of the supernatural, the paranormal, ghosts, and haunted houses note steady subtlety. As Thomas describes it, the supernatural in folklore does little more than "make itself known" (2007, 29). It's mundane, understated, muted (Goldstein, Grider, and Thomas 2007, 212), an eerie presence here, a scurry seen out of the corner of the eye there. American monsters don't *do* much, and thus their legends consist mostly of the radical idea that a particular monster exists, perhaps including an explanation of its habits, habitat, or appearance, sometimes constituting only the vaguest explanation of its physical existence. Dramatic or hyperbolic supernatural encounters are usually signs of cinematic or literary treatment. Indeed, to make monsters kinetic, it's often necessary for a legend performer to work intertextually, splicing the monster legend with another urban legend, such as "The Boyfriend's Death," enlivening the nearby monster with motive and deed.[22]

And the *nearby* aspect is particularly important. The local legend genre, of which the legendary monsters in this casebook are a part, offers a connection to local geography. This proximate link, however, hasn't always been the case. Historian Chet van Duzer, in his historical study of monsters and cartography, demonstrates that in the past local monsters were unusual. He observes that "implicit in most accounts of local monsters is the idea that the region near the teller is normal, and the knowledge from the experience of everyday life that monsters aren't commonly encountered there. That is, in familiar areas, monsters are known to be a small percentage of the overall population, whereas at the edges of the world, we hear of little except monsters" (2013, 431). This worldview has transformed in the modern era. In his study of American beasts, Dorson suggests that monsters seem to "live among their chosen folk, intermingle with them, and enter their personal experience narratives" (Dorson 1982, 1). The legendary monsters once "out there" are now "in here." They do not live on distant shores and in far-off places; modern legendary monsters live in our own liminal spaces, at our own social boundaries, on the edges of our own civilization.

In this casebook, legend scholars emphasize native monster habitats, examining *local* North American monster legends, the concept of *local* contrasted with *migratory*. Migratory legends are those legends dispersed widely across space in which the plot remains consistent but the characters and locations are updated to make local sense (see Christiansen 1958), whereas local legends circulate in one region but not necessarily another, as they are intrinsically bound to a particular geographic area. While each author's idiosyncratic conception of "monster" and "monstrosity" varies from chapter to chapter (and a few prefer other terms all together), all featured monsters are grotesque or uncanny beings with devoted legend cycles and deep roots in particular locales. The scope of this casebook, therefore, and the primary criterion for inclusion is *local* legendary monster case studies, that is, attention to monsters with significant geographic attachment and minimal migratory inclination: the *Jersey* Devil, the *Maryland* Goatman, the *West Virginia* Mothman.

MONSTER MATTERS

Legendary monsters reflect attitudes toward the natural landscape—the awe of the vast untapped wilderness, the fear of what may lurk there, the ever-present (and scientifically verified) possibility that unknown creatures and beings are afoot, and the anxiety of humanity's own place amid it all. North American monsters are inevitably found in just those places most taxing to explore, most difficult to know, most challenging to conquer—deep lakes, thick groves, wooded stretches. The endless hunting expeditions for legendary monsters highlight the American discontent with a rigidly rational and positivist worldview, pointing to a romantic urge to believe there are unsolved mysteries, a world beyond scientific explanation. And while the depths of the sea and the expanse of the universe are undetermined and perhaps undeterminable, legendary monsters hint at the romantic and transcendent in a sanitized, rationalistic world, at an urge for adventure, and at a lust for the unknown.

Folklorists appreciate legends not just as amusing or titillating but as meaningful, stories overlooked by an academic world that sees such scuttle-butt and hearsay lurking safely on the other side of the "triviality barrier" (Sutton-Smith 1970). Monsters, in particular, face a steep jump over that barricade. Here's my own attempt to clear it: in a world where belief rules, whether due to information scarcity or information saturation, plausible possibilities—especially those that fit into preexisting worldviews—influence behavior as often as cold, hard fact. And these repeated, narrative, semi-structured plausible possibilities called contemporary legends explore the frightening characters of the world, such as terrorists (Fine and Khawaja 2005; Fine and Ellis 2013; Langlois 2005); murderers, serial killers, and spree shooters (e.g., Bronner 2014; Ellis 1989; Langlois 1978; Mitchell 1979); and rapists, molesters, and pedophiles (Carroll 1987; Wachs 1982; Winick 1992). (Dare I say "monsters" in the metaphorical sense of the word?) Whether or not sightings or stories are believed, the public perception—how legendary monsters are conceptualized, characterized, assigned territories and misdeeds—remains significant. The community-curated narrative tradition that constitutes the monstrous fiends' repertoire offers insight into the human mind. Legendary monsters, often based on honest reports of encounters with natural phenomena, reveal the fears, anxieties, and cultural discontent of the community and particular historical moments. The legends these creatures spawn bring those dark anxieties into the light, providing a suitable target for the discussion of community unease (Cohen 1996a; e.g., Puglia 2019, 156–61).

If legends matter and monsters matter, the study of legendary monsters must matter as well. But to date, legendary monsters remain woefully understudied, their research and analysis left primarily to Forteans, cryptozoologists, and hobbyist hunters. It's my hope the assembled chapters in this casebook will spur folkloristic interest in the scholarly study of legendary monsters, particularly by demonstrating their continued significance in our modern world. One overarching theme found throughout the volume is that legendary monsters help us articulate, manage, and discuss underlying fears and anxieties by naming and giving shape to them. These anxieties often relate to sociocultural and environmental change and to encounters with otherness that challenge our sense of order and identity, that diagnose pressure points for cultural unease, that discern the boundaries of community break down, or that highlight contradictions in life that are difficult to understand or navigate. These legendary monsters offer an opportunity to enhance our understanding of North American landscapes, anxieties, and play, and most monster scholars agree, generally, that monsters provide windows into grander social and psychological concerns, to larger fields such as history, literature, and religion, and to contemporary concerns such as regional identity and ethnic culture.[23]

In fact, some argue that what most trivializes monsters, and the supernatural in general, is the hesitancy of scholars, including folklorists, to treat the subject solemnly (Goldstein, Grider, and Thomas 2007, 8). To summarize Gillian Bennett's vicious-cycle explanation (1987, 13) as to why the supernatural isn't taken seriously: because few are willing to commit to specializing in a disreputable subject, the knowledge produced in that area is limited, and much of what's produced comes from those less concerned with legitimacy, further increasing the illegitimacy of the subject and discouraging folklorists from associating their interlocutors with the subject matter, all of which further decreases the reputation of the field and encourages potential informants to hide their supernatural experiences and deny belief publicly. (Or, as Ames asks sympathetically but bluntly, "To what extent should a scholar risk his or her professional reputation by pursuing non-respectable topics?" [1980, 302].) What remains are books of literary embellished tales, not believable—and never believed by anyone anyway. One glance between the covers, and the cycle continues. Folklorists can do better. The supernatural is both significant and ubiquitous, whether or not we are willing to acknowledge it.[24] The folklorist's task is to embrace, appreciate, and analyze, and while this may be even *more* challenging with legendary monsters than with other already difficult supernatural subjects, their pursuit remains vital for the same reasons as any other paranormal inquiry.

EXPLAINING MONSTERS

The idea that supernatural belief arises predominantly from error rather than reasoned and sober consideration is no longer in vogue. Today's folklorists tend to take their informants seriously, to hear monster accounts as rational sightings honestly reported, and to decipher the intellectual rationale built into the reports themselves. In that case, how do folklorists explain monsters springing to life? Cohen argues that such a question is inherent in the mere proposed existence of a monster (2013, 452). What is it doing here? What purpose does it serve? One possibility is naming, or what folklorist Bill Ellis calls the "Rumplestiltskin Principle," the proposition that monster legends (and other types of legends) are "convenient language for the experiences that lie, actually or potentially, at the very boundaries of existence" (2003, 63). That is, Ellis writes, "the legend as name allows narrators to identify with the otherwise monstrous experience" (64). Foster also muses on "naming" as an important function of monsters, or *yokai*, in Japan. Labeling subtle scary phenomena for which there otherwise is no language, he proposes, gives form to a thought and a feeling (2015, 93). Ellis agrees that legend allows a sense of control over "marginal situations" and permits participants to "comprehend, control, and share anxiety" (2003, 64). Naming monsters, in these cases, fulfills a comforting social and psychological function.

Naming, though, is but one possible justification for the monster phenomenon. There are still many other potential explanations of where legendary monsters come from. Jan Brunvand suggests that whence legends arise is still one of folklore's great mysteries (2003, 4). Some euhemerize, crediting a "kernel of truth," or assume, as Belgian-French cryptozoologist Bernard Heuvelmans did, for example, that legends contain a residue of fact (1958). Others, like Gilmore, lean towards psychological explanations (2003), and some Fortean cryptozoologists take that further to include "psychic projections of a collective unconscious, literal thought forms that take on a solid state of existence" (Coleman 2007, 287–88). Remembering the symposium that led to the book *Manlike Monsters on Trial,* Ames suggests that explanations for monsters fall into two broad (and interrelated) camps: psychological and structural (1980). The former sees humans constructing monsters onto which they can project their fears and anxieties; the latter understands monsters to embody interstices and contradictions in classification systems, monsters forming out of those beings that fall between the cracks.

Structuralists note that monsters account for gaps that defy classificatory systems, that they speak to cultural contradictions, and that they appear in liminal spaces. Cohen suggests that monsters "embody a relentless hybridity that resists assimilation into secure epistemologies" (2013, 452) and "resist attempts to include them in any systematic structuration" (Cohen 1996a, 6).[25] In this way, the work of structural anthropologists like Mary Douglas and Victor Turner prove valuable in the study of monsters. For Douglas, monsters are those beings that transgress cultural categories, and they are both physically and cognitively frightening because their existence threatens the cosmic order of cognitive classification systems (1966). Or in other words, as Cohen writes, the monster exists "to call horrid attention to the borders that cannot—*must* not—be crossed" (1996a, 13). Joseph Campbell used similar reasoning in his definition of monster: "By a monster, I mean some horrendous presence or apparition that explodes all of your standards for harmony, order, and ethical conduct" (1991, 278). Victor Turner emphasized liminal moments, places, and beings to understand monsters. Such liminal moments are betwixt and between, and it's these moments that consistently become the setting for monsters (Turner 1969; cf. Stewart 1982, 40–43). This concept of liminality is oft referenced by folklorists, who note that legendary monsters are found in liminal places (borderlands, bridges, crossroads), appear at liminal times (full moon, twilight, midnight), and are evoked in ambiguous, liminal moments (adolescent slumber parties, summer camp nights, college dorm life). The monstrous body is itself liminal, hybrid, ambiguous, interstitial, haunting the cracks of classificatory systems. Legendary monsters, to cite a literary monster, have a Frankenstein quality to them; they are stitched together, often of human and animal parts, or, to use Foster's phrasing, "sutured together from pieces of animal" (2015, 87). In Lévi-Strauss's term, monsters are "bricolage" (1962, 11); in Gilmore's, scavenged "scraps of reality" (2003, 21). Monsters are fused composites, reshuffled mélanges, conflated agglutinations.

Another notable structural consideration is humans' love-hate relationship with monsters. Humans revile and revere monsters; monsters disgust and enthrall them. There seems to be scholarly consensus that the blending of attraction and repulsion, love and hate, fear and desire is central to the cultural makeup of monsters. Cohen speculates that "this simultaneous repulsion and attraction at the core of the monster's composition accounts greatly for its continued cultural popularity" (1996a), Gilmore observes a "stark dualism, half horror, half reverence" (2003, ix), and Asma suggests a "simultaneous lure and repulsion of the abnormal or extraordinary" (2009, 6). Others have explored the cartoonish dimension of monsters as the "monstrous/cute" (Brzozowksa-Brywczyńska 2007), or what Susan Stewart referred to as "thematic inversion in which the familiar is transformed into its opposite" (1982, 42). The monster is the eternal frenemy— humans love to hate monsters, hate-love monsters or, at times, simply love monsters.

One universally agreed-upon principal in academic monster studies is that monsters are pregnant with meaning. Legendary monsters, especially if read carefully and in context, reveal deeply help cultural assumptions, concerns, and worldviews. Jeannie Banks Thomas lists the interpretive value more succinctly, writing that the supernatural reveals "cultural values" and "cultural stresses and conflicts" (2007, 31), or what Dendle refers to as a "barometer of cultural anxiety" (2007).[26] Anthropologist Rupert Stasch calls monsters "a walking anthropology" (2014, 196); Jack Halberstam labels them "meaning machines" (1995, 22); and Cohen names monsters "an embodiment of a certain cultural moment—of a time, a feeling, and a place" and one that exists "only to be read" (1996a, 4). While particular monsters are not universal, numerous monster critics see a universality in the monster impetus generally. Gilmore goes so far as to claim that the "mind needs monsters" where "fears can safely settle" (2003, 1). Asma, in addition to seeing monsters index the fears of specific eras, also argues that monsters "reflect more universal human anxieties and cognitive tendencies" (2009, 283). And Marjorie M. Halpin, channeling Durkheim, speculates that monster beliefs would not be so tenacious and widespread if they did not serve a special purpose (1980, 10–11), a point folklorists can agree upon.

Legendary monsters, at the very least, speak to four broad themes: socioenvironmental anxieties, otherness, commercial interests, and a sense of regional identity.

SOCIOENVIRONMENTAL ANXIETIES

From these chapters comes forth, then, in their creeping, looming manner, monsters as means of speaking about fear of the unknown, whether it be the physical unknown—thick forests, vast reservoirs, cavernous sewers—or the social unknown—fear of interbreeding, the disfigured, the disabled, the non-normative. Our authors return repeatedly to the theme of community issues and monsters commenting on local concerns: from local environmental consternation for James Leary's Boondock Monster to diminishing local control of land use for John Ashton's Webber; from local pollution for Elizabeth Tucker's Lieby to rising crime rates for David Puglia's Goatman; from community cultural distrust of single, childless women for Mercedes Torrez's Donkey Lady to issues of colonialism and imperialism for Benjamin Radford's chupacabra.

Legendary monsters, therefore, provide commentary on socioenvironmental anxieties and unease. Thomas, for one, has argued that this is a function of the supernatural in general, to "provide a discourse, which often relies on place, to comment on cultural and political issues" (2015, 14). Monster legends, we find, reveal cultural data about landscape, natural phenomena, historical events, rising conflicts, pressure points, and impending change. Ames observes that many of these creatures lurk in wilderness habitats or developing areas "threatened by the expansion of human settlements or resource industries" (1980, 301). The supernatural can assist in the contemplation of nature and place, and for this reason, monster environments and settings deserve special attention for the attitudes they reveal.[27] In cities and urban areas, Karl Bell finds the unease channeled through legendary monsters "frequently signifies a sense of disempowerment in the face of environmental anxieties" (2019, 18). By contrast, in rural landscapes as in much of Canada, Carpenter suggests, legendary monsters represent "the mixture of fear and fascination they [residents] possess towards the land" and "helplessness in the face of the natural world and an inability to control and capitalize upon its power" (1980, 106). Legendary monsters prove to be productive teachers on issues of fear and anxiety as they relate to place and local community.

OTHERNESS

Scholars argue that monsters provide valuable insight into issues of social difference, race, class, gender, disability, non-normative behavior, and those considered "other," often providing a safe space for discussion of topics that would be difficult or uncomfortable to discuss more directly.[28] While frequently emblems of racial or ethnic prejudice, monsters are perhaps most incisive as indicators of ableism, where legend depicts monsters, especially the humanoid variety, as deformed, disfigured, or disturbed, their atypical corporeality conflated with moral deformity. Cohen argues that monsters are "difference made flesh" and the "dialectical other," asking us to "reevaluate our assumptions about race, gender, sexuality, our perception of difference" (1996a, 20). Monsters, Musharbash agrees, are marked by their "monstrous bodies," ones that don't neatly fit into native classification schema. Understanding monsters is emic and contextual, and the way monsters resist cultural mores "make[s] sense only in particular societies" (2014, 11). And these understandings are themselves in flux, based on ever-evolving conceptions of what's human and what's not, what belongs and what doesn't, what's invited and what's intruding.

Indeed, it's difficult to talk about monsters without discussing some form of social or cultural difference. By studying legendary monsters, we discern what does not gel with the classificatory culture of a group, whether that be race, gender, ability, or another cultural category. Contemplating race and world monstrosity, Friedman observes that "everyday cultural difference in such things as diet, speech, clothes, weapons, customs, and social organization were what truly set alien people apart from their observers in the classical world, and the power of these cultural traits to mark a race as monstrous persisted in the Middle Ages and beyond" (2000, 26). These differences are culturally bounded, culturally marked, and make sense only within particular cultural contexts and logics. Folklorist Elizabeth Tucker encourages attending to the supernatural for its surprising, incisive commentary on persecuted minority groups (2007, 11), and folklorist Claudia Schwabe contends that, in an ideological shift, Americans have begun reimagining and rehabilitating once-infamous folkloric monsters as a means of embracing diversity and promoting tolerance toward otherness (2019). When folklorists encounter a monster legend, careful analysis of the construction of otherness is essential.

COMMERCIAL INTERESTS

Legendary monsters can be lucrative, and scholars have noted their potential profit margin. Halpin calls monsters a "highly saleable image" and notes that, through commerce, we are "increasingly communicating to each other with symbols from the Goblin Universe" (1980, 22). "Monsters are commodity," Dendle writes, and legendary monsters can be "infantilized, commoditized, and incorporated into the kitsch icons of leisure and entertainment" (2013, 438). This appropriation can be perceived negatively because it tends to "corrupt the 'authenticity' and 'folkloric' value" of monsters, ripping them from their native context and morphing them into ownable commodities (Foster 2015, 79). Taken to the extreme, charlatans can even employ legendary monsters and general belief in the supernatural to swindle the naïve, a trope that concludes most episodes of the *Scooby-Doo* franchise.

As numerous folklorists have argued, when it comes to the supernatural, commercialism and media interest are an expected, if not integral, component of the paranormal process, and the prevailing sentiment has shifted toward "oppos[ing] the a priori notion that folk belief expressed in popular or commodified culture is any less serious, any less important, any less rational, or any less a belief than what is expressed more traditionally" (Goldstein, Grider, and Thomas 2007, 16).[29] In addition to international corporations profiting from local monsters—a legendary monster starring in a Hollywood summer blockbuster, for example—it's also possible for commercial interests in monsters to occur on a much smaller scale: a local town investing in a particular monster, like the Mothman in Point Pleasant or the Hodag in Rhinelander.

Consequently, we encounter legendary monster commerce, where local or tourist interest translates into revenue—the sale of tickets, trinkets, and trips. Legendary American monsters are commercialized and adapted into various forms: festivals, stuffed animals, souvenirs, pamphlets, guidebooks, tours, and signature cocktails. They become emblazoned on T-shirts, enshrined as statues, embodied as mascots of sports teams, paradoxically cursed and reviled while also feasted and fêted. Such commercial attention often feeds back into the legend tradition, birthing monstrous revivals or budding bastard media offshoots. For some monsters, the commercialism is at the heart of the legend, perhaps concerning to purists, but perfectly in line with the commercial motive rampant in the development of the United States. In truth, it would seem downright un-American if some ambitious entrepreneur did not try to boost a town and make a buck off the back of a notorious local demon. And so we see just that, benign in the case of the Hodag in Rhinelander, Wisconsin, or Sharlie in McCall, Idaho, perhaps less so with the Mormon Nessie in Bear Lake on the Idaho-Utah border or the White River Monster in Arkansas.

Along with commercialism and local pride comes regional press interest in local monster legends, which, intentionally or not, perpetuates monster legends, spreading them to the far reaches of the newspaper's circulation empire. Journalists investigate local monsters, transform and disseminate their legends, and often become a part of the legend complex themselves. Chicanery, another recurring theme in these chapters, is initiated by hucksters and schemers with commercial motives, ranging from ambitious local showmen drawing crowds into their sideshows to furtive backwoods moonshiners keeping spectators away from their distilleries. When the

Figure 0.1. Vintage postcard from Rhinelander, Wisconsin, featuring the Hodag statue superimposed over the "Hodag City." Collection of David J. Puglia.

local context evaporates but the commercial impulse remains, the theme, generally stated, of popular culture as a consequential monster progenitor reveals itself, and for that reason, many folklorists trace the lineage of their monster outward, from folk origins to feature films, television series, and comic books.

Sense of Regional Pride and Identity

Some legendary monsters—fangs bared, mouth foaming, tentacles dangling—prove horrifying. But critics note that others are downright amusing. Folklorist Alan Dundes suggests that Americans are not content to stand in wide-eyed terror before their awesome landscape, instead demanding to conquer it (1982, xvii). And while the monsters Americans recount may evoke a wondrous and sprawling landscape, the persistent, ever-present humor and exaggeration captures the American aesthetic style. The American braggart, blowhard, raconteur, or fabulist (chronicled by Dorson 1982, 77–169) is both a well-known American archetype *and* the natural originator and presenter of such sensational monster legends. Richard M. Dorson, it should be noted, developed his own American "comic" monster thesis: the United States, having formed too near modernity to develop a fearsome bestiary, created a comic one instead, a menagerie of critters Americans "yarn about, identify with, hunt for, depict, extol, and chuckle over" (1982, 4). Dundes, a proponent of the "inferiority complex" (1985), discerns American pride in the development of a unique legendary monster menagerie, distinct from the fairies, werewolves, and ogres of Europe. Americans have a long history of comparing themselves to Europeans. Are there commensurate American arts, letters, and sciences? Are there commensurate bogeymen? Americans don't just fear their monsters—if they ever really did—they *celebrate* them. In fact, in contrast to the days of garlic necklaces and silver bullets, celebration of local legendary monsters becomes a central theme explored throughout the casebook—a community embrace of a state, region, or town monster. As local legends, while potentially arousing fear, these monsters also attract a sense of regional pride and distinction.

In that way, monsters feed a sense of regional identity. Legend scholars do see contemporary legend emerging from anxiety and uncertainty, but monsters serve another local function, one that transcends mere dread: the role of local mascot. Foster, for one, notes that in Japan today, monsters hold surprising connections to local conceptions of heritage, where yokai practice is characterized by a sense of tradition, history, and community. Local legends, even the grisly ones, suggest "continuity with the past," which promotes a sense of heritage, an inkling of pride, and the possibility of profit (2015, 78). Japan may be the extreme example; Foster deems monsters "central to Japan's identity as a modern nation-state" (2013, 141), folkloric markers that float about as reminders of "authentic" Japanese heritage. But likewise, on a different continent, Carpenter proposes that British Columbians hold onto their legendary monsters because they are something distinctive, something specific they can claim that others cannot (1980). Several of the monsters in this casebook serve a similar function, probably none more so than the Jersey Devil, which is not only New Jersey's state monster but now also the mascot for New Jersey's National Hockey League (NHL) team. As traditional and place-based lore, legendary monsters serve, perhaps in an underappreciated role, as one element of local tradition.

HERE BE LEGENDARY MONSTERS

North American monster legends exhibit remarkable variation. Each town or region that shares a monster has its own version of that creature, and individuals within the area will have their own idiosyncratic variations within the local tradition. North Americans familiar only with their own regional monsters may not fully appreciate the legendary bestiary present on the continent. By bringing together case studies of local monsters, I hope to demonstrate both the consistent legendary North American impulse in imagining monsters across the continent and the dependable localization of these monsters to meet local needs, local fears, and even local pride.

As legends tend to migrate, it's a rare monster that is peculiar to a single location. The Jersey Devil has its doppelgänger the Snallygaster; the Goatman of Maryland, the Goatman of Kentucky; Lake Erie's Bessie, Lake Tahoe's Tessie. The dependable multiple existences of monsters do not reduce, but rather increase, the importance of studying them. Either monsters really do wander the North American landscape (a possibility folklorists remain open to), or there exists some broad human significance to monster legends, offering an intriguing window into North American culture. And whether or not a local monster is entirely unique—and most are not—only through comparison to other North American monsters can the folklorist determine how that particular legend reflects the locality in question, as opposed to shared cultural concerns.

Conversely, no monster is universal. The U.S. bestiary, for example, has little in the way of unicorns, fairies, or leprechauns. Bigfoot sightings occur frequently in the Appalachians and the Pacific Northwest, but rarely in cities and far fewer in the Southwest than in the Northwest. There may be New Jersey's Leeds Devil, West Virginia's Mothman, and Maryland's Snallygaster flying above, but that is not to say all states have winged monsters. Topographic features are critical to the formation of monster legends, but such environmental influences do not dictate uniformity. Lakes seem to attract lake monsters all over the world, for example, but Nessie, Chessie, Bessie, and Tessie are all locally distinct. Neither unique nor universal, legendary monsters lurk somewhere in between, reflective of local history, culture, and environment.

While monster legends are a global phenomenon, this casebook is restricted to those in North America.[30] To cover every monster in the world would be impossible, but the choice in scope was not due to space considerations alone. The "New World" is a different beast to study than the "Old World." Europe nurtures legendary monsters from antiquity, from myth, from a pagan past; the New World proves even more complex. It hosts Native American monster legends (varying by tribe), Old World monster legends preserved and passed along by migrating settlers, pioneers, and voyageurs, and novel monster legends arising anew from local needs, anxieties, and encounters. So while Europe was a mess of monsters, North American newcomers brought the menagerie with them *and* encountered other cultures' bestiaries *and* discovered or invented new legendary monsters. The discovery, blending, and invention of monster traditions, therefore, are themes that arise throughout this casebook, setting it apart from valuable but fundamentally different Old World monster studies.

What, then, is the American monster, this New World legend? Which legendary monsters can survive in this hemisphere, and which cannot? Fairies, for example, seem to thrive in the British Isles, but not in North America.[31] Secretive, serpentine lake monsters and hairy, apelike wildmen live comfortably on both continents. The chupacabra threatens much of the Americas, but avoids Europe. The presence or absence of these monsters can be a defining aspect of North American landscapes (accounting for local pride in monsters) and relates to Dorson's and Dundes's notion of an inferiority complex or a "Why don't we have monsters like . . . ?" sentiment. Dorson, for example, attempting to account for the lack of Old World monsters in North America, cited the fear of vast oceans and a close connection to birthplaces:

> One question that has always intrigued me is what happens to demonic beings when immigrants move from their homelands. Irish-Americans remember the fairies, Norwegian-Americans the *nisser*, Greek-Americans the *vrykólakas*, but only in relation to events remembered in the Old Country. When I once asked why such demons are not seen in America, my informants giggled confusedly and said, "They're scared to pass the ocean, it's too far," pointing out that Christ and the Apostles never came to America. Apparently the ethnic supernatural figures are too closely associated with the culture and geography of the old Country to migrate.[32] (1971, 36)

Once beyond the tendency to form monsters out of geographic otherness—that is, when discussing the monsters *here*, not *there*—which kinds of monsters are *North American*? Folklorists such as Paul Manning have noted the challenges of establishing a supernatural tradition in a "newer" landscape, or, in Manning's words, "anxieties about the unhauntability of the landscapes of the New World" (2017, 63). Nathaniel Hawthorne, for example, complained of the difficulty of writing haunting literature (or supernatural romance) set "in a country where there is no shadow, no antiquity, no mystery, no picturesque and gloomy wrong" (1961, iv).[33] Manning contrasts the "picturesque ruin" of the Old World with the "sublime wilderness" of the New World (2017, 64–65). Whereas in the Old World, the eerie atmosphere required for the supernatural emanates from the ruins, in the New World, it emanates from the wilderness itself (67) or, perhaps more precisely, monsters haunt the wild places, the places *between* nature and culture (71).

And if that's the case, let's pause and examine this theory in practice. How many monsters in the present casebook derive from the North American wilderness? Of the nineteen case studies, all but three have direct connections to nature and the edges of the wild. The exceptions are vampires, perhaps the monster examined here with the strongest Old World roots; zombies, though I might argue that mainlanders conjure up the Caribbean as a single, strange tropical wild; and Slender Man. While an argument could be made that Slendy developed in the digital wilds of the Internet, at the very least, I would remind readers that when two Wisconsin tweens enacted the Slender Man legend on a friend, the perpetrators first act was to lure their intended victim into the woods. Excluding those three leaves sixteen of nineteen case studies where monsters lurk at the edges of forests, hide in vast (or tiny) bodies of water, or flee to the woods after their traumatic origins.

As a fledgling field, North American legendary monster studies has yet to identify the definitive, unifying characteristics of North American monsters. In other words, we're still trying to figure out what makes an American monster *American*. Examining the phantasmagoria on display in this casebook, the reader will discern a few immediate North American monster patterns: these creatures are deeply connected to their environments, they're horrific yet comic, they're believed in at times but rarely sacred, they're authentic *and* commercial, oral *and* mass-mediated. They are often playful, sometimes parodic, and occasionally hoaxy. But these are no more than initial postulates, set forth to be tested and contested, refined and refuted over generations of sustained research. The contours of the American legendary monster remain vague, and questions linger about its fundamental essence.

And last, I'll offer a brief explanation for the distinct lack of Native American monsters found in this casebook. This choice is not meant as a slight to the continent's original inhabitants or their monsters—in fact, just the opposite. In his study, Bacil F. Kirtley made the same decision to exclude Native American monsters, albeit with a different justification. Kirtley thought information about Native American monsters too abundant and easily accessible in folklore indices to warrant additional consideration (1964, 77–78). While I applaud Kirtley's emphasis on overlooked materials and endeavor to promote the same in this casebook, there exist additional, compelling reasons to be especially careful when considering Indigenous "monsters." As art historian Matthew Looper recalls, explorers found many grotesque creatures in Mayan culture. The alien beings were cast as "monsters," but such problematic classification betrays a colonial, ethnocentric, and racist rhetoric. To the outsider Spanish Christians, these images were monsters, but to the Mayans, they were sacred gods. Looper urges scholars "writing from a position of privilege and authority . . . to consider the legacy of racism and ethnocentrism that the term [monster] invokes when applied to Native Americans and their gods" (2013, 199). In this casebook, therefore, with the exception of the windigo, mention of Native American beliefs most often arrives in the form of non-Indigenous narrators offering "proof" of a monster's long existence through vague reference to Indigenous history and belief, rather than to description of a particular nation's pantheon.

A CONTEMPORARY LEGEND CASEBOOK

Monster books abound, so I expect some readers will demur when I declare this volume the first of its kind. While monster books are plentiful, a careful examination of the monster library shelf reveals distinct subgenres: cultural studies or "monster studies," cryptozoology, skeptical inquiry, monster hunting, encyclopedic approaches, and the history of science. None are legend studies proper, but legend studies can contribute to all six. "Monster studies" is the field that most involves academics from a wide range of disciplines. Cultural analysis of monsters in literature and film—that is, fictional monsters never part of an oral tradition—is valuable for the insights it provides into artistic conceptions of the monstrous, otherness, and concepts of disability, race, and non-normativity. Cryptozoology is the study of unverified animals purported to exist. Although it is often decried as a pseudo-science, supporters will point to nineteenth-century naturalist and twenty-first-century microbiologist findings as legitimate instances of the discovery of unknown creatures. At their best, cryptozoology books question the scientific establishment's hold over knowledge and represent the romantic impulse for exploration of the unknown. The skeptics—rigid, rigorous, and rationalistic researchers—question the methods, the evidence, and the conclusions of cryptozoologists and monster hunters, pointing out logical fallacies, sloppy methods, or shaky evidence, and their books offer prosaic explanations for purported extraordinary beings: mangy coyotes, disoriented bears, frolicking otters. What I refer to as "monster hunter" books are vast compendiums of ostensible monster lore and purported sightings, sometimes serving as do-it-yourself field guides for tracking particular monsters in specific geographic locales. The encyclopedic approach emphasizes taxonomies: collection, classification, and ordering of monster data. Such ordering and organization can improve our intellectual grasp of monsters and assist us in taming an unruly subject but, as a trade-off, encyclopedic approaches extract monsters from their native contexts, thereby obscuring their critical social and psychological underpinnings (Dendle 2013, 438; Foster 2015, 91). Among proponents of monster studies are scholars of the history of science, particularly those studying the inquiries of naturalists during the Scientific Revolution. While scientists explain nature's regularities (e.g., sun rising, stone falling), pre-modern scientists also sought to explain irregularities (e.g., conjoined twins, hermaphrodites, egg-laying mammals like the duck-billed platypus). Monstrous phenomena were valuable cues, signaling deficiencies in theories of nature that did not yet account for all terrestrial beings.[34]

While it can contribute to all of these practices, legend scholarship is distinctly its own field of inquiry with its own approach to monster research. While not as credulous as monster hunters, legend scholars assume as their default position that informants are honestly reporting real sensory experiences to the best of their ability. While not as incredulous as skeptics, when debunking is possible, folklorists are not analytically satisfied with poking holes: legend scholars are primarily interested in why and how the monster legend took hold in the first place, rather than its basis in established fact. While not as scientific as cryptozoologists, who often see themselves as part of the life sciences, legend scholars do adhere to a rigorous set of disciplinary norms and methodologies, including proper data collection and rigorous peer review. While more interested in local context than exhaustive encyclopedic documentation, legend scholars do embrace reference tools, motif analyses, tale-type indices, and cross-cultural comparisons. And while their motives differ from the naturalists of the Scientific Revolution (and the historians of science who study them), folklorists too are intrigued by accounts of Earth's anomalies, legendary monsters being but one of those, and view such legend cycles as the folk's own attempt to reconcile official accounts of how the world works with their own personal and community experiences. So, in sum, while there have been many field guides of North American monsters and many debunkings of the same, there has never been a casebook that, through folkloristic concern with community narrative, belief, and performance, has focused on rigorously fieldworked and duly sourced legendary North American monsters. And that is why I claim this volume is the first of its kind.

What differentiates this casebook is its commitment to *legendary monsters* in their *native habitats* and the *folkloric approach* to studying them. For some, especially those not attuned to folk narrative and belief, I suspect the monsters presented here might initially feel underwhelming. Compared to monsters in other media, folklore monsters tend to be muted, their narratives understated, their legends, at least originally, carried along without screenwriters, novelists, or illustrators who transform subtle legendary monsters into lurid media monsters. Nonetheless, or perhaps for this reason, legendary monsters are welcomed in a wide range of media, and they prove willing travelers, journeying by any means available, rarely ever reaching a final destination. These modes can interbreed, cross-pollinate, feint one way and bolt the other.[35] Monster legends can be passed on in oral form by word of mouth, transmitted visually or digitally, shared one-on-one, performed in front of a large studio audience, streamed across the airwaves to millions at once, or stored asynchronously on a video hosting platform to be stumbled upon years later.

Legendary monsters are particularly intriguing because of the many environments they successfully navigate. Bigfoot, for example, might be the antagonist of a short story, be portrayed in a blurry photograph circulated on the Web, be regaled in legend form around a campfire, or be the star of his own movie. "We cannot say any one of these is the true or original" monster, Foster writes, but "they are versions of each other—the same but different," and it's the "ability to thrive in diverse environments, to perform in multiple platforms" that makes monsters especial interesting (2015, 92). In fact, because a legendary monster can bounce around, though it may lose its local and contextual meaning, its analytic potential only increases as a "free agent" or a "mutable metaphor for all sorts of purposes" (Foster 2013, 139). By contrast, it's important to note that legendary monsters are not lone victims in this folk-media process. Legendary monsters themselves appropriate popular culture, where they "feed themes, motifs, and descriptive details back into the small-group intimate transmission" in an "effortless comingling" (Goldstein, Grider, and Thomas 2007, 5–6). Monsters are at home in many forms of media, and folklorists can and will follow legendary monster dissemination anywhere the monsters lead. Because cinematic, literary, and metaphorical monsters are comparatively well covered in other disciplines, steadfast and careful consideration of folkloric and legendary monsters, wherever they roam, is folklorists' prime contribution to the larger interdisciplinary monster studies endeavor.

LEGENDARY MONSTERS: YESTERDAY AND TOMORROW

And now, I present nineteen monster chapters covering the gamut of legend scholarship, spanning half a century and an entire continent. In the early chapters, readers will encounter standard folkloristic methods in monster research, including fieldwork techniques, interviewing, transcription, participant-observation, motif and tale-type identification, and folklore archive research. They will also glimpse the importance of function, variants, performance, community re-creation, ecotypes, kernels of truth, diffusion, and issues of ethics, rapport, and respect for local cultural knowledge. As the chapters progress and inquiry expands, the questions folklorists pose become increasingly complex, pulling in concepts developing throughout the field in the second half of the twentieth century. Authors tackle ideas of ostension, legend tripping, legend climate, regionalism, cosmology, worldview, memorates, liminality, the experience-centered study of belief, and the invention of tradition. Readers will detect a concern with interrelationships: between legend, myth, and tall tale; between legend, journalism, and newsprint; between legend tourism, brochures, and guidebooks; between legend, film, and television; between legend and anti-legend; even between legend and legend scholars as inadvertent legend instigators. By the final chapters, legendary monster researchers broach the leading questions of the present era, including hybridity, intertextuality, creolization, colonialism, appropriation, artistic license, digital culture, conspiracy theory, fête and festival, celebration, and revival.

I can already hear the lamentations ringing in my ears. "But you left out *my* favorite monster!" My apologies! But I had sensible reasons, I promise. There was the ever-nagging word limit. Fitting in nineteen chapters, each on a different monster, and in a moderately sized, affordable book, was already a tight squeeze. But I agree, the New World has a wondrous menagerie of legendary monsters, and it's heartbreaking to leave out any, especially with such fabulous names as the Abominable Swamp Slob, the Ozark Howler, and the Whirling Whimpus. But North American legendary monsters are underresearched. There were more worthy essays than could fit into a single casebook, but not many more. Legendary monster studies conducted with the folklorist's dedication to fieldwork, oral tradition, variants, and contextualization are few and far between, lost in a sea of amateur monster hunters and midnight creature feature enthusiasts. That's a good thing. As scholars say, there's room here. We need you. Use these chapters as models, and don't allow your town, state, or region's monster to wither in obscurity.

Ideally, I would have included every monster in North America, but as the authors here show, tracking down interviewees, rifling through folklore archives, squinting through microfiche, and searching out monster ephemera requires prolonged toil (and honestly, monster research can be a tough sell to your fiancé's family at the Thanksgiving table). So while any author can crank out search engine results and throw together collected digital tidbits combined with her own literary inspiration—the type of "fakelore" that would have folklore purist Richard M. Dorson not only spinning in his grave but contemplating his own monstrous return—outstanding monster research requires good old-fashioned hard work. Listen to what these monsters have to teach you, and then go out and find your own—and remember to bring your recorder.

NOTES

1. European explorers were primed to encounter monsters and monstrous races, and their subsequent discoveries are frequently discussed in histories of the Age of Exploration and in discussions of monsters and the New World. See, for example, Surekha Davies's (2013) chapter section "Monstrous People at the Ends of the Earth" for a discussion of some of the monster hearsay Columbus encountered (63–71). Magellan's shipmate and voyage chronicler Antonio Pigafetta documents their meeting giants (*giganti*) in his *Magellan's Voyage around the Word* (Pigafetta 1906, 49–61).

2. For more on the idea of native inhabitants *as* monsters, see Friedman 2000; Looper 2013.

3. Pinzón's "strange Monster" and other New World sightings and depictions are reported and discussed in van Duzer (2013), 423–29; Columbus's "mermaid" report can be found in the *Journal of the First Voyage of Columbus* under his entry for "Wednesday, 9th of January" (see Markham 2010, 154).

4. A comprehensive and thoroughly useful overview of this history is Thomas Friedman's *The Monstrous Races in Medieval Art and Thought* (2000).

5. For a quick introductory overview of monstrous births, see Weinstock 2020, 6–12.

6. For a compelling example of monster analysis embedded in a much larger ethnographic study, see Pritchard's *The Nuer* (1940).

7. The most frequently cited is Cohen's own chapter from that collection, "Monster Culture (Seven Theses)."

8. Similarly, in his monster studies collection, one that emphasizes theory, Weinstock (2020) observes, "One difficulty confronting monster theory researchers . . . has been the dispersed nature of the scholarship—a difficulty exacerbated by the transnational and transdisciplinary nature of the investigation" (1).

9. The folkloristic study of legendary ghosts boasts a more prolific literature than legendary monsters. For a sampling of how folklorists approach ghosts, see Bennett 1999; Bronner 2012, 277–342; Browne 1976; Ellis 2003, 117–41; Goldstein, Grider, and Thomas 2007; Harris 2015; Hufford 1995; Iwasaka and Toelken 1994; Jones 1944; McNeil 1985; Montell 1975; Tucker 2007. In addition, metaphorical ghost spectrality literature (what Roger Lockhurst recognizes as meta-gothic haunted modernity literature) mingles with literal ghosts and invokes haunting metaphors but fails to investigate folklorists' core concerns. For commentary on metaphorical ghost spectrality, see Fisher 2017; Luckhurst 2002a; Stevens and Tolbert 2018.

10. For example, in the introduction to a monster anthology published just before this casebook went to press, Weinstock (2020) breaks monster studies into three parts: teratology, mythology (folklorists would much prefer "folklore"), and psychology. He further breaks mythology into monstrous races, monsters from myth and fantasy, and cryptids.

While contemporary folklorists can contribute to the latter two categories, it's the study of cryptids, broadly conceived, where folklorists can be of greatest service to the monster studies movement.

11. As ethnographers, folklorists no longer bother with the charade of detached and ostensibly objective indifference—the folklorists in this casebook, for the most part, are indelibly entangled with their monsters.

12. Or, as Susan Stewart describes the legend's distinctive impending and threatening temporal characteristics, "the listener's welfare becomes increasingly implicated as the narrative sequence proceeds" because "audience time and narrative time collapse into each other as the story-teller proceeds" (1982, 33–34).

13. Foster's research specifically addresses "yokai," which are indeed Japanese legendary monsters, but can encompass an even larger spectrum of beings, including ghosts and animals. As Foster is one of the premier folklorists working in this subfield, almost all of his thinking applies equally to Western monsters. Therefore, I use the words *yokai* and *monster* synonymously in this chapter, but I acknowledge they are not necessarily always a one-to-one comparison.

14. In his establishing essay (1996a), Cohen highlights "Do monsters really exist?" as the question that will come up in any serious monster discussion.

15. Woolley's work was first brought to my attention by Dendle (2013).

16. Carpenter wrote in a similar vein that "the actual existence of these extraordinary beings does not concern me here at all," only the "cultural phenomenon" that cannot be denied (1980, 98).

17. For a sample of the pivotal works resituating the field of folklore from text to social interaction, see Abrahams 1968; Bauman 1975; Ben-Amos 1971; Georges 1969; Hymes 1968.

18. For the full list of Hufford's scholarship applicable to monster studies, see "Recommended Reading List" in this casebook.

19. Or, as Goldstein, Grider, and Thomas write, there is a common "academic belief that supernatural tradition is antithetical to modern thought and therefore destined for imminent demise as technology and education increase" (2007, 19).

20. Dendle notes how technology feeds belief in UFOs and aliens, which he calls "the signature folklore of the technological age" (2013, 446; see also Clarke and Roberts 2007).

21. Susan Stewart referred to the legend in oral form as existing in the "peculiar place between the real and the fictive" (1982, 35).

22. See Puglia's Goatman essay (chapter 12) in this casebook for an example in action.

23. Cohen, in his third of seven monster theses, writes that the monster is a "messenger" or "harbinger of category crisis" that embodies "a relentless hybridity that resists assimilation into secure epistemologies" (2013, 452). Similarly, Mittman sees monsters as "theatrical constructs by which we might gain greater understanding of the cultures by which they are produced" (2013, 9). And Gilmore argues that the universality of monsters alone proves they "must reveal something about the human mind" (2003, ix). Dendle sees importance not in monsters' fictitious nature but rather in their brilliant and constant navigation of the boundaries between real and imaginary (2013, 448). Goldstein, Grider, and Thomas write of how the supernatural has the intriguing power to both "reflect cultural values and simultaneously shape and maintain those values" (2007, 16). In her explanation, Barbara Walker focuses less on the importance of the monster and more on the groups that maintain that supernatural belief. She writes, "The events and phenomena reported or described within a

group give us evidence of a particular way of perceiving the world. It provides insight into cultural identity and a greater awareness of the breadth and quality of human experiences and expressions. How groups regard the supernatural contributes to thought and behavior, and by attending to those patterns, we gather a fuller understanding of what's meaningful to the group, what gives it cohesion and animation, and thus we develop a rounder perspective of cultural nuance, both within the group and cross-culturally" (1995, 4). Canadian folklorist Carpenter similarly argues, "Extraordinary beings are a surprisingly profitable area of investigation since they are a part of the people's own culture—the un-official or folk level of culture—which persists not through official or institutional support, but because it's of particular and peculiar importance to the people themselves" (1980, 106). Likewise, writing about the folkloric treatment of American animals, Gillespie and Mechling argue that "American symbolic discourse about an animal is, simultaneously, American symbolic discourse about human relations" (1987, 1). It follows then, I would argue, that North American symbolic discourse about monsters is North American symbolic discourse about human relations, too.

24. Nonetheless, Barbara Walker notes how little this skepticism really matters to the supernatural beliefs that actually do pervade our daily lives. Regardless of the scientific consensus, people wake up, put on their lucky socks, walk to work while avoiding ladders and black cats, zip past the nonexistent thirteenth floor on the elevator, rub their lucky crystal before meeting with the boss, come home, make a quick call to the psychic hotline, and then feel the presence of their great-uncle before praying and going to sleep beneath their dream catcher. As Walker puts it, "Whether I'm skeptical or not really doesn't matter because these things are a part of my immediate world regardless" (1995, 4).

25. In his *Monster Theory Reader*, Weinstock gives the concept of monster hybridity a generous section of his introduction (2020, 12–15).

26. Dendle was referring specifically to zombies.

27. Put briefly, "aspects of the environment" or "attitudes towards the environment" (Thomas 2015, 44).

28. For further commentary on monsters, otherness, and alterity, see Camille 2004; Friedman 2000; Stewart 2014; Vernant 1991; Vernant and Doueihi 1986; Vidal-Naquet 1998. Weinstock has a brief but intriguing section on the theme of monster otherness, subtitled "Monster Politics," where he considers how monsterizing promotes imperialist political agendas, a common theme of contemporary monster theory essays (2020, 38–39).

29. For a sampling of this line of contemporary folkloristic thought on the supernatural, see Foster 2015; Goldstein, Grider, and Thomas 2007; Thomas 2015.

30. Perhaps it was overly restrictive to title this casebook *"North American" Monsters*, as what's American is also global, a thriving media industry having encouraged transnational proliferation. Monsters travel easily, encouraged by commerce, bouncing from country to country through different media outlets. But there does seem to be some minor difference by continent, and I will attempt to comment based on the general scholarly consensus. Breaking it down by continent, it might be fair to say that Asia has a closer and more playful relationship with its teeming monsters (the yokai in Japan, the dragon in China); Europe's monsters primarily existed on the fringes of civilization and later "elsewhere," such as in Africa and the Americas; Latin American and Caribbean monsters are a commentary on colonial and imperialist relations; and the United States, because of its late development, has a pantheon of "comic" creatures that nonetheless seem to comment on sociopolitical and environmental anxieties.

31. Except, of course, in Newfoundland, an island that seems to exist to be the exception to North American rules. For examples of the fairylore in Newfoundland, see Butler 1997; Narváez 1997; Rieti 1997. For other exceptions to the North American "No Fairy Zone" rule, see Wells 1997; Woodyard and Young 2019.

32. Dorson's passage has received international attention after best-selling fantasy author Neil Gaiman opened his novel *American Gods* (2001) with it. Folklorists noticed (see Evans 2018; Manning 2017).

33. For generations, folklorists have noted how ballads and legends lose some of their supernatural characteristics as they transplant into the New World. Drawing attention to the logic in Dorson's informants' explanation, Manning writes, "Creatures [that] embody and animate landscape features of uncanny alterity can scarcely be more portable than those landscape features themselves" (2017, 69).

34. While admittedly given scant attention in this casebook, science and technology studies and the history of science do not think monsters trivial. In fact, those disciplines share with folklore and anthropology a disinterest in debunking ghosts, monsters, or the supernatural. While the scholarship is oriented toward the ghost/technology interface, there is also a small literature on monsters (e.g., see Bynum 1997; Daston and Park 2001; Park and Daston 1981).

35. Folklorists Angus Gillespie and Jay Mechling identify legends of American creatures carried on, at the very least, in conversational genres, oral narrative, children's literature and film, popular, mass, commercial culture, performances (like tour guides), elite culture, and science (1987, 4–8). Foster calls this "media mix," the idea that "the same character can perform on many different platforms" (2015, 92–93).

REFERENCES CITED

Abrahams, Roger D. 1968. "Introductory Remarks to a Rhetorical Theory of Folklore." *Journal of American Folklore* 81 (320): 143–58.

Ames, Michael M. 1980. "Epilogue to *Manlike Monsters on Trial*." In *Manlike Monsters on Trial: Early Records and Modern Evidence*, edited by Michael M. Ames and Marjorie M. Halpin, 301–15. Vancouver: University of British Columbia Press.

Ames, Michael M., and Marjorie M. Halpin, eds. 1980. *Manlike Monsters on Trial: Early Records and Modern Evidence*. Vancouver: University of British Columbia Press.

Asma, Stephen T. 2009. *On Monsters: An Unnatural History of Our Worst Fears*. Oxford: Oxford University Press.

Bauman, Richard. 1975. "Verbal Art as Performance." *American Anthropologist* 77 (2): 290–311.

Bell, Karl, ed. 2019. *Supernatural Cities: Enchantment, Anxiety, Spectrality*. Woodbridge: Boydell.

Ben-Amos, Dan. 1971. "Toward a Definition of Folklore in Context." *Journal of American Folklore* 84: 3–15.

Bennett, Gillian. 1987. *Traditions of Belief: Women and the Supernatural*. New York: Penguin.

Bennett, Gillian. 1999. *"Alas, Poor Ghost!" Traditions of Belief in Story and Discourse*. Logan: Utah State University Press.

Blank, Trevor J., and Lynne S. McNeill, eds. 2018. *Slender Man Is Coming: Creepypasta and Contemporary Legends on the Internet*. Logan: Utah State University Press.

Bronner, Simon J. 2012. *Campus Traditions: Folklore from the Old-Time College to the Modern Mega-University*. Jackson: University Press of Mississippi.

Bronner, Simon J. 2014. "'The Shooter Has Asperger's': Autism, Belief, and 'Wild Child' Narratives." *Children's Folklore* 36: 35–53.

Browne, Ray. 1976. *"A Night with the Hants" and Other Alabama Folk Experiences.* Bowling Green, OH: Popular Press.

Brunvand, Jan Harold. 2003 [1981]. *The Vanishing Hitchhiker: American Urban Legends and Their Meanings.* New York: Norton.

Brzozowksa-Brywczyńska, Maja. 2007. "Monstrous/Cute: Notes on the Ambivalent Nature of Cuteness." In *Monsters and the Monstrous: Myths and Metaphors of Enduring Evil,* edited by Niall Scott, 213–28. Amsterdam: Rodolpi.

Butler, Gary R. 1997. "The *Lutin* Tradition in French-Newfoundland Culture: Discourse and Belief." In *The Good People: New Fairylore Essays,* edited by Peter Narváez, 5–21. Lexington: University Press of Kentucky.

Bynum, C. W. 1997. "Wonder." *American Historical Review* 102 (1): 1–26.

Camille, Michael. 2004. *Image of the Edge: The Margins of Medieval Art.* London: Reaktion Books.

Campbell, Joseph. 1991 [1988]. *The Power of Myth.* New York: Anchor Books.

Carpenter, Carole H. 1980. "The Cultural Role of Monsters in Canada." In *Manlike Monsters on Trial: Early Records and Modern Evidence,* edited by Michael M. Ames and Marjorie M. Halpin, 97–108. Vancouver: University of British Columbia Press.

Carroll, Michael P. 1987. "'The Castrated Boy': Another Contribution to the Psychoanalytic Study of Urban Legends." *Folklore* 98 (2): 216–25.

Christiansen, Reidar Th. 1958. *The Migratory Legends.* Folklore Fellows Communications 175. Helsinki: Suomalainen Tiedeakatemian.

Clarke, David, and Andy Roberts. 2007. *Flying Saucerers: A Social History of UFOlogy.* Loughborough, UK: Alternative Albion.

Cohen, Jeffrey Jerome. 1996a. "Monster Culture (Seven Theses)." In *Monster Theory: Reading Culture,* edited by Jeffrey Jerome Cohen, 3–25. Minneapolis: University of Minnesota Press.

Cohen, Jeffrey Jerome, ed. 1996b. *Monster Theory: Reading Culture.* Minneapolis: University of Minnesota Press.

Cohen, Jeff Jerome. 2013. "Postscript: The Promise of Monsters." In *The Ashgate Research Companion to Monsters and the Monstrous,* edited by Asa Simon Mittman and Peter J. Dendle, 449–64. Aldershot, UK: Ashgate.

Coleman, Loren. 2007. *Mysterious America: The Ultimate Guide to the Nation's Weirdest Wonders, Strangest Spots, and Creepiest Creatures.* New York: Paraview Pocket Books.

Daston, Lorraine J., and Katharine Park. 2001. *Wonders and the Order of Nature, 1150–1750.* Cambridge, MA: Zone Books.

Davies, Surekha. 2013. "The Unlucky, the Bad, and the Ugly: Categories of Monstrosity from the Renaissance to the Enlightenment." In *The Ashgate Research Companion to Monsters and the Monstrous,* edited by Asa Simon Mittman and Peter J. Dendle, 49–76. Aldershot, UK: Ashgate.

Dendle, Peter. 2007. "The Zombie as Barometer of Cultural Anxiety." In *Monsters and the Monstrous: Myths and Metaphors of Enduring Evil,* edited by Niall Scott, 45–57. Amsterdam: Rodolpi.

Dendle, Peter. 2013. "Conclusion: Monsters and the Twenty-First Century: The Preternatural in an Age of Scientific Consensus." In *The Ashgate Research Companion to Monsters and the Monstrous,* edited by Asa Simon Mittman and Peter J. Dendle, 437–48. Aldershot, UK: Ashgate.

Dorson, Richard M. 1971 [1959]. "A Theory for American Folklore." In *American Folklore and the Historian,* 15–48. Chicago: University of Chicago Press.

Dorson, Richard M. 1982. *Man and Beast in American Comic Legend.* Bloomington: Indiana University Press.

Douglas, Mary. 1966. *Purity and Danger: An Analysis of Concepts of Pollution and Taboo.* London: Routledge.

Dundes, Alan. 1982. Introduction to *Man and Beast in American Comic Legend*, by Richard M. Dorson, ix–xix. Bloomington: Indiana University Press.

Dundes, Alan. 1985. "Nationalistic Inferiority Complexes and the Fabrication of Folklore." *Journal of Folklore Research* 22: 5–18.

Eastman, Charles R. 1915. "Early Portrayals of the Opossum." *American Naturalist* 49 (586): 585–94.

Ellis, Bill. 1989. "Death by Folklore: Ostension Contemporary Legend, and Murder." *Western Folklore* 48 (3): 201–20.

Ellis, Bill. 2003. *Aliens, Ghosts and Cults: Legends We Live.* Jackson: University of Mississippi Press.

Evans, Timothy H. 2018. "Slender Man, H. P. Lovecraft, and the Dynamics of Horror Cultures." In *Slender Man Is Coming: Creepypasta and Contemporary Legends on the Internet*, edited by Trevor J. Blank and Lynne S. McNeill, 128–40. Logan: Utah State University Press.

Fine, Gary Alan, and Bill Ellis. 2013. *Global Grapevine: Why Rumors of Immigration, Terrorism, and Trade Matter.* Oxford: Oxford University Press.

Fine, Gary Alan, and Irfan Khawaja. 2005. "Celebrating Arab Terrorists: Rumor and the Politics of Plausibility." In *Rumor Mills: The Social Impact of Rumor and Legend*, edited by Gary Alan Fine, Véronique Campion Vincent, and Chip Heath, 189–205. New Brunswick, NJ: Aldine Transaction.

Fisher, Mark. 2017. *The Weird and the Eerie.* London: Repeater.

Foster, Michael Dylan. 2008. *Pandemonium and Parade: Japanese Monsters and the Culture of Yokai.* Logan: Utah State University Press.

Foster, Michael Dylan. 2013. "Early Modern Past to Postmodern Future: Changing Discourses of Japanese Monsters." In *The Ashgate Research Companion to Monsters and the Monstrous*, edited by Asa Simon Mittman and Peter J. Dendle, 133–50. Aldershot: Ashgate.

Foster, Michael Dylan. 2015. *The Book of Yokai: Mysterious Creatures of Japanese Folklore.* Berkeley: University of California Press.

Friedman, John Block. 2000. *The Monstrous Races in Medieval Art and Thought.* Syracuse: Syracuse University Press.

Gabriel, Elun. 2007. "The Anarchist as Monster in Fin-de-Siècle Europe." In *Monsters and the Monstrous: Metaphors of Enduring Evil*, edited by Niall Scott, 103–20. Amsterdam: Rodolpi.

Gaiman, Neil. 2001. *American Gods: A Novel.* New York: William Morrow.

Georges, Robert. 1969. "Toward an Understanding of Storytelling Events." *Journal of American Folklore* 82 (326): 313–28.

Gillespie, Angus K., and Jay Mechling, eds. 1987. *American Wildlife in Symbol and Story.* Knoxville: University of Tennessee Press.

Gilmore, David D. 2003. *Monsters: Evil Beings, Mythical Beasts, and All Manner of Imaginary Terrors.* Philadelphia: University of Pennsylvania Press.

Goldstein, Diane. 2007. "Scientific Rationalism and Supernatural Experience Narratives." In *Haunting Experiences: Ghosts in Contemporary Folklore*, edited by Diane Goldstein, Sylvia Grider, and Jeannie Banks Thomas, 60–78. Logan: Utah State University Press.

Goldstein, Diane, Sylvia Grider, and Jeannie Banks Thomas. 2007. *Haunting Experiences: Ghosts in Contemporary Folklore.* Logan: Utah State University Press.

Halberstam, Jack. 1995. *Skin Shows: Gothic Horror and the Technology of Monsters*. Durham, NC: Duke University Press.

Halpin, Marjorie M. 1980. "Investigating the Goblin Universe." In *Manlike Monsters on Trial: Early Records and Modern Evidence*, edited by Michael M. Ames and Marjorie M. Halpin, 3–26. Vancouver: University of British Columbia Press.

Harris, Jason. 2015. "Shadows of the Past in the Sunshine State: St. Augustine Ghost Lore and Tourism." *Western Folklore* 74 (3–4): 309–42.

Hassig, Debra. 1995. *Medieval Bestiaries: Text, Image, Ideology*. Cambridge: Cambridge University Press.

Hawthorne, Nathaniel. 1961[1860]. *The Marble Faun*. New York: New American Library.

Heuvelmans, Bernard. 1958. *On the Track of Unknown Animals*. Translated by Richard Garnett. London: Rupert Hart-Davis.

Hufford, David. 1977. "Humanoids and Anomalous Lights: Taxonomic and Epistemological Problems." *Fabula* 18 (1): 234–41.

Hufford, David J. 1982. "Traditions of Disbelief." *New York Folklore* 8 (3): 3–4, 47–55.

Hufford, David J. 1995. "Beings without Bodies: An Experience-Centered Theory of the Belief in Spirits." In *Out of the Ordinary*, edited by Barbara Walker, 11–45. Logan: Utah State University Press.

Hymes, Dell. 1968. "The Ethnography of Speaking." In *Readings in the Sociology of Language*, edited by Joshua A. Fishman, 99–138. The Hague: Mouton.

Iwasaka, Michiko, and Barre Toelken. 1994. *Ghosts and the Japanese: Cultural Experience in Japanese Death Legends*. Logan: Utah State University Press.

Jones, Louis C. 1944. "The Ghosts of New York: An Analytical Study." *Journal of America Folklore* 57 (226): 237–54.

Jones, Louis C. 1983 [1959]. *Things That Go Bump in the Night*. Syracuse: Syracuse University Press.

Kirtley, Bacil F. 1964. "Unknown Hominids and New World Legends." *Western Folklore* 23 (2): 77–90.

Lang, Andrew. 1894. *Cock Lane and Common-sense*. London: Longman's.

Langlois, Janet L. 1978. "Belle Gunness, the Lady Bluebeard: Community Legend as Metaphor." *Journal of the Folklore Institute* 15 (2): 147–60.

Langlois, Janet L. 2005. "'Celebrating Arabs': Tracing Legend and Rumor Labyrinths in Post-9/11 Detroit." *Journal of American Folklore* 118 (468): 219–36.

Lévi-Strauss, Claude. 1962. *The Savage Mind*. Chicago: University of Chicago Press.

Looper, Matthew. 2013. "The Maya 'Cosmic' Monster as a Political and Religious Symbol." In *The Ashgate Research Companion to Monsters and the Monstrous*, edited by Asa Simon Mittman and Peter J. Dendle, 197–216. Aldershot, UK: Ashgate.

Luckhurst, Roger. 2002a. "The Contemporary London Gothic and the Limits of the 'Spectral Turn.'" *Textual Practice* 16 (3): 527–46.

Luckhurst, Roger. 2002b. *The Invention of Telepathy*. Oxford: Oxford University Press.

Manning, Paul. 2017. "No Ruins. No Ghosts." *Preternature: Critical and Historical Studies on the Preternatural* 6 (1): 63–92.

Manning, Paul. 2018. "Spiritualist Signal and Theosophical Noise." *Linguistic Anthropology* 28 (1): 67–92.

Markham, Clements R., ed. 2010 [1893]. *The Journal of Christopher Columbus (during His First Voyage, 1492–93)*. Cambridge: Cambridge University Press.

McNeil, W. K. 1985. *Ghost Stories from the American South*. New York: Dell.

McNeill, Lynne, and Elizabeth Tucker, eds. 2018. *Legend Tripping: A Contemporary Legend Casebook*. Logan: Utah State University Press.

Meurger, Michel. 1989. *Lake Monster Traditions: A Cross-Cultural Analysis*. Translated by Claude Gagnon. London: Fortean Tomes.

Mitchell, Roger E. 1979. "The Press, Rumor, and Legend Formation." *Midwestern Journal of Language and Folklore* 5 (1–2): 1–61.

Mittman, Asa Simon. 2013. "Introduction: The Impact of Monsters and Monster Studies." In *The Ashgate Research Companion to Monsters and the Monstrous*, edited by Asa Simon Mittman and Peter J. Dendle, 1–16. Aldershot, UK: Ashgate.

Montell, William Lynwood. 1975. *Ghosts along the Cumberland: Deathlore in the Kentucky Foothills*. Knoxville: University of Tennessee Press.

Musharbash, Yasmine. 2014. "Introduction: Monsters, Anthropology, and Monster Studies." In *Monster Anthropology in Australasia and Beyond*, edited by Yasmine Musharbash and Geir Henning Presterudstuen, 1–24. New York: Palgrave Macmillan.

Musharbash, Yasmine, and Geir Henning Presterudstuen, eds. 2014. *Monster Anthropology in Australasia and Beyond*. New York: Palgrave Macmillan.

Musharbash, Yasmine, and Geir Henning Presterudstuen. 2020. *Monster Anthropology: Ethnographic Explorations of Transforming Social Worlds through Monsters*. London: Bloomsbury Academic.

Narváez, Peter. 1997. "Newfoundland Berry Pickers 'in the Fairies': Maintaining Spatial, Temporal, and Moral Boundaries through Legendry." In *The Good People: New Fairylore Essays*, edited by Peter Narváez, 336–68. Lexington: University Press of Kentucky.

Oring, Eliott. 1990. "Legend, Truth, and News." *Southern Folklore* 47 (2): 163–77.

Park, Katharine, and Lorraine J. Daston. 1981. "Unnatural Conceptions: The Study of Monsters in Sixteenth- and Seventeenth-Century France and England." *Past & Present* 92 (1): 20–54.

Parrish, Susan Scott. 1997. "The Female Opossum and the Nature of the New World." *William and Mary Quarterly* 54 (3): 475–514.

Peck, Andrew. 2015. "Tall, Dark, and Loathsome: The Emergence of a Legend Cycle in the Digital Age." *Journal of American Folklore* 128 (509): 333–48.

Pigafetta, Antonio. 1906. *Magellan's Voyage around the World*, vol. 1., Edited and translated by James Alexander Robertson. Cleveland: Arthur H. Clark.

Poole, W. Scott. 2011. *Monsters in America: Our Historical Obsession with the Hideous and the Haunting*. Waco: Baylor University Press.

Pritchard, E. E. Evans. 1940. *The Nuer: A Description of the Modes of Livelihood and Political Institutions of a Nilotic People*. Oxford: Clarendon.

Puglia, David J. 2019. "The Goatman and Washington, D.C.: Strange Sightings and the Fear of the Encroaching City." In *Supernatural Cities*, edited by Karl Bell, 145–64. Woodbridge, UK: Boydell & Brewer.

Quinn, Dennis P. 2010. "Culture of an Unwitting Oracle: The (Unintended) Religious Legacy of H. P. Lovecraft." *PopMatters*. https://www.popmatters.com/cults-of-an-unwitting-oracle-the-unintended-religious-legacy-of-h-p-lovecraft-2496158350.html.

Rieti, Barbara. 1997. "'The Blast' in Newfoundland Fairy Tradition." In *The Good People: New Fairylore Essays*, edited by Peter Narváez, 284–98. Lexington: University Press of Kentucky.

Schwabe, Claudia. 2019. *Craving Supernatural Creatures: German Fairy-tale Figures in American Pop Culture*. Detroit: Wayne State University Press.

Stasch, Rupert. 2014. "Afterword: Strangerhood, Pragmatics, and Place in the Dialectics of Monster and Norm." In *Monster Anthropology in Australasia and Beyond*, edited by Yasmine Musharbash and Geir Henning Presterudstuen, 195–214. New York: Palgrave Macmillan.

Stevens, Vanessa, and Jeffrey A. Tolbert. 2018. "Beyond Metaphorical Spectrality: For New Paranormal Geographies." *New Directions in Folklore* 16 (1): 27–57.

Stewart, Charles. 2014. "The Symbolism of the Exotiká." *Semiotic Review* 2. https://www
.semioticreview.com/ojs/index.php/sr/article/view/21/21.

Stewart, Susan. 1982. "The Epistemology of the Horror Story." *Journal of American Folklore*
95 (375): 33–50.

Sutton-Smith, Brian. 1970. "Psychology of Childlore: The Triviality Barrier." *Western
Folklore* 29 (1): 1–8.

Thomas, Jeannie Banks. 2007. "The Usefulness of Ghost Stories." In *Haunting Experiences:
Ghosts in Contemporary Folklore*, edited by Diane Goldstein, Sylvia Grider, and Jeannie
Banks Thomas, 25–59. Logan: Utah State University Press.

Thomas, Jeannie Banks. 2015. Introduction to *Putting the Supernatural in Its Place: Folklore, the
Hypermodern, and the Ethereal*, edited by Jeannie Banks Thomas, 1–23. Salt Lake City:
University of Utah Press.

Thompson, Stith. 1955–1958. *Motif-Index of Folk-Literature*. Bloomington: Indiana
University Press.

Tolbert, Jeffrey A. 2013. " 'The Sort of Story That Has You Covering Your Mirrors': The
Case of Slender Man." *Semiotic Review* 2. https://semioticreview.com/ojs/index
.php/sr/article/view/19.

Tucker, Elizabeth. 2007. *Haunted Halls: Ghostlore of American College Campuses*. Jackson:
University Press of Mississippi.

Turner, Victor. 1969. *Ritual Process: Structure and Anti-structure*. London: AldineTransaction.

Van Duzer, Chet. 2013. "Hic Sunt Dracones: The Geography and Cartography of
Monsters." In *The Ashgate Research Companion to Monsters and the Monstrous*, edited by
Asa Simon Mittman and Peter J. Dendle, 387–436. Aldershot, UK: Ashgate.

Vernant, Jean Pierre. 1991. "Death in the Eyes: Gorgo, Figure of the Other." In *Mortals
and Immortals: Collected Essays*, 111–38. Princeton, NJ: Princeton University Press.

Vernant, Jean Pierre, and Anne Doueihi. 1986. "Feminine Figures of Death in Greece."
Diacritics 16 (2): 54–64.

Vidal-Naquet, Pierre. 1998. "Land and Sacrifice in the *Odyssey*: A Study of Religious and
Mythical Meanings," in *The Black Hunter: Forms of Thought and Forms of Society in the
Greek World*, translated by A. Szegedy-Maszak. Baltimore, MD: Johns Hopkins
University Press.

Wachs, Eleanor. 1982. "The Crime Victim Narrative as a Folkloric Genre." *Journal of the
Folklore Institute* 19 (1): 17–30.

Walker, Barbara, ed. 1995. *Out of the Ordinary: Folklore and the Supernatural*. Logan: Utah
State University Press.

Weinstock, Jeffrey Andrew. 2020. "Introduction: A Genealogy of Monster Theory." In
The Monster Theory Reader, edited by Jeffrey Andrew Weinstock, 1–55. Minneapolis:
University of Minnesota Press.

Wells, Rosemary. 1997. "The Making of an Icon: The Tooth Fairy in North American
Folklore and Popular Culture." In *The Good People: New Fairylore Essays*, edited by
Peter Narváez, 426–54. Lexington: University Press of Kentucky.

Winick, Stephen. 1992. "Batman in the Closet: A New York Legend." *Contemporary Legend*
2: 1–21.

Woodyard, Chris, and Simon Young. 2019. "Three Notes and a Handlist of North
American Fairies." *Supernatural Studies* 6 (1): 56–85.

Woolley, Jacqueline D. 1999. "Thinking about Fantasy: Are Children Fundamentally
Different Thinkers and Believers from Adults?" In *Annual Progress in Child Psychiatry
and Child Development*, edited by Margaret E. Hertzig and Ellen A. Farber, 57–88.
Philadelphia: Brunner/Mazel.

1

The Boondock Monster of Camp Wapehani

James P. Leary

PREFACE

As a first-semester doctoral student, James P. Leary enrolled, against the better judgment of his peers, in legend doyenne Linda Dègh's legend seminar. For his term paper, which Dègh would later publish in *Indiana Folklore*, Leary recalled his days as a Boy Scout in his native Wisconsin and the stories of the Swamp Man that haunted Camp Phillips. Supposing his was not the only camp threatened by monsters, he searched the Indiana University Folklore Archives for reports of monstrous camp denizens, where he found variants with recurring motifs: looming, murderous dark-woods creatures who could be avoided by steering clear of particular off-limits areas. Leary hypothesized that such legends functioned to warn of dangerous areas and inhibit wayward campers (of which he presents several frightening and hilarious examples). Not satisfied with archival materials alone, though, Leary began interviewing local scoutmasters and spending time around campfires.

At Camp Wapehani, he learned his supernatural Swamp Man of the 1950s had become the mortal lunatic Boondock Man of the 1960s, who then vanished entirely in the 1970s. Here, Leary's research question came into focus as his interests turned diachronic. How and why do camp monsters change, and when do they die off? Leary's research method relied on chronicling, via interviews, the Boondock Monster in the 1950s, 1960s, and 1970s, with the ultimate goal of explaining its disappearance. Documenting the change over time, Leary's presentation relies heavily on verbatim interview transcriptions, a practice that later folklorists would deem essential to legend study.

https://doi.org/10.7330/9781646421602.c001

Leary found camp legend content corresponded closely with the pre-occupations of particular decades, explaining the monster's transformation and eventual disappearance as the legend's response to contextual and environmental changes. The legends, by avoiding precise monster descriptions or set narratives, were adaptable to contemporary needs and circumstances. By alluding to the Boondock Monster rather than insisting upon it, scout-masters allowed campers to do the heavy intellectual work in forming the "reality" of the monster. Leary's essay proves exemplary not only as a dia-chronic study of a camp legend but as an interview-based examination of how monster legends form, spread, thrive, and expire.

ESSAY

In the summer of 1962 I was a Boy Scout attending Camp Phillips which is situated west of Haugen, Wisconsin. During my tenure in the camp I encountered various fragmented narratives concerning a creature called the Swamp Man. Apparently he was a human who, for reasons never fully explained, decided to lead a hermit's existence in the swamps surrounding the camp. Somehow, either through a pact with the Devil or as the result of some supernatural event, the Swamp Man metamorphosed into an immortal being. It was his custom to roam the fringes of campsites at night in search of wayward Boy Scouts who, if caught, were carried off, never to be seen again.

The Swamp Man's story was never fixed, nor was it ever officially told around campfires; rather it was spread through conversation and allusion. Generally older Scouts dropped oblique references to the Swamp Man in the presence of younger boys. Supposedly various artifacts and documents concerning the Swamp Man—articles of clothing, photographs, newspaper clippings—were kept in the camp's main office. Only experienced Scouters were privy to these articles.

As I recall, fear of encountering the Swamp Man effectively kept us from wandering the woods at night. Our behavior was further altered as we, too, joined in speculations about the Swamp Man. We even matched our conjectures with actions as, one night, we locked a resisting fellow camper in the latrine that stood on the swamp's edge as bait for the Swamp Man. Of course, no monster appeared and, after a few hours, our victim's angry demands for release were complied with.

However, my experiences with the Swamp Man led me to suppose that similar monsters might be present at other camps. A survey of materials in Indiana University's Folklore Archives bore this supposition out. Some ten entries deal with monsters which supposedly attack young campers.

Invariably told by Scoutmasters and older Scouts, these narratives have certain common elements. They all say that some kind of terrible creature exists in the dark wood; it is usually stated directly or implied that one should avoid this area and that failure to keep out of the monster's domain leads to dire consequences. These narrative elements suggest Alan Dundes' motifemic sequence "Interdiction, Violation, Consequence";[1] a basic structure which suggests that the legends might function primarily for admonitory purposes. Another dimension is added by postulating that underlying this form is the legend-teller's desire to control potentially unruly campers. My own experience with camp monster legends tends to corroborate the hypothesis that this was indeed their major function.

It was with this knowledge in mind that I contacted Dr. Larry Steele, a local Scoutmaster, on 1 October 1973. Steele related to me a long account of a creature which inhabited the swampy regions around Camp Wapehani, just west of Bloomington, Indiana, in the mid-1950s. The creature was known to Steele as the Boondocks Monster.[2]

During the weekend of 5th-6th October 1973, local Boy Scouts converged on Wapehani and from older Scouts and staff members I gleaned texts which concerned the monster in the mid-1960s. Already certain differences were apparent between the two sets of narratives. The monster of the mid-1960s had changed from a supernatural being to a demented human: the "Boondocks Man."

I was eager to discover how contemporary Scouts conceived of the creature and so I arranged to spend time around the campfire with Bloomington's Troop 118. To my surprise, none of the dozen Scouts, whose ages ranged from twelve to fifteen, had even heard of any bizarre creature roaming the swamps around the camp. What developments had obliterated its presence?

In order to explicate this mystery, I intend first of all, to present the monster as he appeared in each decade, and, secondly, to set forth possible explanations for the Boondocks Monster's devolution. Such a discussion will not only examine the use of monster legends as a means of social control, but will also necessarily relate directly to the processes of legend formation, transmission and sustenance.

THE MONSTER IN THE MID-1950s

Actual descriptions of the monster occurred at various times during my conversation with Dr. Steele. I will summarize them in the interests of clarity: the monster is a supernatural creature, possibly from outer-space; he leaves enormous footprints in swampy areas around the camp, but avoids the dry ones. If any venture into his realm, they risk their lives. (1) (Numbers refer to informants in the appendix.)

THE MONSTER IN THE MID-1960S

When they were building the lake, this dude takes, this bulldozer down there and he gets it stuck. So he freaks out and he went crazy and he just lives down there in the swamp and is human, y'know. And he'd creep around at night and grab campers and take 'em back there and eat 'em . . . or somethin' . . . I don't know what he'd do with 'em . . . it used to leave seaweed, well you know, this kind of water weed in front of their tent or in their hair when they woke up. (6).

I can tell you about my tangle with the Boondocks Man. I was out one night swimming with a couple guys—skinny dippin'. Anyway there was this big thing . . . we saw it comin' through the water, it looked like a big turtle. And we were swimmin' toward it—galump, galump through the water. This guy with me was thinking he was pretty brave and so he said "I'll grab that turtle." So then he swam over toward the dark spot and it pulled him down into the water. He was never seen again. Happened right out there. (4)

THE MONSTER IN 1973

As stated previously, contemporary Scouts told no tales concerning a creature in the boondocks. However, they did tell several legends which were related to the camp and their camping experience.

INFORMANT: A long time ago there used to be—this guy and his wife used to live around here and they were trappers. And sometimes they'd see the Indians. The lady's husband would sometimes go away for a month or two. And one time he went away, he was gone for about three months and he still hadn't come back and she'd thought that he'd been scalped by Indians. And then that lady would come every night—is it a Tuesday or a Thursday—she's supposed to come to this area and scalp somebody each night or something like that. (8)

COLLECTOR: Yeah, what does she do that for?

INFORMANT: Well, it's supposed to be some spirit of revenge or something.

COLLECTOR: Does that sound silly to you?

INFORMANT AND OTHERS: Yeah.

At this point there was general laughter and several scouts said "Tell him about Draper Cabin. Haw, Haw."

Well, Draper is out at Morgan Monroe and we go campin' there a lot in the winter. And they have remains of an old dam where it used to be, where it dams up this creek. This guy used to do a lot of trapping and fishing out there and, anyway, one night his grandson was staying with him. They just went to bed and his grandson lays closest to the lagoon and they heard steps out in the leaves, walkin'. He looked up above the window where his grandfather was sleeping and there was this monster just broke the window—he reached in and grabbed him and dragged him out. When the boy saw that he opened the door and took off running real fast. Ran out to some highway close to there—five or six miles. They said he was in a daze. Some guy picked him up—took him to the police station. Three, four days before they could get him to talk.

Anyway he told 'em what had happened and where it was at and they went out there and checked it. They found this type of algae out on the glass of the window that was left. And then they saw where he'd been drug into the lagoon. So nobody went out to that place for about two or three years. Then a few Scouts—they didn't believe it—so they thought they's go out and fix the place up. That night, after they'd got it cleaned up, they decided to sleep in it that night. So during the night one kid had to go out to the restroom, so he told his buddies, "I've gotta go to the restroom, I'll be back in a few minutes." So he went out lookin' for it. His friends lay there about an hour, but he never did come back. So they told the Scoutmaster and went out lookin' for him and all they could ever find was his shoe left on the bridge that went out over the lagoon. So after that the police, they didn't know what to think. And they said there hasn't been nothin' goin' on there ever since. (9)

Scary stories did not hold the interests of the Scouts for long. After telling a few they shifted to a more preferred genre—"dirty jokes." Among the jokes told around the campfire were several which may well be classified as humorous "negative legends."[3] Here is one:

There were these guys in this house y'know. They were building this house and so forth. It was really late at night and, it wasn't really rainin' or nothin', but they didn't decide to go home. And so, they decided they'd stay the night. When they did they heard this noise; says (sung) "When the wall rolls over we will all be dead." And so they just don't worry about—they act like they didn't hear it. They're all sleepin' by the side of each other—they're actin' like they're asleep. And it says again (sung) "When the wall rolls over we will all be dead." Now they all knew that everybody heard it. So they were just sayin' "Do you hear that? . . . yeah, yeah, yeah" and all this. So they heard it again and said we'd better go investigate or else it's best to leave. There were these kids there. You know, they were playin' King of the Mountain that day and so forth and everything. Since they knew these guys were sleepin' there they decided to spy. And so while these guys were walkin' around tryin' to find what noise they'd heard, the kids were spyin' on them and when the kids heard that noise they hopped on that one bike and just flew away. And so they were all huntin' around and everything and they went in the bathroom and saw this turd with three ants on it singin', "When the wall rolls over we will all be dead." (12)

ANALYSIS

The above texts indicate a chronological devolution of the monster from a supernatural being to a man to a nonentity. Explanation and exposition are necessary to establish exactly why this has occurred; there are three sets of impressions, but the dynamic processes which engendered the Boondocks Monster's legendary complex, and which led to its subsequent disappearance have not been fully investigated. On the basis of text alone one might note that the campers of the '70s told only stories from which they were separated by time and place and, hence, postulate that they consider horror stories as fictions which do not figure in their real experience. The telling of jocular negative legends—which build up fearful suspense only to dissipate it through humor—lends further credence to this assertion through the supposition that contemporary Scouts are so sophisticated that they poke fun at scary stories. However, such statements may well be premature. Speculations about the '70s should be put aside until the '50s and '60s have been investigated.

With the exception of the account concerning the turtle-monster—a formalized narrative which was coherently presented as an actual experience related specifically to time, place, and persons—legends about the Boondocks Monster seem to conform with Leopold Schmidt's idea that a legend is all content with no fixable form at all.[4] This fact tends to indicate that the boondocks creature had a functional existence beyond his appearance in narrative.

In order to illustrate this it is useful to refer to my initial theory about the primary function of the monster's legend: social control. In her study of the use of ghost stories by southern slave-owners in order to exert control over their chattels, Gladys-Marie Fry makes this observation:

> The master's technique of utilizing the supernatural for the purposes of slave control employed three associated methods: first, the systematic use of simple narrative statements concerning the appearance of supernatural figures, such as ghosts and witches; second, the designation of purportedly haunted places usually located strategically along heavily traveled roads; and, third, actually masquerading as ghosts in order to employ any one of these methods, or all of them.[5]

The simultaneity of these factors is vividly present in Larry Steele's description of the Boondocks Monster:

> Well, I started on the camp staff in '55. I was fourteen at the time and we had an area in the camp that was very swampy; it was by the lake. You had to go through it to get to your cabin, and we had a problem one year with one troop making raids on another, staying out after taps, and doing other things—nothing malicious, but it really was a bummer because the kids weren't getting enough sleep. So, there had been a legend there about someone down in the boondocks which was what the swampy area was called . . . so some of the older staff members told some of us younger staff members that we had to stop the kids from making their midnight raids. So we told 'em that during the evening, when it was beginning to get dark, the Boondoggle came out of the boondocks, or the Swamp Monster as some of them called it, and it roamed the area. There had been a few kids who had been lost for several days and then they mysteriously reappeared and didn't remember what had happened.

COLLECTOR: Really? Wow.

INFORMANT: Yeah. Anyway the older staffmen told us that the easiest way to keep the kids in their tents at night was to explain the Swamp Monster or the Boondoggle never came out into the areas because he didn't like the dry areas around the campsites, but if people went out into the woods where it was moist and there was dew on the ground, then there was a possibility of running into him. And we have found articles of clothing down in the swamp, half-stuck in the mud; mysterious footprints that went into the mud then stopped all of a sudden.

COLLECTOR: These were things that were really there?

INFORMANT: Really were happening? Yes. And whether they were kids that had been walking in the marshes and jumped into a canoe in order to leave their footprints or what happened, we didn't know. But it always led for an interesting basis for our stories. So, the Swamp Monster was perpetuated and we told the kids about it and it worked. And the one story in particular which we really built up—this was at the time in the '50s when the flying saucers were the big thing. And Frank Edwards was talking about his *Strange As It Seems* around here,[6] which were many legends about things happening around this area. The quarries in this area are notoriously beautiful hiding places for flying saucers because, uh, because the saucers can land and go underwater and hide and nobody can ever—this is one reason why the temperature of different quarries varies, because if a saucer's been in there recently it's a warmer quarry than the other places where it's cooler. And it also cools off the metal on the spaceship. These are the things that we always . . .

COLLECTOR: . . . Fog rises and so you can't see anything?

INFORMANT: Right, right. Of course, you see, there's no shore for the waves to beat up against so you can't tell that something's landed cause it's, it's stone all the way around. And so this one time, it was close to the end of camp and sort of a "boress" [joke] and sort of as a fun thing for us, but to scare the hell out of the kids, we had this plastic Cub Scout—Johnny Cub Scout was his name—he was originally intended to be stood upon the front end of the dining hall porch. He had been mutilated through the years with his fingers cut off and moustaches drawn on and the statue had been defaced to the point where . . .

COLLECTOR: . . . it wasn't good for anything.

INFORMANT: Right, and it was really a shame having it around, so they told us to destroy him—to take him out and dump him in the lake cause he was of a wire frame—you couldn't bury him. In the center of our lake is reputed to be a quarry of some sort cause it's forty to fifty feet deep. Anyway the staffmen all prepared themselves for this, this Thursday night. And we put Johnny Cub Scout on the stretcher and draped him with black cloth and then the staffmen had prepared a tape. I had a big tape recorder there that year and we had, we took an electric razor and turned it on and dropped it down into a metal pitcher that we used in the dining hall and it made an eerie buzzing sound. And we took two Coke bottles and banged them together and blew on the Coke bottles which you got a—like you would take two steel ball bearings and click them together, you get a reverberation of sound. And then we put all this on tape in sequence. Like there was a whirring sound which was this razor in the pitcher, then there was this clicking sound which was like someone walking down steps and walking through the woods. Then we played this at half speed, cut it back, put this in the showerhouse and this was the background for our funeral procession through the camp.

COLLECTOR: And did—was the showerhouse a concrete place so that it would . . .

INFORMANT: . . . Yes, reverberate over the whole camp, over the whole sixty acres. And so we had a time, we knew that it would take us about fourteen minutes to walk around to all the units. And so we had fourteen minutes of this eerie sound. And we'd taken—we had a kid over by the dam with a glow from behind the dam. And we put on black blankets, dressed in black blankets as monks. And we had Indian dance bells which we taped around so that they didn't ring but they rattled. And we went through all the units and then went down to the dam and slid Johnny Cub Scout into the lake and then played muffled taps and then the flares went off. And then this tape recorder had the walking sound and then we all disappeared. Well, the next day there were dozens of stories of how the kids imagined what had happened because we really had built up the story of the Boondoggle that week. Very few Scoutmasters were pleased with what we had done because many of the kids were petrified and wanted to go home. Now I could understand why they would do that. But that sort of enlarged the story about the Boondoggle in that he had a clan of followers.

COLLECTOR: Now the Boondoggle—were they supposed to believe that he had originally come from outer space?

INFORMANT: That was one of the most prominent stories because—there were some that he was some kind of undersea monster, which the kids wouldn't believe anyway because there was no connection between our lake and any other body of water where he could get in there. So he had to come from somewhere and the easiest thing at that time, in our period of development, in the middle '50s, was flying saucers, y'know?

COLLECTOR: Yeah. He couldn't have just been an old man who was somehow a hermit?

INFORMANT: No, no he was, he was something supernatural, something away from the human type situation. His footprints were always bigger than a dog's prints, but these big footprints—and they could have been somebody with a lot of mud stuck to their galoshes and then made footprints that way, but they were—even kids would try to put their feet in the Boondoggle's footprint and it was too big. And it had hairy things around the edge of it which could have been . . .

COLLECTOR: . . . Now they were really . . .

INFORMANT: Yeah, they were there. But see we have friends of Scouting who go out there and frog gig and hunt turtles and things and could easily have had galoshes on.

COLLECTOR: Hip boots or something?

INFORMANT: Yeah and made these footprints. But there would be times when they would go out in a marshy area and, all of a sudden, stop. And the kids would say that either he was assumed into his subterranean something or other, or he was zapped into the sky and . . .

COLLECTOR: You'd hear them talking about this?

INFORMANT: Yes. Well, see all of these things then really blew up the next day because they then said that the Boondoggle had his cohorts come down and buried him and would put a substitute there sometime in the future. Other kids said that this was a situation where finally somebody was killed and so they came down and buried this somebody to destroy the evidence.

COLLECTOR: And that this somebody was a Scout?

INFORMANT: Was a Scout? Yeah. But they didn't know who was under the blanket, they could just see that it was in the form of a body. It kept going and even the next year the kids talked about that funeral procession and, unfortunately, we had some kids who didn't come back because they were afraid to come back to camp. The kids did not relate at all to us artificially preparing the sound. That sound was real. (1)

Steele continues with various observations on the impact of the funeral procession. Apparently, the event succeeded in not only terrorizing the Scouts, but it also had repercussions among its initiators: "We not only frightened the kids, but we got staff people and older adults who were aware of how we'd done the thing. They were still a little bit on edge because people couldn't explain the UFO's."[7]

We emerge from Steele's account with a clear picture of just how the three methods outlined by Fry might be effectively employed. Narrative statements about the mysterious Boondoggle were spread around, the swamp and quarry were alluded to, and staffmen enacted a multi-media charade. All three ultimately fused to create an intensely frightening experience. However there are dimensions of this experience which go beyond the methods noted by Fry: (1) there actually were mysterious footprints and bits of rotten clothing in the swamps and—if Scoutmasters could be believed—several Scouts really did disappear for several days; (2) the prevalence of UFO's at that time increased belief in the possibility of the Boondoggle's existence; and (3) the Scouts were young boys who were both unfamiliar in the nocturnal woods and gullible enough to believe any plausible tale about so strange an environment. Thus, in the case of the Boondocks Monster, we see concrete (sites, artifacts, footprints), narrative (stories and references concerning the Boondoggle), and contextual (the immediate aura of the dark scary woods and the larger atmosphere of uncertainty accompanying UFO sightings) elements synthesized and crystallized in a dramatic performance which both actualizes the legend and gives rise to subsequent legendry.

This performance is of particular importance because it effectively creates what may be called the legend atmosphere fraught with "mysterious ghostlike" sounds (E402), inexplicable lights (E530.1), strange dark figures (E446.4), and a graveyard ritual.[8] Furthermore, the practical material components figuring in the ritual—bells, blankets, pitchers, electric razors, Coke bottles, flares, a mannikin, and a tape recorder—were not exotic importations, rather they were everyday objects.

On perhaps a less elaborate level the performance phenomenon continued into the '60s. A giant metal foot was attached to a broom handle and stamped into soft, swampy ground; older Scouts smeared their faces with mud and scurried through the woods shaking bushes and leaving trails of waterweed; stories were circulated and Scoutmasters made concerted efforts to cow boisterous Scouts:

> I was workin' with a troop from Mooresville. And there was a Scoutmaster there that deliberately set up some really harrowing experiences for these kids which I participated in I'm ashamed to say, but so did the camp chaplain. About midnight one night the Scoutmaster was goin' "Hey, there's monsters around here. White Lady's gonna get you and the Boondocks Monster's s'posed to come out tonight" and stuff like that. So, long about midnight one of the counselors threw a poncho on and a ghostly lookin' mask and the camp chaplain threw a sheet over his head and had a flashlight down there [under the sheet] and they just scared the p——— outa those kids. (6)

Here we will recall that the Boondocks Monster was a demented man and that the UFO element was not present. This shift might be explained in the following manner: in the mid-1960s there was less public preoccupation with UFO's; since it was no longer quite so effective to speak of the boondocks creature as a being from outer space, his origin and presence were logically credited either to insanity or to the existence of a mysterious man-like animal.

Numerous modern legends involve madmen rather than supernatural beings.[9] Hairy monsters (F531.1.1.1.1.6.3 "Giants with shaggy hair on their bodies") resembling the Himalayan yeti or the Sasquatch of the Pacific Northwest[10] have long been supposedly present in the central United States.[11] Consequently, as had been done in the '50s, Scoutmasters concocted their monsters out of the most logical and available materials and brought them to life whenever the situation demanded their existence.

The ability to make monsters was important to Scoutmasters not only because it enabled them to control their Scouts, but also *because of the way* in which it allowed them to exercise control. Since Scoutmasters' jobs depended on rapport between them and their campers, it behooved the clever Scoutmaster to discipline his Scouts through indirect means whenever possible. A conversation with Larry Steele demonstrates this:

> This is one thing I've learned not to do, is to let a Scout get you into a corner, especially with discipline. If you say, "Do this something wrong and I'll have your b——," well that can mean a thousand things. But if I say, "If you do this, I'll fine you or kick you out" or something like that, you see they've backed you into a corner.
>
> COLLECTOR: But if you tell 'em this story then . . .
>
> INFORMANT: . . . Yeah—see then there's no way for them, you aren't backed into a corner. You can take 'em down there and show 'em the footprints. You can slip some moss on the showerhouse and tell 'em next morning the Boondoggle was up on top of the showerhouse lookin' around for somethin' to eat. (1)

Thus, through the story of the monster, the Scoutmaster could let the legend do his work for him.

That Scoutmasters were able to conjure up monsters and utilize them almost at will suggest that they, albeit unconsciously, possess sophisticated knowledge of what has been termed the "legend process." Linda Dègh and Andrew Vázsonyi have observed that "the procedure by which legends are being generated, formulated, transmitted and crystallized by means of communication through the legend conduit might be called . . . legend process."[12] This process is activated when a legend core based on common knowledge is fed into the legend conduit; once it is begun, the following is likely to occur: "the legend carriers—believers or non-believers—usually accept, pass on and are fed back the verbal communication they themselves have launched."[13] Since the legend is based on shared knowledge it is seldom transmitted by means of a narrator addressing an audience. In fact, because of its basis in shared knowledge, the legend is seldom articulated with artistic clarity and depth. The legend of the Boondocks Monster illustrates the legend process.

The monster's presence—both real or fictive—was acknowledged by everyone, and all engaged from time to time in speculation about the monster. Such speculations were encouraged by the fact that the boondocks creature was never brought into visual focus through precise definition; neither was the monster the subject of a set narrative, rather he was something about which a group of people commented within the course of conversation.

> I don't know how it started . . . First thing I heard when I got here was, well, there's this monster back there so you gotta be really careful. Seemed like everybody that came would make up their own story . . . because no one knew, there was no clear definition, there was no Boondocks Monster story. We just knew that there was one down there. (6)

Indeed, once established, the concept of a boondocks creature was maintained effectively through constant verbal communication between those at the camp. However, occasionally, a Scoutmaster would disrupt the legend process by jarring the legend from its group context to the extent that he became an inept performer in the face of an increasingly skeptical audience:

> Well the reason it failed is cause they talked too much about it. They said, "Hey, you hear about this?" They just spread it around too much. You know, if someone's like, if they keep repeating it—a good story's like when you're talking to another person and they overhear what you're saying. And that's how it first starts. And then you let the boys talk on their own. Let them figure it out. (7)

The clever Scoutmaster did not upset the legend process with heavy-handed talk, but was content with dropping a few subtle allusions here and there; then he allowed the Scouts' imagination and opinions free expression in a discussion of the monster's reality.[14]

Additionally, Scoutmasters were able to perpetuate the monster through enlisting older Scouts to do the work of monster-mongering. This partnership was developed to the point where the monster legend's primary function of social control took on a secondary, initiatory function. Older Scouts became junior custodians and agents of the legend, often activating it out of boredom or in order to assert dominance over younger Scouts. Consequently, as was the case with Scoutmasters, it was in the self-interest of older Scouts to maintain the legend.

Given the universality of the monster legend and its inextricable relationship with the dynamics of camp life throughout the 1950s and '60s, it is curious that no trace of the monster was to be found among members of 1973's Troop 118. Various questions come immediately to mind: are there no longer any plausible elements about the camp out of which to construct the monster; have Scouters lost their understanding of the legend process; have the old Scouts revealed their esoteric knowledge to younger campers; or, as suggested earlier, are contemporary Scouts simply too sophisticated to believe in monsters at all?

The answer would appear to be none of these; rather it is limited to two factors—one minor, the other of major importance. The first factor to consider is the partial destruction of the monster's original legend context. During the past four years Camp Wapehani has been used sparingly, if at all, for Scout functions. The appearance of apartment construction near the camp and numerous other circumstances have brought about the purchase of a new Scout camp south of Bloomington. Older Scouts are likely to say that, with the abandonment of Wapehani, the monster has disappeared. One Scouter showed me a twisted mass of wrecked lumber that once was a bridge and commented:

> Yeah, the Boondocks Man did it. Guess he was mad about the camp being deserted. Rumor has it that he moved out to the new camp. Wish I could remember more of those stories. Boy, they scared the s out of some of those Scouts . . . but he's gone now. Left when they started construction here. (4)

Meanwhile, when I confronted members of Troop 118 with a reference to a monster in the swamp, the first response to greet me was, "There's no swamp around here is there?" (10). Obviously, the Boondocks Monster could not survive without a familiar and ongoing social context.

Yet this explanation of the monster's disappearance is somewhat feeble. Why couldn't the monster be resurrected to fit the new situation; surely the legend is adaptable to conditions in the '70s? The solution to this dilemma becomes apparent when we take cognizance of what has become a trend in Scouting in recent years. This trend has positive and negative dimensions. It is opposed to the use of scary stories as reaction against the fact that, in the past, monsters made a camper's experience unnecessarily frightening:

> I don't believe scare or ghost stories have a place in any Scout camp. I gave a session once many years ago in a camp and was up almost all night with

scared boys and staff, and since that time gave up the practice of telling scare tales. (2)

On the other hand, progressive Scouters state that they would prefer it if the boys ran around the woods, since such experiences enabled them to get to know the woods and feel comfortable in it (3, 5). On the basis of accumulated data it would appear that the phenomenon of a monster lurking in the Boy Scouts' swamp is a constant which may be brought into palpable existence or shunted into near-oblivion according to the inclinations and talent of particular Scoutmasters.[15]

APPENDIX (INFORMANTS)

All informants were white. While some were sons of professors or were, themselves, involved in academia, others were of blue-collar backgrounds.

Scoutmasters
1. Larry Steele, 34, Bloomington, Indiana.
2. Bob Finehout, 3?, Bloomington.
3. Dick Martin, 28, Bloomington.

Staff members
4. Ron Rogers, 20, Bloomington.
5. Jim Svenstrup, 19, Bloomington.
6. Dave Schrodt, 20, Bloomington.
7. Nyle Johnson, 15, Bloomington.

Boy Scouts
8. Ray Keller, 13, Bloomington.
9. Bruce Foster, 15, Spencer.
10. Bill Oliver, 13, Bloomington.
11. Curtis Kruger, 14, Bloomington.
12. Fred Demscher, 12, Bloomington.
13. Tom Heise, 12, Bloomington.
14. John Heise, 12, Bloomington.
15. Chris Baker, 14, Ellettsville.
16. Kevin Coghlan, 12, Bloomington.
17. Bruce Shertzer, 12, Bloomington.

NOTES

1. Alan Dundes, *The Morphology of North American Indian Tales* (Helsinki: Suomalainen Tiedeaketamia, 1964).

2. The word "boondocks" refers to "an isolated forest, swamp, mountain, or jungle region" and is derived from the Tagalog "bundok," meaning mountain. *Dictionary of American*

Slang, ed. by Harold A. Wentworth and Stuart Berg Flexner (New York: Thomas Crowell Co., 1960), p. 54.

3. Similar narratives are examined in John M. Vlach, "One Black Eye and Other Horrors: A Case for the Humorous Anti-Legend," *Indiana Folklore* 4:2 (1971), 95–140. More recently Linda Dègh and Andrew Vázsonyi—"The Dialectics of the Legend," *Folklore Preprints Series* 1:6 (1973), 12–16—have challenged the application of the term "anti-legend" to such narratives, suggesting that "negative legend" is more appropriate.

4. Linda Dègh and Andrew Vázsonyi, "Legend and Belief," *Genre* 4:2 (1971), p. 281.

5. Gladys-Marie Fry, "The Night Riders: A Study in the Social Control of the Negro," PhD dissertation, Indiana University, Bloomington, 1967, p. 74.

6. Frank Edwards, now deceased, was an Indianapolis newscaster who devoted a show to documenting UFO's and other unusual phenomena.

7. For a discussion of UFO's see C. G. Jung, *Flying Saucers. A Modern Myth of Things Seen in the Skies* (New American Library, 1959).

8. Stith Thompson, *Motif Index of Folk Literature* (Bloomington: Indiana University Press, 1955–58).

9. For examples of madmen in modern legends see "The Laughing Woman," "The Hook," and "The Boyfriend's Death"—all from *Indiana Folklore* 1:1 (1968); see also Linda Dégh, "The Roommate's Death and Related Dormitory Stories in Formation," *Indiana Folklore* 2:2 (1969), 55–74.

10. For a discussion of these Alpine monsters see John Green, *Year of the Sasquatch* (Agassiz, British Columbia: Cheam Publishing Lt., 1970) and *The Track of the Sasquatch* (1971): see also John Napier, *Bigfoot* (London: Jonathan Cape, 1972).

11. John Green (1971) reproduces records of a "wild man of the woods" of "gigantic stature" and "covered with hair" from the *New Orleans Times Picayune*, 16 May 1851; additional references to the *Memphis Enquirer* and the *Galveston Weekly Journal* suggest the monster was a survivor of an 1811 earthquake disaster in rural Arkansas. More recent articles—Otto Ernest Rayburn, "Some Fabulous Monsters and Other Folk Beliefs from the Ozarks," *Midwest Folklore* 10:1 (1960) and Ronald L. Baker, "Monsterville: A Traditional Place-Name and its Legends," *Names* 20:3 (1972), 186–91—chronicle hairy monsters in Arkansas and Indiana. A few of the clippings sent to the Indiana University Folklore Archives by Loren C. Coleman (Decatur, Illinois) indicate such a monster's prevalence throughout the U.S.: French Lick, Indiana (March, 1965); Albuquerque, New Mexico (October, 1966); Decatur, Illinois (August, 1968); Flagstaff, Arizona (January, 1971); Texarkana, Arkansas (May, 1971), Marshall, Michigan (October, 1971); Pine Bluff, Arkansas (June, 1973); Murphysboro, Illinois (June, 1973); and Latrobe, Pennsylvania (August, 1973). Elsewhere an early and popular work—William T. Cox, *Fearsome Creatures of the Lumberwoods* (1910)—describes a hairy ape-like creature which inhabits the Cumberland mountains of Tennessee and is often held responsible for the disappearance of hunters and wanderers in the woods. The creature's name—the "Whirling Whimpus"—is remarkably similar to the "Golly wompus" said to roam Camp Louis Ernest near Dupont, Indiana.

12. Dégh and Vázsonyi, "Legend and Belief," p. 283.

13. Ibid., p. 284.

14. This open-ended form with its invitation to discussion and debate is discussed in Dégh and Vázsonyi, "Dialectics," particularly pp. 29–31.

15. For a further discussion of such "extinct," "dormant," and "active" legends, see Dégh and Vázsonyi, "Dialectics," pp. 10–11.

EDITOR'S SUGGESTIONS FOR FURTHER READING

Bronner, Simon J. 2006. "'And Then He Heard These Footsteps': Tales and Legends." In *American Children's Folklore*, 143–59. Atlanta: August House.

Ellis, Bill. 1981. "The Camp Mock-Ordeal Theater as Life." *Journal of American Folklore* 94 (374): 486–505.

Ellis, Bill. 1982. "'Ralph and Rudy': The Audience's Role in Recreating a Camp Legend." *Western Folklore* 41 (3): 169–91.

Hawes, Bess Lomax. 1968. "La Llorona in Juvenile Hall." *Western Folklore* 27 (3): 153–70.

Mechling, Jay. 1999. "Children's Folklore in Residential Institutions: Summer Camps, Boarding Schools, Hospitals, and Custodial Facilities." In *Children's Folklore: A Sourcebook*, edited by Brian Sutton-Smith, Jay Mechling, Thomas W. Johnson, and Felicia R. McMahon, 273–92. Logan: Utah State University Press.

Stewart, Susan. 1982. "The Epistemology of the Horror Story." *Journal of American Folklore* 95 (375): 33–50.

2

The Cropsey Maniac

Lee Haring and Mark Breslerman

PREFACE

Like the Boondock Monster, Cropsey is a murderous camp fiend, stalk-ing the surrounding woods, preying on wayward campers, his raison d'être an eternal desire for revenge. The present study of Cropsey resulted from a student-professor collaboration, with student Mark Breslerman on data collection and folklore professor Lee Haring on analysis. Methodologically, Breslerman pursued the Cropsey legend strictly through elicited interviews, eschewing journalism, popular media, folklore archives, or ethnography of performance—a sanctioned scholarly approach, but one that would likely be too narrow for a longer study. Breslerman's fieldwork offers evidence that Cropsey circulated in New York, New Jersey, and Pennsylvania, with the hearth of the tradition located in New York summer camps in and around the Catskill Mountains. Haring analyzed the legend both struc-turally, breaking it down by motifs (the building blocks of legends), and functionally, explaining how the legend permits imagined escapism from structured and monitored camp life, encourages solidarity among campers, initiates the constant flow of new campers into the long-standing tradi-tions of the camp, and implicitly warns against wandering off the camp-grounds. Invoking Stith Thompson's motif and tale-type indices, Haring demonstrates how killing a child for revenge and murder by knife, ax, and immolation have deep roots in narrative tradition.

Noting the dates (data collected in 1966, article published in 1977), some readers will also discern the folk inspiration for the archetypical slasher film *Friday the 13th* (1980)—a haunted summer camp on a lake, an accidental death, a homicidal yearning for revenge, and a murderous annual anniversary remembrance. Another of these standby motifs, the "perennial

https://doi.org/10.7330/9781646421602.c002

return of the victim," will also translate into film, with Cropsey (as *Friday the 13th* baddie Jason Voorhees) now in its twelfth installment. Haring and Breslerman's essay stands the test of time due to wide-ranging fieldwork, careful examination of verbatim texts, and dutiful consultation of folklorists' bibliographic resources.

ESSAY

Children in New York's summer camps yearly learn or hear again the story of the Cropsey Maniac, a respected member of the community whose insane desire to avenge an accidental death prompts him to stalk the outskirts of the camp property as a revenant. The camper who strays off the grounds needs to beware of Cropsey, who is probably carrying an ax. Here is a sample text, collected from Peter Sherman, a former camper and counselor at Camp Lakota on Masten Lake at Wurtsboro, New York.

> George Cropsey was a judge. He had a wife and two children, all of whom he loved very much. He owned a small summer cottage along the shores of Masten Lake. His wife and children would go there for the summer months, and he would come up to visit with them on weekends . . . One night two campers snuck away from the camp's scheduled evening activity and went down to the lake to roast some marshmallows. The fire they built went out of control and there was a big fire on the lake. George Cropsey's family was burnt to death. When Cropsey read the report in the newspaper, it is said he became completely white and disappeared from his home. Two weeks later one of the campers from Lakota was found near the lake chopped to death with an ax. There was talk of closing the camp for the remainder of the summer but they didn't.
>
> The camp owners insisted upon constant supervision of the campers, there were state troopers posted in the area, and each counselor slept with either a knife, an ax, or a rifle. One night at about three in the morning, one of the counselors was awakened by the screams of one of his campers. He put his flashlight in the direction of the screams and saw his camper bleeding to death, and, standing over him, a man with chalk-white hair, red, bloodshot eyes, and swinging a long, bloody ax. When the maniac saw the light, he ran from the bunk, but the counselor chopped at his leg with the hatchet he was armed with. The man got away but left a trail of blood into the woods. The state troopers were called, and followed the trail into the woods. They called to Cropsey to surrender, but all they heard was a crazed laughter. They determined his position, and when he would not give himself up, they built a circle of fire around him. When the fire had subsided, they searched the woods for his remains but could find nothing. The police closed the file on George Cropsey, assuming him to be dead . . .

It is said that on the evening of the anniversary of the death of judge Cropsey's family, you can see the shadow of a man limping along the shores of Masten Lake.

Versions of the Cropsey story collected from eleven New York City informants display interesting variations but preserve a consistent plot structure. Some information about our informants: Diane Spiegel Horowitz, a thirty-three-year-old graduate of Portland State Teachers College, heard the Cropsey story at Crystal Lake Camp in Roscoe, New York. Roy Steinbach is a twenty-one-year-old former camper at Lake Tagola, at Sackett Lake in the Catskills. Harry Wilson, thirty-six, heard the story while working at a refreshment stand in Beaverkill State Park. Linda Lau, twenty-three, from Hewlett, Long Island, attended Camp Glenmere in Great Barrington, Massachusetts, for seven years, and heard the story there. Steve Ross, twenty-six, worked for four summers on the waterfront staff at Camp Lenox, Monterey, Massachusetts, where he heard the tale. He heard no versions of it during his four years at Murray State College in Kentucky. Barry Weiss, twenty-five, heard the story as a counselor at Camp Kahagon in Bucks County, Pennsylvania. Richard Banks, twenty-two, from West Long Branch, New Jersey, learned the story as a Boy Scout. Kenny Levine, twenty-six, heard the story as a student at Syracuse University. Joan Kaplan, sixteen, heard the story as an eleven-year-old pupil at Brooklyn Ethical Culture School from one of the older pupils. Priscilla Rambar, twenty-two, heard the story as a student at Harcum Junior College in Bryn Mawr, Pennsylvania. Informants who heard the story in a camp setting localize it near their camp; those who heard it at school localize it near their schools.

The central character of the Cropsey maniac story is always a respected adult male typifying the values of the older generation from a middle-class adolescent's point of view. He was one of the best-liked men in the town, the owner of a large hardware store and member of the city council; he had a wife and one child (Diane Spiegel Horowitz). He was a Sullivan County judge with a wife and three little boys who rented a summer cottage near the place where the story is told (Harry Wilson). He was a retired businessman whose money supported a friend's livery stable named Cropsey's Barn in gratitude; with his wife and two children he lived in a large home near the place where the story is told (Linda Lau). He was a brilliant, civic-minded judge who lived with his wife and two children in a large frame house near the camp (Barry Weiss). He was a judge; his two sons were Boy Scouts, like the informant (Richard Banks). He was a Brooklyn judge whose daughter attended the same school as the informant (Joan Kaplan, Brooklyn Ethical).

Two informants connected Cropsey more closely with their institutions: he was a guard at the camp, a "nice old guy, liked a lot," a widower with one daughter (Roy Steinbach); he was the head of security police at the informant's junior college, kindly, well-liked, with a wife and one child (Priscilla Rambar, Harcum Junior College).

The death which is the first move of the story is always accidental. Cropsey's only child is drowned while boating with one of the campers (Diane Spiegel Horowitz). His daughter, the only member of his family, is drowned during a cookout (Roy Steinbach). His daughter, out walking during her school lunch hour, is frightened by boys making a fire. Running away, she falls and is knocked unconscious, then burnt as the fire spreads (Joan Kaplan). One of Cropsey's three sons, falling down the side of a hill accidentally, is instantly killed by a skull fracture (Harry Wilson). His younger child is killed when a camper at the rifle range misfires (Linda Lau). A campfire out of control kills both children (Steve Ross). A campfire out of control kills everyone on an overnight hike including Cropsey's two sons (Richard Banks). A wood fire started by campers, illicitly smoking, incinerates the house where Cropsey's wife and two children are visiting (Barry Weiss). His wife and child die in childbirth (Kenny Levine). A collision with a car driven by three Harcum girls kills wife and child (Priscilla Rambar).

Cropsey reacts pathologically to the news of death. He turns pale with horror and runs wildly from home (Linda Lau). He goes to pieces, runs from home swearing revenge against all Harcum girls (Priscilla Rambar). He "went crazy, he started beating up the owner, he beat him over the head with a club a lot of times and then fled from the camp grounds" (Roy Steinbach). He "went out of his mind. He started yellin' and screamin' and swore that he'd get revenge against all Boy Scouts" (Richard Banks). Or he just stares into space, doesn't speak for some time, then disappears (Diane Spiegel Horowitz, Harry Wilson). He doesn't speak, he turns white, "a certain numbness came over him," he walks out of the camp and is not heard from for several weeks (Steve Ross). His complexion turns white, his hands tremble, he begins to breathe heavily, then disappears for two weeks (Barry Weiss). He turns white and stands trembling, then breaks down crying; he is never heard from again by friends or business associates (Kenny Levine). He disappears and is not heard from (Joan Kaplan).

Then Cropsey commences his bloody revenge. A girl is found stabbed at the same spot as the previous action; after a police search, a second girl is stabbed in the same place (Priscilla Rambar). A girl student is found stabbed in the woods near the school; after an attempt at capture, a second girl student is stabbed walking with a friend who survives to say that George

Cropsey was the killer (Joan Kaplan). A hiking camper is stabbed in the area of the previous action; a card with the name "Cropsey" is found next to the body. On another hike he is discovered stabbing a second camper; after the stabbing of a third, a man is seen limping away and another "Cropsey" card is found near the body (Richard Banks). A camper is found stabbed in the woods with his face burned; written in blood on his stomach is the name "Cropsey." All that takes place again (Barry Weiss). The maniac is discovered one night laughing hysterically and stabbing a third camper to death (Steve Ross). A girl camper is found stabbed in the woods; within sight of a counselor Cropsey strangles another girl (Linda Lau). A child from his daughter's bunk is found stabbed; another is found with a knife in her chest and a pillow "covering her face to muffle her screams" (Roy Steinbach). A boy at the same bungalow colony is found dead in the road, his head run over by a car; a second boy is stabbed (Harry Wilson). All these deeds of revenge illustrate Motif S115, murder by stabbing, which we may denote the core motif for Cropsey's revenge. Others appear when Cropsey chops a camper to death with an ax in Peter Sherman's text above (Motif S139.4, Murder by mangling with an ax), or when he shoots a camper boy, is heard laughing weirdly from the woods and screaming "I'll have my revenge," then strangles a second camper in the woods two days later (Motif 5113, Murder by strangulation; Steve Ross). A local high school student is strangled in the street; "Cropsey" is written on his forehead in blood (Motif S113; Kenny Levine). The body of a missing camper is found with "Cropsey" burnt into her arm. Cropsey burns a camp cabin with two counselors and seven campers inside, leaving a message "Cropsey's revenge" written in flour on the ground in the middle of the camp. Several times a week thereafter, small fires burn in the woods and "shrieking, dreadful laughter" is heard (Motif S112, Burning to death; Motif E402, Mysterious ghostlike noises heard; Diane Spiegel Horowitz).

Authorities attempt to capture the crazed avenger, who eludes them after death. After the stabbing of one camper, he can't be found. Camp counselors block the cabin door with their beds and sleep with hatchets.

That night about two in the morning someone was heard climbing through the window. All the counselors were up, and when he got inside they all jumped him. He was crazy, though, and had superhuman strength. He got away. But as he was running one of the counselors threw his hatchet and hit him in the leg. Since he now had to limp, it was easy to follow him into the woods. The police joined the search, and he was soon cornered in the woods. He wouldn't give up, so they set fire to the woods where they knew he was. Soon terrifying screams for help were heard. When the fire was ended the next day, they searched the woods completely but couldn't find him. They figured he was dead, but they never found his body. (Roy Steinbach)

After the deaths of two children, the police place themselves in the cottage where a third child lives. The judge enters and stabs a dummy they have planted in bed (Type 1115, Attempted murder with hatchet). When they seize him, he escapes and plunges over a cliff, screaming for help. The body disappears (Harry Wilson). The camp owner fires at Cropsey; the wound leaves a trail of blood into the woods. The trail is traced "to the foot of a cliff," but no body is found (Linda Lau). Shot while starting a fire, Cropsey limps to the lake; his boat is shot and sinks; the search party hears the words "Cropsey's revenge shall not be denied" as the boat goes down. Dragging the lake yields no body (Diane Spiegel Horowitz).

Further examples: a twenty-four-hour police guard is set and the camp counselors are armed. Upon discovery, Cropsey is stabbed in the leg by a counselor. The police chase him into the woods. Twice he screams, "I'll have my revenge!" They build a circle of flames around him (as in the Peter Sherman text above); he calls for help and screams a last time. No remains are found (Steve Ross). A twenty-four-hour police guard is set. When Cropsey appears, the police grab him but he escapes into an old shower house. From there he fires at police with a rifle. They set fire to the shower house; Cropsey keeps shooting and yells for help; a final scream is heard. No body is found (Barry Weiss). After a first death, a city-wide manhunt begins. Summoned by the cries of a second victim, a policeman shoots Cropsey in the leg. He drives to the lake with police in pursuit and jumps in, leaving a trail of blood. No body is found in a search of the lake (Kenny Leanne). Unsuccessful in finding the murderer of two victims, the local chief of police sets a trap.

> He said the next day a student from the school should go walking in the park, and he'd have policemen all around dressed like regular people and not in their uniform.

Cropsey appears, attacks the student, is chased away and shot, and disappears into the ground of Brooklyn's Prospect Park.

> This is the place where grass will not grow any more. We all call it Cropsey's Plot. (Joan Kaplan)

The terminal marker exemplifies Olrik's observation that folk narratives often end with "a locally established continuation of the plot," such as "the perennial return of the victim."[1]

In our other example using a school locale, police fail to find the first murderer and a second stabbing occurs. Police station themselves behind houses as a girl student walks down the street. As Cropsey attacks her, he is wounded but not killed and limps away, leaving a trail of blood. Chased into a deserted lot, he is repeatedly shot, gives a dreadful scream, and disappears (Priscilla Rambar).

As the final move of the tale, Cropsey haunts the neighborhood (Motif E275, Place of great accident or misfortune haunted by a ghost). Informants do not use the word *ghost* for Cropsey, citing his wounds and disappearance and the failure of authorities to find a body as evidence that Cropsey is still at the place where the murders occurred. "Strange voices" and "low terrifying laughter" are heard in the woods near the camp the rest of that summer and for two summers more (Diane Spiegel Horowitz). Cries are heard every hour on the anniversary of Cropsey's death; a voice is heard to yell that "he'd be back, and that no child in the area would escape his revenge . . . I coulda sworn I heard desperate cries for help in that valley" (Harry Wilson). People at camp now believe "Cropsey's Barn" to be haunted, saying Cropsey swore revenge and would come back from the grave to achieve it (Linda Lau). The camp people had an eerie feeling Cropsey would return (Steve Ross). "Any time any Boy Scout goes on a hike, there's a chance of being attacked by the Cropsey maniac" (Richard Banks). Cropsey is assumed dead although his body is never found (Priscilla Rambar).

The Cropsey story fulfills several important functions for the campers and counselors who transmit it. For one, it permits a few moments of imagined melodrama as an escape from the scheduled life under constant surveillance that characterizes camp and school. In style it may conform to the mass-culture melodramas of television, as when Peter Sherman says, "The police closed the file on George Cropsey . . ." Enhancing the entertainment function of the story, the narrator often aims at frightening his audience. "Our counselor told it to us one night to get even with us" (Diane Spiegel Horowitz). "It spooked me" (Roy Steinbach). Campers "were scared to death" (Steve Ross). In one performance, the narrator "let out with a loud scream in an effort to scare the listeners" (Kenny Levine).

A second function is to promote a feeling of solidarity among the hearers: the setting and main actor of the story appear *outside* the camp or school grounds, and the action of mayhem and insanity is of a type solidly condemned by the society to which the hearers belong. A third function is to integrate new campers into the camp society by imposing on them the local traditions. Thus, camp society ingeniously solves the problem of continuity in a situation of yearly change. Finally, of course, the story explicitly tries "to insure conformity to the accepted cultural norms,"[2] in this case the prohibition against leaving the camp grounds. "Camp Tagola is very strict" (Roy Steinbach).

> LINDA LAU: No one would go near [Cropsey's Barn] at night. They say Cropsey swore revenge against all campers from Glenmere, and would come back from the grave if necessary to achieve it.
>
> MARK BRESLERMAN: Would you go near Cropsey's Barn?
>
> LINDA LAU: No!
>
> . . .
>
> JOAN KAPLAN: Now if anyone from Ethical Culture walks by Cropsey's plot alone, Cropsey will get them.
>
> MARK BRESLERMAN: Then you would never walk past there alone?
>
> JOAN KAPLAN: Of course not. Not with my friends either.

Over the endings of all our versions hangs Motif Q553.4, Death of children as punishment.

These eleven versions give a clear outline of the Cropsey maniac story, though further collecting would be bound to increase our understanding of some points. Most coherent and consistent in the New York versions, it is a New York State story, known today to many city undergraduates who have had summer camp experience in the Catskills. It continues to be transmitted each year and is a vital piece of modern folklore.

NOTES

1. Axel Olrik, "Epic Laws of Folk Narrative," in *The Study of Folklore*, ed. Alan Dundes (Englewood Cliffs: Prentice-Hall, 1965), p. 132.

2. William R. Bascom, "Four Functions of Folklore," in *The Study of Folklore*, p. 297. Our discussion of the functions of the Cropsey story is based on this essay and on Dundes's headnote (pp. 277–278).

EDITOR'S SUGGESTIONS FOR FURTHER READING

de Vos, Gail. 2012. "Cropsey (2009)." In *What Happens Next? Contemporary Urban Legends and Urban Popular Culture*, 40–42. Westport, CT: Libraries Unlimited.

Koven, Michael, J. 2003. "The Terror Tale: Urban Legends and the Slasher Film." *Scope: An Online Journal of Film Studies*. https://www.nottingham.ac.uk/scope/documents /2003/may-2003/koven.pdf.

Koven, Michael J. 2007. "Studying the Urban Legend Film." In *Film, Folklore, and Urban Legends*, 99–111. Lanham, MD: Scarecrow.

Tucker, Elizabeth. 2006. "Cropsey at Camp." *Voices: The Journal of New York Folklore* 32 (3–4): 42.

Vitale, Meredith. 2014. "The Cropsey Maniac." *Artifacts* 11. https://artifactsjournal.mis souri.edu/2015/01/the-cropsey-maniac/.

Zeman, Joshua, and Barbara Brancaccio, dirs. 2009. *Cropsey*. Philadelphia: Breaking Glass Pictures.

3

Alligators-in-the-Sewers
A Journalistic Origin

Loren Coleman

PREFACE

This editor can attest that New Yorkers still recount legends of sewer-dwelling albino alligators, blindly slithering beneath the streets of the Big Apple, feeding on rats and unwary sanitation workers (along with the many other beings that are purported to live beneath the streets of Gotham). In New York City, the campers' woods becomes the city dwellers' sewers—the unknown and the out of bounds breed legends of frightening, lurking possibilities. Investigating these subterranean reptilian claims, Loren Coleman, the world's leading cryptozoologist and director of the International Cryptozoology Museum, takes a historical, archival, and literary approach, focusing on texts from popular literature and the news media. Coleman's purpose was to match a persistent urban legend to a historical incident, and his findings landed in American folklorists' flagship journal, the *Journal of American Folklore*.

The search for origins in legend study can be a fool's errand. Variants found in print are often derived from oral tradition, a tradition likely inspired by an even earlier genesis. Sometimes, however, there is a traceable "kernel of truth" in a legend. Folklorists agree legend will gladly travel long distances carried on the backs of mass media. Coleman is careful here, admitting that his search for a verified account of an alligator in the New York City sewers is only a "possible origin of the tale" and acknowledging that the published story could itself be the stuff of legend. Alligators are often found in odd places, including community ponds, hot tubs, and bathrooms. A sewer incursion sounds only reasonable.

As a side note, several cited authors, and even Coleman himself, refer to alligators-in-the-sewers as a "folktale," a misnomer best avoided in formal

https://doi.org/10.7330/9781646421602.c003

folkloristic study. *Legend* refers to plausible stories told as true, whereas *folktale* properly references only fictional tales told for entertainment. Baba Yaga is a Slavic folktale monster; the sewer-surfing alligators are New York creatures of legend.

In the 1935 *New York Times* article Coleman unearthed, a group of boys shoveling snow into a manhole in Italian Harlem spot an alligator thrashing in the waters below. The boys pull the alligator from the sewer, the frightened alligator attempts a pitiful attack, and the boys put it down with their snow shovels. Now, in the vein of Richard M. Dorson's legendary comic creatures, New York City has memorialized its sewer alligators with their own bronze sculpture on the subway platform at 8th Ave. and 14th St., and New Yorkers celebrate a strictly unofficial Alligators in the Sewers Day (February 9). Whether his discovery is the "origin" of the alligators-in-the-sewers legend is unknowable, but Coleman has proven that when New Yorkers claim to have "seen it in the papers," they speak the truth.

ESSAY

The story of alligators haunting the sewers of major American cities is a modern urban legend. But what of its origin? Thomas Pynchon has written:

> Did he remember the baby alligators? Last year, or maybe the year before, kids all over Nueva York bought these little alligators for pets. Macy's was selling them for fifty cents; every child, it seemed, had to have one. But soon the children grew bored with them. Some set them loose in the streets, but most flushed them down the toilets. And these had grown and reproduced, had fed off rats and sewage, so that now they moved big, blind, albino, all over the sewer system. Down there, God knew how many there *were*. Some had turned cannibal because in their neighborhood the rats had all been eaten, or had fled in terror.[1]

With those words, Pynchon propelled the persistent rumors of alligators in the sewers of New York City into a major work of fiction. Pynchon's retelling of this folktale is at once concise, complete, and elaborate. He envisioned an Alligator Patrol going into the depths of the sewers, working in teams of two, with one man holding a flashlight while the other carried a twelve-gauge repeating shotgun. Pynchon's fascinating novel wove the fabric of the alligators-in-the-sewers motif throughout the pages of his book, and thus brought this tale into modern popular culture as no one before him had.

Folklorists to herpetologists have acknowledged the widespread distribution of this peculiar alligators-in-the-sewers story, but many researchers have been vague as to the origins of the tale. Without giving a citation, Richard M. Dorson noted marijuana harvesters, in pursuit of the elusive strain "New York White," had difficulties

> because, according to a newspaper story, full-grown alligators prowled the sewers of New York. It seems that Miami vacationers returning to New York in the winter brought back baby alligators as pets for their children. The more the alligators grew the less ideal they appeared as playmates, and their owners, too tenderhearted to skin them for their hides, mercifully flushed them down the toilet. Some survived in their new environment and confronted sewer maintenance workers, who publicly protested at this unnecessary additional hazard to their occupation. The newspapers published the matter, and the tales began to circulate.[2]

In Jack Horn's 1975 review of *Urban Folklore from the Paperwork Empire*, the "blind white alligators that live in New York sewers" are mentioned as an example of urban folklore, but Horn's "source" of the tale does not go further than the Florida souvenir and the flushing toilet.[3]

In the world of zoology, we find the same meanderings, for the herpetologists Sherman and Madge Rutherford Minton have written:

> One of the sillier folk tales of the late 1960s was that the New York sewers were becoming infested with alligators, presumably unwanted pets that had been flushed down the toilet. In some accounts, these were growing to formidable size from feeding on rats. We have been unsuccessful in tracing the source of these legends but would assure New Yorkers that alligators are not among their urban problems.[4]

My search, therefore, was for an apparently "real" account of an alligator in a sewer—a journalistic vehicle—as the possible origin of the tale. As I have written elsewhere

> crocodilians fall from the sky, and materialize inside cotton bins and in washrooms from Texas to France. They slither and slink to the horror of humans from basement drains and sewers anywhere from Kansas to New York City. Unlike some mystery animals,[5] alligators are caught, killed, and placed in museums. Although actual alligators seem to appear and persist in northern winters (e.g., sightings and finds for Oakland County, Michigan, 1953–1957) to the dismay of herpetologists, random out-of-place finds seem to be the rule.[6]

Figure 3.1. Tom Otterness brought the alligators-in-the-sewers legend to life in his "Life Underground" bronze sculpture series, readily viewable at 14th Street/Eighth Avenue, New York City. (Creative Commons Attribution 2.0 Generic.)

Some of these alleged discoveries are unusual, as, for example, the "alligator five and a half feet long . . . found near the bank of the Rock river, at Janesville, Wis., frozen to death," in 1892.[7]

I have compiled a list[8] of seventy-plus encounters with erratic alligators for the years 1843–1973, but the actual, supposedly true recording of an alligator in a sewer proved to be a rare occurrence. I was able to discover just such an event, nevertheless, recorded as fact from, not surprisingly, New York City.

The incident may or may not have taken place, but its publication in a no nonsense fashion in a highly regarded and respected newspaper must have lent much credibility to the story. In contrast to the common notion that the alligators-in-the-sewers motif is a product of the sixties, the following article is from the *New York Times* of February 10th, 1935, and is given here in its entirety:

ALLIGATOR FOUND IN UPTOWN SEWER

Youths Shoveling Snow Into Manhole See The Animal Churning In Icy Water.

SNARE IT AND DRAG IT OUT

Reptile Slain by Rescuers When It Gets Vicious—Whence It Came is Mystery.

The youthful residents of East 123rd Street, near the murky Harlem River, were having a rather grand time at dusk yesterday shoveling the last of the recent snow into a gaping manhole.

Salvatore Condulucci, 16 years old, of 419 East 123rd Street, was assigned to the rim. His comrades would heap blackened slush near him, and he, carefully observing the sewer's capacity, would give the last fine flick to each mound.

Suddenly there were signs of clogging ten feet below, where the manhole drop merged with the dark conduit leading to the river. Salvatore yelled: "Hey, you guys, wait a minute," and got down on his knees to see what was the trouble.

What he saw, in the thickening dusk, almost caused him to topple into the icy cavern. For the jagged surface of the ice blockade below was moving; and something black was breaking through. Salvatore's eyes widened; then he managed to leap to his feet and call his friends.

"Honest, it's an alligator!" he exploded.

OTHERS LOOK AND ARE CONVINCED

There was a murmur of skepticism. Jimmy Mireno, 19, of 440 East 123rd Street, shouldered his way to the rim and stared.

"He's right," he said.

Frank Lonzo, 18, of 1743 Park Avenue, looked next. He also confirmed the spectre. Then there was a great crush about the opening in the middle of the street and heads were bent low around the aperture. The animal apparently was threshing about in the ice, trying to get clear. When the first wave of awe had passed, the boys decided to help it out. A delegation was dispatched to the Lehigh Stove and Repair Shop at 441 East 123rd Street.

"We want some clothes-line," demanded the delegation, and got it.

Young Condulucci, an expert on Western movies, fashioned a slip knot. With the others watching breathlessly, he dangled the noose into the sewer, and after several tantalizing near-catches, looped it about the 'gator's neck. Then he pulled hard. There was a grating of rough leathery skin against jumbled ice. But the job was too much for one youth. The others grabbed the rope and all pulled.

Slowly, with its curving tail twisting weakly, the animal was dragged from the snow, ten feet through the dark cavern, and to the street, where it lay, non-committal; it was not in Florida, that was clear. And therefore, when one of the boys sought to loosen the rope, the creature opened its jaws and snapped, not with the robust vigor of a healthy, well-sunned alligator, but with the fury of a sick, very badly treated one. The boys jumped back. Curiosity and sympathy turned to enmity.

"Let 'im have it!" the cry went up.

RESCUERS THEN KILL IT

So the shovels that had been used to pile snow on the alligator's head were now to rain upon it. The 'gator's tail swished about a few last times. Its jaws clashed weakly. But it was in no mood for a real struggle after its icy incarceration. It died on the spot.

Triumphantly, but not without the inevitable reaction of sorrow, the boys took their victim to the Lehigh Stove and Repair Shop. There it was found to weigh 125 pounds; they said it measured seven and a half or eight feet. It became at once the greatest attraction the store ever had had. The whole neighborhood milled about, and finally, a call for the police reached a nearby station.

But there was little for the hurrying policemen to do. The strange visitor was quite dead; and no charge could be preferred against it or against its slayers. The neighbors were calmed with little trouble and speculation as to where the 'gator had come from was rife.

There are no pet shops in the vicinity; that theory was ruled out almost at once. Finally, the theories simmered down to that of a passing boat. Plainly, a steamer from the mysterious Everglades, or thereabouts, had been passing 123rd Street, and the alligator had fallen overboard.

Shunning the hatefully cold water, it had swum toward shore and found only the entrance to the conduit. Then after another 150 yards through a torrent of melting snow—and by that time it was half dead—it had arrived under the open manhole.

Half-dead, yes, the neighborhood conceded. But still alive enough for a last splendid opening and snapping of its jaws. The boys were ready to swear to that.

At about 9 p.m., when tired mothers had succeeded in getting most of their alligator-conscious youngsters to bed, a Department of Sanitation truck rumbled up to the store and made off with the prize. Its destination was Barren Island and an incinerator.

The article makes exciting reading and probably had people of its day talking about alligators-in-the-sewers for some time. Indeed, the reported encounter may have, for years, spawned similar reports from New Yorkers and other readers of the paper. As far as this writer can establish, this account is the first documented source of this particular motif.

NOTES

1. Thomas Pynchon, *V* (New York: Bantam Books, 1964), p. 33.

2. Richard M. Dorson, *America in Legend: Folklore from the Colonial Period to the Present* (New York: Pantheon Books, 1973), pp. 291–292.

3. Jack Horn, "White Alligators and Republican Cousins—The Stuff of Urban Folklore," *Psychology Today*, November 1975, pp. 126, 130.

4. Sherman A. and Madge Rutherford Minton, *Giant Reptiles* (New York: Charles Scribner's Sons, 1973), p. 34.

5. Here I am attempting to make a distinction between such "mystery animals" as Bigfoot, Thunderbirds, Lake Monsters, and so forth and captured, out-of-place animals.

See Jerome Clark and Loren Coleman, *Creatures of the Outer Edge* (New York, Warner Books, 1978), for more complete insights into "mystery animals."

6. Loren Coleman, "Erratic Crocodilians and Other Things," *The Info Journal*, 3, No. 4 (February, 1974), 12.

7. "News Briefly Stated," *Chicago Citizen*, February 27, 1892, p. 3; from Larry A. Viskochil, personal communication, March 24, 1971.

8. Coleman, "Erratic Crocodilians," pp. 13–18.

EDITOR'S SUGGESTIONS FOR FURTHER READING

Coleman, Loren. 2006. "Alligators in the Sewers." In *Mysterious America: The Ultimate Guide to the Nation's Weirdest Wonders, Strangest Spots, and Creepiest Creatures*, 67–75. New York: Pocket Books.

Daley, Robert. 1959. "Alligators in the Sewers." In *The World Beneath the City*, 187–93. Philadelphia: J. B. Lippincott.

Dorson, Richard M. 1982. *Man and Beast in American Comic Legend*. Bloomington: Indiana University Press.

Fine, Gary Alan. 1980. "The Kentucky Fried Rat: Legends and Modern Society." *Journal of the Folklore Institute* 17 (2–3): 222–43.

Gillespie, Angus K. 1987. *American Wildlife in Symbol and Story*. Knoxville: University of Tennessee Press.

Ingemark, Camilla Asplund. 2008. "The Octopus in the Sewers: An Ancient Legend Analogue." *Journal of Folklore Research* 45 (2): 145–70.

Kilgannon, Corey. 2020. "The Truth about Alligators in the Sewers of New York." *New York Times*, February 26.

Mann, Craig Ian. 2015. "America, Down the Toilet: Urban Legends, American Society and Alligator." In *Animal Horror Cinema: Genre, History and Criticism*, edited by Katarina Gregersdotter, Johan Höglund, and Nicklas Hållén, 110–25. London: Palgrave.

McConnell, Brian. 1982. "Urban Legends in Fleet Street." *Folklore* 93 (2): 226–28.

Meder, Theo. 2007. "The Hunt for Winnie the Puma: Wild Animals in a Civilized Dutch Environment." *Contemporary Legend*, new ser., 10: 94–127.

Stecker, John K. 1965 [1926]. "Reptiles of the South and Southwest in Folk-lore." In *Rainbow in the Morning*, edited by J. Frank Dobie, 56–69. Dallas: Southern Methodist University Press.

4

Sasquatch-Like Creatures in Newfoundland
A Study in the Problems of Belief, Perception, and Reportage

Michael Taft

PREFACE

In his formative years, Michael Taft, later the head of the Archive of Folk Culture at the American Folklife Center, set out to investigate the dearth of Sasquatch findings in Newfoundland. While this essay would mark the beginning and end of his career as a monster researcher, his Sasquatch studies would follow him to the day of his retirement, when colleagues filled his vacant seat with a Sasquatch yard ornament.

Pursuing Sasquatch in Newfoundland seems an odd proposition at first glance. Why would a folklorist, in a region renowned for its fabled supernatural and cryptozoological beings and peopled with talented raconteurs eager to spin wondrous yarns, choose to study a monster *not* reported to exist in Newfoundland? The answer, for Taft, lay in the influence of his mentor, folklorist David Hufford, who sparked his interest in cosmology, worldview, and the experience-centered study of tradition. Taft, who had been working in the Memorial University of Newfoundland Folklore and Language Archive, was familiar with the numerous strange sightings submitted to the archive and realized that anomalous accounts were *not* reported as Sasquatch, despite presenting all the necessary motifs.

In his essay, Taft neither confirms nor denies that Sasquatch lives in Newfoundland, nor does he confirm or deny that Newfoundlanders have witnessed Sasquatch. Taft's interest, instead, lies in Newfoundlanders' ability to report sensory phenomena based on traditional island cultural knowledge, an inquiry that has broad general application to monster sightings across North America. Because Newfoundlanders had no knowledge of Sasquatch,

https://doi.org/10.7330/9781646421602.c004

sightings must by necessity be reported as "wild Indians," ghostly "treasure guards," the bogeyman, local fauna such as bears, or even exotic wildlife such as gorillas. Taft reminds us that, in working with local histories and folklife archives, it is never the sightings themselves but rather the *perceptions* of those sightings that folklorists ultimately encounter in interviews or documented reports. Although local narrators are often teased for misidentifying mundane fauna as monsters, Taft contends that cognitively, it's more likely that people will misinterpret the unknown as the known (mistaking a hairy monster for a bear) than the known for the unknown (mistaking a bear for a hairy monster), thereby decreasing even further the likelihood of receiving Sasquatch reports. Only once folklorists are aware of how Sasquatch-like creatures are perceived and interpreted in Newfoundland, Taft argues, can they accurately sift through the pertinent data in folklife archives, local histories, and oral accounts. Taft has provided future monster researchers with an important intellectual statement that encourages careful consideration of how reporting aligns with local cultural knowledge, whichever their monster of choice.

ESSAY

In the one-thousand-year history of the exploration and settlement of Newfoundland by European peoples, there have been a great many encounters with half-human half-animal creatures and human-like supernatural beings on the island.[1] In about the year 1000 a Norse sailor was killed by an arrow from a sciapod, a hopping one-footed humanoid.[2] In 1610 sailors and dock-workers in the Newfoundland port of St. John's were sent fleeing by a rather malevolent and unattractive mermaid.[3]

The traditional culture of Newfoundlanders allows for the existence of fairies, devils, ghosts, Jack O'Lanterns, spirits, mermaids, witches, magicians, wraiths, and a host of other human, part-human, or human-like creatures. Stories of encounters with these various beings abound in Newfoundland,[4] and these phenomena are recognized by many islanders as distinct and identifiable parts of the world in which they live. For example, fairies are described by Newfoundlanders according to certain rather standard characteristics, behaviour patterns, and places of habitation, and are called "fairies," "little people," or "the good people" to distinguish them from other perceived phenomena. Likewise, the other beings which I listed above can all be described and given a taxonomic name by people within the traditional island culture. In short, the Newfoundlander's world view includes a number of well-defined and taxonomically distinct beings not found in the scientific or "official" lists of island flora and fauna.

One might say that all the above beings are relatively well defined within the "cultural language" of Newfoundlanders.[5] When confronted with a fairy, ghost, or devil, the Newfoundlander recognizes it as such and can report his encounter to others in terms which will properly identify the phenomenon he has observed.

The traditional world view of the Newfoundlander, however, does not include Sasquatch-like creatures; that is, large, human-like bipeds covered with fur or long hair. Unlike certain cultures in the Pacific Northwest or in the Himalayas, there is no word in the Newfoundlander's traditional cultural language (or in his actual language for that matter) which would describe such a creature. Quite simply, the Sasquatch does not exist within the traditional cosmology of the Newfoundlander.[6]

This does not mean that Sasquatch-like creatures do not inhabit the province, nor does it mean that encounters with such creatures have not occurred in Newfoundland. When such encounters are made, however, the Newfoundlander has no way of describing the creature as a distinct phenomenon according to his cultural language and can only perceive and report the encounter in terms which conform to his world view. Toelken, in his excellent essay on the nature of world view and communication, writes that a person is "inclined to view many, if not most, phenomena in those conceptual terms which seem 'logical' to his society; that is, he is taught by his society *how* to see."[7]

Since the world view of the Newfoundlander prevents him from seeing and reporting a Sasquatch as a "Sasquatch," "Bigfoot," or "Yeti," he perceives and reports a creature with which he is familiar, while at the same time he describes a creature with the characteristics of the Sasquatch. I will illustrate this peculiarity of perception and reportage with some examples of Sasquatch-like sightings or encounters in Newfoundland.

One of the more intriguing ways in which Newfoundlanders have perceived and reported the Sasquatch is as an "Indian." The Indigenous Indians of the island were the Beothucks, who were extinct by the third decade of the nineteenth century. Micmac Indians from Nova Scotia settled on the island in comparatively recent times, but their numbers are small and they are not very widespread. The average Newfoundlander, therefore, would have little, if any, knowledge of Indian behaviour or characteristics. Few would have ever met an Indian, and those Indians they did meet were likely to be the highly acculturated Micmacs.

There is, however, an image within the Newfoundlander's cultural language of the "savage" Indian of the wilderness, no doubt created out of a combination of legends about the Beothucks and the popular literature on

Indians found throughout North America. It is this image of the wild, savage, or hostile Indian which some Newfoundlanders have used to describe encounters with Sasquatch-like creatures.

In 1915 James P. Howley wrote a history of the Beothucks in which he compiled many reports, both written and oral, of encounters with this extinct tribe. It is of interest that several of these reports describe these Indians as a tall and massive race of people:

> A man killed in Trinity Bay by the fishermen is described as a huge savage, and another said to have been seen by one Richards, in Notre Dame Bay was pronounced to be seven feet tall.
>
> Mr. Watts remembers many years ago, hearing from a reliable source, that some hunters being in the interior of Labrador near Forteau came across the footprints of men, who judging by their great strides, must have been of immense stature.
>
> One Richmond, a noted Indian killer, told many stories about them [Beothucks]. He said he once saw a dead Indian 7 feet tall.[8]

Although it is true that the Beothucks were somewhat taller than most aboriginal tribes in North America, the above descriptions would seem to be either exaggerations[9] or accounts of beings other than Beothucks.

In the mid to late nineteenth century the following encounter occurred, as described by the grandson of the witness:

> Way back a number of years ago, Indian Head, the northernmost point of White Sands, derived its name from the fact that Indians [were] frequently down there. The first fishermen in that area came from Caplin Harbour and used to moor their boat off shore. Often when the fishermen came back to their camps on shore, they found their fishing gear mutilated. Their fishing gear mutilated, their cooking utensils—but rarely anything stolen, just broken and destroyed. So my grandfather told me that this occurred many times, but they did not see the Indians personally.
>
> When he was some eight years old, he lived in Caplin Harbour. He came up to White Sands fishing with some other men, and, one time, in search of caplin or bait, they went on to and landed on the south side of White Sands, White Sands Beach, and as they rowed in there in the early morning, there were two Indians in the sands. There were two or three boats of them [fishermen] and one of the boats had a gun—an old cap and ball musket, the gun of the era. So, as the two Indians got to their feet to start to retreat towards the bank and forest, one of the men raised the gun and shot one of the Indians.
>
> That Indian, according to my grandfather, was approximately nine feet tall, covered with hair from an inch to an inch and a half. He had on no

clothing whatsoever. They did not take him in their boat, but they towed
it in the water—back to Caplin Harbour and it's buried down in Caplin
Harbour in a place called Shark Cove.[10]

There are, of course, many unanswerable questions about this story. Who
were the Indians who destroyed the gear of the fishermen? The Beothucks
were long gone by the time this encounter occurred. It is conceivable that the
Indians were Micmacs, but it would be more likely that the Micmacs would
have stolen the gear, rather than simply destroying it. The description of the
random destruction of the fishing gear is not unlike similar descriptions of
the destruction of equipment in woods camps in the Pacific Northwest.[11]

The description of the dead Indian displays the characteristics of a
Sasquatch-like creature rather than those of a man. Yet, in attempting to
find a logical explanation for both the random destruction of their gear
and the strange creature which they had killed, these nineteenth-century
Newfoundlanders made use of the image and characteristics of the wild
Indian which was already implanted within their world view.

The following account combines both the large footprint motif and the
sighting of a hairy, human-like creature. The encounter took place sometime in the first half of this century, and the collector of this story tells
us that the narrator-witness is illiterate and has little conception of time
or number:

> "Meself and Mista Jim L. were huntin' this fall 'bout . . . oh . . . twas
> (scratching his head) twenty or forty years ago (he couldn't tell two from
> ten years). Anyway we was walkin' through the woods down in Willwood
> Harbour when bine-by sher I sees this thing runnin' through the woods. It
> had hair on it 'bout ten feet long. He was all covered with long black hair.
> Be gar the reckly he vanished. I says to Mista J. it must be an indin. Well we
> looked around and the reckly I sees his fut print. It was a large fut."
>
> He went on with a lengthy description [of] the foot print which accord-
> ing to him wore tannels. He concluded his description by reminding us we
> had often seen a picture of the indian's foot in the books. I believe every-
> one present had seen a picture of an indian's foot except Mr. W. because
> from his description I know he didn't have a clue.
>
> He continued, "We followed his tracks and then I sees him sittin' up
> in a branch. I took out the horn and put six fingers and two three-quarter
> pistol balls in the musseloader. Mista J. L. fired first. He only scarred him.
> I raised the gun, took good sight and fired. The pistol balls went right in
> his heart. He fell from the branch into a big hole. I started to load again
> but Mista J. told me the gun would bust open. I was just going to fire again
> when he stopped kicking and died (he then removed his cap)."[12]

Whether the narrator-witness was as ignorant of dimensions and of Indians as the collector believed is impossible to determine. The meaning of "tannels" as give in this context is obscure, but it would seem to refer to some kind of footwear.[13] The important fact, however, is that this man truly believed he had shot and killed an Indian, rather than some unknown beast. In a later part of his narrative, he actually warns his audience not to talk too much about the incident, since "you can get strung up for a thing like this."

The perception of a Sasquatch-like creature as an Indian may seem preposterous, yet in the context of traditional Newfoundland culture such a view is not altogether strange. The Indian, whether Micmac or Beothuck, was at home in the wooded and marshy interior of the island, whereas the European was mostly a man of the sea and only occasionally ventured inland. Thus, the Newfoundlander may well have associated Indians with the wild, unknown, and dangerous forests and marshes of the island. At the same time, the Newfoundlander's view of the acculturated Micmacs of the coast was that they were strange and magical persons. There are many stories told among Newfoundlanders connecting Micmacs with witchcraft and black magic.[14]

In the mind of the Newfoundlander, then, the Indian had both human and non-human characteristics—a creature of the woods rather than a dweller on the coast, a witch and a sorcerer rather than a simple mortal. Given this view, an encounter with a half-human half-creature in the woods or on an uninhabited stretch of beach might very well be perceived as an Indian by the Newfoundlander.

The association of Sasquatch-like creatures with part-human part-supernatural beings is evident in other encounter stories. Given a different context in which the creature is seen, the Newfoundlander interprets what he sees in a manner different from the above stories. Note the following narrative of an incident which happened around 1930 to 1935. Again, the narrator is the grandson of the witness:

When they (his grandfather's family) were living down on Battle Point, he used to sell rum—bootleg rum. There were usually rangers on the go and grandfather used to keep his rum buried up in the garden—in different places. One night he went up as usual to get a bottle of rum and just as he had dug up the bottle he saw a very bright light coming towards him. It was so bright he could not look at it. But as it got closer, it sort of got dull enough so that he could look at it and he saw that it was really a monster with two very bright eyes. Grandfather used to say that the creature had eyes like two big saucers. It was about the size of a man—a big man over six feet tall, was very black and hairy all over. Grandfather wasn't frightened—the devil wouldn't frighten him—but he didn't know what to do because the light was so bright he was almost blind. He started digging again just to see what would happen and the light began to get brighter and come closer. He stopped digging—filled in the hole and the monster disappeared. Grandfather was sure that the monster was protecting something that was buried in this spot—and it was afraid that he . . . was going to find it. He figured that there was some treasure buried there by pirates and that they had killed one of the crew and buried him near the treasure to protect it, until the pirates themselves got back. The pirates never came back and so the monster which was really the old pirate was still there.[15]

The story goes on to tell that the man tried again on another night, but the monster or guardian spirit appeared once more. The legend of a pirate's ghost as a guardian spirit over buried treasure is extremely common in Newfoundland.[16] The guardian spirit, however, usually does not have the Sasquatch-like characteristics described above.[17]

What may have been another encounter under similar conditions is described by the same informant in response to questions about his first story:

There's lots of stories like that in Newfoundland [buried treasure stories]. Grandfather knew a man in Otto River somewhere who saw a monster up in the cliff and a few days later when he and some other men went back to the spot they saw where a chest or a trunk had been dragged over the rocks to the water's edge.[18]

The sudden appearance of the creature while the witness was digging, or shortly before a newly dug hole was discovered, as in the above stories, places the anomalous being under the taxonomic designation "treasure guard," according to Newfoundland folklore. Once again, a strange and unexplainable event is rationalized or made logical within the world view of the traditional island culture.

Under other conditions, it is possible that encounters with Sasquatch-like creatures have been perceived and reported as other supernatural beings by Newfoundlanders. But unless the Newfoundlander describes in detail what he saw or heard, rather than simply stating what he assumed the creature to be, it is impossible for the researcher to determine whether the report might be a Sasquatch sighting. Thus, the many times in which Newfoundlanders have reported hearing strange or eerie sounds in the woods may be interpreted by the researcher as the whistling of a Sasquatch, but may be described by the Newfoundlander as music made by fairies.

In an unpublished paper Laurie Lacey discusses the possibility that a large footprint found in Nova Scotia and assumed by the locals to be "the Devil's footprint" may actually be the mark of a Sasquatch.[19] Since "Devil's footprint" legends are quite common in Newfoundland, similar perceptions and reports may have also occurred there.

Of course not all sightings of Sasquatch-like creatures are interpreted by Newfoundlanders in the ways described above. Despite the belief traditions of the island culture, individual Newfoundlanders may not include devils, spirits, and savage Indians within their own personal world views. In addition, encounters with Sasquatch-like creatures may occur under conditions which would not be associated in the mind of the Newfoundlander with any of the above-mentioned creatures. Under such conditions, descriptions of the creature and reports of what it was might differ little from Sasquatch reports in other parts of North America.

The following two accounts exhibit more mainstream North American perceptions of the Sasquatch phenomenon. The first report, dating from the late nineteenth century, occurred in Labrador, the mainland part of the province:

> one afternoon a young girl was playing in front of her parents' cabin when she saw a large animal covered with short white fur, walking erect and appearing to have practically no neck, come out of the forest and start toward her. She very reasonably ran screaming into the house where her mother barred the door and the creature went away. However, it returned at night and walked around the cabin beating on the walls, apparently with a branch or other piece of wood. During the following days the men of the area tracked it hoping to shoot it. They claimed to have seen it at a distance several times, but never got a clear shot at it. For some time it continued to come back at night, frightening the inhabitants of the community, and then at length it simply disappeared. The local people explained it as apparently being a gorilla which had somehow found its way into the local forest.[20]

Note that the creature is perceived as a gorilla in this account.[21] Once again [an] unexplainable phenomenon is seen in terms of an explainable one, according to the world views of the witnesses. As with the image of the wild Indian, the image of the gorilla was probably incorporated into the belief systems of these Labrador inhabitants through popular literature. Under the circumstances of the encounter, which occurred within the community rather than in the wilderness, perceptions of the creature as a spirit, savage Indian, or other such being may not have been appropriate. A "gorilla," however, if perceived as a wild animal which had abandoned its natural habitat and "found its way" into Labrador, might be expected to wander into a community either to seek human companionship or simply out of misdirection.

In the second account the witness does not identify the creature according to any traditional taxonomy, but simply describes it without an accompanying belief statement:

> The man who is supposed to have seen our version of the Abominable
> Snowman was William Decker, who lived in one of the small settlements
> on the Newfoundland side of the Strait of Belle Isle. The time was in the
> 1890s, when Decker was spending the winter in Pistolet Bay, hunting and
> fishing.
>
> One frosty morning he took his muzzle-loader and headed back into
> the country. As he reached a marsh, about 300 yards across, he heard a
> loud and frightening roar. He turned and what he saw made him almost
> faint in his tracks. A huge animal, or huge man, a giant creature anyway,
> was coming at him in gigantic leaps.
>
> Decker had already charged his gun with plenty of powder and shot.
> He knelt down and took steady aim and waited till the creature was very
> close, too close for comfort. Then he fired. The weight of the charge
> brought the beast-man to his knees; but it was up again very quickly. But
> Decker was ready with a second volley and the creature fell the second
> time letting out a bellow that could be heard for miles. Taking no chances,
> he reloaded and fired a third volley. The creature did not stir again.
>
> The story relates that Decker measured the creature. It was ten to twelve
> feet tall, with an outstretched arm-span of fourteen feet. Its feet left tracks
> in the snow that Decker's snowshoes couldn't cover. The body, he said, was
> covered with long hair. He figured the creature weighed about one thousand
> pounds! Apparently. He left the carcase or corpse where it lay . . .[22]

Note that in the above account, the present-day narrator adds a belief statement that the creature was an abominable snowman. Again, he is simply applying his own world view in order to make sense out of an anomalous story. In a later part of this radio script, the narrator gives us a clue as to why he perceives this incident as a Sasquatch encounter:

> the general details are very similar to the other tales that are current with
> respect to the Abominable Snowman and the Sasquatch and a number of
> other frightening apparitions reported from other parts of the world.

Just as previous Newfoundlanders had incorporated the image of the savage Indian and the gorilla into their world views, the narrator took the image of the Sasquatch from popular culture and applied it to a local story as an explanation of the phenomenon.

If we assume, and it can only be an assumption, that all of the above reports refer to a single phenomenon—that is, a Sasquatch-like creature native to Newfoundland—then the major variable present in all these accounts is the different perceptions of the phenomenon. The researcher, looking for evidence of the Sasquatch phenomenon in Newfoundland, must be aware of this variable; otherwise, he will run the risk of rejecting, out of hand, important and useful data for his research.

Because the researcher is likely to have a different world view from the people he is studying, he may mistakenly reject data because it is described in terms which he finds unbelievable or ridiculous. In reference to both Sasquatch-like creatures and U.F.O.'s in Newfoundland, David Hufford has made this very point:

> there is one other logical error to which folklorists and other scholars all too often fall prey when considering belief materials, and which is relevant to the ABSM [Sasquatch] and UFO material. This is the discounting of the possible objective reality of a phenomenon because it is accompanied, either in tradition or the account of the informant, by an unacceptable explanation. For example, the statement that UFO's are spaceships and ABSM's are their occupants may well accompany or even replace an informant's report of having heard recent stories of lights in the sky and having personally seen a large hairy biped. The former is an interpretation which may well derive totally from tradition while the latter is an alleged observation which may or may not come from tradition. Obviously most informants will not make statements with a high degree of phenomenological clarity. Therefore our assessment of likelihood (where appropriate), as well as our need for data relevant to a wide variety of linguistic and cultural questions, requires that we carefully distinguish between interpretation and observation in belief materials.
>
> As soon as we become truly careful about our logic and our understanding of our own assumptive sets we shall be able to begin to work seriously with a huge body of material of great importance within our culture, and to do so in ways that promise a variety of very exciting possibilities.[23]

Bearing in mind the close relationship between belief, perception and reportage, the discovery of accounts of any given phenomenon becomes difficult. For example, the rationale often given for Sasquatch reports by those who cannot accept the existence of such a creature is that the witness mistook a bear or some other animal or object for a Sasquatch. Although, as I shall discuss shortly, there are some problems with such a rationale, some Sasquatch reports may well be cases of a "mistaken bear," and the researcher must be prepared to accept this possibility when gathering reports of Sasquatch sightings.

The "mistaken bear" theory of Sasquatch sightings finds its greatest support in the examination of the Newfoundland psyche. John D. A. Widdowson, in an extensive study of frightening and threatening figures in Newfoundland, demonstrates the various ways in which Newfoundlanders embody or personify fear.[24] In different contexts and under different circumstances, the Newfoundlander's mental picture of fear will vary; thus, parents might use the priest, the devil, Santa Claus, mummers, the policeman, ghosts, fairies, or almost anything else to both threaten and control children. There is, however, one context in which a particular mental image of fear seems to predominate: the threatening figure of the wilderness, when described by parents or children, often resembles a Sasquatch-like creature. In order to understand this, one must know something of the Newfoundland way of life. The Newfoundlander is surrounded by two potentially dangerous wildernesses—the forest (or marsh) and the sea. Stories of misfortune in the wilderness, of both a natural and a supernatural variety, abound in the narrative traditions of the island. The people are well aware of the great risks they take when they leave the relative safety of their community to fish in the sea or hunt in the interior. It is thus quite understandable that Newfoundland parents would do their utmost to keep their children away from the forests and marshes of the interior and the uninhabited landwash or coastline.

The threatening figure used to keep children away from the wilderness is often called the "bogey man" (or some variation on this name), and it is this figure, embodying the fear of the wilderness, which is often pictured as a Sasquatch-like creature.[25] The following mental picture (in this instance called a "boo-bagger") has several Sasquatch-like characteristics:

> The Boo-bagger is similar to the bear—hairy, same height and size, but without claws. It is entirely black with a blunt face rather than a sharp one like a bear. Its tail is like that of a bear's.[26]

In other reports, this threatening figure is described as a "half-human beast . . . covered with long black hair."[27] Others, instead of referring to this figure as a "bogey man," make more direct reference to its characteristics by calling it the "Harry Man" or "the big hairy monster."[28] In at least one instance, the link between the threatening figure and the Sasquatch has been made directly. One Newfoundland college student remembers being threatened with the "abdominal [sic] snowman."[29]

Thus, although the Newfoundlander has no word in his cultural language for a Sasquatch as a true and distinct phenomenon, he does have a word for such a creature within his mental conception of fear. No adult

Newfoundlander believes in the existence of the Sasquatch-like bogey man, yet many have the image of such a creature firmly implanted in their psyches from childhood fears.

Of course, an intriguing question which immediately comes to mind in respect to the Newfoundland bogey man is where this particular image of fear came from. Is a large, hairy, manlike biped a natural and universal symbol of fear among human beings of different cultures—an "archetype of the collective unconscious" in Jungian terms?[30] Or does the image of the bogeyman stem from some natural phenomenon on the island? Is it only a coincidence that both the Newfoundland Sasquatch and the make-believe bogey man inhabit the same wild forests, marshes, and coastline of the island? Just as the image of the wild and savage Indian of the wilderness might be traced partially to memories and legends of the Beothucks, might the image of the bogey man be traced to some other natural island phenomenon?

I am not sure what effect this mental image has upon the actual perception and reportage of a Sasquatch encounter in Newfoundland, but it may indeed add weight to the "mistaken bear" theory as an explanation for such encounters. If the Newfoundlander is in a particularly fearful state while in the wilderness, might not his fear take concrete form, forcing him to perceive a bear or a tree as a bogey man or Sasquatch?

The "mistaken bear" theory, however, may not adequately explain all reports. Others have already pointed out the behavioural and anatomical differences between the creature reported and the bear,[31] but there is another argument against this rationale which has to do with belief and perception. Many of the Sasquatch sightings, both in Newfoundland and elsewhere, were made by hunters, woodsmen, or others familiar with the flora and fauna of the wilderness. Is it reasonable to assume that such experts, well acquainted with bears, would perceive a bear as something other than what it is? In discussing mermaids, Horace Beck has made the same point:

> since the northern fishermen . . . live out their lives in proximity to thousands of seals, it would be ridiculous to think that atmospheric conditions or even strong drink could prompt them to mistake seals for mermaids.[32]

It seems more likely that the reverse situation would occur: when confronted with an anomalous creature, the witness might perceive it in terms of a similar, recognizable creature. Thus, a great problem for the researcher are those witnesses who have seen a Sasquatch, but who assume that they were looking at a bear. Such a rationalization seems quite likely in view of the fact that almost all Newfoundlanders accept the bear as a part of their world view, whereas few accept the Sasquatch. Thus, the simple statement, "I saw a bear in the woods today," may conceal an actual Sasquatch encounter.

The researcher, who may be alert to reports of encounters with spirits, devils, Indians, gorillas, and other such unlikely beings, will still miss reports of bear, moose, or lynx, since these encounters seem "reasonable and normal" according to the researcher's world view. Thus, what may have been a true sighting of a Sasquatch-like creature could, through subsequent tellings, become no more than a story about a frightening encounter with a bear.

The researcher, then, is faced with the problem of a world view which does not accept the Sasquatch when it is actually there, but rather rationalizes it as an Indian, spirit, devil, fairy, or as nothing more than a bear. At the same time, the researcher must deal with the problem of a psyche which might accept the Sasquatch when it isn't there. The Newfoundlander's world view and his conception of fear are in contradiction, so that when confronted with an unexplainable phenomenon, he may well be torn between a cosmological and a psychical rationalization of the event.

The problems of a researcher who attempts to interpret Sasquatch reports in Newfoundland are great. The islander's way of reporting the Sasquatch phenomenon may totally obscure the "actuality" of the event, from the researcher's point of view. In a culture such as that of Newfoundland, these problems may seem insurmountable, yet the reports gathered so far are intriguing, and further work may, in time, overcome the barriers of belief, perception, and reportage.

NOTES

1. I should like to thank David J. Hufford and John D. A. Widdowson for many of the ideas presented in this paper, and for the inspiration to write it. I should also like to thank the Memorial University of Newfoundland Folklore and Language Archive (hereafter MUNFLA) for allowing me access to their collections.

2. Gwyn Jones, ed. and trans., *The Norse Atlantic Saga: Being the Norse Voyages of Discovery and Settlement to Iceland, Greenland, America* (London: Oxford, 1964), pp. 184–85. The sciapod, monocole or footshade man was well known to European culture; see Heinz Mode, *Fabulous Beasts and Demons* (London: Phaidon, 1973), pp. 206–7.

3. Richard Whitebourne, *A Discourse and Discovery of New-Found-Land* . . . (London, 1623), pp. [100–101].

4. The greatest repository for such stories is the MUNFLA collection. All references to stories from this collection will include the MUNFLA accession number.

5. I have taken this term from Barre Toelken, "Folklore, Worldview, and Communication," in *Folklore: Performance and Communication*, eds. Dan Ben-Amos and Kenneth S. Goldstein (The Hague and Paris: Mouton, 1975), p. 267.

6. David J. Hufford has made this same point in "Humanoids and Anomalous Lights: Taxonomic and Epistemological Problems," *Fabula* 18 (1977): 234–41. See also Wayne

Suttles, "On the Cultural Track of the Sasquatch," *Northwest Anthropological Research Notes* 6 (1972): 65–90, for a discussion of belief and perception of Sasquatch among Pacific Northwest Indians. For a good survey of recent folkloristic studies on the relationship of perception to belief, see Donald Ward, "The Little Man Who Wasn't There: Encounters with the Supranormal," *Fabula* 18 (1977): 212–25.

7. Toelken, "Folklore, Worldview, and Communication," p. 265.

8. *The Beothucks or Red Indians: The Aboriginal Inhabitants of Newfoundland* (1915, reprint ed., Toronto: Coles, 1974), pp. 257–58, 266, 273.

9. Ibid., pp. 257–61.

10. MUNFLA Q68-49, p. 12. Names and places have been changed.

11. For accounts of this type of random destruction, see Don Hunter and René Dahinden, *Sasquatch* (Toronto: McClelland & Stewart, 1973), pp. 19–20; and John Green, *On the Track of the Sasquatch* (Agassiz, B.C.: Cheam, 1968), pp. 28–29.

12. MUNFLA Q68-247, p. 12. Names and places have been changed. Middle paragraph and parenthetical remarks are by the collector.

13. I should like to thank William Kirwin for searching, albeit in vain, for this word in the Newfoundland Dictionary Centre, Memorial University of Newfoundland.

14. See Peggy Martin, "Drop Dead: Witchcraft Images and Ambiguities in Newfoundland Society," *Culture & Tradition* 2 (1977): 35–50.

15. MUNFLA 68-17, p. 137. The place name has been changed. Parenthetical remarks are by the collector.

16. See motifs N570ff. in Stith Thompson, *Motif-Index of Folk-Literature*, rev. ed. (Bloomington: Indiana University Press, 1955), for international analogues to this legend.

17. The strange shining eyes have been described in other Sasquatch encounters. See Ivan Sanderson, *Abominable Snowmen: Legend Come to Life* (Philadelphia and New York: Chilton, 1961), p. 122; Hunter and Dahinden, *Sasquatch*, pp. 46, 67; and Green, *On the Track of the Sasquatch*, p. 63.

18. MUNFLA 68-17, p. 137. The place name has been changed.

19. "Sasquatch/Bigfoot: A Canadian Perspective," typescript, 1976. See motif A972.2.2. *The Devil's Footprint* in Thompson, *Motif-Index*.

20. As quoted in Hufford, "Humanoids," p. 236. Hufford was unable to track down the source of this story, noting that, according to his informant, it appeared in an "old travel book." Another account of the "Traverspine Gorilla" of Labrador is given in Elliott Merrick, *True North* (New York: Scribner's, 1933), pp. 24–26.

21. Similar perceptions of the Sasquatch as a gorilla occurred in the report of the capture of a creature, subsequently named Jacko, in British Columbia in 1884; see Hunter and Dahinden, *Sasquatch*, pp. 22–25. See also Green, *On the Track*, p. 41, for a similar perception.

22. *Abominable Snowman in Newfoundland*, writ. & narr. Michael Harrington, CBC Radio, St. John's, Jamboree—Friends and Neighbors, 8 June 1977. The source of this story is not given. I should like to thank CBC St. John's for allowing me access to the radio script.

23. Hufford, "Humanoids," p. 241.

24. "Aspects of Traditional Verbal Control: Threats and Threatening Figures in Newfoundland Folklore," Ph.d. diss., Memorial University of Newfoundland 1972. A slightly abridged version of this dissertation has been published as *If You Don't Be Good: Verbal Social Control in Newfoundland*, Social and Economic Studies, No. 21 (St. John's: Institute of Social and Economic Research, Memorial University of Newfoundland, 1977).

25. Hunter and Dahinden, *Sasquatch*, p. 35, allude to the bogey man–Sasquatch relationship, but do not explore the question.

26. MUNFLA Q67-213, as quoted in Widdowson, *If You Don't Be Good*, p. 166.

27. MUNFLA Q63B, as quoted in Widdowson, *If You Don't Be Good*, p. 179, and MUNFLA 67-1, as quoted in Widdowson, "Aspects," p. 367, respectively.

28. MUNFLA Q67-158, as quoted in Widdowson, *If You Don't Be Good*, p. 195, and MUNFLA Q67-427, as quoted in Widdowson, *If You Don't Be Good*, p. 151, respectively.

29. Reported by the student in a class on Newfoundland Folklore at Memorial University of Newfoundland, taught by Herbert Halpert, in the autumn of 1972.

30. See C. G. Jung, *The Archetypes and the Collective Unconscious*, trans. R.F.C. Hall, *The Collected Works of C. G. Jung*, vol. 9, part 1 (London: Routledge & Kegan Paul, 1959). For a discussion of the ape as a universal "figura diaboli," see H. W. Janson, *Apes and Apelore in the Middle Ages and the Renaissance*, Studies of the Warburg Institute, No. 20 (London: Warburg Institute, University of London, 1952), pp. 13–27.

31. Green, *On the Track of the Sasquatch*, pp. 33, 41–42; and Bernard Heuvelmans, *On the Track of Unknown Animals*, trans. Richard Garnett (New York: Hill and Wang, 1965), pp. 91–92.

32. *Folklore of the Sea* (Middletown, Conn.: Wesleyan University Press for the Marine Historical Assn., Mystic Seaport, 1973), p. 228.

EDITOR'S SUGGESTIONS FOR FURTHER READING

Ames, Michael M., and Marjorie Halpin, eds. 1980. *Manlike Monsters on Trial: Early Records and Modern Evidence.* Vancouver: University of British Columbia Press.

Bayanov, Dmitri. 1982. "A Note on Folklore in Hominology." *Cryptozoology* 1: 46–48.

Bowman, Matthew. 2007. "A Mormon Bigfoot: David Patten's Cain and the Conception of Evil in LDS Folklore." *Journal of Mormon History* 33 (3): 62–82.

Buhs, Joshua Blu. 2010. *Bigfoot: The Life and Times of a Legend.* Chicago: University of Chicago Press.

Buhs, Joshua Blu. 2011. "Tracking Bigfoot through 1970s North American Children's Culture: How Mass Media, Consumerism, and the Culture of Preadolescence Shaped Wildman Lore." *Western Folklore* 70 (2): 195–218.

Hufford, David. 1977. "Humanoids and Anomalous Lights: Taxonomic and Epistemological Problems." *Fabula* 18 (1): 234–41.

Hunter, Don, and Rene Dahinden. 1993. *Sasquatch/Bigfoot: The Search for North America's Incredible Creature.* Rev. ed. Richmond Hill, ON: Firefly Books.

Kirtley, Bacil F. 1964. "Unknown Hominids and New World Legends." *Western Folklore* 23 (3): 77–90.

McLeod, Michael. 2009. *Anatomy of a Beast: Obsession and Myth on the Trail of Bigfoot.* Berkeley: University of California Press.

Milligan, Linda. 1990. "The 'Truth' about the Bigfoot Legend." *Western Folklore* 49 (1): 83–98.

Murad, Turhon A. 1988. "Teaching Anthropology and Critical Thinking with the Question 'Is There Something Big Afoot?'" *Current Anthropology* 29 (5): 787–89.

Suttles, Wayne P. 1972. "On the Cultural Trail of the Sasquatch." *Northwest Anthropological Research Notes* 6 (1): 65–90.

Suttles, Wayne P. 1980. "Sasquatch: The Testimony of Tradition." In *Manlike Monsters on Trial: Early Records and Modern Evidence*, edited by Michael M. Ames and Marjorie Halpin, 245–54. Vancouver: University of British Columbia Press.

5

The "Char-Man"
A Local Legend of the Ojai Valley

Charlie Seemann

PREFACE

Much as James Leary had done with the Swamp Monster, Charlie Seemann
summoned early memories to fulfill a graduate school research assignment,
recalling the Char-Man from his Southern California childhood. Seemann
begins with autoethnography, recounting a verbatim text of the Char-Man
legend as he would perform it: a man, scorched in a California wildfire,
retreats to the hills, living out life as a wildman, occasionally making frightening appearances or giving chase to teenagers. Seemann demonstrates how
the Char-Man oral tradition encouraged ostension (specifically, legend tripping), which itself encouraged local newspaper reports. Seemann finds two
"kernels of truth," one in a 1948 brushfire that destroyed many homes in
the Shelf Road area and another in a severely disfigured skin-cancer victim
who would walk his dog late at night in the same darkened, secluded lanes
where teenagers would park.

This chapter, originally published as a research note, proves that legend
studies need not be long to be effective. In fact, in just a brief article, Seemann
touches on numerous key legend terms and concepts, including migration,
function, localization, recurring motifs, legend climate, and legend tripping.
Seemann's central question is migration: how a legend from Shelf Road relocated to and localized on Old Creek Road and other new areas across the
Ojai Valley (a question Puglia will also ask about the Maryland Goatman
decades later). Seemann argues that the legend climate is pivotal: when Shelf
Road was compromised by urban sprawl, the legend migrated to more fertile
grounds that allowed for the same essential motifs (fires, bridges, forests,
dark roads, and wildmen) and the same basic function—"providing young

people an excuse for a journey to a remote locale in search of adventure" or, put simply, an ideal location for legend trips.

Similar to the Boondock Monster's changing legend climate, as urban sprawl eroded the fertile legend environment and Shelf Road ceased to provide the necessary legend climate, the Char-Man legend attached itself to a new location, similar in setting to the original: a remote, hilly, wooded, uncivilized, yet accessible stretch of road. Researchers across North America can emulate Seemann's careful study of a community monster legend, both in method and in concept, and apply it to their own local settings.

ESSAY

The legend of the "Char-Man" was in wide circulation when I was a high school student in the Ojai Valley, a small, quiet, mountain-ringed community about fourteen miles inland from Ventura, California. I have heard the story many times from my peers, and my version seems to be very typical. Here is the story as I remember it from high school days in 1963 or 1964:

A

Back in 1948 there was a big brush fire in the Ojai Valley, which burned a good part of the valley and destroyed many homes. It was several days after the fire before anyone could get around to all the burned homes in the surrounding foothills to see if everyone was all right. There was a man living with his son in an isolated cabin in the hills south of town. Their house was burned in the fire, the father was killed in the fire, and the son was badly burned. When someone finally got out to the remains of the cabin, they found that, apparently, the son had gone crazy from the experience, for he had hung the body of his father by the feet from what was left of a nearby tree and had stripped all the burned skin from it. After skinning his father, he fled into the hills down on Old Creek Road, where he has lived in his "charred" condition ever since. Every once in a while he comes close enough to town to encounter someone, occasionally chasing people and such. The police have been sent out to look for him, and although they have caught glimpses of him, and found traces of him, they have never been able to catch him.

I became interested in seriously studying the legend years later, because as I considered a number of variants, an interesting pattern of migration began to emerge. In this paper I will trace this legend from its apparent origin and location, on one side of the Ojai Valley on Shelf Road, through its various forms and migration to the Old Creek Road area, all the way across the valley. I will also examine the influences of function and symbolism on

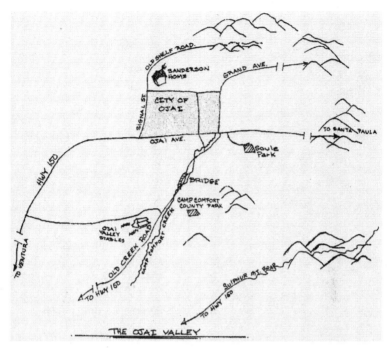

Figure 5.1. Hand-drawn map of the Ojai Valley, with key locations marked.
(Illustration by Charlie Seemann.)

the migration and eventual localization of the legend on Old Creek Road,
the area with which it is now associated. In presenting variants related to me
by informants, I will begin with the earliest versions I collected.

A woman who works for the *Ojai Valley News*, a local weekly paper, told
me that her sons learned the story when the family first moved to Ojai in
1961. Her boys were eight and eleven years old at the time. They told her
the following story:

B

Supposedly this Char-Man lived in the foothills in the area between the
ends of Signal Street and Daly Road. He was in his house in the big fire of
1948, and as my kids put it, he was "burned to a crisp." He had been living
there, I guess in the ruins of the house, ever since. He was all covered with
bandages, and was afraid to come out into town because he was so terribly
disfigured. My eight year old said he had seen the house where the Char-
Man lived, but he never saw the Char-Man.

I might say here that Signal Street becomes, at its extremity, a small dirt
road known as Shelf Road, as shown on the map. (The map is not drawn to

scale, but is merely intended to indicate the topographical relationships of the places mentioned.)

An interview with Sergeant Bill Klamser, a long-time member of the Ojai Police Department, also places the "Char-Man" at the end of Signal Street:

C

Back a few years ago, in the early '60s, probably 1961 or '62, we got a report from some teen-agers that they had been parked up at "the point," a sort of look-out spot overlooking the valley up on Shelf Road, and that their car had been approached by an "awful looking creature," which they said had the appearance of being badly burned and deformed. They used the word "charred." Well, this first report was more or less just brushed aside, but soon we had more similar reports, and then some parents came in complaining that their kids had been frightened by a similar man near Shelf Road. We started an investigation, patrolling the Shelf Road–Signal Street area, looking for this "charred" man. Of course, by this time the stories of this "awful creature" had spread among the kids in the valley, and some- how he got named the "Char-Man." Eventually the individual who was the source of these reports was found. He was an elderly man, who lived alone with his dog, near Signal Street. He had cancer, apparently some kind of bad skin cancer, and his face and one arm were badly deformed. He was so ugly that he didn't like to be seen, and so he only went out for walks at night or early in the evening, with his dog, up on Shelf Road, away from town. It was while he was walking up there that he would sometimes be seen by kids parked at "the point." Anyway, pretty soon the kids were saying that this man had been burned up in the big 1948 fire, and that he was still living there. That was about as far as the whole thing went, until four or five years ago this Char-Man turned up down on Old Creek Road. Then things got out of hand, with dozens and dozens of kids going down there looking for the Char-Man, until it was necessary for our department, and the Sheriff's Department, to send men down there to keep them away.

Sergeant Klamser is certain that the cancer victim involved in this series of incidents on Shelf Road was the original inspiration for the "Char-Man" legend.

The next most closely related version was told to me by Mrs. Lynn Leikens, a long-time valley resident:

D

I knew the "Char-Man" story from several years ago, but exactly when I first heard it, or where, I don't recall. I just remember that he had been burned in his house, and was called the "Char-Man." I think he lived up on Sulphur Mountain somewhere.

I have included this variant here, as being most closely related to the Shelf Road versions, because the story has not been shifted to Old Creek Road. While it is not a Shelf Road version, it still places the "Char-Man" on one of the lonely roads (Sulphur Mountain Road) circling the rim of the valley in the mountains, as shown on the map.

While I was interviewing Mrs. Leikens, her twelve year old son came in the room; curious about the currency of the legend in his age group, I attempted to interview him. He responded:

E

Yeah, I know the story. He [the Char-Man] lives in an old rock house down on Creek Road. My brother, Chip, seen him one day in the bushes out in Soule Park [see map]. My brother was in Soule Park with some friends when this monster-guy came running at them out of the bushes. He was all burned looking and was wearing an old ripped-up windbreaker, made out of cloth.

In a hurry to go somewhere, he departed, leaving me with that as his entire account. Unfortunately, his brother was unavailable for interview.

The apparent significance of this variant seems to be that although the Char-Man lived on Old Creek Road, he was not confined to that area and could travel to other parts of the valley, even to such an unlikely place as Soule Park.

The next variant is from Mr. Joseph Weaver of Ojai, an attendant at Camarillo State Hospital. His version was as follows:

F

There was this guy who was burned in a big fire and lives in the mountains around Ojai. Sometimes campers see him, and sometimes he comes down and scares them.

Mr. Weaver couldn't remember where he heard the story, but he thought a lot of people knew it.

Variants D, E, and F seem to follow a trend toward a generalized spread of the story from the specific locale of the Signal Street–Shelf Road area to other areas of the valley and "the mountains around Ojai." In other words, the legend seems to become detached from its place of origin and "float" freely about the Ojai Valley area.

The other variants I collected were similar to variant A and show a later localization of the legend on Old Creek Road, near Camp Comfort County Park. The first informant with this version was 19 year old Michael Neuron of Ojai.

G

In the big fire in the '40s, a lot of houses in the hills around town were
burned, and there was a man and his son living down by Camp Comfort
Creek, and his house was burned in the fire. The father was killed and
his son was burned real bad. He flipped out and hung his father in a tree
and skinned him. They found him hanging there when they got out to his
house. If you go down to the bridge on Old Creek Road, by Camp Comfort, and yell "Help! Help!" sometimes he will come down to the bridge.
Sometimes he comes down and chases people.

Neuron couldn't remember where he heard the story, but he says, "A lot of
people say they've seen him."

Tom Weddle, a resident of the Ojai Valley "riverbottom," in the community of Meiner's Oaks, tells a very similar story, but he remembers where
he heard it.

H

There was a fire in which the house that a young man and his parents were
living in was burned. Both of the guy's parents were burned to death,
and he was burned badly. He hung both of his parents and went into the
mountains, near Old Creek Road, and has been living there ever since.

Tom Weddle first heard the story from Mark Gates, when Gates recounted to him how he went down to the Old Creek Road bridge with some
friends and was attacked by the Char-Man; one of them had his jacket
ripped off by the Char-Man while they were trying to get away. Weddle was unable to remember exactly when this occurred, somewhere he
thought between 1965 and 1968. He said that Mark Gates related this adventure to his friends and schoolmates, and everyone started going down
to the bridge and screaming "help" to see if they, too, could produce the
Char-Man. Mr. Weddle said the police came and spent several nights chasing everybody away.

The next account is one I stumbled on quite inadvertently. Attempting
to locate and interview Mark Gates, I called his home. A person, who has
requested anonymity, answered, said Mark wasn't there, and asked what
I wanted. I told him I wanted to talk to Mark Gates about his encounter
with the Char-Man. He said he could probably tell me more about the
Char-Man than Mark could, and much to my surprise, declared: "I was
the Char-Man." He then proceeded to tell me his version of the legend
and then to relate the events which had occurred at the bridge on Old
Creek Road:

I

There was a big fire, and a man and his wife who were living in a cabin down by Camp Comfort Creek had their house burned. The guy's wife was burned to death in the cabin, and the man got burned real bad trying to get back in to save her. She was screaming "Help, Help!" but he couldn't get to her. He went insane, and now he goes down to the bridge, and if you holler "Help, Help!" he comes down to the bridge and goes crazy.

At this point, the individual told me how he and a couple of his friends had perpetrated a Char-Man hoax, not only upon Mark Gates, but on a good portion of the county, as well.

We had heard about the Char-Man and we was drivin' around one night, and decided to pull off this Char-Man thing. We arranged it so I would wear this pig mask and hide up the river [Camp Comfort Creek], and limp up when they yelled "Help, help!" They [Mark Gates and his friends] drove up to the bridge, turned off their lights, and yelled "Help, help!" and I came limping up and tore Eddie White's jacket off him. They still don't know we did it. It was a real big deal; the cops came down, it was in the paper and on the radio and everything. It was really far-out.

An account of the incident did, in fact, appear in the 6 July 1967 Ventura County *Star-Free Press.*

THE CHAR-MAN MAY BE LURKING SOMEWHERE IN THE OJAI VALLEY
By Jerry Thomas

Has Ventura County youth discovered another summertime spook fad? Or is there actually a frightening hermit prowling the backcountry roads, ranting at intruders and howling in the night? County lawmen regard recent reports as a combination of a little bit of fact, and a whole lot of youthful vivid imagination. They pleaded that the spook spot not be specifically identified for fear that thousands of teen-agers with summer leisure time on their hands would flock to the area in search of the figure that has been described as something akin to a werewolf. If such an anti-social figure exists, they point out, the hordes of thrill-seekers will make his life even more frantic. One night this week, as many as 60 county youths drove to the meccas of mystery, somewhere in the mountains near Ojai Valley, looking for someone they describe as the Char-Man, a purported anti-social individual who resists intrusion by howling at interlopers, banging on cars, and giving bodily chase. One Ojai policeman said "almost every kid in town has gone into the area" looking for something unexpected and eerie. One teen-ager is convinced a recluse lives along a winding creek bed. He is Eddie White, 18, of 68 Burnham Road, Oak

View. White maintains he had his sheepskin jacket torn from his back "when something ran across a bridge and grabbed my neck." This incident reportedly occurred 10 days ago. The boy and seven companions returned last Saturday night. With flashlights trained along the creek bottom, the youths picked up a figure walking up stream. "I guess it was a man," White recalled. "We jumped into the car and locked the doors. He banged on the trunk and windows." The youth described the angry face as "distorted, scarred, and old." White admits "we kids bother him and he no doubt resents our intrusions." The accepted method of rousing the hermit is to have someone get on the bridge and yell "Help!" White said the man always replies with another "Help!" Authorities are mindful that last year a "haunted house" tale lured hundreds of youths to the Saticoy area. Reports of ghosts and spooks drew the curious by the carload. No one found any supernatural being but many found a convenient haven for parking and romancing, deputies said.

This account of the incident led me once again to contact the Ojai Police. This time I spoke with officer Gene Meadows, who had personally chased the Char-Man on several occasions and was one of the officers who responded the night Eddie White reported he had been attacked. Officer Meadows's recollection of the event was rather vague because of the time elapsed—he thought it had been "about four years"—but he remembered going out to the bridge after receiving a report of a boy having his jacket ripped off. However Meadows said he remembered the person responsible as being a sort of "wild looking colored man" from Los Angeles, who just happened to be down in the creek bed when the boys started yelling "Help!" He thought they really needed help, so he came running up; the boys were frightened, and a scuffle of some sort ensued, during which the jacket was ripped off. He said the rest of the problem, trying to keep people from congregating down at the bridge, was handled by the County Sheriff's Department, because it was in their territory.

It is not my intent to try to resolve the discrepancies between the various accounts of this incident. What is important is the role this incident, and its coverage in the local news media, had in helping to localize the legend on Old Creek Road.

The last interview I conducted [was] at the Ojai Valley Stables, which lie just down the road from the bridge on Old Creek Road. Riders from the stables ride extensively in the area, and I had heard that occasionally riders, and their horses, had been frightened by the Char-Man. I went to the stables and talked to two young men who were working there. Together, they related the following variant:

J

The Char-Man was burned in the big fire in the '40s; he killed his brother and went off to live in the hills. Supposedly he lives down by the bridge somewhere. Just a couple of weeks ago, a 14 year old girl, who leads trail rides for us, came back to the stables and said she had seen the face of the Char-Man in the window of a little rock house down by the bridge. She won't go down there anymore. Sometimes people who come here to ride ask if it's safe to ride down Camp Comfort Creek because of the Char-Man.

CONCLUSIONS

The growth and migration of the "Char-Man" legend and its eventual localization to the bridge on Old Creek Road have in large measure been determined by the story's functions and symbols, which it shares with other frightening local legends and which help explain its development and popularity.

According to Linda Dégh, "scary" stories like the "Char-Man" tale are especially prevalent among teen-agers, filling for them a need for adventure in an otherwise "dull" world. With newfound mobility, teen-agers can drive to locales of extraordinary and frightening events in search of the "chill of fear." Visits of the "whole gang" to these locales, as in the "Char-Man" account, also serve, argues Dégh, as a rite of passage, as a chance for participants to challenge danger and prove their courage.[1]

The "Char-Man" story shares not only common functions with "scary" legends but at least three major symbols as well. The first is the bridge where the legend is now localized (Variants A, E, F, G, H, I, and J). In an article on haunted bridges, Dégh speaks of a "cluster" of bridge legends which have two parts: first, an account of a supernatural or extraordinary "event that occurred in the past and . . . [explains] a present phenomenon attributed to it"; second, a personal experience of the narrator "as he explores the phenomenon" (in our "Char-Man" account this experience is often related second or third hand and is not usually that of the immediate informant).[2] The bridge in the story, Dégh points out, is a universal symbol of the passageway between life and the world beyond. She cites several examples of this association in German and English folklore and notes that bridge stories are prevalent in North America, as shown by the number of references made to them in Baughman's *Type and Motif Index of the Folktales of England and North America*.[3]

The second and third symbols in the "Char-Man" legend are the "forest" and the "dangerous wild man." In discussing the legend of the

"Laughing Woman," C. Richard K. Lunt states that stories of lost, wild people are frequent in tradition. He also speaks of the "ancient literary motif of the forest that harbors ancient and death dealing creatures" and the "equally ancient and lingering distrust and fear of those persons whom we judge insane."[4] In our legend, the primeval forest is simply the heavily wooded and remote area of Old Creek Road, and of course the Char-Man is the insane and dangerous creature who lurks there. There seems to be no special symbolism or motif involved in the fact that the Char-Man was disfigured by fire. The combination of the bridge and the forest creates a favorable "legend climate," which contributes to the setting necessary for a good scare.

The "Char-Man" legend, then, originated with the events on Shelf Road and was initially associated with the 1948 fire and the ruins of the old Sanderson home. In the early 1960s the Sanderson home was fairly remote. As Ojai grew, it expanded into this territory; as a result, the home is now well within the fringes of the town. This circumstance interfered with the legend's function of providing young people an excuse for a journey to a remote locale in search of adventure. Furthermore, the setting had been impaired by the building of other homes in the area so the mood could no longer be the same. With the Char-Man no longer associated with Shelf Road and freed to wander in any remote area of the valley, these functions could be restored. The Char-Man could be easily invoked anywhere. However, the legend was thus removed from a concrete and real setting, impairing its credibility. It would seem only natural, therefore, that the story would tend to become attached to some other suitable location. Old Creek Road is remote, a short drive out of town being necessary to get there. The area is about as much a "forest" as there is within the valley, and the relatively heavily-wooded, hilly landscape provides a good habitat for a Char-Man, furnishing him with protection from civilization, yet at the same time affording ample opportunity for his occasional encounters with travelers in the area. The symbolic value of the bridge on Old Creek Road also plays an important role in the story's being located there. So too does the bridge's functional value. From it, it is possible to play out the rite of passage, to challenge danger without venturing too far from one's car. The car can be parked on the bridge, and the ritual of crying "Help, help!" can be carried out without actually venturing into the woods. Dégh mentions the motif of the automobile being strangely considered as adequate protection from similar dangers, and Eddie White, in his account of his "attack" in the *Star-Free Press* article, says that they locked themselves in the car and the Char-Man banged on the windows and trunk but apparently could not get to them.

The importance of the "Char-Man" legend lies in the "living laboratory" it provides us, with all the events taking place since the fire of 1948, well within the memories of most adults and well within the comprehension time of younger people. It is not too removed chronologically to seem remote or impossible. The migration of the legend gives an excellent opportunity to observe first-hand the processes and influences involved in the legend's origin and development. The evidence from these observations indicates that both function and symbolism are important in this legend's formation, migration, and localization. We also have an excellent example of the importance of a printed newspaper account in the reinforcement of a local legend; although arising from a contrived prank, the newspaper article helped to further establish, stabilize, and lend credibility to the legend.

ACKNOWLEDGMENTS

Thanks are due Linda Dégh and Wayland Hand for reading preliminary drafts of this paper and for making valuable suggestions regarding layout and integration of the text.

NOTES

1. Linda Dégh, "The Belief Legend in Modern Society" in *American Folklore Legend*, ed. Wayland Hand (Los Angeles, 1971), 64–68.
2. Linda Dégh, "The Haunted Bridges Near Avon and Danville and Their Role In Legend Formation," *Indiana Folklore* 2 (1969): 77–78.
3. Ibid., 89.
4. C. Richard K. Lunt, "The Laughing Woman," *Indiana Folklore* 1 (1968): 80.

EDITOR'S SUGGESTIONS FOR FURTHER READING

Bishop, Norma. 1984. "The Ingleby Monster and the Penns Valley Legend Complex." *Keystone Folklore* 3 (1): 24–31.

Harling, Kristie. 1971. "The Grunch: An Example of New Orleans Teen-Age Folklore." *Louisiana Miscellany* 3 (2): 15–20.

Hudson, Arthur Palmer, and Peter Kyle McCarter. 1934. "The Bell Witch of Tennessee and Mississippi: A Folk Legend." *Journal of American Folklore* 47 (183): 45–63.

Langlois, Janet L. 1978. "Belle Gunness, the Lady Bluebeard: Community Legend as Metaphor." *Journal of the Folklore Institute* 15 (2): 147–60.

Osbone, August Knapp. 1955. "The Green Fly Monster." *New York Folklore Quarterly* 2: 214–15.

Rhone, George E. 1963. "The Giwoggle." *Keystone Folklore Quarterly* 8 (1): 44–48.

6

The Jersey Devil

Angus Kress Gillespie

PREFACE

Angus Kress Gillespie originally published his Jersey Devil research in the little-circulated, short-lived, now-defunct, nearly inaccessible *Journal of Regional Cultures*. Along with James F. McCloy and Ray Miller Jr., Gillespie has become the authority on the Jersey Devil, among other Jerseyana, guest-starring on television shows such as *History Hunters* and *MonsterQuest*. The popular attention Gillespie has received should not overshadow the important folkloristic monster thesis he developed: that a little-known local legend, the Leeds Devil, became a statewide phenomenon and mascot not because of its deeds or cultural significance but because of its easily identifiable and widely applicable sobriquet, the *Jersey* Devil.

Folklorists have many useful concepts for referring to the relationship between folklore and popular culture, including fakelore, folklure, folklorism, the folklore continuum, hypermodern folklore, and the folkloresque. Here Gillespie uses another, "poplore," (coined by Archie Green) to examine and account for the transformation of the folk Leeds Devil into the popular Jersey Devil, the official state demon of New Jersey. Like many monsters in this anthology, at least part of the Jersey Devil's life was lived through newspapers. All Jersey Devil researchers point to the events of 1909 as the Jersey Devil's statewide debut. Somewhat unusual in this instance was the prominence and quantity of newspapers reporting sightings (albeit with bemused incredulity), giving no indication the phenomenon was a hoax or deliberate misrepresentation.

In response to innumerable requests for interviews from journalists, Gillespie offers the most succinct and accurate undressing of lay monster questions versus folkloristic monster questions ever put to paper. Journalists

https://doi.org/10.7330/9781646421602.c006

ask if the Jersey Devil exists and what evidence there is for its existence; folklorists ask who tells the legend, when, and why. While Gillespie acknowledges McCloy and Miller's *The Jersey Devil* as a comparatively competent and sympathetic study of the Jersey Devil, he criticizes their aversion to fieldwork and verbatim texts and demonstrates how the authors tend to only acknowledge variants within streamlined summaries. Gillespie also criticizes ambiguous or absent sourcing, a problem that plagues many popular treatments of monster legends.

Gillespie summons folklorist Carl Wilhelm von Sydow to differentiate between the Jersey Devil's active and passive tradition-bearers. Active Jersey Devil tradition-bearers grew up with the legend, learning it from family and friends in or from the Southern New Jersey Pine Barrens, and can perform the legend themselves. Passive tradition-bearers have heard of the Jersey Devil, likely through mass media, but cannot recount the legend with any particular detail. The popular press, the mass media, the state legislature, and even Gillespie's article will not create any more active tradition-bearers, but they certainly have created more passive ones. The Jersey Devil's popularity has caused consternation for folklorists. With such a rash of literary and popular treatments, it becomes difficult to decipher what emanates from folk tradition, what has been fabricated whole hog, and what, perhaps, is a muddled and befuddled conjoining of the two. Gillespie admits, however, that even the Pineys themselves, active tradition-bearers, take part in the folk processes of contextualization and localization, using it (i.e., changing the legend's function) to accomplish their own goals, such as keeping children (and perhaps treasure hunters and maybe even prohibition agents) out of certain parts of the woods.

Gillespie's study also demonstrates the importance of establishing rapport and trust with informants rather than ransacking towns for legends. Gillespie's students have attempted quick Jersey Devil fieldwork raids and failed; Gillespie established some Pine Barrens rapport and experienced some success; folklorist Herbert Halpert and famed author John McPhee achieved near-insider status and were both granted near-full narratives.

Employing a common convention of legend case studies, Gillespie concludes with an overview of how the folk legend has seeped (or perhaps more accurately, been vigorously yanked) into statewide popular culture. He argues that, though the Jersey Devil may still exist in oral tradition, statewide popular culture's embrace has decreased its folk vigor. While folklorists may cringe at the popularization of once-cherished local tradition, commercial appropriation appears to be a common trajectory of the legendary monster within advanced consumer culture. This process itself, if somewhat removed from their traditional realm of folkloristic inquiry, still requires folklorists' committed attention.

ESSAY

The story of the Jersey Devil when it was first told in the 1730s was of great interest only to a few people in a handful of sparsely settled communities in South Jersey. Now some 250 years later the story is of casual interest to millions of people throughout all of New Jersey. Thus, the Jersey Devil has undergone a transition from being a creature of folklore to being a creature of poplore.[1] In becoming a household word known to millions, the Jersey Devil has lost some of his original surrounding awe and mystery. In this essay we shall neither mourn the loss of his mystique nor celebrate his popularity. Instead, we shall try to explain the change. To do so requires some understanding of the way in which a legend functions.

By definition a legend is a prose narrative that has been handed down orally generation after generation. It generally is regarded by its tellers as true. Unlike myth, which usually deals with something far away and long ago, legend is concerned with the immediate historical past. Legend is sometimes referred to as folk history, but, of course, it is history as changed through oral transmission. Because legends deal with beliefs, they sometimes are called belief tales.[2]

For many years the legend of the Jersey Devil functioned in just the way the definition suggests. Related from father to son and from mother to daughter, it helped to explain the otherwise inexplicable. The major change took place around the turn of the century. The moment of change can be pinpointed with some precision. In 1909 a number of Philadelphia newspapers picked up the story and reported a number of "sightings." The quiet, mysterious, rural legend became a media event. The way which the "sightings" were reported is significant. Sophisticated urban reporters did not report the events as straight news. Instead, the tone they adopted was one of bemused and condescending feature story. Since that time the story has resurfaced from time to time in the media throughout the twentieth century, almost always being treated with tongue-in-cheek.

Why has interest in the Jersey Devil continued to increase? I think that part of the explanation may lie in the name—the *Jersey* Devil. Originally back in the 1700s the story was often referred to as the Leeds Devil or as the Shourds Devil and only occasionally as the Jersey Devil. But when the Philadelphia newspapers picked up the story, the name became standardized as the Jersey Devil. The new name is actually somewhat misleading

Figure 6.1. Drawing of the Jersey Devil based on witness descriptions. (*Philadelphia Evening Bulletin* [1909].)

since it seems to suggest a statewide demon. But traditionally the Jersey Devil always was identified with a very particular place—Leeds Point, not far from present day Atlantic City, which, of course, did not exist at that time. Even today at Rutgers, the State University of New Jersey, I notice in my introductory folklore courses that the students from South Jersey are often much more knowledgeable about the Jersey Devil than students from North Jersey. Until the local professional hockey team adopted the name "New Jersey Devils" most students from North Jersey never had even heard the word, let alone know the story. But that name does lend itself to statewide identification and recognition. One might speculate: if the name had remained the Leeds Devil, would the story have entered popular culture? I doubt it.

When I started teaching folklore at Rutgers about ten years ago, I began to receive a few questions about the Jersey Devil, and so I took some time to look into the matter. Now it is almost routine: every October I get a few calls, usually from journalists, about the Jersey Devil. To my distress I find that most reporters, however well-meaning and well-informed, usually ask what to me are the wrong questions. Most newspaper stories about the Jersey Devil go astray in one of two ways: (1) the story trivializes the legend by attempting to make it light and humorous, or (2) the story attempts to explain away the legend through a misapplication of the scientific method. In the first case there is no attempt to deal with the legend in a serious way. In the second case the method is inappropriate to the subject matter. Instead of asking questions like this: Does the Jersey Devil exist? What proof is there for the existence of the Jersey Devil? Are there plaster casts of the footprints? Are there verified photographs? Let us try an entirely different set of questions: Who tells the legend of the Jersey Devil? What are the circumstances of the telling? Who makes up the audience? What function does the legend serve? Why has it lasted more than two hundred years?

With this new set of questions, we are on the road to learning something useful. The Jersey Devil has been sighted hundreds of times by all sorts of people. Let us examine some of the early accounts to get a fix on the story. The earliest version I have found comes from the 1790 diary of a woodsman named Vance Larner. In the section of his diary marked "October" Larner wrote:

> It was neither beast, nor man, nor spirit, but a hellish brew of all three. It was beside a pond when I came upon it. I stopped and did not move. Nay, I could not move. It was dashing its tail to and fro in the pond and rubbing its horns against a tree trunk. It was as large as a moose with leather wings. It had cloven hooves as big around as an oak's trunk. After it was through with the tree, it yielded an awful scream as if it were a pained man, and then flew across the pond until I could see it no more.[3]

The woodsman Larner told everyone about the creature he saw, and gradually a story about its birth developed. It was said that a woman who was expecting an unwanted child wished that it would be born a devil. Over time people added more and more details to the story.

Nearly seventy years after Vance Larner recorded seeing the Jersey Devil in his diary, an account of the legend appeared in the *Atlantic Monthly* in 1859:

> There lived in the year 1735, in the Township of Burlington, a woman. Her name was Leeds, and she was shrewdly suspected of a little amateur witchcraft. Be that as it may, it is well established, that, one stormy gusty night, when the wind was howling in turret and tree, Mother Leeds gave

birth to a son, whose father could have been no other than the Prince of Darkness. No sooner did he see the light than he assumed the form of a fiend, with a horse's head, wings of a bat, and a serpent's tail. The first thought of the newborn Caliban was to fall foul of his mother, whom he scratched and bepommelled soundly, and then flew through the window out in to the village, where he played the mischief generally. Little children he devoured, maidens he abused, young men he mauled and battered; and it was many days before a holy man succeeded in repeating the enchantment of Prospero. At length, however, Leeds devil was laid—but only for one hundred years.

During an entire century, the memory of that awful monster was preserved, and, as 1835 drew nigh, the denizens of Burlington and the Pines looked tremblingly for his rising. Strange to say, however, no one but Hannah Butler has had a personal interview with the fiend; though, since 1835, he has frequently been heard howling and screaming in the forest at night, to the terror of the Rats in their encampments. Hannah Butler saw the devil, one stormy night, long ago; though skeptical individuals affirm, that very possibly she may have been led, under the influence of liquid Jersey Lightning to invest a pine-stump, or, possibly, a belated bear, with diabolic attributes and a Satanic voice. However that may be, you cannot induce a Rat to leave his hut after dark,—nor, indeed, will you find many Jerseymen, though of a higher order of intelligence, who will brave the supernatural terrors of the gloomy forest at night, unless secure in the strength of numbers.[4]

Folklorist David Cohen has pointed out that the *Atlantic Monthly* account does not have the flavor of oral tradition. With allusions to Shakespeare, it is clearly literary. The author does not even like the Pineys; he refers to them as "Pine Rats." In addition, it is clear that the author does not believe in the Jersey Devil; he simply dismisses it as an hallucination. Cohen complains: "Most of the published accounts of the Jersey Devil have been written by unbelievers. These writers have trivialized what was originally an authentic folk legend and folk belief."[5]

What is it that bothers David Cohen about these published accounts? Unfortunately, it is all too easy to find examples of the sorts of things that Cohen disparages. Let us consider two examples, both of which are conspicuously absent from the bibliography of David Cohen's recent and authoritative book, *The Folklore and Folklife of New Jersey*. The first example is quite clear-cut. Let us look at the description of the Jersey Devil that is given in Walker D. Wyman's *Mythical Creatures of the U.S.A. and Canada*:

JERSEY DEVIL (TERATOS INCOMPREHENSIBILIS)

This creature was first reported in Northern New Jersey in the 1920s and 1950s. Since it was such a terrifying monster in general appearance, it defied description by those who may have seen it. The public was aroused until someone pointed out that it always appeared just at the time that the annual supply of bootleg applejack came from the illegal stills in the hills. After Prohibition was repealed, the Jersey Devil seems to have disappeared.[6]

In this case it is clear from the start that the author is not serious; indeed, he is poking fun at the whole business. We are tipped off from the very start by the phony Latin name. Hardly anything in the account is correct. The author mistakenly places the Jersey Devil in Northern New Jersey rather than in Southern New Jersey; in terms of time, he is two hundred years off the mark. This example is easy to dismiss. Let us now turn to a case that is far more subtle.

In 1976 the publication of *The Jersey Devil* by James F. McCloy and Ray Miller, Jr. was a major event for folklorists interested in New Jersey lore. It was an informative work, set in effective prose and tastefully produced. McCloy and Miller put together a considerable amount of information about the Pine Barrens, about the origins of the Jersey Devil, and about major historical accounts of its sighting. In their preface the authors explain, "we have attempted to focus on the essential points of the Jersey Devil's history and meaning." In this limited sense the authors did fulfill their intentions quite creditably. Their conclusions on "What is the Jersey Devil?" present reasonable hypotheses and interpretations of data that are at best ambiguous. Their treatment of the numerous sightings of January 1909 are a positive contribution. The book's thirteen drawings and five maps contribute to its usefulness, and the nine photographs help to evoke the desolate spirit of the Pine Barrens.

McCloy and Miller are knowledgeable and effective in presenting variants of the Jersey Devil legend. It is a given that oral transmission invariably creates different versions of the same text. The authors do not present individual verbatim "texts" or "versions." Instead they present a digested or compiled account—introducing minor varying details into the body of the main text. Let us see how this style works by examining a short passage:

> *Some say* that this cursed being was born horribly deformed, while *others say* it was natural at birth and afterward took on fiendish characteristics. Then, according to *some accounts*, Mother Leeds confined [it] in the attic, or the cellar, for a number of years until it made its escape up the chimney, or out the cellar door, during a raging storm. Curiously little is said about Mr. Leeds at any point, although *some people* talk of a horned being secretly visiting the unfortunate mother.[7] (Italics mine)

The trouble with this method is that we never get to connect specific informants with specific variants; nonetheless, while this procedure lacks rigor, it does make it abundantly clear that different versions do exist.

The publisher's dust jacket says, "This is the first booklength treatment of a legend that has endured for more than two centuries." While this statement is true, it is also a bit misleading. Despite the work's obvious charm and appeal, one is troubled by its brevity. Only 121 pages in length with large type and wide margins, printed on heavy stock, the work might more accurately be called a booklet with hard covers—directed toward a popular rather than a professional audience. The bibliography reveals a working familiarity with the relevant books and newspapers. However, the scholarly reader will be disappointed by the conspicuous absence of footnotes, so that in places the source of the information is simply not clear. It is disturbing to think that publication of this book may preclude other publishers from releasing a more scholarly work for fear that the market already has been saturated.

For folklorists the most disappointing aspect of the book is the absence of any fresh fieldwork. There are no verbatim presentations of the legend as found in the field. Does this mean that the authors prefer to do library research? Or that they have no training in folklore fieldwork? Or does it mean that they tried to collect living oral versions of the legend and failed? The latter question is not frivolous, since my own experience in gathering materials for the Folklore Archives at Rutgers shows that many people in the Pine Barrens are fed up with the intrusive questions of strangers. Feeling that they have been misrepresented or patronized too often in the popular press, many "Pineys" find it easier not to cooperate with anyone from the outside world.

So far we have seen that the story of the Jersey Devil is legendary and that it goes back over two hundred years. With the passage of time, the story has undergone the process of change. In addition, most of the printed accounts are disappointing in some fashion. The definitive book on the Jersey Devil has yet to be written. In some ways New Jersey's problem with the Jersey Devil is unique.

Just about every state in the union has an official state bird, not to mention a state tree and sometimes a state animal. But New Jersey is unique. We have the Jersey Devil, who was adopted as the *official state demon* in 1939. This action on the part of the state legislature is not without significance. Why would the state lawmakers do such a thing? In the first place it is a painless piece of legislation. It costs nothing since it requires no appropriation. There is no organized political resistance. It involves no tradeoffs of opposing interest groups. But in the second place, and more important, it ratified what already had taken place in the newspapers. By 1939 the Jersey Devil had enjoyed thirty years of media coverage. Not only had there been sightings from time to time, there had also been at least one celebrated case of a "museum exhibit" in Philadelphia, which later turned out to be a hoax. The state legislature simply was making "official" a legend which already had been embraced by the people, or at least by the people of South Jersey. The bill actually may have been a gesture of good will on the part of delegates from the northern (richer and more populous) part of the state toward their fellow lawmakers from the southern part of the state, who traditionally complain of neglect and poor treatment. It was an intriguing historical sequence: an obscure localized down-to-earth South Jersey legend was picked up by the Philadelphia media, which brought it to the attention of South Jersey lawmakers, who brought it to the attention, at least briefly, of the entire state. To this very day there basically are two classes of people who deal with the story. There are the active tradition-bearers who grew up with the story in family, home, and community in South Jersey. These are people who know him as the Leeds Ghost, the Monster of Leeds, the Devil of Leeds Point, or the Leeds Devil. He is part of their legendary heritage. His name is inextricably linked to the swamps, bogs, salt marshes, and lonely stretches of beach to be found in South Jersey.[8] Then there are the passive tradition-bearers who perhaps have heard of the story, usually through the mass media. These people may *know* about the story, but they do not really *care* about the story.

As an example of the sort of problem that the contemporary folklorist faces, let us consider the following, which was taken from a longer text:

> Halloween, naturally, is time for the Jersey Devil—the elusive demon who has been winging his way though Jersey history for more than 200 years.
>
> A witch at Leeds Point in Atlantic County in 1735 was overheard saying her 13th child would be a devil, folks say. A shy and gentle imp was born to her one stormy night with clown-hoofs and a long tail, a kangaroo body, bat wings, the face of a horse, and the head of a dog. He looked at his mother, flew up the chimney and disappeared into the Pine Barrens. The Jersey Devil's loud shrieks were heard at night in the swamps for several years.[9]

A rather standard Jersey Devil anecdote. Does it come from oral tradition? Was it collected with a tape recorder from the lips of an old-time resident of the area? Or is it simply culled from a dry academic textbook on New Jersey history? The answer, as you may by now have suspected, is neither.

It is taken from a short article in New Jersey Bell's *Tel-News*, an envelope stuffer sent out monthly with the telephone bills throughout the state, and much of the information in the *Tel-News* release appears in a longer treatment in the *Burlington County Herald*.[10]

Both note that after 1790 the Devil was not sighted until 1840, and only became widely known in 1960 when a newspaper report of the Devil appearing near a farmer's barn touched off hysteria in the area:

> People as far away as West Orange claimed to have seen the Devil Himself, or at least his tracks.
>
> Rewards were offered for the Devil's capture. A circus man offered $100,000 for him—dead or alive. Another man put up $500 for the Devil which he said was a rare vampire. Rewards were never claimed.
>
> A Philadelphia publicist charged gullible people money to catch a glimpse of the Jersey devil he'd captured—a small kangaroo painted green with a snapped on pair of large wings.[11]

With this kind of mass dissemination it becomes harder and harder to tell what is authentic oral tradition and what is not. From a folkloristically pure point of view, the legend has been hopelessly "contaminated" by its repeated circulation in print.

Despite this handicap the Jersey Devil legend continues to capture our imagination and is a popular subject for investigation by beginning students in folklore at Rutgers. Students often run into considerable difficulty in trying to collect Jersey Devil stories. The people of the Pine Barrens are very suspicious of outsiders. Examination of the New Jersey Folklore Archives at Douglass College reveals a number of cases in which students were rebuffed by Pineys. Other students have had better luck. It is important to point out in this context that professors do not grade papers on the basis of "success" or "failure" in field collecting projects. An "unsuccessful" interview may in itself reveal a great deal about the attitudes of the people of the area. Nonetheless, it is satisfying for everyone when a cooperative informant is discovered. Some of the most cooperative informants whom Rutgers students have encountered are children, who typically alter the Jersey Devil legend to suit their own purposes. They explain grotesque and unusual events in their own lives by attributing them to some intervention by "the Jersey Devil." Often the story is localized, placed in their own home town. In the Folklore Archives at Douglass there are dozens of different versions of the Jersey Devil legend. They differ on many key points of the story. No aspect of the story is more cloudy than the matter of the Jersey Devil's origin. Some say that it was born deformed; others say that it took on devilish characteristics after it was born. Some say that the mother was a Mrs. Leeds; others say it was a Mrs. Shourds. And so it goes. Every time you hear the legend it seems that there is a new twist.

It is revealing to compare these student reports with my own field notes from South Jersey. It is true that I have had more experience than most of them in folklore collecting. However, my findings on the Jersey Devil legend have all the same shortcomings. The material I have collected is partial and fragmentary. None of the stories I have collected is a fully developed narrative. What I have collected has come in bits and pieces—just as it has for the students. For instance, let us consider a story told to me by someone who has lived in the Pines all his life—Merce Ridgway, Jr., of Waretown, New Jersey. Ridgway is a bayman, a clammer by trade, and he knows many of the songs and stories of the area. His story is told in a very roundabout manner. Essentially it is based on a conversation he had heard as a child of seven or eight some forty years earlier:

> We didn't have very much company. About once a year my Uncle Augie and Aunt Viola would come around. We lived up on Route Nine. It was all woods. There weren't any houses around. They used to send us youngsters out of the house when they talked, so they could have their private adult conversations. I was the oldest kid. For some reason, I had gone back in the house. I went back in the hallway, and they were talking about this particular thing that happened up by Bamber Lake in the wintertime. There was snow on the ground, and the lakes were frozen. They were skating on the lake after dark as people used to do. On the way home they had a dog with them. The dog got nervous and cringing and whining and hanging on their feet, you know. It was a houndog. He acted like he was scared, and the gist of it seemed to be that something ran across the road. The whole party was very nervous and upset. They saw something, but they weren't sure what it was. They went back the next day and investigated. They found footprints there. It was something that was unfamiliar, and they had lived in the woods all of their lives. Years went by, and I tried to talk to Mom and Pop about that, and they just wouldn't talk about it. They never would discuss it.[12]

Merce Ridgway's story is tantalizing and frustrating. We are left hanging because of his parents' refusal to explain what had happened. Another story told by another Waretown oldtimer raises more questions than it answers. It was related to me by Joe King, a Navy veteran who has worked construction and served as a jack-of-all-trades. A sometime bluegrass musician, King knows and loves the woods. His story went like this:

Well, this thing happened a long time ago. I heard this through a conversation with Louis Kramer. He lived down near Leeds Point, or in that
area—Smithville, or somewhere. He used to run a winter netline for
flounders. He went down one night to pull his nets or to check his nets.
You know you get in the sand, and you get bogged down. The road wasn't
very good at that time, and his car got bogged down. It was Model A or
Model T. He couldn't get it loose. So he got out and started to walk. First
he heard a crashing in the woods—something coming through the woods.
He figured it was somebody coming through there with a truck jacking
deer; and he stopped and he waited, but he didn't see anything. He could
still hear the crashing. He walked on a little farther, and he heard a man.
Something went across the road. They found him on what is now Route
Nine. He was talking incoherently. He had seen the Jersey Devil. He ran
from that road to Route Nine.[13]

Joe King's story also is frustrating. Since the victim is rendered incoher-
ent by the sighting, we get no description of the legendary creature. Like
the rest of us, Pineys try to figure out an explanation for the origin of the
Jersey Devil. One particularly intriguing explanation was suggested to me
by Gladys Eayre of Forked River, New Jersey. Eayre is a lifelong resident
of the Pines who plays guitar with the well-known Pineconers, an old-timey
string band from Ocean County, New Jersey. She is a veritable storehouse
of South Jersey lore, and she shared this explanation for the Jersey Devil
with me:

Like I showed you on that map in there, all of Longbeach Island from the
lighthouse to Oldbrook was a famous spot where the pirates of Barnegat
would signal the ships to come ashore, and they'd beach them and then
plunder them. They would burn hay stacks because they would think that it
was the deep water off Barnegat Light. It would bring them in off course,
and they'd come ashore on the shoals. They were beached, you know, on
the sand bars and then they'd kill everybody and plunder what they had.
From that, they used to put them in their sail garveys and take them to the
mainland. That would be approximately Tuckerton and south—sometimes
Manahawkin, but in the big swamp and big woods. What would you do if
you had a lot of plunder in the woods? (You want to keep people away?)
Yes, exactly. So from what I can figure out all these years I been living
around here, born around here, it was a damn good story, and they kept a
lot of people out of the woods.[14]

Though the legend of the Jersey Devil may be alive and well in the Pine
Barrens, circulating orally in different traditional variations, it is increasingly difficult for us to collect this material. Indeed, with the passage of

time the Jersey Devil seems to have become more and more a creature of poplore rather than folklore. Contemporary folklorists (or poplorists) may find the Jersey Devil in a wide variety of urban expressive genres. For example, there is Bill Reed's *Mother Leed's Thirteenth Child*, a film produced by the New Jersey Network in 1972, a knowledgeable and sympathetic dramatization based on fieldwork. Then in 1976 there was Bill Mastrisimone's *The Scourge*, an original play directed by Margaret Dawson and produced for the first New Jersey Folk Festival. The play was a dramatic reenactment of the "gypsy curse" version of the Jersey Devil's origins. Later that year a long story appeared in *Philadelphia Magazine* entitled "The Devil Made Me Do It: On the spooky trail of the Jersey demon" by Peggy Morgan. In 1976 the Jersey Devil first appeared as the official logo of the New Jersey Folk Festival in New Brunswick and has been used that way ever since. At the Festival he has appeared on programs, T-shirts and banners.

Tourists in South Jersey inevitably confront a popular culture version of the Jersey Devil. For example, visitors to the town of Smithville, a restoration of an eighteenth-century southern New Jersey community, may stop off at the Gift Shop to purchase Jersey Devil postcards (imaginatively rendered by artist Ed Sheetz) and T-shirts bearing the legend "I'm a Lil' Jersey Devil." After wrapping up these purchases, the visitor may drop into the restaurant to enjoy a Jersey Devil Cocktail. Its ingredients include apple jack, cranberry juice, triple sec, and lemon juice. Just as the legend exists in different oral versions, the cocktail exists in different versions also. If you get off Exit 4 of the New Jersey Turnpike and take Route 73 to the Mount Laurel Travelodge, you can have a Jersey Devil cocktail which is described as "a Bloody Mary with an extra dose of fire and brimstone. For hellraisers only." The most recent popularization occurred in the early 1980s—a professional hockey team took the name "The New Jersey Devils." The team in 1984–1985 played a demanding schedule of forty home games at the Meadowlands Arena in East Rutherford, New Jersey. Perhaps the best shrine for Jersey Devil memorabilia is the Historic New Gretna House "Fine Dining in the Jersey Pines Since 1823" located at Route 9 and North Maple Avenue in New Gretna, New Jersey. In the fall of 1984 on a visit there, I asked the bartender why the oil portrait of the Jersey Devil was unsigned. I should have known better. He told me, "It's a self-portrait!" The Jersey Devil Taproom features a drink called the Jersey Devil made with apple jack, triple sec, and juice of cranberries, oranges and lemon. Not far from New Gretna is the 177th Fighter Interceptor Group of the New Jersey Air National Guard, under the command of Colonel Richard C. Cosgrave. Proudly painted on the tail of each modern F-4 fighter plane is a Jersey Devil. Appropriately enough this outfit is headquartered at the Atlantic City Airport. What gradually has happened is that the Jersey Devil has been transformed from a creature of folklore, a legend found among an enclaved group within the larger society, to a creature of poplore, entertainment and advertising.[15] Naturally, some folklorists are aghast at this drift of the Jersey Devil to becoming a creature of mass society.

Despite this discouraging trend, occasionally one does find a sympathetic and knowledgeable account. John McPhee in his book *The Pine Barrens*, which first appeared in 1967, gave a solid account of the Jersey Devil. McPhee gave the last word to his principal informant:

> Fred Brown believes. "The Jersey Devil is real," he told me. "That is no fake story. A woman named Leeds had twelve living children. She said if she ever had another one she hoped it would be the Devil. She had her thirteenth child, and it growed, and one day it flewed away. It's haunted the earth ever since. It's took pigs right out of pens. And little lambs. I believe it took a baby once, right down in Mathis town. The Leed's Devil is a crooked-face thing, with wings. Believe what you want, I'm telling you the truth."[16]

Why did John McPhee succeed in finding an authentic oral narrative of the Jersey Devil where so many others have failed? I think the real answer is not that he is a good writer, though he is that. The real answer is that he had the patience to take the time to establish rapport. Fred Brown instinctively knew that McPhee was sincere, serious and interested. These stories customarily are not told in front of strangers. This basic fact was explained clearly by Herbert Halpert, who did pioneer fieldwork back in the 1930s. Halpert explained:

> In spite of an occasional questioning of detail, stories of the Devil, witches, and spirits are firmly believed by the Pineys. One important reason for their continuation in Piney tradition is that they are not looked upon as stories meant for entertainment in the way that tall tales and fool stories are. These are veritable facts, and no storyteller can get prestige from telling them. Some indication of this attitude toward them can be seen in the fact that women, who are reluctant to tell many kinds of folktales, tell these freely.
>
> Since they are matters of belief rather than stories told for amusement, they are not told before strangers. I was able to hear them only because I was well-known as a person interested in and sympathetic to all aspects of life in the Pines. This very reluctance to speak of such serious matters before strangers has helped to preserve the stories, since they are not laughed out of belief by an unsympathetic audience.[17]

Halpert's analysis is very helpful in that it stresses the element of belief. This is the heart of the matter. For a legend to be a legend, it should be believed to be true by those who tell it and by those who listen to the telling. But one could reasonably ask whether it is indeed true or not.

"The point is irrelevant," it might be argued, "because it doesn't really matter whether legends are true or whether they are not. The important thing is that they *are true* as far as those who tell and hear them are concerned."[18]

Our attempts at collecting oral versions of the legend in South Jersey have pointed out the increasing difficulty of finding anyone who really believes that the legend is true. Rationalism and secularism have chipped away at the foundations of belief. This tendency toward skepticism already has been noted by other scholars dealing with American legendary materials in general. For example, Richard Dorson, in his *Man and Beast in American Comic legend,* pointed out that the mainstream culture of the United States does not take legendary creatures seriously. He wrote, "We yarn about, identify with, hunt for, depict, extol, and chuckle over these critters. Belief and dread are not wholly absent, but in contrast to the rest of the world, we engage in hoaxes, pranks, tall tales, and tomfoolery with our legendary creatures."[19]

Basically, the twentieth century has had a paradoxical effect on the legend of the Jersey Devil. On the one hand, the mass media have disseminated the story to the point that it has gained a wider range, a broader audience. More people have heard of it. It is more widespread. On the other hand, it has lost most of its original power of terror and dread. As it has become more widespread, it has become trivialized. In its transition from oral narrative to pseudo-folk newspaper feature, it is now comic rather than awesome.

NOTES

1. The term "poplore" was coined by Archie Green. See his *Only a Miner: Studies in Recorded Coal Mining Songs* (Urbana: University of Illinois Press, 1972) 3, 14, 23, 102, 291, 445, 447.

2. Jan Harold Brunvand, *The Study of American Folklore* (New York: W. W. Norton and Company, Inc. 1978) 106.

3. Fred Cicetti, "A Monster of Our Own," *The New York Times,* 18 April 1976, NJ 27.

4. W. F. Mayer, "In the Pines," pp. 566–567.

5. David Steven Cohen, *The Folklore and Folklife of New Jersey* (New Brunswick: Rutgers University Press, 1983) 38.

6. Walker D. Wyman, *Mythical Creatures of the U.S.A. and Canada* (University of Wisconsin-River Falls Press, 1978) 73.

7. James F. McCloy and Ray Miller, Jr. *The Jersey Devil* (Wallingford, Pa.: The Middle Atlantic Press, 1976) 23–24, emphases mine.

8. Norma T. Vivian, "The Jersey Devil," Conservation and Environmental Studies Center, four-page pamphlet, with one illustration, undated.

9. New Jersey Bell, "Jersey Devil: Legend or Not?" *Tel-News*, October, 1975.

10. *Burlington County Herald*, 12 October 1976, 3.

11. *Burlington County Herald*, 3.

12. Merce Ridgway, Jr., personal interview, 1 August 1978, Waretown, New Jersey.

13. Joe King, personal interview, 1 August 1978, Waretown, New Jersey.

14. Gladys Eayre, personal interview, 1 August 1978, Forked River, New Jersey.

15. Green, 445.

16. John McPhee, *The Pine Barrens* (1967, reprinted New York: Ballantine Books, 1971) 82.

17. Herbert Norman Halpert, "Folktales and Legends from the New Jersey Pines: A Collection and a Study," unpublished dissertation, Indiana University, 1947, 285–286.

18. Robert A. Georges, "The General Concept of Legend," in Wayland D. Hand, ed., *American Folk Legend: A Symposium* (Berkeley: University of California Press, 1971), 15.

19. Richard M. Dorson, *Man and Beast in American Comic Legend* (Bloomington: Indiana University Press, 1982) 4.

EDITOR'S SUGGESTIONS FOR FURTHER READING

Beck, Henry Charlton. 1947. "Jersey Devil and Other Legends of the Jersey Shore." *New York Folklore Quarterly* 3: 102–6.

Boyton, Patrick. 2011. *Snallygaster: The Lost Legend of Frederick County.* Published by author.

Gillespie, Angus Kress, comp. 1977. "The Jersey Devil." *New Jersey Folklore: A Statewide Journal* 1(2): 24–29.

Gillespie, Angus Kress. 1993. "The (Jersey) Devil in the Details." *New Jersey Outdoors* (Fall 1993): 40–43.

Halpert, Herbert Norman. 1947. "Folktales and Legends from the New Jersey Pines: A Collection and a Study." PhD dissertation, Indiana University.

McCloy, James F., and Ray Miller Jr. 1976. *The Jersey Devil.* Moorestown, NJ: Middle Atlantic.

McCloy, James F., and Ray Miller Jr. 1998. *Phantom of the Pines: More Tales of the Jersey Devil.* Moorestown, NJ: Middle Atlantic.

Phillips, Tom, dir. 2009. "Devils in New Jersey." *MonsterQuest.* New York: A&E Television Networks.

Regal, Brian. 2015. "The Jersey Devil: A Political Animal." *NJS: An Interdisciplinary Journal* 1(1): 79–103.

Sullivan, Jeremiah J., and James F. McCloy. 1974. "The Jersey Devil's Finest Hour." *New York Folklore Quarterly* 30: 231–38.

7

American Vampires
Legend, the Media, and Tubal Transmission

Norine Dresser

PREFACE

Long before *Twilight, True Blood*, or *Buffy the Vampire Slayer*, folklorist Norine Dresser had pinpointed the importance of the vampire in American culture. While the vampire is ostensibly a European monster, Dresser highlighted its American characteristics: a love of power, a desire for youth, an obsession with sex. In her book *American Vampires: Fans, Victims, Practitioners* (1989), Dresser identified and interviewed vampire fans, vampire followers, vampire victims, and even those convinced they were vampires themselves. Dresser also used an instrument unique in this collection: the social scientist's beloved survey—specifically, a fixed survey with open-ended responses.

Dresser found that American vampires have a native habitat: television. In the second half of the twentieth century, folklorists held extended debates over the dissemination and importance of oral tradition. Alan Dundes and Carl Pagter, for example, argued for the traditionality of copylore, a genre that repeated and varied but did not rely on orality. Other folklorists, too, noticed how television co-opted, embraced, reheated, and even created folklore. Dresser credited "tubal transmission" as the key factor in the dissemination of the American vampire. While there was an accepted body of shared lore surrounding the traits and actions of a vampire, the reference point for that transmission, she found, was television and discussions stemming from television. Writing before interactive social media, Dresser reminds readers that while media flows from broadcasters out to consumers, these were not necessarily "passive" consumers. New-millennium consumers developed social tools to talk back to media, but before then, the folk discussed, analyzed, and reinterpreted media among themselves.

https://doi.org/10.7330/9781646421602.c007

Presented here is an excerpt from Dresser's *American Vampires*. Much can be gained from examining Dresser's methods. First, while not commonplace in folkloristics, surveys prove an effective instrument for sketching the contours of a belief tradition. Researchers might use these to begin to grasp the behaviors and traits of their monsters. Second, the study demonstrates why legend scholars must investigate transmission anew in every era. In our increasingly complex multimedia world, folklore is transmitted in ever novel and varied ways, from the campfire to the television to the Internet. Finally, folklorists might attempt to deduce regional or national cultural influences on monsters. While public perception might cast the vampire as "Transylvanian," monsters often take on the traits of those who celebrate and/or fear them.

ESSAY

There is something about the vampire that promptly engages people's curiosity. Prior to my research, I had assumed erroneously that vampire lore was a thing of the past and that any center of vampire lore was to be found primarily in Eastern Europe. I had totally overlooked the potential significance of all the Dracula films and plays I had seen. I also had completely forgotten a pilgrimage I made over twenty years ago to see a faltering Bela Lugosi in the back room of a tawdry Las Vegas nightclub reenact his famous Dracula-about-to-attack-the-maiden scene. However, Dr. Dolphin's correlation of vampires and porphyria symptoms (1984) and its consequential effect on porphyria patients led me to inquire further into vampire beliefs in the United States, and I soon came to understand the indefensibility of my long-standing assumption that vampires belonged to the past, and to recognize that, as a folklorist, I had overlooked the fact that vampires are a significant phenomenon in contemporary American culture. I came to see that old, scary, sometimes campy movie images set in Transylvania had been transplanted, translated, and transformed. The vampire symbol had begun to take on a new meaning and interpretation—evolving into something one could call the American vampire.

Varied methods of inquiry were utilized before reaching these conclusions. I developed and circulated three different forms of questionnaires. The 574 respondents who answered the student questionnaire about the attributes and reality of vampires came from many places across the United States and from thirty-four other countries as well. I also interviewed porphyria patients by mail and by phone from fourteen different states plus England. I received lengthy responses to a third questionnaire from vampire fans, including those who believe that they are vampires. Physicians and scientists from four states and five countries answered other inquiries. I corresponded with twenty-two heads of organizations and editors of small independent journals. I received phone calls from Germany, France, and Canada. I drove 110 miles to meet with one physician in Santa Barbara and flew 475 miles to meet with another physician and patients in San Francisco. I journeyed cross-country to New York to visit a fan club headquarters.

As is apparent, the data recorded and analyzed came from beyond the Los Angeles area where I live, representing opinions, experiences, and interpretations from all over the world. Most important, a large portion of additional data was taken from the media, thus revealing interests representative of the entire nation. Indeed, it is the media—radio, TV, movies, newspapers, magazines—that have largely shaped our folklore about the vampire today, altering the historical and Old World roots of belief.

Some colleagues wishing to play devil's advocate have asked, "How can you tell that your vampire informants aren't putting you on?" The answer is that there is no way I can tell for sure. Unlike the now almost apocryphal story of the folklorist of the mid-1930s diligently recording the song of black workers only to discover they were singing "White man settin' on wall, white man settin' on wall, white man settin' on wall all day long, wastin' his time, wastin' his time," I haven't yet found that my informants are playing with me. Thus I must believe them. I have always operated under the assumption that informants usually tell the truth—that is, their truth, their interpretation of their own reality. While in this situation informants' claims may seem fanciful, I cannot discount them until I have evidence to do so. My belief is that they are honest in their statements about how they perceive themselves.

And if they were putting me on? How would that affect the research? Would it invalidate it? I don't think so. It would actually dramatize the significance of the vampire symbol. The desire of my informants to identify with these creatures would be so powerful that they actually invented symptoms, behavior, and stories to convince me of their condition.

And so the research adventure described in what follows illuminates the path that, like Dorothy's yellow brick road, led me through a new territory of ideas, encounters with a wondrous assortment of new friends and acquaintances, and ultimately altered my perspective about the culture in which we live. I didn't find the wizard [at] the end of my journey. I discovered the vampire, instead.

Power of the Media

The acceptance of belief in the vampire and its pervasiveness today can be accounted for through the influence of popular culture and the media. They don't permit the vampire to die. They have become the generators of vampire lore and its transmitter and perpetuator through movies, cartoons, headlines, advertisements. Television, in particular, has become the prime mode for the vampire's resuscitations and reincarnations. From seeing old movies, reinforced by animated versions, "Sesame Street," and commercials, the public is continuously bombarded with the vampire image.

In 1978, within hours following the television broadcast of a movie showing a hero driving the vampires out of England by sprinkling pieces of holy wafers on graves, 200 consecrated Holy Communion wafers were stolen from St. Lucy's Roman Catholic Church in Altamont, New York ("Sacrilegious Theft"). Given the proximity in time between the viewing of this program and the robbery, one has to assume a connection. If the act was a serious one, it reveals that the viewer/robber was taking no chances about protection from vampire attacks. If the stolen wafers were taken only as a gag, it nonetheless shows that someone was stimulated sufficiently to commit this offense against the church, inspired by the retelling of an old story.

In a questionnaire distributed to 574 students inquiring whether or not respondents believed in the possibility of the existence of vampires, 15 percent said that they learned about vampires from other people, but 49 percent of the sample reported that they first learned of vampires from television and films. The questions were "Who told you? Under what circumstances?" These are the typical answers:

> I saw the movie "Dracula."
>
> In private discussion with my mother in preparation for a television program.
>
> Alone, just watching TV.
>
> I saw a show on TV.
>
> The late movie—Abbott and Costello.

Fans, those persons who are members of clubs celebrating either Dracula or other vampire characterizations, also credited the media as a major source of learning:

> I had seen some Dracula movies, but Barnabas in "Dark Shadows" had the most effect on me. This was in 1970 sometime when they first ran the show here in Columbus.

I was an avid reader and I remember reading Bram Stoker's Dracula. To be honest, I wasn't overly impressed. But when I discovered "Dark Shadows" on television, they [vampires] began to have greater attraction. Barnabas Collins, ah there was a most elegant vampire and he never frightened me like the later vampires of "Salem's Lot" or "The Nightstalker."

"Bela Lugosi's portrayal of Dracula was my first exposure," another fan admitted. "Considering the number of years that have passed since the first encounter, it would appear that I was hooked for life. It was a Saturday afternoon matinee and in my opinion the best nickel I ever spent."

Another said:

I was six years old and first encountered the vampire via the "Dark Shadows" TV soap opera. I clearly remember asking my stepmother what it was and how it made the "marks" they were always talking about on the show. She explained the best she could at the time and then warned me not to watch the show—but it was too late. I was hooked. At the time I was visiting my father in Seattle. (He and my mother had been divorced for about four to five years.) The anxiety surrounding my visits could, I supposed, have heightened my receptivity to the fantasy of the vampire, but once I returned home, and for the remainder of my life I have been fascinated by this creature.

In many cases, students revealed that the media were responsible for their belief in vampires. "Because I have seen them in the movies." Seeing the image of these creatures projected on a screen, whether at home or in a theater, gives them credibility.

Another example of this comes from a student who said he believed in vampires because "I've seen convincing documentation and movies." Others responded:

Because I heard it on the news.

Because they do [exist]. I've seen them on TV.

Yes, because I have seen many movies and stories about vampires and they are so real. So, I believe it's possible that vampires will exist as real entities.

Indeed, the media provide the proof. Even in analyzing the answers of students who did not believe in vampires, again the media were cited as sources of truth. According to one student, the reason he did not believe in vampires was that if they did exist, he would have seen them on the evening news. Another nonbeliever said, "Because I've never seen one interviewed on TV." A third student explained, "Because I have never seen or heard on the news that someone was bitten on the neck."

. . .

The popular American image of the vampire appears to have had its roots in Bram Stoker's mind. Stoker was inspired by Celtic tales told by his mother; historical knowledge of Vlad the Impaler learned from a Hungarian historian; stories spun for him by the fascinating traveler Sir Richard Burton (who also had very prominent canine teeth); and knowledge about Jack the Ripper, who terrorized London during 1888. If Michael E. Bell's speculation is correct (Dukes 1982), the author may also have been influenced by nineteenth-century New England customs of exhumation and burning of vital organs of recently buried, disease-causing suspects. Stoker took elements, combined and transformed these ideas, then embellished and personified them in Count Dracula. He made changes which have had long-lasting effects. He changed the vampire's color, making him pale. He confined the vampire's activities to nocturnal hours, and turned him into a creature who erotically preys upon virtuous, beautiful maidens. Gone are the traditional motifs of bloatedness and milkless cows.

Stoker's book *Dracula* has never been out of print since first published in 1897. His influence has been so great that when the 574 students in my study were asked where vampires originated, half answered "Transylvania." Stoker selected the Transylvania locale for the setting of his story, but Transylvania was not a center—and certainly not the place—where vampires originated, for vampire tales have been collected from all over the world. Dracula scholars Raymond McNally and Radu Florescu suggest that Stoker chose Transylvania because, to persons from the British Isles, this seemed like an exotic place (1972). Further, McNally has discovered that Stoker had been affected by and used parts of a book called *The Land Beyond* by Emily Gerard, particularly the chapter titled "Superstitions from Transylvania." This, too, possibly influenced his choice of setting for the novel.

Stoker's book has been so influential that, of the 574 students surveyed, almost everyone knew what they were and could accurately describe their characteristics as delineated by Stoker and reinforced by the movies, particularly the Bela Lugosi version. Student surveys were completely open-ended, and informants often wrote "I don't know" as their answer. The least number of "Don't know" answers related to this question: "How are they [vampires] dressed?" Only forty-three students, or 7 percent did not know how vampires are attired. Of those who did know, the most common response was either "black cape" or "cape" (277, or 48 percent).

This was followed by 183 who wrote that vampires were dressed in black and 69 who mentioned white shirts. Other items of clothing mentioned were black pants, black suit, black tuxedo, red lining on cape, black shoes, and tuxedos.

Reference to the cape by 48 percent of the students is significant. The cape was not part of the Bram Stoker creation of Dracula, but was added by actor Hamilton Dane in 1924, when he adapted the book for the London stage. It was worn by Bela Lugosi in the 1931 film version and since then has become standard dress for vampires. The cape was significant for Lugosi offscreen as well. He was buried in it in 1956.

Actor Christopher Lee, who played Dracula in the British film version, was opposed to the outfit popularized by Lugosi, because it deviated from the book. He told writer Leonard Wolf, "Surely it is the height of ridiculous for a vampire to step out of the shadows wearing white tie, tails, patent leather shoes and full cloak." Yet, for Americans, this outfit has become the archetype for attire.

In describing the physical characteristics of a vampire, 249 students wrote "fangs," and 228 mentioned that he/she is "pale." The next most common features named, in descending order were "dark/black hair" (92); "tall" (86) "like a normal person" (75); "'slick, combed-back or greased-back hair" (60); and "thin/slender" (50). Again, this is a perfect description of the Bela Lugosi characterization, later emulated by Christopher Lee, Frank Langella, and even by George Hamilton in the spoof *Love at First Bite*.

How does one become a vampire? Eighty-seven (15 percent) of these students didn't know. Of those who did, 238 said one had to be bitten by one; 42 said one had to be bitten on the neck by one; 31 said one had to be bitten three times; and 21 specified that one had to be bitten on the neck three times. Add to this the three students who said one becomes a vampire by being infected by the bite of one and the two students who said one had to be bitten a couple of times, and the total is 337, or 59 percent, who understood, according to tradition, that being bitten was the way to become a vampire. (There were also 21 students claimed that one had to be bitten by a bat or vampire bat.) Thus, the vampire bite, a characteristic emphasized by Stoker and reenacted in film versions of his novel, though not necessarily found in traditional vampire folklore, is the concept that is more significant in the minds of the survey respondents.

When asked, "Under what circumstances does a vampire appear?" the most popular answer was "night," by 268 students, or 47 percent. This was a big leap from the next most quoted answer, "full moon," by 73 students.

When it's "dark" (62) or when it "needs/wants/is hungry for blood" (55) came next. This again is consistent with Stoker's portrayal.

"What does a vampire do?" Thirty-three percent, or 192 people, answered, "Sucks blood." "Bites necks," said 74 students. "Drinks blood," wrote 64 of them. "How can you protect yourself from a vampire?" Fifty-nine percent of the students (338) wrote either that one had to have a cross or crucifix or that one had to wear one. The next most significant prevention cited was garlic (200). As to how to kill a vampire, 44 percent (252) answered with "a stake through the heart" or "a wooden stick in the heart." Exposure to sunlight/daylight was mentioned by 69 respondents.

The influence of media was also seen in the way students responded in the survey, attaching heavily advertised brand names to their answers. A vampire dressed in a "Pierre Cardin tux." He is fashionable, "like GQ." He wears "Sergio Valente jeans" or "black C&R [an L.A. low-cost men's shop heavily advertised on TV] pants." He wears "trendy/black Reeboks." The way to destroy him is to "Shine a light on him—Duracell."

The media version of Bram Stoker's Count Dracula became personified by Bela Lugosi, not only to the public, but to the actor himself. In compliance with his request, he was buried in his Dracula cape. His grave marker is inscribed "Bela Lugosi, 1882–1956, Beloved Father." Lugosi biographer Arthur Lennig states, "It is not as father to a child that he will generally be remembered; rather as father to a great myth and legend the embodiment of Dracula."

The popularity of the Dracula figure in the United States can be credited in great part to the impact of Bela Lugosi and his pronounced speaking style. Even though he has been dead for over thirty years, Lugosi's accent and portrayal of Count Dracula will be forever perpetuated in popular culture—through the huckstering of such products as cat food, pizza, and snail repellants; through the teach[ing] of numbers to youngsters; in greeting cards ("I vant to suck your blood") and on buttons ("Gooood Eeevening"); through media reruns and future productions; [and] also through oral transmission.

In the study of folklore, the term oral transmission is used to describe a process which has been considered as the primary mode of communication of concepts; stories, custom, games, riddles, jokes, and proverbs. In recent years the term xerography has been added to the folklorist's lexicon. This word describes the process of folklore transmission that occurs in office settings where the presence of the photocopying machine facilitates quick, cheap (at the company's expense), and accessible means of copying and circulating jokes, which may be in the form of cartoons, narratives, or parodies (Dundes and Pagter 1975). There is probably another term which could be added to the folklorist's glossary—tubal transmission. The television tube has become the tribal storyteller. The study detailed here has dramatically revealed its impact. Even if respondents talked about seeing motion pictures, it was rare that they referred to seeing them in movie theaters. Most students and fans mentioned seeing films on television. One student wrote, "I have answered your questions to the best of television's ability."

When a movie is viewed from a location outside the home, as in a cinema setting, there is more of a separation between what is and is not real. The viewer has escaped to a new milieu. She is watching the celluloid in a context quite different from her living room—with strangers, in a formal seating arrangement. The time organization is structured; the viewer dresses more conventionally; outsiders are in control.

In contrast, watching a film in the living room or bedroom makes it become part of one's immediate, familiar, and therefore "real" environment. Here the viewer is alone or in the presence of family or friends. He may stretch out on the sofa, lie on the floor, or pedal an exercise bike. He can even be in his own bed in pajamas or without any clothes at all. The program may have been recorded earlier on a VCR and can be played back at a time convenient to the owner.

Unlike the face-to-face interaction, during which the audience interacts directly with the teller or performer, with tubal transmission the communication is one way only—from tube to the viewer. With the exception of call-in shows, such as Dr. Ruth Westheimer's, and those limited programs from which viewers order merchandise, current technology does not yet permit direct and immediate feedback from the audience to the screen. Yet there can be communication between viewers who are watching the tube at the same time. Viewers who watch alone can, at a later time, share what they have seen or heard when they rehash the previous day's soap or the previous night's news with fellow employees, friends, or family members. This delayed mode of interpersonal communication does not lessen the influence of what has been seen. It may very well enhance it because of the repetition of information. This process creates waves of redundancy.

If not for the power of the television tube, there would not be so many Americans who are aware and knowledgeable about vampires, especially since seven hours and forty-eight minutes is now estimated to be the average daily TV viewing time of Americans. Given the amount of time people watch television and its powerful impact on them, one is immediately aware that the medium has the potential to distend the credibility of viewers.

This stretching of believability through television watching can also be interpreted as the reason that 27 percent of the students polled thought it was possible for vampires to exist as real entities. They have seen so much fantasy on TV that they have difficulty separating real from unreal entities.

Even though the majority of students did not believe in the possibility of the vampire's existence, they do accept his presence in this culture. Media bombardment starts out at a very early age, with TV commercials, films, and shows, supported by chewing gum, trading cards, cereal. The vampire lurks in math workbooks. Further reminders of its presence occur especially at Halloween, a time when Bram Stoker's brainchild rises to a new position as [a] primary holiday character. Whether in the top ten or top twenty in popularity at costume shops, the vampire is on top.

The vampire today has become a stock American Character. He is an everyday phenomenon. A yellow, diamond-shaped sign saying "Dracula on Board" attached to the rear window of an old Ford Fairlane parked on a Los Angeles street exemplified the view that Dracula has become an American icon. He's as ubiquitous as the Big Mac.

The All-American Guy

Unlike the lore of Eastern European vampires, the lore of the American vampire does not bind and unite communities. American vampires have adapted to the soil to which they have been transplanted, reflecting the individualism of the American people.

American vampires do exist—in the fantasy world of those who dress up as Halloween celebrants or pretend like lonely Belle with her make-believe vampire lover. They exist in the real world of others who actually imitate their behavior by drinking blood to bring them something positive in return, solace, comfort, sexual arousal, self-importance—elements we all crave. However, they have created a ritual that feeds that need.

Vampires titillate by their erotic behavior; they kindle the making of verbal sexual innuendos in jest. They have an impact on men of science. They arouse passion and fear. They become a common basis of communication for fans, a gold mine of income and creativity.

Writers, filmmakers, and sponsors can count on the vampires' bankability. They bring in big bucks and fit in neatly with the free-enterprise system. That is why the media are so full of them. In turn the media, particularly television, become the primary channel for indoctrinating youngsters and teaching them how vampires look, behave, and talk. The source for this goes back to Bram Stoker, but its popular manifestation and folklore come from Bela Lugosi's portrayal.

These pop-culture vampires have become a potent part of American culture and beliefs and stories about them are widespread. Vampire tales are thrilling. Regardless of whether they are believed, the information is passed along. This became evident in the student survey conducted. Even though only 27 percent believed it was possible for vampires to exist, most of the rest knew all about their media-defined characteristics.

From their first arrival on these shores vampires have been linked with witches and the devil, and this association has remained. But there is a difference. American vampires have become less lethal and more benign than their Old World antecedents. They are more sympathetic characters.

American vampires are appealing because of the humor associated with them. They permit and stimulate laughter. They give a laugh to the first-graders doing their sums; Count Chocula makes breakfast more entertaining; they give a chuckle to the computer users of DRC. Unlike their European, Latin American, African, and Asian counterparts, the fun they inspire in everyday conversation about them is one of their most desirable qualities. Although fans overlooked this aspect of their appeal in their official responses, their letters, asides, and fun-filled conventions and publications strongly reflect this humor. However, fans did corroborate in part what experts have declared—that the sexual, powerful, immortal elements of the vampire are what most strongly draws them to him.

While on the surface it at first seemed incongruous that vampires were so prominent in this technologically advanced society, after carefully examining and analyzing the data, I believe one can see that they seem to exemplify American ideals and values. Sexuality, power, and immortality were listed as the top attractive qualities of the creature by fans. This is congruent with the interest often attributed to the larger American society.

That American culture places great emphasis on sexuality and sexual prowess is evident. The proliferation of sexual manuals and how-to books as well as the presence of pundits like Dr. Ruth, who publicly gives advice on how to repair faulty sexual relationships, are testament to this preoccupation. From the bombardment of sexual innuendos in television ads ("Nothing comes between me and my Calvin's") to the more blatant expositions becoming prevalent (a career woman telephones her handsome lover still in bed and slyly refers to the great night they spent together) sexuality is promoted as an activity that adults should be involved in. Fear of AIDS may be inhibiting some of this activity, but for most the only change has been an emphasis on "safe sex."

Power, too, is a hallmark of the vampire and lures the fans. Some of those who identified with the vampire by imitating his behavior or calling themselves vampires demonstrate that the power it brought them was pleasing. There is no denying that the power is highly valued in our society. For that is what competition is all about—winning and losing. Only the winners gain the power. An informant tells about the corporate event where games were being played and the captain of the losing team cried out, "Second sucks!" Like Hertz, he wanted his team to be number one. He, like most Americans, could not be consoled with the Avis philosophy, "We Try Harder."

Another important characteristic that draws fans to the vampire symbol is his immortality. That, too, is a trait that resounds in contemporary American culture. Indeed, we have almost a fetish about preserving youthful appearances and behavior, to postpone aging and death. Why else would Retin-A be considered such a breakthrough? News of its ability to smooth rough skin, fade spots, and reverse wrinkles was given prominent space on TV news shows, in newspapers, and in magazines—"A Facelift Out of a Tube"; "Retin-A: New Hope for Aging Skin." Is this so far removed from the vampire?

The three major attractions of the vampire are totally compatible with American ideals of power, sex, and immortality. Sometimes it is difficult to separate these three from one another because the idea is that with power you can have sex, and the aging process limits or eliminates both power and sexual abilities and opportunities.

To be a vampire, then, isn't so terrible. With his elegant presence and his sophisticated ways, he need never worry about wrinkles. His only concern is finding the next victim, and that's not so bad because he always emerges victorious. He gets what he wants. He can't help it if he breaks society's rules. His compulsion is out of his control; he's not responsible for any of the unhappiness, fear, or discomfort he might cause others. And he's oh-so-attractive!

Power, sex, and immortality are the qualities of vampires that Americans relate to. They are sentiments that are echoed in all the film and book variations. Students and fans are intrigued by these desired qualities as well. Apparently these vampires satisfy the American public, for it seems they never tire of the tale. And so it appears that American vampires are perfectly suited to this culture. They reflect those values which many Americans hold dear. They like to succeed. They always get the girl. Their fans never see vampires suffer anxiety about retirement, convalescent homes, and whether or not their social security checks will be enough to cover their needs. Vampires have magically bypassed the struggles that Americans face on a daily basis. Uniting themselves with the vampires, the American public leaves their burdens behind—borne away by this alluring, omniscient presence. American vampires are indeed an appropriate symbol for American life and hold an important and beloved place in society.

BIBLIOGRAPHY

Dolphin, David. 1984. "Porphyria, Vampires, and Werewolves: The Aetiology of European Metamorphosis Legends." Paper presented at the American Association for the Advancement of Science, Los Angeles, California.

Dresser, Norine. 1989. *American Vampires: Fans, Victims, Practitioners.* New York: W. W. Norton & Company.

Dukes, Paul. 1982. "Dracula: Fact, Legend, and Fiction." *History Today*, 32 (July): 44–47.

Dundes, Alan, and Carl R. Pagter. 1975. *Urban Folklore from the Paperwork Empire.* Publication of the AFS Memoir Series, ed. Hugh Jansen, 62. Bloomington, IN: American Folklore Society.

Gerard, Emily. 1888. *The Land Beyond the Forest: Facts, Figures, and Fancies from Transylvania.* New York: Harper & Brothers.

McNally, Raymond T., and Radu Florescu. 1972. *In Search of Dracula: A True History of Dracula and Vampire Legends.* Greenwich, CT: New York Graphic Society.

"Sacrilegious Theft." 1978. Associated Press, Altamont, New York, March 27.

Stoker, Bram. 1965. *Dracula.* New York: New American Library.

EDITOR'S SUGGESTIONS FOR FURTHER READING

Cleto, Sara. 2013. "'Darkness Has Too Much to Offer': Revising the Gothic Vampire." *Supernatural Studies* 1 (1): 53–64.

Dresser, Norine. 1989. *American Vampires: Fans, Victims, Practitioners.* New York: Vintage Boks.

Dundes, Alan, ed. 1998. *The Vampire: A Casebook.* Madison: University of Wisconsin Press.

Gallehugh, Joseph F., Jr. 1976. "The Vampire Beast of Bladenboro." *North Carolina Folklore Journal* 24 (2): 53–58.

Laycock, Joseph P. 2009. *Vampires Today: The Truth about Modern Vampirism.* Santa Barbara, CA: Praeger.

McNeil, Lynne. 2015. "Twihards, Buffistas, and Vampire Fanlore: The Internet." In *Putting the Supernatural in Its Place: Folklore, the Hypermodern, and the Ethereal,* edited by Jeannie Banks Thomas, 126–45. Logan: University of Utah Press.

Milspaw, Yvonne J., and Wesley K. Evans. 2010. "Variations on Vampires: Live Action Role Playing, Fantasy and the Revival of Traditional Beliefs." *Western Folklore* 69 (2): 211–50.

8

The Ways and Nature of the Zombi

Hans-W. Ackermann and Jeanine Gauthier

PREFACE

The following essay, published in a premier folklore journal, was penned not by researchers formally designated as folklorists but rather by a virologist, Hans-W. Ackermann, and a nurse, Jeanine Gauthier. In this excerpt, Ackermann and Gauthier share their "personal investigations," the results of field interviews with Haitian *houngans* (Vodou priests). The zombie that emerges from these interviews appears markedly different from the mindless, reanimated corpses plodding ever forward in an endless search for human flesh. From *Night of the Living Dead* to *Resident Evil* to *The Walking Dead*, zombies have been and remain prevalent across numerous media platforms. Born in Haiti and frequently tied to narratives of exploitation and colonialism, the zombie serves an important function beyond its native soil as an evolving index of American social fears, forming what Peter Dendle referred to as a "barometer" of cultural anxiety. The appropriation and popular conception of the zombie are significant and worth studying, but so too are the native beliefs Ackermann and Gauthier reveal.

The authors explain why certain beliefs, even of familiar legendary monsters like zombies, might go underresearched. Despite zombies' broad appeal, studying Haitian zombies in their native habitat necessitates a litany of skills and access not easily attainable. First, reviewing Haitian zombie literature often requires the ability to read French. Second, interviewing informants demands a working knowledge of Haitian Creole. And third, assuming they have both of those skills, researchers still need access to Vodou communities, ones willing to speak about zombies. When those inroads are made, folklorists and their ilk prove their worth. As Ackermann and Gauthier demonstrate, even fashionable media monsters like zombies

https://doi.org/10.7330/9781646421602.c008

can be valuably researched at their folk source material, perhaps revealing a living tradition quite different from the one embedded in the popular imagination.

ESSAY

Zombis, or Zombies, the living dead, have always created much morbid interest. Recent media events have brought the topic to the forefront again. A captivating if sensationalist and problematic book entitled *The Serpent and the Rainbow* presented a possible pharmacological explanation of zombification (Davis 1985). This was followed by a horror movie of the same title (1987) and another book, *Passage of Darkness*, in which certain pharmacological and ethnological findings were more fully explained (Davis 1988a:107). Wade Davis, the author of both books, was attacked for less than rigorous scientific methodology, and a controversy ensued (Booth 1988; Davis 1988b; Kemp 1989).

Davis's inquiry was triggered by the discovery, in 1981, of a man named Clairvius Narcisse, who claimed to be a flesh-and-blood zombi who had been drugged, buried alive, taken out of the grave, and enslaved. There was even a medical record to prove it (Davis 1985:28, 1988a:1, 82; Diederich 1984; Pradel and Casgha 1983:40). This news caused much commotion. One wild book claimed that "thousands of drugged slaves worked on the plantations of certain Vodun dignitaries" (Pradel and Casgha 1983:130). Another book, a general study of Haiti, offered a medical explanation. Zombis were said to be poisoned and somehow maintained in a cataleptic state (Saint-Gérard 1984:117). Davis set out to find a pharmacological basis for zombification and, in doing so, obtained several samples of different "zombi powders." One ingredient of these powders could plausibly induce a state of apparent death. Narratives persistent in Haiti were thus vindicated and given a rational basis. However, during his inquiry, Davis soon found that there were two kinds of zombis: a material and an immaterial variety, namely, a zombi of the body and a zombi of the soul (Davis 1984, 1985:186, 1988a:60).

Many scholars have long been aware of the dualism of the zombi concept; however, this has gone largely unnoticed by the general public outside of Haiti. Most investigators have focused on the flesh-and-blood zombi, a body without a soul, the same type of zombi that has become famous through portrayal on film. The other variety of the zombi, a soul without a body, remains little known if at all, both to scholars and to the general public. Indeed, the whole subject of zombiism is even dismissed as an exploitation of the cult of the dead (Paul 1978:259). Our understanding of the subject has not been helped by the fact that much of the relevant literature is difficult to retrieve or has been published in French and may therefore escape the average English speaker. In addition, non-Haitian investigators may be led into error by difficulties with the Creole language and dependency on interpreters.

Although Elsie Clews Parsons (1928), over 60 years ago, pointed to the possible relationships between the Haitian zombi and the West Indian *duppy*, or ghost, African connections and New World ramifications of the zombi concept have generally been overlooked. Only Dewise (1957:97) has made an effort to find parallels in the folklore of other nations. The zombi concept is thus considered to be purely Haitian, a secondary belief derived from an African concept of death (Laroche 1975). Consequently, in view of the Haitian revolution against slavery, the zombi is sometimes seen as a symbol of the slave, of alienated man reduced to slavery, an incarnation of fate with Promethean overtones (d'Ans 1987:292; Laroche 1975). Considering the widespread belief in zombi-like entities, these interpretations are difficult to justify.

Thus, a review of the zombi concept is due for several reasons: (1) a recent investigation tried to explain zombification by modern pharmacology; (2) there are several types of zombis in the literature (this is supported by our own investigations); and (3) African and Caribbean parallels of the zombi concept have been neglected. The purpose of this article is to review the literature on the zombi concept and to report new data on the zombi of the soul.

PERSONAL INVESTIGATIONS

In February 1989, we made a series of tape-recorded interviews in Port-au-Prince and its vicinity. The informants included three houngans.[1] Our objective was to record legends and supernatural tales. The subject of zombis came up constantly. These zombis were mentioned only briefly. The informants said that if someone, preferably a strong young man, died after a quarrel with another, a houngan could take him out of the grave, beat him, walk him past his house, and make him work in his garden. Such a zombi would work until the time of its natural death; however, if given salt, it would become a *zombi gâté*, or "spoiled zombi," and might kill its master. All this is classical zombi lore. We were also told of a zombified man who had been interviewed on the radio, obviously Clairvius Narcisse (Davis 1985:28, 1988a:78; Diederich 1984; Pradel and Casgha 1983:65).

Zombification by poisoning was explicitly denied. By contrast, information on zombis of the soul was abundant and varied, and fell basically into the following categories:

Nature

All humans have a zombi within themselves, regardless of religion or nationality, or whether they believe in Vodun or not. Specifically, one has both a zombi and a spirit. The zombi is like a soul; one can also say that everybody becomes a zombi at death. Werewolves, so frequent in Haitian folklore, have zombis because they are basically human. Even animals have zombis, but plants do not.

Destiny

At death, the zombi instantaneously leaves the body and flies away. It then attends the prayers at its own funeral for nine days (the novena of Catholic ritual). Unless captured, it may become a butterfly or small bird. Certain zombis, those that inaugurate a new cemetery, become Baron Samedi, a death spirit governing graveyards. Zombis of Vodun priests go under water for a year, after which time they are retrieved. In a general way, zombis remain on Earth and only go to Heaven when their time has come. Haiti is populated by zombis of Indians, Spaniards, French colonists, and, of course, ancestors of present-day Haitians.

Attributes and Ways

A spirit zombi is immortal and does not age, generally keeping human form and the aspect of its dead owner. It is never ill (even if it was frequently during its lifetime), does not eat, and is able to move. Many zombis live and sleep in cemeteries. All are at home between three o'clock and three-thirty in the morning. Some live in caves, but never under the water (unlike Vodun gods). In the evening, they may go to church. Zombis walk with their heads down, speak with a nasal voice (normally a property of zombis of the body), and manifest themselves in dreams. On this occasion, a zombi may speak with its former family. Generally, zombis are not affected by noise, but are afraid of living people and flee them if they can. They also are afraid of red objects. For example, if a mother dies leaving a child, the child has to wear red tights for one year and one day lest the zombi of the mother torment it. Spirit zombis are invisible unless they want to be seen; however, if captured, they are visible to their masters. If called by name, a zombi will appear as a cock or hen according to its sex and take human form as it approaches the caller. Zombis are also visible to people born with a "caul" (fetal membranes on the head) and, after a special, difficult ceremony, to houngans and ordinary people. We were offered the opportunity to observe zombis for $200 but did not take it.

The good news is that zombis can now make love. In the case of a dead couple, both partners can make love to each other. If only one partner dies, his or her zombi can return to the surviving spouse. A male zombi can impregnate his former wife. Her belly swells and diminishes, but there is no birth (clearly, this is a rationalization of hysterical pregnancies, spontaneous abortions, and, possibly, miscarriages). To prevent a dead husband from making love to his living wife, she can put on red underwear to repulse him.

Capture and Its Prevention

The spirit zombi may be captured during its owner's lifetime—especially during illness. The body continues to work and may live on for two to five years. If the zombi is mistreated by its captor, its rightful owner may fall ill or die. Capture is always achieved by knowledgeable professionals, but is difficult if the captor does not know the victim. After death, the most critical period is the novena. The captured zombi can be recovered for its relatives, knowing that it must attend the novena, prepare a jar filled with water. The zombi then enters the jar as a fly, cockroach, cricket, or ant. The jar is then solidly plugged, and the zombi is now withdrawn from the influence of its captor. It is freed again a week later by breaking the jar at a crossroad.

Capture may also be prevented by confining the zombi in a bottle immediately after death. This is done in the following manner. A bottle is "clad" in white and red tissue, and the body of the dead is measured with a string with seven knots. String, finger and toe nail clippings, and one hair each from the head, the pubic area, and the axilla are put into the bottle. Baron Samedi is then asked to put the zombi therein. He is paid with *clairin* (raw rum), some sweets, and small change. Alternatively, a dead person can be armed in the grave by giving it two sour oranges with three needles in each. When the prospective captor calls the zombi by name as required, the zombi stands up and kills the captor with the two oranges. Coconuts are equally suitable.

Varied Uses

A captured zombi may be put to work, but only after sunset. For example, a zombi transformed into a horse may be put to work in a sugar mill. This is said to happen especially in the region of Les Cayes, a town in the south of Haiti. Houngans may also use zombis to serve their guests. The zombis are kept in submission by blows to the head. In addition, a captured zombi may

be sent to attack and kill people. Such a death can be prevented with coun-
termagic. In a special ceremony, the zombi is returned to Baron Samedi,
who ties it up and frees the intended victim for some money. However,
the power of zombis seems to be limited. It is said that if someone does
not believe in them, they can do no harm. An enslaved zombi may also be
posted over treasures as a guardian. Legend has it that the fleeing French
colonists interred their treasures and killed a slave over them to acts as
a guardian. If the zombi of such a slave likes someone, it will help this
individual in exchange for clothes (by definition, slaves were poor and had
no clothes). Finally, and more benignly, a free zombi may be asked by its
relatives to guard their houses or children. It must be contacted at its tomb.

Discussion

Our fieldwork confirms beliefs in the existence of a spirit zombi, already
postulated by many authors. It was surprising that so much information was
obtained about this relatively unknown entity. In particular, we discovered
that the spirit zombi was a zombi from the start and not a zombified soul.
The Ti Bon Ange and the Gros Bon Ange were never mentioned in our
interviews, and knowledge of these terms was expressly denied. However,
the dualism of the Haitian soul was acknowledged, and the zombi as a normal part of a human was rather new. Only twice in the literature do we find
a brief mention that a part of the Haitian dual soul, the Ti Bon Ange, may
be called a zombi (Huxley 1966:93; Planson 1974:253).

Some of our findings are reminiscent of common beliefs mentioned
above: storing souls in jars, visibility of zombis to people born with a caul,
gatherings of zombis at cemeteries, special treatment of the souls of Vodun
priests, and the central role of Baron Samedi in black magic (Herskovits
1975:247; Hurbon 1972:168; Kerboull 1973:94; Métraux 1968:237; Philomé
1980). Other observations were variants of pervious findings, for example
the guarding of treasures by *baka*, or evil spirits, said to be souls of particularly vicious slaves (Herskovits 1975:242; Métraux 1953). Similarly, arming
of the dead with specially prepared oranges relates to arming them with a
knife (Hurston 1939:182; Métraux 1968:250).

Many other findings appear to be new. Are they? It was said above
that zombis could make love and were afraid of the color red. However,
a tradition of the Akan tribe of Ghana and the Ivory Coast has it that the
soul of a man may have sexual intercourse with a woman. This is fatal for
the man if he is alive and the woman is dead; conversely, if the man is dead
and the woman is alive, she becomes barren (Parrinder 1951:32). A similar
belief has been recorded in Jamaica. The principal motive of the Jamaican

duppy in returning to its former home is to have sexual relations with its spouse. A duppy husband, in making love to his wife, will make her barren or beget dead children. The first nine nights (again the novena) are said to be the most dangerous time, but red knickers will afford protection because ghosts dislike red (Leach 1961; Newall 1981). The color red is also used in the Ruanda-Burundi area to repel evil spirits (Bourgeois 1956:159). Finally, Jamaican duppies speak with a nasal voice and may be prevented from returning by measuring the body of the deceased during the funeral (Newall 1981). All these beliefs clearly have a common origin, and it is probable that many more West African or New World parallels to Haitian folklore can be found.

Why did so many beliefs reported here, particularly that the zombi is a normal human constituent, go unnoticed? First, we believe that Haitian folklore is extremely rich and never had been investigated fully. So far, investigators have concentrated on Vodun religion and children's tales and have neglected other subjects. There are many other reasons why these beliefs may have escaped attention: fragmentation of beliefs due to the mountainous terrain of Haiti and consequent difficulties in traveling, rapid evolution of belief in the absence of written records, communication problems of foreign investigators due to the complexity of the Creole language, persecution of Vodun by government and church officials, and, possibly, traditional bias of the Haitian "elite" against anything called "superstition." It is clear that we encountered only a small sample of what may actually be found in a more thorough investigation.

CONCLUSIONS

African Origins of the Zombi

Zombis of all types, bodily or bodiless, and zombi-like entities appear as variations of the same theme and are equally fictitious. The zombi concept is essentially one of enslavement by magic, be it of the body or of the soul. Regardless of the country, zombis can be made to work for a master, and, sometimes, they even share such characteristic attributes as nasal voices and a special relationship with salt.

Our literature survey clearly shows that all components of the zombi concept—name, duality of the soul, bodily and spirit zombis—are African in origin. A likely area of origin is the coastal region of West and Central Africa. From there, it was transported to the New World by slaves, apparently with little variation. Thus, the Haitian zombi appears to be an immigrant to the West Indies.

If the Haitian zombi is usually considered to be a specifically Haitian invention, it is probably because of the overexposure of Haiti in the press and a relatively large volume of ethnological research on this country. There are considerably fewer investigations of zombi-like entities in other areas, notably the French Antilles (Pollak-Eltz 1977:215). More studies are needed, especially in the Caribbean outside of Haiti and the putative African area of zombi origin. These investigations should concentrate on the little-known specifics such as salt eating, fear of the color red, nasal voice, and the magical rituals of zombification. It is probable that such research would uncover an even greater dissemination of the zombi concept than is now apparent.

Its wide distribution in Africa suggests two conclusions. First, the zombi concept is very old and possibly predates the historical Bantu migration. Second, and most important in this context, it makes the poison hypothesis of zombification unlikely, unless one supposes the existence of numerous agents able to induce a lethargic sleep or even a lively trade in puffer fishes.

Genesis of the Zombi Concept

The primary belief from which all others derive seems to be that the soul can be influenced by magic. Capture or enslavement of the soul, from either a dead or living victim, and the use or misuse of the soul appear as further developments. Misuse of the soul may derive from compacts with evil spirits. It is semantics whether a soul begins as a zombi or becomes one by magic.

From zombification of the soul, it is only a small mental step to zombification of the body. Logically, this must be a secondary belief because the feat is much more difficult to accomplish. Anyone can attempt to capture a soul, but zombifying a body is a different matter. Resurrecting a real corpse would overtax the best sorcerer, and inducing a state of apparent death would require a sophisticated knowledge of pharmacology. This secondary belief could have originated from three sources:

a.   Observation of imbeciles or certain mentally ill people, especially catatonic schizophrenes, demented or amnesic, who wandered off and were sighted later. In countries where illness and premature death are commonly attributed to magic, it would only be logical to explain the vagrant mentally ill as resurrected dead without a soul. This would be a purely popular belief; sorcerers could have contributed nothing but rumor.

b.   Observation of grave robbing for magical purposes.

c.   Attempts to harm or capture the soul using magical powders that contain poison. It would be natural to compose such powders from noxious or toxic substances. A small, symbolic dose would suffice.

Mentally ill persons with a history of hospitalization constitute between 28% and 44% of the homeless in the United States (Gelberg et al. 1988; Koegel et al. 1988). About 12% to 17% of these are schizophrenes (Breakey et al. 1989; Koegel et al. 1988). A description of their behavior almost reads as does the list of zombi cases (Davis 1988a:66; Dewisme 1957:139; Pradel and Casgha 1983:64). Incidentally, one famous "zombi" was diagnosed long ago as a wandering schizophrene (Mars 1945, 1947:76), and a houngan from Port-au-Prince stated that zombi tales could be explained by the peasant habit of using imbeciles to guard their fields (Dewisme 1957:130). We are not overly impressed by the fact that a medical death certificate accompanied the case (and only this one) of Clairvius Narcisse. Hospital folklore abounds with horror stories, for example, of babies exchanged at birth and reattributed to their mothers just before discharge. They are told with great relish.

Zombi Powders

Haitian folk medicine is replete with symbolic powders and liquids (Kerboull 1973:88). However, there are magical powders whose only use is malevolent. If they are deposited on the doorstep of the victim's house or with its belongings, this is called a *coup de poudre*, or "blow by powder." Ingredients are numerous and diverse, including, among others, powdered remains of snakes or toads and irritating plant products (it may be remembered that Haiti has no poisonous snakes). These powders are said to cause illness and even death. If the powder, this time also containing saliva collected from a corpse, is projected into the air, this is a *coup d'air*, a "blow by air." It is said to cause pulmonary edema, a lethargic state and possibly death (Delbeau 1990:142).

There are irresistible similarities between magical powders from Africa and the zombi powders collected by Davis. Except for puffer fishes and human remains, zombi powders have similar ingredients, are applied as a coup de poudre, and are said to cause a lethargic state as in a coup d'air. We suggest that the puffer is an ingredient of some zombi powders because it is known to be toxic, not because it induces some state of lethargy. In other terms, it is there for its magical virtues, and the quantity or even the presence of tetrodotoxin is unimportant. This would explain many above-noted problems with Davis's zombi powders: the necessity of capturing the soul of the victim, the presence of human remains, the variety of real or supposed poisons, the presence of tetrodotoxin in two samples and in small amounts only, and a questionable mode of application. Zombification thus appears as a case of sympathetic magic, a kind of perverse homeopathy. If such a zombi powder is really lethal and its victim dies, this may be unintended, but the powder still serves its original purpose: by separating body and soul of the victim, it facilitates capture of the soul. Davis can be credited with starting the first serious investigation of zombification, but lethargy-inducing zombi powders have yet to be found.

NOTE

1. Data on zombis were obtained from four informants: (1) Cayer Jolicoeur, 83, houngan in Darbonne near Léogâne, tape II; (2) Jacques Mercier, 66, houngan, masseur, and healer, La Plaine 19, Port-au-Prince, tapes V to VII; (3) Jules Quatre-Hommes, about 70, houngan in Bizoton, Port-au-Prince, tape VIII: and (4) Jean Surin, 45, waiter, Mariani, Port-au-Prince, tape II. The houngans, each of whom had a small *houmfort*, or temple, were recruited through personal contacts and were paid for their interviews. Recordings were in Creole. French transcripts are available on request.

REFERENCES CITED

Bourgeois, R. 1956. *Banyarwanda et Barundi: Religion et Magie.* Vol. III. Brussels: Académie Royale des Sciences Colonials.

Booth, William. 1988. Voodoo Science. *Science (Washington)* 240:274–276.

Breakey, William R., Pamela J. Fisher, Morton Kramer, Gerald Nestadt, Alan J. Romanoski, Alan Ross, Richard M. Royall, and Oscar C. Stine. 1989. Health and Mental Health Problems of Homeless Men and Women in Baltimore. *Journal of the American Medical Association* 262:1352–1357.

d'Ans, André-Marcel. 1987. *Haiti: paysage et société.* Paris: Karthala.

Davis, Wade E. 1984. The Ethnobiology of the Haitian Zombie. *Caribbean Reviews* 12:18–21 and 47.

Davis, Wade E. 1985. *The Serpent and the Rainbow.* New York: Simon & Schuster.

Davis, Wade E. 1988a. *Passage of Darkness: The Ethnobiology of the Haitian Zombie.* Chapel Hill: University of North Carolina Press.

Davis, Wade E. 1988b. Zombification. *Science (Washington)* 240:1715–1716.

Delbeau, Jean-Claude. 1990. *Société, culture et medicine populaire traditionnelle: Etue sur le terrain d'un cas: Haiti.* Port-au-Prince: Henri Deschamps.

Dewisme, C.-H. 1957. *Les zombis ou le secret des morts-vivants.* Paris: Bernard Grasset.

Diederich, Bernard. 1984. On the Nature of Zombie Existence. *Caribbean Reviews* 12:14–17 and 43–46.

Gelberg, Lillian, Lawrence S. Linn, and Barbara D. Leake. 1988. Mental Health, Alcohol and Drug Abuse, and Criminal History Among Homeless Adults. *American Journal of Psychiatry* 145:191–196.

Herskovits, Melville J. 1975 [1937]. *Life in a Haitian Valley.* New York: Octagon Books.

Hurbon, Laënnec. 1972. *Dieu dans le vaudou haitien.* Paris: Payot.

Hurston, Zora Neale. 1939. Voodoo Gods: An Inquiry into Native Myths and Magic in Jamaica and Haiti. London: J. M. Dent.

Huxley, Francis. 1966. *The Invisibles.* London: Rupert Hart-Davis.

Kemp, Mark. 1989. Chemistry of Voodoo. *Discover* 10:26–28.

Kerboull, Jean. 1973. *Le vodou: Magic ou religion?* Paris: Robert Laffont.

Koegel, Paul, M. Audrey Burney, and Rodger K. Farr. 1988. The Prevalence of Specific Psychiatric Disorders Among Homeless Individuals in the Inner City of Los Angeles. *Archives of General Psychiatry* 45:1085–1092.

Laroche, Maximilien. 1975. Mythe africain et mythe antillais: Le personage du zombi. *Canadian Journal of African Studies* 9:479–491. (English translation in *Exile and Tradition: Studies in African and Caribbean Literature* [1976], ed. Rowland Smith, pp. 44–61. Dalhousie, N.S.: Longman & Dalhousie University Press.)

Leach, MacEdward. 1961. Jamaican Duppy Lore. *Journal of American Folklore* 74:207–215.

Mars, Louis P. 1945. The Story of Zombi in Haitie. *Man* 45:38–40.

Métraux, Alfred. 1953. Croyances et Pratiques dan la Vallée de Marbial, Haiti. *Journal de la Sociétés des Américanistes de Paris* 42:135–198.

Métraux, Alfred. 1968 [1958]. *Le vaudou haitien*. Paris: Gallimard. (English translation by Hugo Charteris [1972], *Voodoo in Haiti*. New York: Schocken Books.)

Newall, Venetia. 1981. West Indian Ghosts. In *The Folklore of Ghosts*, ed. Hilda R. Ellis Davidson and W. M. S. Russell, pp. 73–93. Cambridge, England: D. S. Brewer.

Parrinder, Geoffroy. 1951. *West African Psychology*. London: Lutterworth Press.

Parsons, Elsie Clews. 1928. Spirit Cult in Haiti. *Journal de la Société des Américanistes de Paris* 20:157–179.

Paul, Emmanuel C. 1978 [1962]. *Panorama du folklore haitien (presence africaine en Haiti)*. Port-au-Prince: Editions Fardin.

Philomé, Bellard. 1980. Les expeditions (essai sur la magie offensive). In *Cahier de folklore et des traditions orales d'Haiti*, ed. Max Benoît, pp. 62–83. Port-au-Prince: Imprimerie des Antilles.

Planson, Claude. 1974. *Vaudou—un initié parle*. Paris: Jean Dullis.

Pollak-Eltz, Angelina. 1977. *Cultos afroamericanos (Vudu y herchicería en las Américas)*. Carácas: Universidad Católica Andrés Bello.

Pradel, Jacques, and Jean-Yves Casgha. 1983. *Haiti, la république des morts-vivants*. Monaco: Editions du Jour.

Saint-Gérard, Yves. 1984. *Haiti: L'enfer au paradis*. Toulouse: Eché.

EDITOR'S SUGGESTIONS FOR FURTHER READING

Compora, Daniel. 2013. "Undead America: The Emergence of the Modern Zombie in American Culture." *Supernatural Studies* 1 (1): 31–38.

Dendle, Peter. 2007. "The Zombie as Barometer of Cultural Anxiety." In *Monsters and the Monstrous: Myths and Metaphors of Enduring Evil*, edited by Niall Scott, 45–57. Amsterdam: Rodopi.

Hurston, Zora Neale. 1938. "Zombies." In *Tell My Horse: Voodoo and Life in Haiti and Jamaica*, chap. 13. Philadelphia: J. B. Lippincott.

Koven, Mikel. 2008. "The Folklore of the Zombie Film." In *Zombie Culture: Autopsies of the Living Dead*, edited by Shawn McIntosh and Marc Leverette, 19–34. Lanham, MD: Scarecrow.

Koven, Mikel. 2015. "Tradition and the International Zombie Film: The Movies." In *Putting the Supernatural in Its Place: Folklore, the Hypermodern, and the Ethereal*, edited by Jeannie Banks Thomas, 90–125. Salt Lake City: University of Utah Press.

Owens, Trevor. 2015. "Lego, Handcraft, and Costumed Zombies: What Zombies Do on Flickr." *New Directions in Folklore* 13 (1–2): 71–92.

Parsons, Elsie Clews. 1928. "Spirit Cult in Hayti." *Journal de la Société des Américanistes de Paris* 20: 157–79.

Roth, LuAnne K. 2017. "'You Are What Others Think You Eat': Food, Identity, and Subjectivity in Zombie-as-Protagonist Narratives." In *What's Eating You? Food and Horror on Screen*, edited by Cynthia Miller and Bow Van Riper, 271–92. London: Bloomsbury.

Roth, LuAnne K., and Kate Shoults. 2015. "'Three Men, and the Place Is Surrounded': Reel Women in the Zombie Apocalypse." In *. . . But if a Zombie Apocalypse Did Occur: Essays on Medical, Military, Governmental, Ethical, Economic and Other Implications*, edited by Amy L. Thompson and Antonio Thompson, 227–45. Jefferson, NC: McFarland.

9

Ecotypes, Etiology, and Contemporary Legend
The "Webber" Cycle in Western Newfoundland

John Ashton

PREFACE

In contrast to globally notorious monsters like Bigfoot and the chupacabra, many lesser-known monster legends thrive quietly in small towns across North America. Researchers of such monsters usually boast a close connection to the town, living there themselves, becoming aware of the legend through community life (or, sometimes, community students). The late John Ashton, a folklore professor at Sir Wilfred Grenfell College and resident of Stephenville, Newfoundland, studied precisely this variety in the Webber monster legend, an ill-defined, woods-dwelling, hybrid man, possibly with webbed feet.

A diligent scholar, Ashton begins by laying out his theoretical framework and the literature he is indebted to, proceeds to offer a detailed contextual background of his setting and thorough analysis of variant texts, and concludes with a forceful delineation of his own contribution to legend scholars' understanding of ecotypes. Ashton's mission was ultimately conceptual. The Webber provided a prime example of how legend ecotypification works, a process that transforms monster legends to exude a local logic but also, as Ashton claims, to reflect local consciousness and cultural values, including local cultural ecology. Some monsters are truly local, others are local but their purported acts and behaviors are migratory, and a third variety are migratory with only basic adjustments for setting and cultural logic. A loose and diffuse narrative without an essential core, the Webber legend did demonstrate recurring motifs, including a car accident, disfigurement,

https://doi.org/10.7330/9781646421602.c009

life in the woods, and body hybridization. The one constant, though, was the Webber as local Stephenville bogeyman, cropping up as intertextual reference and assumed perpetrator in localized variants of migratory legends, such as "The Boyfriend's Death."

Folklorist and urban legend elder statesman Jan Brunvand had argued that the fusion of localized legend with migratory legends was part of the ecotypification process of increasing credibility, but here Ashton disagrees. While Brunvand sees local monsters as adding to community maintenance of contemporary legends, Ashton points to cultural ecology and the natural environment (the *eco* in Carl von Sydow's ecotype) as the engine of local monster legends. Ashton's interpretation emphasizes the clash of civilization, an overriding theme in Webber legends and in Stephenville generally. Following structural changes in the local economy, the Webber became the metaphor for both the life-sustaining and life-taking dangers of the wilds *and* that wilds' expected progeny.

ESSAY

Most students of the contemporary legend would agree that one of the genre's defining characteristics is what may be variously termed its flexibility, malleability, plasticity or mutability.[1] The fairly small group of identifiable, relatively stable, migratory narrative patterns upon which the literature has focused (Brunvand 1993b:325–347) has revealed itself to be readily transformed by localization and the proclivities of individual narrators.

Contemporary legend scholarship has devoted extensive consideration to the interchangeability of details of spatial and temporal setting, *dramatis personae* and other situational elements as texts are transmitted from person to person and place to place. Somewhat less attention appears to have been given to the transformative and shaping effects of the relatively widespread circulation and longer-term currency of particular legendary traditions within a community or region. The regionalization of contemporary legend, in Suzi Jones' (1976) sense of its creative manipulation to articulate regional consciousness, has been best exemplified in the recent work of Diane Goldstein (1996) and Gary Alan Fine (1992).

In her study of Newfoundland variants of the ubiquitous "Welcome to the World of Aids" legend, Goldstein demonstrates how the narrative has been "molded and shaped in narrative tradition to reflect regional and cultural values" to such an extent that it ". . . points to crucial issues in Aids education and provides a clear example of the applied potential of contemporary legend" (1996: 211). Gary Alan Fine meanwhile examines legend texts recorded in South Africa during the 1980s, texts which, while similar to those collected in North America and Western Europe, ". . . comment on the specific socio-political situation and fears of southern African populations." Fine goes on to observe that "The socio-political context shapes the locally produced content of contemporary legends and rumours by a process akin to [Carl von Sydow's (1934)] concept of ecotypification" (1992:54).

I would like to add my own voice to those of the writers quoted above in adopting a regional perspective on the study of contemporary legend as I consider a legendary tradition, perhaps more precisely an intertextual legendary tradition, from an area of Western Newfoundland including and immediately surrounding the town of Stephenville at the head of St. George's Bay. This tradition, while embracing several items from the canon of Western contemporary legend, articulates the beliefs, attitudes and cultural values of the local population and, I suggest, further upholds the utility of Von Sydow's concept of the ecotype as an analytical tool in contemporary legend research.

The town of Stephenville is situated approximately fifty miles southwest of the city of Corner Brook at the head of St. George's Bay and lies close to the isthmus of the largely French-speaking Port au Port Peninsula. Initially known as "Indian Head," it was first settled by Acadian French immigrants who engaged in a small-scale herring and lobster fishery as well as both commercial and subsistence agriculture. The name "Stephenville" first appears in the census for 1874.

The development of a forest industry, centered upon the activities of a newly constructed paper mill in Corner Brook, stimulated a growth in the town's population during the 1920s and 1930s, but a more important stimulus emerged with the Second World War and the construction in 1941 of the Harmon Air Field which became the largest American Air Force base outside the continental U.S. and a major re-fueling stop for both military and commercial aircraft en route to Europe. The town was provided with a rail link to the trans-island railway, and Stephenville's population quickly grew to more than 7,000.

Between 1941 and the closure of the air base in 1966, Stephenville was home to as many as 5,000 American service personnel as well as between 7,000 and 9,000 permanent residents. Since the departure of the Americans, the air base has been converted into a commercial regional airport and the town's economy has been dominated by the service industries as well as a newsprint manufacturing facility which was built in the 1970s as part of a government-sponsored program to develop and diversify the provincial economy (Bennett 1979; McGrath 1992; Moores 1994).

Each year a number of students from the Stephenville area enroll in courses at Sir Wilfred Grenfell College, the Western Newfoundland campus of Memorial University. Students in my introductory folklore courses are sometimes asked to locate the text of a contemporary legend in any one of a variety of acceptable sources and to discuss the ways in which the text exemplifies the characteristic features of the genre as enumerated in lectures and a variety of assigned readings. In the fall of 1998 a female student from Stephenville submitted the following text in fulfillment of that assignment:

> . . . two lovers were driving down a dark road near the Stephenville mill when they ran out of gas. The man got out and went to get some gas while the girl stayed in the car and locked the doors. She fell asleep, only to wake up and find no sign of her boyfriend. She decided to walk home hoping to meet him on the way. She looked up to find the headless body of her friend swinging from a rope. She tripped and fell and the Webber grabbed her and killed her. [SWGC 01–002][2]

The young lady offered the following etiology in support of what the reader will immediately recognize as a version of "The Boyfriend's Death" (Brunvand 1981:5–10).

> No-one knows for sure how the legend of the Webber came to be. There are, however, many possible origins where the Webber is said to have come from. Various stories circulated around the town of Stephenville and surrounding area to give rise to its possible origin. Some say it originated one day when a couple and their son were driving in the woods and a storm hit. There was a flash of lightning and the lightning hit a tree. When the tree fell it fell on the car killing the mother and father. The son thought it was right to kill. From then on, whoever went into the woods where he lived he would kill them. [SWGC 01–002]

My student claimed that she had heard "The Boyfriend's Death" legend and the narrative explaining the appearance within it of a character known as "The Webber" from fellow students at the junior high school she had attended in Stephenville. Further interrogation yielded the fact that the Webber appears or appeared in several other contemporary legends in local circulation and that there is a multi-variant etiological legend tradition explaining who the Webber is, how he acquired his distinctive physical features and why he appears as the perpetrator of crimes in versions of "The Boyfriend's Death," "The Babysitter and the Man Upstairs," and "The Roommate's Death" (Brunvand 1981:5–10, 53–56, 57–61; 1986:202–204).

Another student provided me with the following description of the Webber derived from the stories she had heard circulating in the adjacent but smaller community of Stephenville Crossing:

> It's half man and half reptile. It only comes out at night. People have spotted it only on the part of town labeled Seal Cove [This part of town is very swampy]. This creature supposedly comes from an accident that happened late one night on that road. The person was never found and after this accident weird occurs *[sic]* started to happen. No-one has ever been hurt by this creature but may have been chased. The top half of the creature is man and the bottom half is reptile. [SWGC 01–002]

I have subsequently discovered that such has been the currency of the Webber stories in the Stephenville area, that they have been featured in local newspaper reports and on the Western Newfoundland broadcasts of CBC radio, that they have been incorporated into the script of a radio play conceived and performed by local students, and that they have been immortalized in literary form by a local poet. Jessie Fudge (a Stephenville school teacher, local historian and graduate of Memorial University's folklore program) has recorded more than fifty versions of these stories since the early 1970s.[3]

The earliest recorded version of a story featuring the Webber that I have so far encountered was collected by the then Dean of Graduate Studies at Memorial University in a questionnaire about "Strange and Unusual Animals" which he had distributed throughout the island of Newfoundland in 1968. One informant provided the following response:

> The only strange or unusual animal I have ever heard of in Newfoundland is that of the Webber people. These Webber people are supposedly the off spring *[sic]* of a man named Webber and a bear. As the story was told to me . . . this man Webber was in a car accident somewhere out around Stephenville and the accident left him grossly disfigured so he never came home, he lived in the woods. The story says that the man mated with the bears and this creature resembles a mixture of a man and a bear. However, I do not know of anyone who has seen this animal and I think it may just be a folktale. (MUNFLA Q 73-B)

Subsequent elaborations on the Webber theme may be grouped into four basic subsets. In the first subset, a woman abandons her deformed baby in the woods or in a local park. The baby survives by fending for himself and evolves as a half man, half beast character with webbed feet. In the second subset, a handicapped or deformed child escapes from a caring home environment through an open window and wanders off into the woods where he survives by scavenging and eating dirt, developing webbed feet in the process. In the third subset the Webber is a victim of an unsuccessful murder attempt. His parents tie him in a sack and try to drown him in a local pond, but he escapes, lives in the nearby woods, grows webbed feet and returns to wreak revenge on his parents. In the fourth subset, the Webber is the infant survivor of a traffic accident in which his parents are killed. He crawls off into the woods evading searchers' efforts to locate him. He learns how to survive in a forest environment, in the process growing webbed hands and feet or becoming half man, half reptile. In each of the four cases, the Webber's physical and cultural development may or may not be furthered by the assistance of bears or other woodland creatures.

Over the last thirty years there appears to have been a fusion of this presumably independent local legend tradition and a series of the more widely known migratory narratives familiar to all contemporary legend scholars. This coalescence is manifested in two ways. In its simplest form, a well-known contemporary legend concludes with a suggestion or statement to the effect that the Webber is the perpetrator of the crime, usually a murder that is depicted in the text. The appearance of webbed footprints on the ground or the roof of a car is frequently adduced in support of the accusation:

> three boys were camping in the Cold Brook area when they heard on the radio that some unidentified object was killing things in the woods. They locked themselves in a cabin and when they opened the door in the morning they saw a boy with his head cut off. That night the boys said they saw an object with web feet. [SWGC 01–002]

Alternatively, references to the Webber may appear at the beginning and end of the story producing the classic symmetry effected by other narrative framing devices:

> A boy and girl were out on the road. They had just heard on the radio that the Webber was in the woods they were traveling besides. So, they headed back to the nearest gas station. They ran out of gas so the boy said he would be back in a while and to cover up in a blanket. So, after a while she fell asleep. A while later she woke up. She heard this scraping sound on the roof and a thump three times every few minutes. She heard the siren of the police. They told her to slowly get out of the car and not to look back. It was her boyfriend's foot thumping on the car but the scratching was the Webber trying to get her. He had a few inches left to go and he would have killed her too. [Fudge, 7]

The Webber character intrudes more strikingly into locally circulating texts of migratory legends when a complete etiological account is embedded within a more complex exposition of the contemporary legend canon:

Along time ago there was a lady named Mrs. Webber and a man named Mr. Webber who were back from the hospital after the birth of their first child. They were traveling on a narrow road which was very dark. All of a sudden their car went off the road and Mr. and Mrs. Webber were killed but their son wasn't.

Not many people drove on the road so Mr. and Mrs. Webbers' bodies were left there. The boy was very young and he didn't know what he was supposed to do. Many years after the accident the young boy (now five years old) got adapted to the forest. He got webbed feet and hands, he started to get lumps on his face and he ate seeds and berries for food.

Ten years after the Webber started to kill all people who traveled on that road. One dark night, two people were driving down the long narrow road when all the lights went out in their car. They couldn't see where they were going. The man got out of the car and went to the front of their car and opened the hood. Then he realized that they were also out of gas. He got back in the car and told his wife that they were out of gas. He then got out of the car and started walking down the road with a flashlight in his hand, to find the nearest gas station.

A couple of hours later the lady noticed a police car coming towards their car. The police officer stepped out of his car and said to the lady, "We will take you home and please don't look back." She looked back with terror. She screamed as loud as she could when she saw her husband's body all splattered over the trunk of the car. The Webber was at it again. [Fudge, 2]

The intrusion of a locally known and named character into otherwise standard texts of contemporary legends is a phenomenon by no means restricted to Stephenville, or Newfoundland for that matter. Jan Brunvand, for one, provides examples of this phenomenon in the various compendia of what he prefers to call "urban legends." He cites, for example, the New Jersey Devil's infiltration of various legend texts, including a version of "The Boyfriend's Death" (1993a:96–97). He also refers to a New Orleans version of a legend in which "The Boyfriend's Death" is incorporated into a local tradition about "The Grunch," a half sheep, half human monster that haunts specific local sites (1981:9–10). Brunvand's discussion of these deviations from the traditional norm restricts itself to the suggestion that they represent the "localized details inserted by individual tellers" by which a folk legend "acquires a good deal of its credibility and effect" (1981:9–10).

Newfoundland variants of contemporary legends which feature the Webber are clearly the product of localization and often display the contextual specificity so characteristic of the genre's concrete style. Local place-names and landmarks are invoked for example. The events take place "Near Cold Brook," in "West Haven Park," at "Seal Cove," or on "The Old Mill Road." But the attachment of the Webber to widely circulated contemporary legends represents more than the mere supplementation of local detail to an otherwise migratory tradition by narrators who reside in the area of its most immediate dissemination. It is rather, in my view, a manifestation of the organic relationship between environment and expressive culture to which Carl Von Sydow was alluding in his elaboration of the concept of "ecotypes" in relation to the transmission and modification of migratory narrative folklore traditions (1934).

As Timothy Cochrane's excellent discussion (1987) of Von Sydow's work has illustrated, the concept of the ecotype has been variously understood by Western folklorists and is the subject of an extensive interpretative literature. I would contend, however, that it represents nothing if not the application of what anthropologists term "cultural ecology" to the study of folklore, an application Lauri Honko has dubbed "tradition ecology" in which, according to him, the student of variation "attempts to allow for three factors simultaneously. The tradition itself, the community maintaining it and the natural environment embracing them both" (1986:116).

The Webber stories represent the type of "milieu morphological" adaptation, to use Honko's phraseology (1986:116), that Von Sydow had in mind when he coined the term "oicotype" in the 1930s. The unique form of these tales embodies the formation of an ecotype, perhaps a series of ecotypes, resulting from the sustained interaction between a narrative tradition and a distinctive material environment as well as the locally prevailing environmental beliefs and attitudes that cluster around it.

Somewhat ironically, it is the more stable narrative elements, rather than the more variable ones, that support this observation. Throughout all the Webber texts I have seen to date, the creature is depicted as a human being transformed by his adaptation to a wilderness environment. He is most decidedly a creature of forest and wetland who emerges to prey upon local residents in brief forays into their urban milieu as in "The Babysitter and the Man Upstairs" (Brunvand 1981:53–56) or, more frequently, who ambushes unsuspecting travelers or campers who have unwittingly strayed beyond the confines of their safe urban environment into his woodland domain.

The Webber's victims may be just unlucky enough to be in the wrong place at the wrong time, but they most often fall prey to their own shortcomings as travelers or campers: running out of gas or firewood, getting lost in the woods or traveling in territory which is unfamiliar to them. It is interesting to note that when place-names are alluded to in these stories they are invariably those of out-of-the-way locations on the very margins of the community itself.

The town of Stephenville, like virtually all the communities of Newfoundland, is a product of the peculiar settlement history and patterns of resource exploitation that have bequeathed to the island much of its cultural distinctiveness and homogeneity. It is a relatively small coastal settlement which was quite deliberately situated in immediate proximity to the marine resources whose exploitation provided its initial *raison d'etre*. It is otherwise completely encircled by a wilderness environment of boreal forest and wetlands. Even today, the boundaries between town and country are sharply drawn and immediately apparent. The omnipresence of the encircling wilderness environment is regularly reinforced by news reports of incursions into the town of such woodland dwellers as moose, caribou, black bears, foxes and so on. With some frequency, the potential dangers of the country are driven home by stories of hunters, hikers, skiers and snowmobilers who lose their way in the woods or suffer other mishaps of various kinds.

For the first one hundred years of its existence, the town of Stephenville and its residents shared in Newfoundland's tradition of economic and occupational pluralism, itself an adaptive strategy in the face of the island's maritime and boreal forest ecologies. They shared also the system of cultural values emphasizing wilderness skills and environmental competence which grew up in support of this tradition. These features of Newfoundland's social and cultural fabric are voiced in expressive culture (Ashton 1998; Byrne 1991) and well documented in social scientific research (Omohundro 1994; Sinclair, *et al.* 1989). So too is their jeopardization by the recent decline in Newfoundland's resource-based industries and endeavours to replace them by government-financed public works projects and social welfare schemes and repeated attempts at industrial development.

I believe that the Webber stories are not, strictly speaking, "urban" legends but rather narratives that are at least in part about the inherent tensions between town and country, urban and rural lifestyles, popular and traditional culture and cultural values. That they should enjoy a particular currency and a distinctive, ecotypical form in the vicinity of Stephenville should come as no surprise since this community, more perhaps than any other in Newfoundland, has experienced these tensions first hand throughout the course of its history. It has evolved from a fishing and farming settlement through the culturally transformative experience of the oft locally dubbed "American Invasion" to replace American money and jobs with new, non-traditional industrial enterprises after the closure of the U.S. Air Force base in the mid-1960s.

The Webber is both the product and symbol of the juxtaposition of the urban and natural worlds. A physically ambiguous creature, he lives on the margins, stalking those in transition between town and country. The Webber tales have circulated as exemplary narratives about the life-sustaining potential of a wilderness which simultaneously poses unseen dangers, particularly to those failing to subscribe to traditional values and lacking the co-requisite environmental skills. In functional terms, the tales may represent a modern-day equivalent to an older narrative tradition in Newfoundland in which berry-pickers who inadvertently wandered too far into the woods were abducted or led astray by fairies (Narváez 1991).

When viewed in this light, the Webber cycle of contemporary legends represents a localized pattern within a more widely diffused narrative tradition which reflects the environmental and cultural particularities of the region in which it resides. As such, I suggest, it illustrates the enduring utility to folklorists of Von Sydow's concept of the ecotype, an old idea which may be worth taking out and dusting off every now and again.

NOTES

1. For a survey of the underlying characteristics of contemporary legends and literature devoted to them, see Bennett and Smith (1996) and Smith (1997).

2. Archival materials cited are housed at the Sir Wilfred Grenfell College Folklore Archive and Resource Centre and the Memorial University of Newfoundland Folklore and Language Archive. References to both collections employ the archives' standard accession numbers (e.g. SWGC 01-002, MUNFLA 75-137, etc.).

3. Items from this collection hereafter cited as Fudge 5, Fudge 14, etc.

REFERENCES

Ashton, John. 1998. "Hunters, Jinkers, Sealers and Squealers: Wilderness Skills, Cultural Values and Local Song-Making in Newfoundland." Paper presented at the Annual Meeting of the American Folklore Society, Portland, Oregon.

Bennett, Gillian and Paul Smith. 1996. "Introduction." In *Contemporary Legend: A Reader*, eds. Gillian Bennett and Paul Smith, pp. xxi–xlvii. New York: Garland Publishing.

Bennett, Wayne. 1979. "Stephenville." Unpublished Ms. St. John's: Maritime History Group, Memorial University of Newfoundland.

Brunvand, Jan Harold. 1981. *The Vanishing Hitchhiker: American Urban Legends and Their Meanings*. New York: W. W. Norton.

Brunvand, Jan Harold. 1986. *The Mexican Pet: More "New" Urban Legends and Some Old Favorites*. New York: W. W. Norton.

Brunvand, Jan Harold. 1993a. *The Baby Train and Other Lusty Urban Legends*. New York: W. W. Norton.

Brunvand, Jan Harold. 1993b. A Type-Index of Urban Legends. In *The Baby Train and Other Lusty Legends*, pp. 325–347. New York: W. W. Norton.

Byrne, Patrick 1991. "Tall Are the Tales that Fishermen Tell: Manifestations of the Tall Tale Impulse in Selected Examples of Contemporary Newfoundland Writing." In *Studies in Newfoundland Folklore: Community and Process*, eds. Gerald Thomas and J.D.A. Widdowson, pp. 309–328. St. John's: Breakwater Books Ltd.

Cochrane, Timothy. 1987. "The Concept of Ecotypes in American Folklore." *Journal of Folklore Research* 24:33–55.

Fine, Gary Alan. 1992. "Rumours of Apartheid: The Ecotypification of Contemporary Legends in the New South Africa." *Journal of Folklore Research* 29:53–71.

Goldstein, Diane E. 1996. "Welcome to the Mainland, Welcome to the World of Aids: Cultural Variability, Localization and Contemporary Legend." In *Contemporary Legend. A Reader*, eds. Gillian Bennett and Paul Smith, pp. 209–224. New York: Garland Publishing.

Honko, Lauri. 1986. "Types of Comparison and Forms of Variation." *Journal of Folklore Research* 23:105–124.

Jones, Suzi. 1976. "Regionalization: A Rhetorical Strategy." *Journal of the Folklore Institute* 13:105–120.

McGrath, T. M. 1992. *History of Canadian Airports*. Toronto: Lingus.

Moores, Barry. 1994. "Stephenville." In *The Encyclopedia of Newfoundland and Labrador*, ed. Cyril F. Poole, pp. 303–304. St. John's: Harry Cuff Publications Ltd.

Narváez, Peter. 1991. "Newfoundland Berry Pickers 'In the Fairies': Maintaining Spatial, Temporal and Moral Boundaries Through Legendry." In *The Good People. New Fairylore Essays*, ed. Peter Narváez, pp. 336–368. New York: Garland Publishing.

Omohundro, John T. 1994. *Rough Food: The Seasons of Subsistence in Northern Newfoundland*. St. John's: Institute of Social and Economic Research, Memorial University of Newfoundland.

Sinclair, Peter R., Robert H. Hill, Cynthia Lamson, and H. A. Williamson. 1989. *Social and Cultural Aspects of Sealing in Atlantic Canada*. St. John's: Institute of Social and Economic Research, Memorial University of Newfoundland.

Smith, Paul. 1997. "Contemporary Legend." In *Folklore: An Encyclopedia of Beliefs, Customs, Tales, Music and Art*, ed. Thomas A. Green, pp. 493–495. Santa Barbara, California: ABC-Clio.

Von Sydow, Carl Wilhelm. 1934. "Geography and Folktale Ecotype." *Béaloideas* 4:344–355.

EDITOR'S SUGGESTIONS FOR FURTHER READING

Atwood, Margaret. 1994. "Canadian Monsters: Some Aspects of the Supernatural in Canadian Fiction." In *The Canadian Imagination: Dimensions of Literary Culture*, edited by David Staines, 97–122. New York: Routledge.

Carpenter, Carole Henderson. 1980. "The Cultural Role of Monsters in Canada." In *Manlike Monsters on Trial: Early Records and Modern Evidence*, edited by Marjorie M. Halpin and Michael Ames, 97–108. Vancouver: University of Vancouver Press.

Henderson, M. Carole. 1976. "Monsters of the West: The Sasquatch and the Ogopogo." In *Folklore of Canada*, edited by Edith Fowke, 251–61. Toronto: McClelland & Stewart.

Ransom, Amy J. 2015. "The Changing Shape of a Shape-Shifter." *Journal of the Fantastic in the Arts* 26 (2): 251–75.

10

The Lake Lieberman Monster

Elizabeth Tucker

PREFACE

Much like the Webber, the Lake Lieberman monster, or Lieby, is an extreme local, confined to a single drainage ditch. (Legends of bottom-dwelling monsters, on the other hand, lurk in lakes worldwide.) Unlike lake monsters elsewhere, no seeker yearns to verify Lieby's scientific existence. Rather, in this article, folklorist Elizabeth Tucker offers a case study of the monster legend itself, tracing Lieby's genesis, rise, decline, and revival on her campus in the Southern Tier of New York. Folklorists have noted the importance of folklore to college life generally, and here, Tucker argues for campus monsters as valuable historical data, demonstrating the "wildness, wit, and irreverence" characteristic of Binghamton University campus life in the 1970s, especially in Newing College, BU's "animal house" residence area.

Tucker speculates that the 1969 hiring of folklorist W.F.H. Nicolaisen prepared the way for the Lieby. Scouring the *Lake Lieberman Gazette*, she chronicles the Lake Lieberman monster from its birth—fledgling in 1969, fully matured by the 1970s—a documented "inventing" of tradition that is part and parcel of the modern folklore process. Richard M. Dorson might deride Lieby as fakelore, spurious fiction passed off as homey folk tradition, but his student Alan Dundes encouraged folklorists to embrace fakelore and analyze its meaning and function. Indeed, Dorson must agree that Lieby qualifies as one of his American comic creatures: an odd but amusing lark, pregnant with possibilities of pranks and tomfoolery. BU journalist Mark Halperin's admitted motive as one of the legend's propagators—"a new school has to develop legends fast"—even shows shades of folklore's romantic role in European nation-building of yore, albeit on a much smaller scale.

https://doi.org/10.7330/9781646421602.c010

In addition to their role in campus rituals and community building, contemporary legends adapt to and comment on sociopolitical climates. Lieby embraced that function, critiquing pollution, mercury seafood contamination, and higher education budget cuts. Campus administrators were less enamored of Lake Lieberman's contribution to campus life. Citing new construction, litter, and pollution, they initiated a plan to drain the dirty water hazard, transforming the lake into a swamp. And, as was the case with Leary's Boondock Monster, the destruction of the monster's home led to the extinction of the monster, save for the occasional revival by nostalgic alumni (or Libby Tucker herself). Researchers can appreciate Tucker's detailed historical study not as an investigation of a monster's physical existence, but rather as an exploration of its artfully crafted legendary existence, its showcasing of student character, and its integral role in campus ritual, school narrative, and community building.

ESSAY

Encircled by green hills in Upstate New York, Binghamton University has four large residential areas: Hinman College, Newing College, College-in-the-Woods, and Dickinson Community. During my twenty five years of teaching at Binghamton, Newing College has been known as the "wild" residential area, the "animal house" where fun-loving students congregate. At the edge of the woods behind Newing College lies a wet, grassy depression covered by weeds. Beneath the green surface, embedded in layers of ooze, sprawl wooden planks, rubber tires, bicycles, and a rusted-out vending machine. Mosquitoes swarm there. When rainfall is heavy, one can almost imagine a swamp monster raising its head to greet students walking by.

In fact, this little-known but significant swamp is actually a lake: Lake Lieberman, where the Lake Lieberman Monster entertained students in the 1970s and 80s. At a folklore conference in the summer of 2003, John McDowell, then Chair of Indiana University's Folklore and Ethnomusicology Department, said that archives of student life "seemed trivial to people before" but are "priceless now." Agreeing with McDowell's statement, I want to explore a small part of American college life: the creation of monster lore. Monster lore not only encapsulates eras and attitudes, but also expresses a certain wildness intrinsic to campus social life. In many respects, the Lake Lieberman Monster typifies the kind of wildness that is among the most cherished memories of many college graduates.

Previous scholarship on college student folklore has included discussion of wild and domestic animals on campus. James P. Leary's article "The

Notre Dame Man: Christian Athlete or Dirtball?" lists some of the animals who run in Notre Dame's spring animal race: snakes, turtles, ducks,
and cockroaches (1978:141). In Simon Bronner's *Piled Higher and Deeper:
The Folklore of Student Life*, two of the more memorable college festivities
are the Running of the Rodents and the Rat Ball at Spalding University in
Kentucky (1995:95). Bronner describes college pranks that involve smug-
gling cows, pigs, and other farm animals into college buildings, noting that
such pranks disrupt the power relationship between faculty and students
(1995:114). Colorado College students have rebelled against administrators
"by secretly moving the Palmer museum's stuffed animals to various inappropriate locations around the campus" (Loevy 1999:250). At Shenandoah
University, the code of student conduct decrees that "animals, live or dead,
may not be used in pranks or otherwise for amusement or ceremony in
connection with any institutional group function or activity" (2003). The
writers of this rule seem to have had plenty of experience with students'
use of animals and do not seem eager for more.

More fanciful animals can be found in the domain of college mascots. According to Glenn Street, owner of a Canadian company that creates
mascots for two thousand clients, college students "prefer characters with
edge." Testudo the Terrapin, mascot of the University of Maryland, has
recently become an intimidating beast, as has Attila the Duck at Stevens
Institute of Technology in Hoboken, New Jersey. Students like tough,
wild mascots, such as Villanova's wildcat and Brigham Young's cougar.
Texas Christian University recently replaced its Superfrog mascot with "a
monster-like reptile with spiny horns protruding from its head" (Johnson
2001). And Binghamton University, where the Lake Lieberman Monster
once held sway, is now the home of the Bearcat, a predatory creature with
sharp fangs and menacing eyes.

BIRTH OF A MONSTER

Drawings in the *Lake Lieberman Gazette*, Newing College's student newspaper, show that the Monster began to hatch from its egg in 1969 and
emerged, fully formed, in 1970. It is tempting to connect the Monster's
advent with the arrival of my colleague W.F.H. (Bill) Nicolaisen, who came
to Binghamton University on December 5, 1969. Bill's daughter Birgit
[2003] was able to tell me the exact date of his arrival, because she remembered her father searching for candy to fill his daughters' shoes on Saint
Nicholas Day. When asked about the Monster's genesis, Bill did not claim
any credit; he recalled that students who told him about the Monster in

the 1980s felt a creature conceived in the 1970s was too old to be interesting (Nicolaisen 2003). Nonetheless, I find it likely that Bill's early folklore classes, with their intriguing blend of European and American material, made the Binghamton University campus a more comfortable spot for the Monster's birth.

Described in a 1978 newspaper article as "the one and only sacred, fire-breathing dragon who is the mascot for all of Newing College," the Lake Lieberman Monster owes its form to European dragon lore and, in particular, to the Loch Ness Monster. Numerous mentions of the "Loch Lieberness Monster" and the "Lack Lieberschnitzel Monster," as well as the nickname "Lieby," show a droll mixture of cultures, but Loch Ness was clearly the main location the students had in mind. What did it matter that Lake Lieberman was muddy and shallow, while Loch Ness was so vast that its depths had never been charted? Who would object if a fire-breathing monster suddenly emerged from the lake to become the focus of playful new traditions?

No one on the Binghamton campus objected in the 1970s, but I can hear one voice rising in objection now: the voice of Richard M. Dorson. "Fakelore!" his voice shouts. In his proseminar at Indiana University, Dorson carefully trained other students and me to discriminate between authentic folklore and spurious traditions deliberately created by artful talespinners such as the creators of Paul Bunyan. Mindful of Dorson's voice, which is growing louder as I look deeper into the Monster's provenance, I take comfort in the fact that Dorson was one of the first serious analysts of student folklore (1949:671–677); he would understand the humor behind the Monster's creation. As I listen, his objection dissolves into a hearty laugh.

In fact, monster lore provokes such a mixture of veneration and humor that it is difficult to stay serious for long. The Loch Ness Monster, nicknamed Nessie, has become an icon of Scottish culture, with a booming tourist industry specializing in boat rides, artifacts, and stuffed Nessies of various sizes and shapes. When my husband, my son, and I visited Loch Ness in the summer of 1998, we purchased, at my son's insistence, enough stuffed Nessies for all his schoolfriends. Other tourists have done the same. Recently Kevin Carlyon, High Priest of British White Witches, renewed his spell to protect the Loch Ness Monster, encouraging it to make an appearance ("Ritual Appearance" 2003). Nessie piquantly inspires both protective loyalty and tourist kitsch.

Other famous monsters include Champ of Lake Champlain in New York, Ogopogo of Canada's Lake Okanagan, and Storsjoodjuret of Lake

Storsjon in Sweden. Monsters have been spotted in Ireland, Denmark, Finland, Italy, Norway, and Wales. Usually the monster's domain is a deep, cold lake rumored to have no bottom. Often the monster is thought to be a mysterious survival from a primeval past (Costello 1975). The phrase "trapped in the lake" frequently comes up, the underlying explanation being that a pathway to the ocean closed up, so there was nowhere else for the monster to go. "Mystery" is probably the most accurate keyword for a lake monster. Coming from an unknown past and inhabiting a lake of uncharted depths, a monster of this kind represents what cannot be known across a continuum of time and space, tantalizing its fans to find answers that are virtually impossible to discover.

Certainly the creation of the Lake Lieberman Monster and the naming of its habitat were deliberately shrouded in mystery. As Mark Halperin and Jeannette DeLisa explained in a *Lake Lieberman Gazette* article in 1970:

> Few facts are as shrouded in myth as the truth of the naming of Lake Lieberman. Everyone has his own pet myth to explain the christianing [sic] of the Lake. Personally, I have always felt that the name was derived from the twelfth book of the Bingiad in which the country of Bingia having defeated its neighbors goes down to what at that time was a mere pond, and dancing around it they proclaimed themselves to be a free band of men. In the original Latin the term "free band" reads "liber manus." I think that it is obvious that the name has stuck from that day to this. (p. 9)

This amusing account of the lake's naming puts Lake Lieberman in a mock-medieval European setting, with its own authoritative historical document and Latin etymology. Seventeen years after the story was published, Mark Halperin explained that he helped create Lake Lieberman legends because "a new school needs to develop legends fast" (1987). The State University of New York at Binghamton was founded in 1950. Newing students, aware of the relative newness of their surroundings, successfully added a dimension of historical depth to their residential college. Administrators, responsible for maintaining historical accuracy, would not have felt free to make up such a story. With tongue-in-cheek humor and pride, the students of Newing came up with a set of legends that remained vivid through the mid-1980s.

One of the most reliable signs of a legend's vitality is how much it varies, adapting to changing circumstances. Legends of Lake Lieberman's early days vary widely, but many of them focus on an intriguing figure: Elliot Lieberman, namer of the lake. According to Halperin and DeLisa, "Elliot was the first person thrown in the lake. One story claims that he lived in the same room facing the lake for four years and so they decided to name it after him (the lake, not the room)" (1970). Other stories tell of Elliot taking women up to his room "to see his lake" and staving out on the lake's shore in all kinds of weather. One of the more colorful variants explains that when Elliot was a senior, he "walked around the lake three times with his girlfriend without asking her to marry him. She pushed him in after the third time around and the Lake got its name" (Halperin and DeLisa 1970). In a text collected eight years later, Elliot's name becomes Harry, and his claim to fame becomes an accidental death after an all-nighter: "When he woke up he ran to his final, but fell on his fountain pen in front of the Library Tower and died" (Lonky 1978). By 1978, the lake's naming had become less important than the sensational (and quite improbable) death connected with its namer.

When I began my research on Lake Lieberman's origins, I called our university's alumni office to ask whether Elliot Lieberman was a real person. It did not take long to learn that he had graduated from Binghamton in 1966 and had worked for the Environmental Protection Agency for many years. Due to the felicity of e-mail, I was able to obtain Elliot's own story of the lake rather quickly. He explained that in the fall of 1963, when he was a sophomore, his dormitory room overlooked a large drainage ditch. While trying to persuade an attractive young woman to come up to his room, he told her, "Oh it's great. You ought to come over to see it . . . It overlooks . . . Lake Lieberman." That winter, Elliot's friend Betty posted signs across Newing College announcing a skating party on Lake Lieberman. In the spring, his friend John created a sign with the lake's name, "modeled carefully after official campus signs. He made it over a holiday at home, and erected it at 2 a.m. one morning after returning to campus. John recalls, 'I was sure that the pounding of my hammer to get it into that rock hard soil would have half the dorm up, and a security guard at my side. But all went well'" (2000a).

In the midst of all these incidents involving Elliot, who remembers being praised in the campus newspaper as a prophet with the "eyes of a Lincoln, a Washington, a Mighty Joe Young," where was the Monster? Although no printed record tells of its first appearance, its earliest pictures in the *Lake Lieberman Gazette* show a smooth, reptilian creature whose humps barely break the surface of the lake. In the *Gazette* of October 10, 1974, the Monster waits with open jaws while a student rides up a ramp on a bicycle: a willing victim on the way to an early demise.

By March 29, 1976, however, the cover picture of the *Gazette* shows students throwing the Monster itself into the lake. In an inversion of the familiar human sacrifice paradigm, the Monster has taken the role of a Newing College student. This transformation happens gradually. In the Halloween issue of 1974, the Monster is shown putting on a "Human Being Costume":

trying on the life of a student, so to speak. And on December 12, 1974, the Monster stands ready to jump off the Library Tower. The caption under its picture states, "As we last encountered our hero, finals had become too much to bear; is this really the end?" Both victim and demander of sacrifice, the Monster epitomizes the tensions of student life. It also provides a focal point for wit and ribald fun.

VESTAL VIRGINS

Since the Binghamton University campus is located in Vestal, New York, there could hardly be a more appropriate term for the Monster's victims than Vestal Virgins. In the late 1960s and early 1970s, a sexual revolution took place on America's college campuses. Moving away from the rigid sexual mores of the 1950s, students discovered new license for sexual experimentation. According to Binghamton folklore of the early 1970s, the Pegasus figure on the Fine Arts Building would spread its wings and fly away if a virgin ever graduated from the university. Apparently, the Lake Lieberman Monster did its part to make sure that no virgin remained untouched. In the early 1970s, sacrifices at the lake were elaborate and exciting. Torch-bearers and priests, varying in number and in garb, would accompany the Vestal Virgin to the lake and toss him or her in, with great fanfare and an enormous amount of splashing.

One of my first folklore students collected a detailed report of the ritual that surrounded the Monster's activities:

> For each school year two dedication ceremonies over the lake are held. The first is held during Orientation Week in order to "open" the lake and to ensure the blessing of the Lake Lieberman Monster. The second, according to Newing College's constitution, must be held during the first weekend in May. The purpose of this three day ceremony, also known as Newing Navy Weekend, is to "close" the lake for the summer and to give thanks to the monster. Both ceremonies are basically the same. There are three priests, one being the highest, a torch bearer, and a vestal virgin (preferably an unwilling freshman) who is to be sacrificed to the Lake Lieberman Monster in exchange for his blessing and watching over of Newing College. (Landi 1978)

These carefully structured rituals occurred only in the spring and fall, although older students could toss freshmen into the lake whenever the urge struck them (primarily when wild parties were taking place). Rites of spring, designated as "riots," "rites," "flings," "storms," and "fevers," occur on college campuses all around the United States, and these spring festivals offer release of tension before final exams (Bronner 1995:93). In the fall, opening weekend festivities, athletic events, and homecoming parties mark the academic year's beginning.

While Newing's lakeside rituals fit the pattern of seasonal "flings," their most important element seems to be the Vestal Virgin, whose sacrifice ensures blessings for everyone else. This pattern brings to mind the story of the Dragon Slayer (AT 300), in which a brave young hero saves the dragon's victim from an untimely death. Nobody saves the Vestal Virgin from being dunked in the lake. What happens is symbolic initiation into college life, with strong sexual overtones. Legions of folklorists have pointed out the association between water and fertility in young people's rituals (note, e.g., Newall 1971). However, Newing College's rituals are not just pale imitations of well known initiatory patterns. They are witty and humorous ceremonies with one underlying purpose: everyone present should get soaked and have a memorably fine time.

ENVIRONMENTAL MONSTROSITIES

In the early 1970s, many college students participated in demonstrations against environmental pollution. "Save the Whales" became a familiar slogan; marine life was endangered, as was the health of people who ate tainted seafood. In the spring of 1971, Binghamton professor Bruce McDuffie became worried about the level of mercury in local fish. Samples showed that his concern was justified, and similar tests in other parts of the United States gave environmentalists cause for alarm. Playfully responding to local and national stress, the Lake Lieberman Monster became a poster child for environmental advocacy.

On March 3, 1971, the *Lake Lieberman Gazette* published an exchange between the Monster and an unidentified student. The student wrote

> Dear Monster,
> How much mercury is there in you? Does Dr. McDuffie plan to test you?
> Signed,
> H.G. Compound

The Monster's reply to this student with the name symbolizing mercury was

> Dear H.G.,
> See "Quote of the Week" on page 1.
> Contaminatedly yours,
> T*H*E* M*O*N*S*T*E*R

The "Quote of the Week" was as follows: "As soon as we catch him, we'll test him.—Dr. Bruce McDuffie when asked to investigate mercury content of Loch Lieberness Monster." The Monster, accustomed to demanding human sacrifice from the student body, had become a sacrificial victim to an environmental monstrosity.

The plot thickened when the Lake Lieberman Monster found a girlfriend: the Tainted Tuna of Hinman College. Kenneth Anderson, Master of Newing College, addressed the following memo to Hinman Master Christian P. Gruber:

> From time to time, the *Lake Lieberman Gazette* has reported sightings of an unidentified creature from the Hinman swamp cavorting in the waters of Lake Lieberman and fraternizing with our Loch Lieberness monster. These reports have not alarmed us until recently when we learned from highly reliable sources that the swamp creature [is] in fact, huge, and undoubtably [sic] tainted, tuna. Its continued presence thus threatens to contaminate the pure waters of the lake and sully the character of our monster.
>
> We, therefore, feel compelled to insist that Hinman College make arrangements to confine its mercuric and unholy mackerel to the borders of the Hinman swamp. For its part, Newing College [is] prepared to take all appropriate measures to preserve the integrity of its territorial waters, and prevent further encroachments by your aggressive and tainted tuna. These measures could include call-up of the Newing Navy, in which enlistments are at an all-time peak, and an appeal to our environmental specialists, Drs. Battin, Cooper, and McDuffie.
>
> It is our fervent hope that you will heed our demand, so that such further drastic measures will not be necessary. ("Letters to the Monster" 1971)

This humorous memo draws boundaries of war between the beloved Lake Lieberman (or Loch Lieberness) Monster and the "unholy mackerel" of the Hinman swamp, offering relief from tension about environmental pollution. In contrast to the students' letters in the *Lake Lieberman Gazette*, the letter from Newing's Faculty Master locates contamination in [a] rival residential area, whose "aggressive and tainted tuna" [is a] menace to the lake's purity and the Monster's character. Drawing upon well-known rivalries makes [the] vague threat of pollution more familiar and much funnier. More humor is added by the letter's title, "Sorry, Charlie!" [Anderson 1971], alluding to a character in a familiar advertisement for Starkist canned tuna.

Sixteen years after the mercury scare, Newing alumnus Al Kalter [1987] fondly remembered "the scandalous relationship between our beloved Loch Lieberness Monster and that mercury-laden tuna fish from the Hinman swamp," showing that this bit of college humor had had lasting meaning.

"Scandalous" is a significant word here. On college campuses, as in small villages, illicit relationships fascinate people. Who is dating whom? Which relationships seem normal, and which do not? The relationship between the Monster and the tuna serves as a metaphor of college social life, in which all sorts of surprising liaisons occur.

MONSTROUS LEAP

On October 12, 1974, a new visitor approached the Monster's lake. This was no mercury-laden tuna, but a freshman known by the pseudonym "Goodnis Knoodnis." Anyone who remembers Evel Knievel will understand the inversion of this name. Evel Knievel was famous for jumping his motorcycle over what looked like impossible barriers: a line of thirteen cars in Seattle, a flotilla of fifty cars in Los Angeles, and a phalanx of fourteen Greyhound buses in King's Island, Ohio. All of those jumps were successful, but some subsequent attempts resulted in serious injury. Knievel was an unlikely hero, a daredevil well suited to the optimism of the early 1970s. At Newing College, students who had followed his exploits used them as a model for a new chapter in Lake Lieberman's mythology.

Goodnis Knoodnis's quest, celebrated by Newing students and faculty members, was "to leap the slimy waters of Lake Lieberman." When asked why he wanted to do such a thing, Goodnis replied that he was doing it "for the glory of the Endicott underground"—in other words, to enhance the prestige of students who lived in the basement of Endicott Hall. Preparations for his jump involved building a wooden ramp and finding a "$5, second-hand, specially remodeled bicycle." For protection, Goodnis planned to wear a special Goodnis Knoodnis helmet and uniform. Replying to a *Lake Lieberman Gazette* reporter's question about his earlier jumping experience, he reminisced about his childhood in Staten Island. "'I had a puddle,' Goodnis explained modestly. And when he was asked about how he would prepare spiritually for the jump, he answered, 'I intend to get high'" ("Goodnis" 1974).

An eyewitness to this momentous jump was Augie Mueller, who later became Master of Newing College. Mueller recalled:

> He built a huge ramp that went from the courtyard down to the lake, And on a Saturday morning, with many of us lined up to look on, he raced down the ramp on his bicycle, complete with mask and flying hood, to the place on the ramp where it went up slightly, gave the pedals a push to go up that last little bit, and promptly plunged down into the muddy lake. It was quite a sight. (2000)

This vivid description makes it clear how important Goodnis Knoodnis's jump was—but why did it mean so much to Newing's future Master and the students? Was it because Goodnis, a young and relatively innocent freshman, was an unlikely hero who dared to attempt the impossible? Or was it because Goodnis braved the wrath of the Monster, who awaited him in the depths of the lake? No records tell of a tussle between this stalwart young man and the Monster, but his descent into the depths of the muddy lake brings to mind watery initiations of spring and fall. Goodnis successfully proved his bravery (or foolhardiness), and college life went on.

MONSTER TAKEOVER

One of the Monster's greatest adventures took place in the spring of 1976, when students went on strike in protest against state budget cuts. Waiting for the Faculty Senate to show support for their strike proposal, student leaders were disappointed to find that some faculty members and administrators took a more moderate view of what should be done. Zack Bowen, chairman of the English Department, proposed that students hold seminars on their own time and that professors be allowed to cancel classes. The students' subsequent demonstration and takeover of the Administration Building is described succinctly by Newing reporter Lauren Fleishman: "Point of order, student demands, point of information, meeting with Clark, phone call from New Paltz, Columbia of the sixties, point of order, phone call from Old Westbury, smoke bomb, vegetarian lunch, court order, Clark, WHRW, Lisa Chason, court injunction, point of order, clean up, leave" (1976). This was an intense period of student activism, with some residential colleges sharply disagreeing with each other. It was time for the Lake Lieberman Monster to take a political stand.

For the "April Fool" issue of the *Lake Lieberman Gazette*, Lauren Fleishman wrote about a new campus crisis: the "Monster Takeover." Her article began dramatically:

> FLASH—The Lake Lieberman Monster arose last night at 7 PM and swallowed, intact, an entire dormitory, Broome Hall. "It was amazing," said Newingite Joseph Koole. "We were practicing co-rec Softball for our big game against Endicott's dynamic team the Vegetables, when suddenly we heard a series of unearthly bellows coming from the vicinity of the lake. Before we could turn around we heard a tremendous SHLURP!! And the next thing we knew, Broome Hall was gone!!!!!!!!!!!" (1976)

After swallowing Broome Hall, the Monster called a press conference and formally presented four demands: sacrifice of more Vestal Virgins, mobilization of Space Ship Earth to clean up the lake, re-establishment of a committee of faculty, students, and aquatic creatures, and restriction of access to Broome Hall except for cleaning personnel and suppliers of Drakes Cakes. Robert Pompi, Newing's Master at that time, negotiated with the Monster and worked out a compromise: "the monster would regurgitate all of Broome Hall, with the exception of the vending machines. These would be returned, one at a time, in exchange for each Vestal Virgin thrown into the lake. It was also agreed that no academic penalties would be suffered by students who missed any classes because the monster swallowed them" (Fleishman 1976).

"Monster Takeover" is an inspired parody of political activism with a tinge of wish-fulfillment. Who would not like to get everything that could be desired by swallowing a hall in one fell gulp? The Monster's quick adaptation to a volatile political situation proves its protean shape as a vehicle of student folklore.

DECLINE AND FALL

By the early 1980s, the Lake Lieberman Monster was beginning to lose its appeal. Writing anonymously, a student boasted, "I have never been sacrificed to the monster and I will go so far as to say that my skin has not even made contact with the waters of Lake Lieberman." However, that same student suggested, "IF there is a monster in Loch Ness, which I happen to know there is, then there is no law that says we can't have one too" (1982). Students of the early 1980s were no longer immersed in the sexual revolution and political upheaval of the previous decade. The idea of sacrificing virgins to a monster no longer had the same appeal; the Lake Lieberman Monster was such a familiar figure that the excitement of lakeside ceremonies was beginning to fade.

Another reason for the Monster's downfall was the raising of the drinking age from eighteen to twenty-one in 1986. This new law took its toll on Newing's rituals, which now had to be alcohol-free. In the spring of 1986, Newing staff members planned a treasure hunt to replace the revelry of Newing Navy ("Newing Treasure Hunt" 1986). Although students declared the treasure hunt a success, something important had been lost: the wild, outrageous party during which person after person would be thrown into the lake. Although participants in Newing Navy still made floats resembling monsters, the intensity of the spring ritual had diminished.

Contributing to the Monster's decline was the fact that Lake Lieberman itself was starting to deteriorate. Students built fires in the overflow pipe in winter, clogging up the system and making the water level recede. New construction of nearby residence halls and a parking lot added contaminants to the lake, which, Augie Mueller said, had become a dirty and unsafe body of water (2000). Administrators drew up plans to fill in Lake Lieberman and turn it into a park or a playing field, but nothing came of the plans. At the end of the 1990s, while not a site for student activities, Lake Lieberman was still recognized as a campus landmark. Newing secretary Judy Libous spoke nostalgically of the days when students skated across Lake Lieberman and played tug-of-war, stretching ropes from one side of the lake to the other (1999). But when I asked Newing students what they knew about the Lake Lieberman Monster, most of them asked "What monster?"

RETURN

In the spring of 2000, Binghamton University celebrated its fiftieth anniversary. As a member of the Fiftieth Anniversary Planning Committee, I decided to invite Elliot Lieberman to attend the festivities. After all, his naming of the lake had spawned a series of legends and rituals that had lasted more than twenty years. Kindly agreeing to attend the celebration, Elliot joined Newing staff members and me for an early-afternoon commemoration of the lake's naming. Standing on the shore of Lake Lieberman, slapping mosquitoes, we watched as three of my students dramatized the Monster's initiatory antics. Janet, dressed as a High Priestess, performed a blessing while Jodi, wearing a fearsome swamp monster costume borrowed from the Theater Department, dragged Stacy, a reluctant victim, to the edge of the lake. Because of the algae and suspected pollution, the Monster did not throw Stacy into the lake's fetid waters. Newing students walking by, on their way to a late brunch, smiled and shrugged their shoulders. What archaic ritual was this? It probably did not seem any stranger than other elements of college life to which they had already adjusted.

When the short play was over, Elliot read a poem that he had written for the occasion:

Old crusty lake,
For your sake
We, this solemn promise make:

Standing here upon your shore,
Like all those who came before,

Figure 10.1. Binghamton University alumnus Elliot Lieberman, namesake of Lake Lieberman, hails the legendary Lake Lieberman monster during Homecoming 2000 festivities. (Photograph by Evangelos Dousmanis and courtesy of Binghamton University.)

Fearsome Lieby at our side,
Breathing fire, commanding pride,
We will never fear life's blasts.
Your great waters raise our masts.

Having seen the morning sun
Glisten upon your watery scum,
We know life's not always pretty.
Like your shore it's rough and gritty.
Mosquitoes bite and flies abound,
The smell of sewage all around.

Yours is not a noble splendor,
Abandoned bikes with rusted fenders,
But your soulful calm inspires
To push ahead with Lieby's fire.
For we are your faithful band,
Fighting crud where e'er we can,
Children of Lake Lieberman. (2000b)

I should have guessed that Elliot, progenitor of the lake's legends and ritu-als, was an English major. His spirited poem brought back memories of the Monster's various incarnations: deflowerer of virgins, environmental advocate, political activist, and daredevil. Since Elliot is a researcher for the Environmental Protection Agency, it was only fitting that he emphasized "fighting crud" above all else. His poem will be cherished by the guardians of Binghamton University history.

The ferocious and fun-loving Lake Lieberman Monster epitomizes stu-dent spirit in a college community where wildness is valued highly. In 1987, Newing alumnus Keith Weingold recalled that Newing was "the wild place" (1987); his fellow alumnus W. B. Gerard said that Newing was "full of life, with a spirit all its own" (1987). Often the words "zoo" and "animal" would come up in descriptions of Newing. So would the term "summer camp," which showed how much the lake affected Newing's way of life (Gerard 1987; Weingold 1987). Most students liked their community's raucousness in the mid-1980s, and many of them continue to enjoy it now. The peren-nial popularity of the film *Animal House* (1978) seems to indicate that col-lege wildness is here to stay, no matter which incarnations of student spirit rise and fall.

As I finish this piece of writing, the British Broadcasting Corporation is announcing that there is no Loch Ness Monster: six hundred sonar beams have "found no trace of the legendary monster in Scotland's famous loch" ("BBC Debunks" 2003). Those of us who love Nessie will not let this edict bother us; her traditions remain strong. At Binghamton University, no one is undertaking a sonar scan of Lake Lieberman to see if its Monster truly exists; the Monster belongs to campus history. But its essence—a celebra-tion of wildness, wit, and irreverence—lives on.

ACKNOWLEDGMENTS

I would like to dedicate this article to W.F.H. Nicolaisen, my colleague and friend, and to Elliot Lieberman, who gave Lake Lieberman its name in 1963. My thanks go to both of them for providing valuable information for this article. I would also like to thank John McDowell, Birgit Nicolaisen, Augie Mueller, and Judy Libous for their kind assistance.

REFERENCES

Anderson, Kenneth. 1971. Sorry, Charlie! *The Lake Lieberman Gazette* 3 (March 11).
Animal House. 1978. dir. John Landis. Its sequel, *The Yearbook: An 'Animal House' Reunion* (1998) was directed by J. M. Kenny.

BBC Debunks Loch Ness Monster Myth. 2003. http://www.washtimes.com/upi-breaking /2003027-06262 1 8217r.htm. Accessed 29 July.

Bronner, Simon. 1995. *Piled Higher and Deeper: The Folklore of Student Life*. Little Rock: August House.

Costello, Peter. 1975. *In Search of Lake Monsters*. St. Albans: Granada Publishing Limited. Another good source of information on this subject is http://www.strangemag .com/nessie.home.html.

Dorson, Richard M. 1949. The Folklore of Colleges. *American Mercury* 68:671–677.

Fleishman, Lauren. 1976. Monster Takeover. *The Lake Lieberman Gazette* 8:24 (April 1).

Gerard, W. B. 1987. Through the Glass, Dimly. *The Lake Lieberman Gazette* 20:1 (August).

Goodnis Takes a Flying Leap!!!!! 1974. *The Lake Lieberman Gazette* 7:7 (October 10).

Halperin, Mark. 1987. Fall '69–Spring '70. *The Lake Lieberman Gazette* 20:1 (August).

Halperin, Mark and Jeannette DeLisa. 1970. The Legends of the Lake. *The Lake Lieberman Gazette* 2:9 (April 23).

Johnson, Darragh. 2001. Like Other Mascots, Terrapin Has Become a Tough Guy. http:// www.dodgeglobe.com/stories/033002/spo-mascots.shtml. Accessed 30 July.

Kalter, Al. 1987. Fall '71–Spring '72. *The Lake Lieberman Gazette* 20:1 (August).

Lake Lieberman Monster. 1982. *The Lake Lieberman Gazette* 15 (September 9).

Landi, Susan. 1978. Collection Project on the Folklore of College Campuses. Unpublished student paper, Binghamton University.

Leary, James. 1978. The Notre Dame Man: Christian Athlete or Dirtball? *Journal of the Folklore Institute* 15:133–145.

Letters to the Monster. 1971. *The Lake Lieberman Gazette* 3:15 (March 11).

Libous, Judy. 1999. Personal interview. December 16.

Lieberman, Elliot. 2000a. E-mail communication. February 29.

Lieberman, Elliot. 2000b. E-mail communication. May 7.

Loevy, Robert D. 1999. *Colorado College: A Place of Learning 1874–1999*. Colorado Springs: Colorado College.

Lonky, Larry. 1978. Folklore at SUNY-B: Three Examples. Unpublished student paper, Binghamton University.

Mueller, August. 2000. E-mail communication. January 12.

Newall, Venetia. 1971. *An Egg at Easter*. Bloomington: Indiana University Press.

Newing Treasure Hunt Arrives! 1986. *The Lake Lieberman Gazette* 19:9 (January 30).

Nicolaisen, Birgit. 2003. E-mail communication. June 17.

Nicolaisen, W.F.H. 2003. E-mail communication. July 29.

Ritual Appearance: White Witch Casts a Spell on Loch Ness. 2003. *The Scotsman* (June 14).

Shenandoah University Student Conduct Policies. 2003. http://www.su.edu/studaffs/hb4 .asp. Accessed 28 July.

Weingold, Keith. 1987. Spring '83. *The Lake Lieberman Gazette* 20:1 (August).

EDITOR'S SUGGESTIONS FOR FURTHER READING

Blank, Trevor J., and David J. Puglia. 2014. "Terrapin Tales: The University of Maryland's Campus Legends" and "Strange Bedfellows: The College Park Cuddler." In *Maryland Legends: Folklore from the Old Line State*, 67–82, 117–22. Charleston, SC: History Press.

Bronner, Simon. 1995. "Legends." In *Piled Higher and Deeper: The Folklore of Student Life*. Little Rock: August House.

Bronner, Simon J. 2012. "Legendary Locations, Laughs, and Horrors." In *Campus Traditions: Folklore from the Old-Time College to the Modern Mega-University*, 277–342. Jackson: University Press of Mississippi.

Thomas, Jeannie B. 1991. "Pain, Pleasure, and the Spectral: The Barfing Ghost of Buford Hall." *Folklore Forum* 24 (1–2): 27–38.

Tucker, Elizabeth. 2005. *Campus Legends: A Handbook.* Santa Barbara, CA: Greenwood.

Tucker, Elizabeth. 2007. *Haunted Halls: Ghostlore of American College Campuses.* Jackson: University Press of Mississippi.

11

A Nessie in Mormon Country
The Bear Lake Monster

Alan L. Morrell

PREFACE

In his account of the Bear Lake Monster, Alan Morrell, curator of Mormon history for the Church of Jesus Christ of Latter-day Saints, digs through his church's archives to unearth numerous Mormon reports of a lacustrine cryptid inhabiting the Idaho-Utah border, often corroborating these supposed sightings via reference to native belief in a monster living in the lake. While local tribes did host a menagerie of legendary and mythic creatures distinct from their European counterparts, in most cases, ascribing North American legends indigenous origin stories is a legend-telling legitimization tactic rather than an accurate representation of native lore.

Morrell shows that as early as 1868 the Bear Lake Monster legend spread through a combination of newspaper and oral reporting. In this case, the credibility factor was high. Reports came by way of the church-owned *Deseret Evening News*, Utah's oldest daily newspaper, which to this day has the second-highest circulation in the state. Unlike many monster legends, these accounts were not attributed to a friend of a friend (or FOAF) but rather to abundant firsthand reports. Multiple reputable parties testified to seeing a strange monster lurking in the lake, and one purported witness, Joseph Rich, was the son of a member of the Quorum of Twelve Apostles, the governing body of the church. A Church investigation concluded that the accounts were genuine, and later, a traveling contingent of apostles provided additional confirmation when it sighted something large and strange in the lake. Even Brigham Young, it seems, took an interest in the Bear Lake Monster. There was reason to believe a remarkable creature really did haunt the lake—that is, until the monster was exposed as a P. T. Barnum-esque

https://doi.org/10.7330/9781646421602.c011

hoax, an early example of pseudo-ostension, where a perpetrator uses a legend to fuel a ruse.

Morrell assigns the legend's life and appeal not to a Mormon proclivity for the supernatural but to the context of its historical era. British colonialism, imperialism, and exploration provided one explanation for why Americans were primed to believe in the existence of legendary creatures. The "kernel of truth" lay in the regular discovery and report of new monstrous creatures across the globe. Explorers continued to discover never-before-seen creatures abroad, including the Australian kangaroo and the African gorilla. New scientific discoveries and new technology stoked the public's anxiety about progress, resulting in monster legends that tested the boundaries and possibilities of the "known" world. P. T. Barnum, perhaps as much as anyone, bears responsibility for conflating legend and new scientific discoveries, displaying both rare specimens and rarified humbug. In the case of the Bear Lake Monster, Joseph Rich was Utah's Mormon answer to Barnum.

ESSAY

In the August 3, 1868, edition of the *Deseret Evening News*, the Bear Lake Valley correspondent Joseph C. Rich noted:

> All lakes, caves and dens have their legendary histories. Tradition loves to throw her magic wand over beautiful dells and lakes and people them with fairies, giants and monsters of various kinds. Bear Lake has also its monster tale to tell, and when I have told it, I will leave you to judge whether or not its merits are merely traditionary.

The twenty-seven-year-old son of Mormon apostle Charles C. Rich further explained that the local Indians believed in a "monster animal" that had been known to capture and carry away individuals who swam in the lake. Although the Indians had not seen the monster in several years, they described it as being serpentine with legs about eighteen inches long, which allowed it to crawl short distances on the shore.[1]

In the five years since the Mormons had settled the valley, several persons had reported seeing a "huge animal of some kind that they could not describe." Since the observers had no corroborating witnesses, the reports were easily dismissed. Three weeks before Rich's article, S. M. Johnson of South Eden was riding near the lake when he saw what he thought was a drowned person. As he got closer, he realized the body was in fact an animal, which raised its head two or three feet out of the water. Because it did not drift onto shore with the waves, he concluded that its large body must have rested on the lake floor.

The next day, a man and three women saw a large animal of the "monster kind" swimming "faster than a horse could run on land." These two independent reports revived the monster question, and several who had earlier seen the purported leviathan once again brought forward their claims. A short time later, N. C. Davis and Allen Davis of St. Charles, Idaho, and Thomas Slight, J. Collins, and six women of Paris, Idaho, saw the creature. Slight said that he distinctly saw its sides and supposed it was not less than ninety feet in length. N. C. Davis could not be certain of its length but said that it traveled faster than any locomotive that he had ever seen. Judging by the waves and wake that it created, he estimated it was of a significant size. This final sighting also confirmed that there was more than one mysterious beast in the lake. According to the witnesses, six smaller creatures, each about the size of a horse, followed in the wake of the larger.

Joseph Rich explained to the readers of the *Deseret Evening News* that Davis and Slight were "prominent men, well known in this country, and all of them are reliable persons whose veracity is undoubted. I have no doubt they would be willing to make affidavits to their statement." He concluded by stating,

> There you have the monster story so far as completed, but I hope it will be concluded by the capture of one sometime . . . Is it fish, flesh or serpent, amphibious and fabulous or a great big fish, or what is it? Give it up but have hopes of someday seeing it, if it really exists, and I have no reason to doubt the above statements.

Rich's well-placed father added a postscript to the article, stating, "I have talked with some of the parties in relation to the monster story, and it is as Joseph has stated." The senior Rich's apostolic stamp of approval no doubt carried great weight in the Latter-day Saint community.[2]

The article was very convincing. Joseph Rich did not claim to have seen the monsters but was simply reporting the stories as they had been told to him. Furthermore, the testimonies were from several highly respected individuals in the community. Although Apostle Rich had not confirmed the existence of the creature, he had nonetheless verified that the reporting itself was accurate. To the casual reader, it would seem probable that some unusual phenomena were occurring in Bear Lake.

The article created quite the stir in Salt Lake City. Three days after Rich's report, an editor for the *Deseret Evening News* wrote:

> EXCITED—Various and sundry parties . . . are manifesting a degree of
> excitement, altogether unwarranted under the circumstances, concerning
> the description of the Bear Lake Monster by our esteemed friend, J. C. R.
> and endorsed by Pres. C. C. Rich . . . We sustain the tangibility and reality
> of those mysterious denizens of Bear Lake.[3]

Enthusiasm for the sightings was growing and now begged the judgment of
the Latter-day Saint leadership.

At a regional church gathering (a "stake" conference) in Logan a couple
of weeks after the initial report, several leaders from Salt Lake City spoke
firsthand with residents of Bear Lake. They reported that they had "had
conversation with brother Charles C. Rich and other brethren from Bear
Lake Valley, respecting the monsters which have been seen in the lake" and
that they all believed the account as published. They considered the testimony that had been given "by so many individuals, who have seen these
creatures in so many places and under a variety of circumstances, indisput-
able."[4] The reporter concluded:

> Our readers who are familiar with the accounts we have published of these
> creatures, can form their own conclusion respecting them. The accounts
> are fishy, decidedly so; but we cannot dispute the persons who make them.
> Some of the persons who have seen them we know, and their truthful-
> ness is unquestionable. We must believe they saw something remarkable,
> whether monsters or not we hope time will soon decide.[5]

Taking exception to the dubious characterization of the monster, Rich
penned a defensive letter to the *Deseret Evening News* stating that

> I noticed with feelings of profound regret that there existed in Utah
> certain persons disposed to doubt the veracity of the published account
> regarding the monsters of Bear Lake. I supposed the mere fact of the
> appearance of my initials to any communication or statement, however
> incredible apparently, would have rendered its authenticity indisputable.

He further explained that he felt bad for the unfortunate person who might
come up to Bear Lake and be "gobbled up by the 'Water Devil'" while
out for a swim. This correspondence included even more sightings of the
monster and several plans of how the local residents were going to catch
one of them.[6]

Over the next three years, several articles dealing with the Bear Lake
Monster, and other monsters, appeared in local papers. A few of the highlights from those years include the sighting of serpentlike monsters in Utah

Lake described as having a head shaped like a large greyhound, with the "wickedest black eyes" that the witness had ever seen.[7] One writer noted that based on witness testimony, he was certain that the monsters were nothing more than members of the seal family who had been trapped in Bear Lake when the waterways that had once connected it to the ocean receded.[8] In July of 1871, the *Salt Lake Herald* cited the *Corinne Journal* in announcing that one of the monsters had been captured. It was reported to have been about twenty feet in length and to have possessed "a mouth sufficiently large to swallow a man without any difficulty."[9] Sightings of monsters in the confluences of the Bear and Weber rivers and in the Great Salt Lake led several locals to wonder if some great underground channel connected those waters to Bear Lake. The *Daily Corinne Reporter* claimed that Brigham Young actively preached this channel theory, although some critics of the Mormon "prophet" wondered if he had concocted the whole affair so he could steal cattle and blame the monsters for their disappearances.[10]

While Young's teachings about subterranean waterways cannot be confirmed, there is evidence that he had a personal interest in the Bear Lake Monster. In the summer of 1869, the *New York Times* reported an interview with Brigham Young Jr. in which he stated that his father was going to investigate the claims to determine whether the story was "an honest tale of a serpent, or only a fish story."[11] Supporting this claim is a letter to the *Deseret Evening News* from Brigham Young and his traveling party, which mentioned that they stopped at Bear Lake to see if they could spot the elusive creature.[12] In his personal correspondence with church leader David P. Kimball of Paris, Idaho, Young mentioned sending a large rope to the local community to aid in capturing the monster.[13] The anti-Mormon newspaper *Daily Corinne Reporter* also noted that Brigham Young mentioned the existence of the monsters in his sermons.[14]

Perhaps even more interesting was the apparent sighting of the monster by church apostles John Taylor, George Q. Cannon, Wilford Woodruff, Lorenzo Snow, Franklin D. Richards, John H. Smith, and Joseph F. Smith. They reported in the *Deseret Evening News* that "while on the way from Fish Haven, a number of the party saw what they supposed was the celebrated Bear Lake monster. It was described as a large undulating body, with about 30 feet of exposed surface, of a light cream color, moving swiftly through the water, at a distance of three miles from the point of observation." While never declaring the watery beast to be legitimate, church leaders nonetheless seemed as fascinated with the monster as the general membership.[15]

In spite of initial interest, enthusiasm for the Bear Lake Monster eventually declined. The lack of new sightings and the subsequent silence of

Mormon authorities on the topic helped the phenomenon fade from public memory. Unlike many supernatural mysteries, however, the Bear Lake Monster has an explanation. Twenty-six years following his provocative allegations, Joseph Rich finally admitted that it had all been a "wonderful first class lie."[16] A closer look at Joseph Rich's life demonstrates that he was, in fact, a prankster at heart. Even at his funeral, his close friend and apparent co-conspirator, Thomas Slight, stated that Rich would be well remembered for his joking.[17]

Perhaps Rich's greatest lark was his "prophesying hen." Joseph Rich was a leading merchant in the Bear Lake Valley and owned the area's first store. Among the local products that he sold were the unusually large brown eggs of Mrs. Clifton's Plymouth Rock hen. One day, mysterious messages began appearing on the shells. A consummate showman, Rich drew large crowds to the store where he dipped the eggs in a special solution to reveal their otherworldly messages. Scriptures, philosophy, and personal advice all materialized for the local Saints. Eventually, prophecies of future events started to appear, generating a great deal of excitement in the community. Perhaps tiring of his son's mischief, Apostle Charles C. Rich declared at a public gathering that when the Lord wanted something revealed he would do it by way of proper authority and not through the hind end of a chicken. Soon after, Joseph Rich put away his invisible ink.[18]

In spite of Rich's hoax, Mormon belief in the Bear Lake Monster opens a window on a world where the nascent sciences vied for supremacy with less critical views of the universe. It was a world where new wonders and ideas appeared alongside frauds, hoaxes, and humbugs. It was a world that was, perhaps, best symbolized by the lifework of Brigham Young's contemporary, P. T. Barnum.

One of the reasons for the wild success of Barnum's notorious American Museum in New York City was the blossoming popularity of natural history in the Victorian world. People of all classes were busy collecting specimens, attending museums, and reading the latest travel adventures of daring explorers. As one observer pointed out,

> by the middle of the century there was hardly a middle-class drawing room
> in the country [in this case, England] that did not contain an aquarium, a
> fern-case, a butterfly cabinet, a seaweed album, a shell collection, or some
> other evidence of a taste for natural history, and at the same time it was
> impossible to visit the seaside without tripping over parties of earnest
> ladies and gentlemen, armed with a book by Mr. Gosse and a collection of
> jam jars.[19]

British imperialism brought with it "discoveries" from the newly conquered lands. In 1770, a British sea captain noticed an animal off the northeastern coast of Australia that was "as large as a grey hound, of a mouse color, and very swift." It was later observed that it had a long tail and jumped like a hare or a deer. One of the crew finally shot one of these curious animals, and upon examination, it was determined that they had never seen an animal quite like it.[20] Throughout the nineteenth century, several "new" animals joined the kangaroo. In 1861, just seven years before Joseph Rich wrote about the Bear Lake Monster, explorers discovered an animal whose existence had been long rumored but never substantiated—the gorilla.[21] Other discoveries in the natural world continued throughout the century.

Barnum's museum exhibited numerous animals from abroad, including lions, tigers, ostriches, elephants, rhinos, giraffes, and the first hippopotamus seen in America. In 1857, he inaugurated the "Ocean and River Gardens" at the museum, in which aquariums displayed a collection of exotic fishes, sharks, porpoises, sea lions, and a beluga whale.[22] Yet Barnum is not generally remembered for his zoological collections, but for his humbugs. Alongside the odd but authentic, Barnum displayed his gaffes, such as the Feejee Mermaid, unicorns, frogs with human hands, phoenixes, and other curiosities.[23] But what was genuine and what was counterfeit in the American Museum? The bearded woman, rumored to be nothing more than a man dressed in women's clothing (a rumor started by Barnum himself), turned out to be legitimate.[24] Despite having staged numerous hoaxes and written a book about humbugs, Barnum was convinced by the countless reports and legends of sea monsters from various locations across the globe that they must exist. In a rare moment of candor, he offered $20,000 for an authentic specimen.[25]

In many ways, Barnum's American Museum served as a microcosm for the Victorian world. It was an age of discovery, not only in the natural world, but in all areas of knowledge. The professionalization of the sciences, including zoology, paleontology, and anthropology, was just beginning.[26] At the same time, technological advances created a world almost beyond belief. Just a year before the arrival of the Bear Lake Monster, the *Deseret Evening News* carried an article that stated, "But if this is an age of humbug, it is also an age of wonders." The reporter then described his visit to the Western Union Telegraph Company headquarters in New York City where news from around the world arrived within seconds.[27]

Latter-day Saints and other Americans were a part of this wider world of discovery. A week after the report of the Bear Lake Monster, the *Deseret Evening News* carried an article about a giant snake caught in Tennessee that had terrorized a community for years. When finally caught, it measured almost thirty feet long, thirty inches around, and had a mouth twenty-six inches across "armed with a most formidable set of teeth and four large tusks."[28] If Tennessee could reportedly discover such a land animal, why couldn't the newly settled area of Bear Lake produce an even larger and more terrible sea animal? Dinosaur bones being pulled from the earth at an ever-increasing pace also suggested that giant animals fitting the description of the lake monsters once existed.[29]

Similar to other facets of the supernatural world, monsters were something Latter-day Saints were prone to believe in. Rather than making the Mormons unusual, such views made them typical of their time. Although other aspects of supernatural folklore crept into the beliefs and doctrines of early Latter-day Saints, the Bear Lake Monster left barely a trace. Perhaps Mormons, like the visitors to Barnum's American Museum, were willing participants in a hoax that both thrilled and enriched the mysterious and unpredictable world around them.

NOTES

1. "Correspondence: Monsters of Bear Lake," *Deseret Evening News*, August 3, 1868. For additional context on Bear Lake Monster lore, see Bonnie Thompson, *Folklore in the Bear Lake Valley* (Salt Lake City: Granite Publishing, 1972), chap. 2.

2. Ibid.

3. "Local and Other Matters," *Desert Evening News*, August 6, 1868.

4. *The Latter-day Saint Millennial Star*, October 10, 1868, 642.

5. Ibid.

6. "Correspondence," *Deseret Evening News*, September 25, 1868.

7. "Brigham Young's Trip North," *Deseret Evening News*, August 27, 1868.

8. "Bear Lake Monsters," *Deseret Evening News*, March 29, 1870.

9. "Monster Captured," *Salt Lake Herald*, July 9, 1871.

10. *Daily Corinne Reporter*, May 20, 1871.

11. "The Mormons," *New York Times*, August 31, 1869.

12. "Editorial Correspondence," *Deseret Evening News*, June 23, 1869.

13. Brigham Young to David P. Kimball, February 23, 1871, Brigham Young Office Files, Church History Library.

14. *Daily Corinne Reporter*, May 20, 1871.

15. "President Taylor's Tour," *Deseret Evening News*, August 17, 1881.

16. "Joseph C. Rich Addresses the People of Bear Lake Valley," Joseph Coulson Rich Collection, Church History Library, The Church of Jesus.

17. "Funeral Services Held Over the Remains of the Hon. Joseph C. Rich in the Stake Tabernacle at Paris, on Wednesday Afternoon, October 21, 1908," Joseph Coulson Rich Collection, Church History Library.

18. Leonard Arrington, *Charles C. Rich: Mormon General and Western Frontiersman* (Provo, UT: Brigham Young University Press, 1974), 314.

19. Lynn Barber, *The Heyday of Natural History, 1820–1870* (London: Cape, 1980), 13.

20. Harriet Ritvo, *The Platypus and the Mermaid, and Other Figments of the Classifying Imagination* (Cambridge, MA: Harvard University Press, 1997), 1–2.

21. Barber, *Heyday of Natural History*, 67.

22. A. H. Saxon, *P. T. Barnum: The Legend and the Man* (New York: Columbia University Press, 1989), 90–95.

23. Ibid., 97, 119.

24. Andrea Stulman Dennett, *Weird and Wonderful: The Dime Museum in America* (New York: New York University Press, 1997), 28.

25. Saxon, *P. T. Barnum*, 96.

26. See James Edward McClellan and Harold Dorn, *Science and Technology in World History: An Introduction* (Baltimore, MD: Johns Hopkins University Press, 2006); Peter Whitfield, *Landmarks in Western Science from Prehistory to the Atomic Age* (New York: Routledge, 1999); and Paul Bahn, *Archaeology: A Very Short Introduction* (New York: Oxford University Press, 1996).

27. "The Cable: An Age of Wonders," *Deseret News Semi-Weekly*, January 15, 1867.

28. "A Snake Story," *Deseret Evening News*, August 10, 1868.

29. See Mark Jaffe, *The Gilded Dinosaur: The Fossil War Between E. D. Cope and O. C. Marsh and the Rise of American Science* (New York: Crown, 2000).

EDITOR'S SUGGESTIONS FOR FURTHER READING

Bassett, Fletcher S. 1885. *Legends and Superstitions of the Sea and of Sailors in All Lands and at All Times*. Chicago and New York: Belford, Clarke, and Co.

Beck, Horace Charleton. 1973. *Folklore and the Sea*. Middletown, CT: Wesleyan University Press.

Costello, Peter. 1975. *In Search of Lake Monsters*. St. Albans, UK: Granada.

Douglass, Harry S. 1956. "The Legend of the Serpent." *New York Folklore Quarterly* 12 (1): 37–42.

Fife, Austin E. 1948. "The Bear Lake Monsters." *Utah Humanities Review* 2:99–106.

Gatschet, Albert S. 1899. "Water-Monsters of American Aborigines." *Journal of American Folklore* 12 (47): 255–60.

Harris, William. 1977. "The White River Monster of Jackson County, Arkansas: A Historical Summary of Oral and Popular Growth and Change in a Legend." *Mid-South Folklore* 5: 3–23.

Hawley, Herbert J. 1946. "The Sea Serpent of Silver Lake." *New York Folklore Quarterly* 2: 191–96.

Kimiecik, Kathy. 1998. "The Strange Case of the Silver Lake Sea Serpent." *New York Folklore* 9 (2): 10–11.

Meurger, Michel, and Claude Gagnon. 1989. *Lake Monster Traditions: A Cross-Cultural Analysis*. London: Fortean Tomes.

Mitchell, Pat. 1989. "Of Sea Serpents and Sinkhole Sam." *Kanhistique* 15 (3): 2–3.

Radford, Benjamin, and Joe Nickell. 2006. *Lake Monster Mysteries: Investigating the World's Most Elusive Creatures*. Lexington: University Press of Kentucky.

Van Duzer, Chet A. *Sea Monsters on Medieval and Renaissance Maps*. London: British Library, 2013.

12

Getting Maryland's Goat
Diffusion and Canonization of Prince George's County's Goatman Legend

David J. Puglia

PREFACE

As in Angus Gillespie's Jersey Devil case study, folklorist David J. Puglia questions, and then investigates, how a cryptid, the Maryland Goatman, became the state's foremost hobgoblin. Working backwards, Puglia's research begins in his own era, when the Goatman has already established itself as unofficial state monster. Searching for origins, Puglia turns to yet another lovingly preserved folklore collection, the Maryland Folklore Archives, which offers a window into the early days of the Goatman legend, its diffusion, and its interplay with regional newspapers. Peering in, Puglia develops a Goatman legend microhistory.

Existing quietly for decades before galloping onto the statewide scene, the Goatman begins his rapid ascent when a journalist, hunting for a Halloween story, finds early Goatman legends preserved in the Maryland Folklore Archives. From there, the Goatman is revived by regional reporting, reinvigorated by frenzied teenage legend-trippers, returned to the folklore archive by a new generation of folklore students, and requisitioned by the worlds of television, film, and print.

To explain the idiosyncrasies of the Goatman legend, Puglia uses Richard M. Dorson's concept of the "popular legend," distinguishing a type of legend that is not only oral or only literary, but relies on a dynamic relationship between the two. Much like the Jersey Devil, the Goatman's name (and what can be deduced from it) seems to outpace active bearers of his legend; much like Char-Man, the Goatman diffuses to three separate Maryland towns, always along some desolate wooded backstretch of road, in ecotype form, localizing to each new setting. Puglia's research demonstrates

https://doi.org/10.7330/9781646421602.c012

the direct relationship between monster legends and newspapers and shows how the collection and preservation of legend texts can perpetuate the spread of monster legends, calling into question the ostensibly neutral role of legend collectors. Folklorists' products, from books to interviews to folklore archives, are part and parcel of the monster legend process.

ESSAY

Similar to Maryland's State Flower, the black-eyed Susan, its State Bird, the Baltimore oriole, and its State Crustacean, the blue crab, the Goatman has achieved the unofficial status of Maryland's state monster.[1] He stars in magazines, television shows, comic books, movies, haunted houses, and *Wikipedia*. On the other hand, few know the Goatman legend in any detail. Did Maryland's most famous monster have a life as a folk legend prior to his encapsulation as a "legend" in popular culture? Does the Goatman have a definitive starting point? Did he ever live primarily in oral tradition? How did the legend spread across Prince George's County, and later across Maryland?[2]

I attempt to answer these questions by tracing the legend diachronically, from folk legend to popular legend to Maryland popular culture. Although contemporary legend is often international in scope, the Goatman is an example of a local contemporary legend, focused primarily in Prince George's County, adjacent to Washington, D.C. The earliest formation of the Goatman legend is beyond scholarly reach, but a combination of folklore archives, newspaper articles, and reminiscences reveal the key moments in the legend, as the Goatman rears his horned head, trots across the county, and permanently lodges himself into Maryland popular culture.

In this essay, I perform a microstudy of the historical sources that brought this local legend to the forefront of the state's canon of legend materials. I argue that the Goatman legend is an example of Dorson's "popular legend"—one that is neither exclusively oral nor purely literary, but relies on the synergy between the two. The story begins in the small town of Clinton, Maryland, where University of Maryland college student George Lizama completed a fieldwork project for his Introduction to Folklore course. From there, journalist Karen Hosler reported Lizama's findings in the county newspaper, sparking ostension from a couple of local boys in Bowie, Maryland. The resulting news story created such fervor that Goatman legend-tripping became a mainstay of Prince George's County teenage life in the 1970s. While the folklore archive files show the original legend contents succumbing to the newspaper coverage almost immediately,

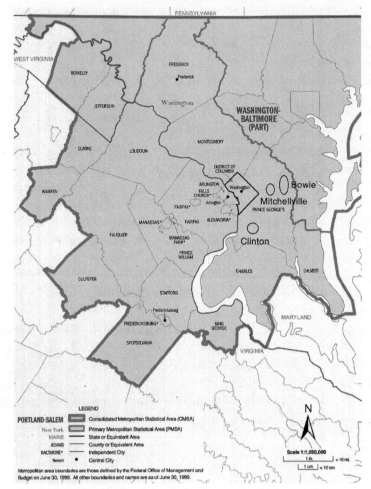

Figure 12.1. Adjacent to the nation's capital, Prince George's County, Maryland, is home to the three most common Goatman legend locations: Clinton, Bowie, and Mitchellville. (Map courtesy of U.S. Census Bureau. Annotation by David J. Puglia.)

the excitement alone entrenched Goatman in Maryland popular culture, even after specific details of Goatman's crimes faded from memory.

THE GOATMAN

According to legend, the murderous Goatman lurks in the woods of Prince George's County, emerging to prey on household pets and lusty teenagers. Depictions of Goatman vary from image to image, but there are some general consistencies. The Goatman walks upright like *homo erectus*, but has the head and the hooves of a goat. His face ranges from human with goat features to purely goat. He always sports a goat's beard and large, curving horns on his head. His torso is nearly human, but his legs are the crooked, hirsute legs of a goat. Often holding a weapon, usually a large axe,[3] his stance is aggressive, and his eyes are menacing. The Goatman is reminiscent of Pan of Hellenic lore (top human, bottom goat) or Baphomet of Christian lore (top goat, bottom human). Those unfamiliar with Goatman might assume they are looking at the western depiction of Satan.

This frightening creature may have had more benign origins. In 1971, Clinton, Maryland local Josiah Proctor told George Lizama that an old, black, self-sustaining hermit with a long white beard lived in a little hut near a bridge. The teenagers called him Goatman.

> Yes I've heard of the Goatman from time to time. You know that the road isn't very far from here. The legend is only partly a story some of it is true. There really is a Goatman of Tucker Road. He is an old man, an old black man with a real long white beard—like a goat. He's a hermit who lives by the bridge in a little shanty. He grows all his food and hunts for his meat and in order to do so must cross the narrow bridge from time to time. This is probably when everyone sees him and as they pass he smiles and then everyone in the car gets bent-out-of-shape and goes around screaming Goatman. I've gone down the road and never met up with him, but relatives have and they're all still alive. (Lizama 1971)

There are additional hints that that man or other itinerants served as the starting point for embellished Goatman legends. Student Frank Caherty titled his Introduction to Folklore research project "Goat-Men, Hermits, & Murderous Woodsmen: Strange Tales and Curious Happenings," but it ultimately had little to do with "goat-men" or "murderous woodsmen" (Caherty 1977). His research shows he was primarily interested in chronicling the large number of local hermits residing in the Prince George's County woods and periodically scaring children. The Prince George's County Police's Bowie District Commander Captain Lawrence Wheeler told *Washington Post* reporter Ivan G. Goldman he "had heard there really was an old man who used to live in a shack in the woods." "Kids would come around," says Captain Wheeler simply, "and once in a while he would come out and scare them" (Goldman 1971). Local Priest Father Joe Jenkins distinctly remembers indigent trappers roaming the surrounding Prince George's County woods with menacing tools of their trade during his childhood (Jenkins 1998). In fact, because they wore thick hide coats in the searing summer heat, children would sometimes refer to them as "Coatman," possibly leading to "Goatman."

Regardless of its origins, this small, unusual legend spread across the state and became a regional symbol of horror in Maryland. I will demonstrate that through a combination of pre-existing oral tradition, sensationalistic journalism, local ostension, and teenage legend-tripping, the Goatman cut his way to the forefront of Maryland's legend canon in less than a year.

George Lizama and "The Goatman of Tucker Road"

When twenty-one-year-old George Lizama turned in his Introduction to Folklore project on May 18, 1971, the University of Maryland upperclassman did not realize the effect his research would have on the future of Maryland's Goatman legend. The final product would be the catalyst to a series of events that would spread the Goatman legend across Prince George's County and into the canon of Maryland popular culture. Lizama had decided to investigate "The Goatman of Tucker Road." He collected eight Goatman legends for his project—seven of a single type. Eighteen-year-old Patricia Isidro's version was the "most common during [his] interviews" (Lizama 1971).

> Yes I've heard of the Goatman. Of course he died a long time ago. He was killed in a fire and burned to crisp [sic]. I'll tell you what I know. Tucker Road is a long tree laden road that is very very narrow. A lot of the kids go out there to park and I think that's how the legend got started. It seems there lived an old man who had the face of a goat and the body of a man. At the time of a full moon he would come out onto the bridge to ward off people, because it was his bridge. He always had a kind of wicked grin on his faced [sic] and called out like a real goat would. I've heard where cars have gone off the road because of the Goatman and that a few people a couple of years back were even killed and no trace of them was found.
>
> Kids say that he always carries bricks and that lots of cars have come off the bridge with busted windshields and the strangest thing is that not a sound was heard of bricks hitting glass or the shattering of glass. He only comes out at night and when the moon is bright. People say that he used to be a goat herder and that after all his goats died he almost turned into one. Some of my friends say they saw his eyes glowing at them at one time or another, but no one has really seen him. (Lizama 1971)

The seven legends that form this most common type share numerous typical motifs. Each includes most, although not necessarily all, of the following: (1) The Goatman is an old hermit with the head of a man and the body of a goat or the head of a goat and the body of a man (2) who lives in a shack near a one lane bridge on Tucker Road, a dark, narrow, treacherous road. (3) He was a goat herder in the past. (4) During one of the moon's liminal moments (e.g. full, eclipsed), (5) he stands at the bridge and (6) throws bricks or rocks at passing cars, (7) while bleating like a goat. (8) He has damaged passing cars and forced a few off of the bridge. (9) The Goatman may have been killed when children set fire to his shack. (10) The informant has never seen Goatman but knows others who have.

NEWSPAPERS AND LEGEND DIFFUSION

How does a small, quirky, local legend from a small, rural town spread across the county and eventually come to be known across the state? In this instance, while oral tradition was important, the newspaper was the vehicle of transmission from town to town. Folklorists have been studying the dynamism between legends and the newspaper for decades. Since the mid-twentieth century, folklorists like Linda Dégh and Richard Dorson have acknowledged the importance of newspapers in tracking the ebb and flow of legends. In 1973, Linda Dégh and Andrew Vázsonyi argued that "legend makes a part of its way—presumably the lesser—on foot and continues on the longer trail through the speedy modern vehicle" of the mass media (37). Conceding that the media were central to legend transmission did not diminish the importance or traditionality of legend, but instead allowed folklorists to engage with the implements of the modern world. Attempting to define the American folk legend, folklorist Richard Dorson found it necessary to "distinguish legends perpetuated through town histories, tourist brochures, local-color literature, Sunday supplements, and similar printed channels from spoken legends" (Dorson 1971:160). He coined the term "popular legend" to refer to legends that are neither exclusively oral nor purely literary, but rely on the synergy between the two. An excellent example of Dorson's popular legend, the Goatman existed in Prince George's County oral tradition prior to journalist Karen Hosler's newspaper coverage, detailed in the next section, but the legend spread rapidly and came to the forefront of the Maryland legend canon only after the media attention. Ever since, the interplay between oral tradition and media interest would be the legend's greatest strength.

Continuing this line of inquiry, Paul Smith encouraged legend scholars to consider all possible transmission channels. By looking only at oral channels, scholars constructed legend as a unique phenomenon disconnected from everyday life. In truth, Smith argued, legends are transmitted through any means available. Like Dégh, Smith agreed that, beyond oral tradition, "the major disseminators of contemporary legend are the news gathering agencies" and "possibly newspapers are the largest carriers of contemporary legends" (Smith 1992:42). In Prince George's County, the newspaper did not give life to the Goatman legend—that credit goes to the legend tellers on the ground—but it allowed the legend to flourish across the county and across the state in ways that it had not in oral tradition.

In a case study of legend and news coverage surrounding serial killer Ed Gein, Robert E. Mitchell suggested that most sensational events that enter into American legend can attribute part of their success to media enhancement of the legend process. Mitchell contends that journalists are "second to none when it comes to filling the information vacuum for a news-deprived public; and since circulation is the media's life blood, much gets published for no more weighty reason than it is presumed to be something the public wants to hear" (Mitchell 1979:6). Mitchell pushed Dégh's argument that the media carry legend further, arguing that the media are not only of central importance in legend transmission, but that "in selected instances the media can be seen as a prime factor in the shape of the legend itself" (Mitchell 1979:7). In Prince George's County, for example, Hosler's reporting spreads the Goatman legend to a broader segment of the county, but also sets the legend's structure and central motifs for future oral tradition.

The Goatman began in oral tradition as Dorson's "folk legend." But as Dégh pointed out legends were prone to do, the Goatman traveled his greatest distance on the back of the media. Far from trivializing the legend, this moment marked the pinnacle of the legend's importance. The Goatman became Dorson's "popular legend," and through the 1970s, the interplay of folk and popular sources gave the legend its strength. By acknowledging both the oral sources and the newspaper sources, as Smith has encouraged scholars to do, researchers can approach Goatman as locals approached the legend, rather than in a synthetic mode pleasing to purists. As Mitchell predicted, after the initial story, both Hosler and the public attempted to fill the "information vacuum" for Goatman news. Legend tellers and newspapers combined to transform the Goatman from an obscure local legend to an unofficial state creature.

KAREN HOSLER AND THE GOATMAN CRAZE

George Lizama's professor placed Lizama's Goatman collection in the Maryland Folklore Archives. It would have fallen into obscurity like many of its donations if it were not for an eager reporter searching for an eye-catching story. The *Prince George's County News'* Karen Hosler visited the Maryland Folklore Archives—at the time merely several filing cabinets in the University of Maryland's resident folklorists' office. By October 27, 1971, Hosler was ready to announce "University Archives Reveal: Boaman, Goatman, and Ghosts Still Haunt Area."[4] Although she does not use his name, Hosler is referring to Lizama's Goatman collection from Clinton, Maryland—the only one in the archive at this date. But instead of placing the legend on Tucker Road in Clinton, Maryland, Hosler reports the location as Fletchertown Road in the larger Bowie, Maryland, a half an hour's drive north.

> The woods around Fletchertown Road have other strange inhabitants, folklore records indicate. One is a Goatman, half-man, half-goat who supposedly once was a researcher at the Beltsville Agricultural Farm. The story goes that the man experimented on goats. One day he went insane and ran into the woods. He grew all his hair until it covered his body . . . other accounts say he lives in an old shack and beats upon parked cars with an axe.

A version of the Goatman legend likely circulated in Bowie at the time, and Hosler probably came into the archive with that version in mind. This small change—one word and twenty-three miles—would cause major excitement in Bowie, lead to ostension by Bowie residents, encourage legend-tripping among Bowie teens, and associate Goatman with the town for the rest of the century.

The first important event following Hosler's story was an act of ostension from three Bowie residents. On the night of Wednesday, November 3, 1971, sixteen-year-old Old Bowie residents April Edwards, John Hayden, and Willie Gheen heard strange noises in their rural backyard that abutted Goatman's purported woods. Hayden remembered seeing "an animal . . . six-foot, something like that, and hairy, like an animal . . . it was on two feet. I remember it made a high-pitched sound, like a squeal" (Opsasnick 2007:72). The following morning, Edwards found her ten-month-old puppy Ginger missing. Armed with baseball bats, Hayden and Gheen set out to investigate. Near the Penn Central railroad tracks, they found Ginger's severed head. Several yards away, they found the rest of her. Less than two weeks after her first story, Karen Hosler would report again. This time the headline read "Residents Fear Goatman Lives: Dog Found Decapitated in Old Bowie." Decades later, the *Washington City Paper* revealed that this was all a hoax, an act of ostension by Hayden and Gheen. ("The whole fuckin' thing was, the dog got hit by a train," John's older brother Raymond Hayden told a reporter in 1998, weary of decades of inquiry [Daly 1998]). But in 1971, Hayden and Gheen implicated the Goatman and his known modus operandi.

Regardless of the boys' motives, the hoax would not come to light for many years. Hosler's grisly report sent an electric wave of excitement through Bowie's teenage population over the next year, documented by the numerous Goatman collections that would soon join the Maryland Folklore Archives. The first was student Clay Schofield in 1972, who went searching for Goatman legends in Bowie just months after Hosler's second report. A sign that the media artificially moved the Goatman legend into Bowie, Schofield found plenty of teenagers who had "heard" of the Goatman (passive tradition carrier), but none who could perform the legend (active tradition carrier) (von Sydow 1999:143–44). The one local who could tell the legend performed a rendition of the ubiquitous contemporary legend "The Boyfriend's Death,"[5] but inserted a "half-man, half-goat" antagonist (Schofield 1972). The Goatman and "The Boyfriend's Death" continued to be a common conflation among legends tellers outside of Clinton, Maryland in the following decades.

In her first article, Hosler had characterized the Goatman legend as "an old one that periodically dies down, then revives." Although there is no reason to doubt Hosler's claim—it seems she already knew the Goatman legend before seeing Lizama's collection—the Goatman legend had not received anything beyond local attention prior to 1971. Maryland state folklorist George Carey was researching two books that included substantial sections on Maryland legends, *Maryland Folklore and Folklife* and *Maryland Folk Legends and Folk Songs*, immediately preceding these events (Carey 1970; 1971). Carey covers a wide range of Maryland legends, including Prince George's County legends, but never mentions the Goatman. This is despite George Carey working at the University of Maryland at the time, located in Prince George's County. Other early, prominent Maryland folklore collections, such as Madeleine Vinton Dahlgren's *South Mountain Magic: Tales of Old Maryland* (1882) and Annie West Whitney and Caroline Canfield Bullock's *Folk-Lore from Maryland* (1925), make no mention of the Goatman either. In comparison, the present-day status of the legend compelled *Weird Maryland* to dedicate two separate sections to the Goatman and include an illustrated rendition of him on the title page (Lake 2006). The Goatman could have existed throughout Prince George's County, but the seminal event for the Goatman legend in Prince George's County was Hosler's first two articles in the fall of 1971.

The Clinton, Maryland legend led to a county-wide newspaper article, and that article led to ostension in Bowie, Maryland. After an act of ostension triggered another newspaper article, teenage legend-tripping ensued en masse. The original legend may have been lost in the shuffle, but a new, vague one formed in its place. A part man, part goat lurked around Fletchertown Road, mutilating animals and maybe teenagers too. It was enough. One of these students remembers the era: "In our high school, we had a Goatman Squad, composed of lots of guys in our high school who were determined to catch him. They sent out literature telling people what he was like, what he liked to eat, and so forth" (Wilson 1990). Bowie resident and future Goatman researcher Mark Opsasnick reminisces that one had to "experience Goatman mania firsthand to fully comprehend the aura surrounding the creature and its stomping grounds" (Opsasnick 2007:69).

While the newspaper articles were the catalyst to the legend-tripping, they also became the subject of more newspaper articles. Two weeks after reporting Ginger's decapitation, Hosler penned a third article, this time condemning the "Pranksters and Thrill-Seekers: The Real Monsters of Fletchertown Road" (1971c). Now paved in empty beer cans, Fletchertown Road was playing nightly host to cavorting teenagers drinking, hunting Goatman, and infuriating property owners. Hosler detailed one particularly egregious occurrence where teenagers abandoned two cars and a truck in the middle of Fletchertown Road, blocking local residents from returning to their homes, while the teenagers pursued a suspected Goatman sighting into the woods.

Even if Karen Hosler was living to ostensibly regret the consequences of her articles, other reporters were eager to join the fervor. On the last day of November, Ivan G. Goldman penned an article for the *Washington Post* announcing "A Legendary Figure Haunts Remote Pr. George's Woods" (Goldman 1971). If the *Prince George's County News'* comparatively small circulation had been any sort of a detriment to the proliferation of Goatman's existence, this article knocked down all barriers. Even if the tone of his article left plenty of room for skepticism, Goldman introduced Goatman to a broad region.

The Goatman legend had followed a complex but decipherable route of diffusion. George Lizama collected Goatman legends from Clinton, Maryland for his folklore class. Karen Hosler, seeking a macabre "human"-interest news story for the Halloween season, examined Lizama's collection and reported the existence of Goatman, albeit in Bowie and conflated with her own preexisting knowledge of the legend. John Hayden and Willie Gheen read or heard Hosler's October 27, 1971 report, both of a "half-man, half-goat" and that

Goatman "once picked up a dog and carried it into the woods" and that "only half the dog was found." Ginger's decapitation provided supporting evidence for the Goatman legend, and the same journalist, Karen Hosler, covered that incident as well. The morbid excitement drove Bowie teens wild—so wild that the nearby *Washington Post* decided to pick up the story. Future Goatman legend tellers who claim they "saw it in the paper" speak the truth.

The Goatman of Lottsford Road

At the same time, seven miles south of Bowie, the Goatman legend appeared on Lottsford Road in Mitchellville, Maryland, completing the Goatman trinity of Tucker Road (Clinton, Maryland), Fletchertown Road (Bowie, Maryland), and Lottsford Road (Mitchellville, Maryland). Like Tucker Road and Fletchertown Road, Lottsford is a long, dark, narrow, rural road snaking through thick woods. The road was fertile ground for taking on the Goatman legend due to a rash of corpses—no less than four in the ten years previous, and fourteen more in the years to follow—dumped from bridges into streams (Meyer 1984). The *Washington Post*, for example, reported "Lottsford Road: Local Legend Says It's a Trail of Terror" not because of the Goatman, but because it has "a macabre reputation as a dumping ground for bodies" (Meyer 1984). Local resident Shirley Hutchinson complained that "finding dead bodies in the road and all" put a damper on the whole neighborhood (Meyer 1984).

Every violent city has its notorious dumping ground. Baltimore has Leakin Park, where a legend tells of an instructor lecturing police recruits practicing evidence retrieval that they are looking for a specific body, not just any body. New York has cement shoes and the East River. Las Vegas has shallow graves sprinkled throughout the surrounding desert. Washington, D.C., has Lottsford Road. Mount Rainier Police Chief Dennis Husk, who patrolled Lottsford Road when he was with the Prince George's County Police Department, remembers "every time [we]'d turn around, [we] were finding either a prostitute from the District or a dope dealer from downtown." Hosler's newspaper reports, the Goatman legend, and the area's violent reputation combined to make a fertile *terroir* [legend climate] for a Goatman variant.

While Mitchellville teenagers "parked" and partied on Lottsford Road before this, Goatman and the rash of murders made the trips more exciting. The "Hatchet Man" legend, the local term for "The Boyfriend's Death," was, as in Bowie, an established legend. After Hosler's sensational articles, in Mitchellville, the Goatman simply supplied the implicit antagonist. For example, seventeen-year-old Stephen L. White, after telling a typical variant of "The Boyfriend's Death," in which he never mentioned the Goatman, commented on the legend, "I personally have never come in contact with the Goatman. I don't believe in the Goatman" (Hoffman 1974). Similarly, seventeen-year-old Karen Snyder told "The Boyfriend's Death" as well, concluding that the couple had parked "down by Goatman's house" and therefore "her boyfriend was killed by the Goatman" (Hoffman 1974). As in Fletchertown Road, newspaper coverage increased the diffusion of the Goatman character while greatly diminishing the legend's narrative content. The newspapers created a great number of passive bearers and only a few active bearers of the Goatman legend.

LURKING IN THE MAINSTREAM

Although just a few short articles in a small newspaper, a decade later Hosler's stories continue to exert influence over the Goatman legend. For example, in Bowie circa 1983, police officer Thomas Lawler told of Goatman beheading a German Shepherd who had dared to bark at him. The Goatman sent a message by leaving the head "upright in the middle of the owner's backyard" (Lawler 1983). Twelve years later, the breed and the manner of death still correspond with the demise of April Edward's Ginger, but Goatman's presentation of the decapitated head embellished the legend, pushing Goatman beyond a typical violent beast toward something more intentional, more malevolent, and more sinister. By 1986, the Goatman legend began to leave active oral circulation. For example, in 1986, Ian McKeller attempted to collect Goatman legends, but could only find "The Boyfriend's Death" with a nominal relationship to Goatman. One of his informants even prefaced by saying he could not remember if they blamed this one on Goatman or not (McKeller 1986). Almost annual in the 1970s, and frequent in the 1980s, Goatman legend collection ended abruptly in 1990. The oral tradition, active and important but anemic in content since Hosler's second story, ceased in the 1990s. But Maryland's love affair with the Goatman was only beginning. While he began in folk culture, spurred on by newspapers, the Goatman would prove himself equally comfortable in popular culture.

As his life in oral tradition ended, Goatman leapt into print, film, television, and the Internet. Mark Opsasnick published the first investigation of Goatman in a 1994 issue of *Strange Magazine*. In 1997, Goatman made his television debut in The Discovery Channel's *Animal X* (Ambrose 1997). The *X-Files* comic book series starred Goatman (and two Goatwomen) as the tragic hero in "The Face of Extinction" (Rozum, Saviuk, and Magyar

1998). *Searching for Satan* on the British LIVINGtv featured the Goatman in 2007, with the twist that the Goatman may, in fact, be an incarnation of the devil. Goatman is the overriding theme of Goatman Hollow, an interactive haunted house in Maryland.

Goatman also inspired several independent films. *Jimmy Tupper vs. The Goatman of Bowie*, part coming-of-age comedy and part *The Blair Witch Project*, premiered at the AFI Silver Theater and Cultural Center in Silver Spring, Maryland in 2010. *The Blair Witch Project* (a pseudodocumentary set in Burkittsville, Maryland about a "Maryland legend" with no actual basis in oral tradition [Myrick and Sánchez 1999]) also inspired the 2012 *Return of the Goatman* (Parks 2012). Perhaps the pinnacle of Goatman's popular success came from his prominent placement in *Weird Maryland* (2006). Ignored by earlier folklorists, Goatman is now literally front and center, throwing livestock off of a bridge on the book's title page. Through the combined powers of a folklore archive, the local media, ostension, and legend-tripping, a little known local legend had spread across the state and become permanently entrenched in Maryland popular culture.

Conclusion

Little known in 1970, by late 1971, the legend of the Goatman had spread across Maryland. The success cannot be attributed to legend tellers or newspapers alone, but to a dynamic synergy between the two. Notably, the Maryland Folklore Archives played a role in the legend's proliferation. Amateur folklorists, in this case, not only captured the legend for future preservation, but also provided an opportunity for the legend to grow. Legend scholars should continue to evaluate and acknowledge their role not just as researchers but as instigators of contemporary legends.

While Goatman has gained stardom, folklorists may hesitate to validate the Goatman of the twenty-first century as legend. Rather, he is the offspring of a legend, of another Goatman who lived in oral tradition in 1971, before spreading through the assistance of newspaper coverage.

But to understand the diffusion of the Goatman legend, it is not enough to rely on the steady stream of newspaper articles sprinkled through local and regional papers. These only tell half of the Goatman story. While the era has passed and memories have faded, a combination of newspaper reports and folklore archives provides the most complete window into the era, revealing the interplay of the journalists on the one hand and the oral tradition, the ostension, and the legend intertwined with everyday life on the other. The Goatman rises from the Washington, D.C., hinterlands to reach statewide notoriety through dedicated media coverage and earnest public involvement. Together, the two made Goatman Maryland's unofficial state creature.

NOTES

1. A version of this paper was presented at the International Society for Contemporary Legend Research's 29th annual meeting in May 2011. A shorter version meant for the general public forms one chapter in the book *Maryland Legends: Folklore from the Old Line State*. I want to thank Simon J. Bronner and Trevor J. Blank for comments on early drafts of this paper; Libby Tucker, Diane Goldstein, Yvonne Milspaw, and Gail de Vos for helpful comments at the conference; Ian Brodie for assistance during the peer review process; and two anonymous peer reviewers for pushing me to craft a better essay.

2. There are several Goatmans across the country, but these are not cognates to Maryland's Goatman. Some are cryptids, but the best known is an itinerant preacher who traveled the Upland South evangelizing, his cart pulled by goats.

3. The axe is probably due to conflation with another local legend known as the Bunnyman. More often associated with Virginia, the Bunnyman is also known in Maryland and Washington, D.C.

4. My thanks goes to Mark Opsasnick for calling my attention to Karen Hosler's *Prince George's County News* articles, which helped me greatly in making sense of what I was finding in the Maryland Folklore Archives. Opsasnick is not only an early and intrepid Goatman researcher, but also a local, growing up in Goatman Country. His full Goatman accounts can be found in "On the Trail of the Goatman" in *Strange Magazine* (1994) and "Horror on Fletchertown Road: The Goatman of Prince George's County, Maryland" in *The Real Story Behind the Exorcist: A Study of the Haunted Boy and other True-Life Horror Legends from Around the Nation's Capital* (2007).

5. In the traditional "Boyfriend's Death" legend, a couple is on the way to a party when their car breaks down. They are on a dark, secluded road, a couple miles from the nearest service station. The boy tells his girlfriend that he will go for help. He insists that while he is gone she should stay in the backseat with a blanket over her. They establish a code. When the boyfriend returns, he will knock three times. Otherwise, the girl should remain hidden. Soon after her boyfriend leaves, the girl hears a scratching on the roof of her car. Frightened, the girl stays hidden. She soon falls asleep, only to be awakened by the sound of knocking. Thinking it is her boyfriend, she springs up only to find a police officer. He tells her to step out and walk directly to his car, explicitly commanding her to only look straight ahead after exiting the vehicle. Unable to resist, she turns around to see what the police are hiding from her. Hanging from a tree at the side of the road, her dead boyfriend swings in the wind, the tips of his feet scratching the roof of the car. See Brunvand (1981:5–10) for a more thorough overview of the "Boyfriend's Death."

FOLKLORE ARCHIVES FILES CONSULTED

The following is the collection of Goatman files in the Maryland Folklore Archives. The Maryland Folklore Archives is in the Maryland Room at the Hornbake Library, along with the rest of the University of Maryland

Special Collections. To review any of the following files, scholars must write in advance, requesting files by name and location.

Caherty, Frank. 1977. "Goat-Men, Hermits, & Murderous Woodsmen: Strange Tales and Curious Happenings."
Duley, Rose Ann. 1975. "Goatman Tales."
Hoffman, Carolyn. 1974. "Local Legends of Lottsford Road Area."
Lawler, Mark. 1983. "Legends of Bowie Maryland."
Lizama, George. 1971. "The Goatman of Tucker Road."
McGuigan, Mark. 1984. "Local Legends."
McKeller, Ian, 1986. "The Goatman and Crybaby Bridge: Local Legends of Lottsford Road."
Schofield, Clay. 1972. "Legends of Bowie."
Wilson, Trish. 1990. "Bowie Legends."

NEWSPAPERS ARTICLES REFERENCED

Daly, Sean. 1998. The Legend of Goatman. *Washington City Paper,* 18 September.
Goldman, Ivan G. 1971. A Legendary Figure Haunts Remote Pr. George's Woods. *Washington Post,* 30 November.
Hosler, Karen. 1971a. University Archives Reveals: Boaman, Goatman, and Ghosts Still Haunt Area. *Prince George's County News,* 27 October.
Hosler, Karen. 1971b. Residents Fear Goatman Lives: Dog Found Decapitated in Old Bowie. *Prince George's County News,* 10 November.
Hosler, Karen. 1971c. Pranksters and Thrill-Seekers: The Real Monsters of Fletchertown Road. *Prince George's County News,* 24 November.
Meyer, Eugene, L. 1984. Lottsford Road: Local Legend Says It's a Trail of Terror. *Washington Post,* 1 October.

REFERENCES

Ambrose, Melenie, prod. 1997. Goatman, Phar Lap, Psychic Animals. *Animal X* season 1, episode 9. Storyteller Productions.
Blanks, Trevor J., and David J. Puglia. 2014. *Maryland Legends: Folklore from the Old Line State.* Charleston, SC: The History Press.
Brunvand, Jan Harold. 1981. *The Vanishing Hitchhiker: American Urban Legends and their Meanings.* New York: W. W. Norton & Co.
Bowser, Andrew, dir. 2010. *Jimmy Tupper vs. The Goatman of Bowie.* Motion picture. One Small Instrument Pictures.
Carey, George G. 1970. *Maryland Folklore and Folklife.* Centreville: Tidewater Publishers.
Carey, George G. 1971. *Maryland Folk Legends and Folk Songs.* Centreville: Tidewater Publishers.
Dahlgren, Madeleine Vinton. 1882. *South Mountain Magic: Tales of Old Maryland.* Maple Shade, NJ: Lethe Press.
Dégh, Linda, and Andrew Vázsonyi. 1973. The Dialectics of the Legend. *Folklore Preprint Series* 1:6 (December): 1–65.
Dorson, Richard. 1971. Defining the American Folk Legend. In *American Folklore & the Historian,* 157–72. Chicago, IL: University of Chicago Press.

Jenkins, Joseph. 1998. The Goatman of Prince George's County. On *Father Joe: From Silly to Sacred, A Priest Speaks. Blog.* http://fatherjoe.wordpress.com/stories/the-goatman-of-prince-georges-county/. Accessed winter 2011.

Lake, Matt. 2006. *Weird Maryland: Your Travel Guide to Maryland's Local Legends and Best Kept Secrets.* New York: Sterling Publishing Co.

Mitchell, Roger E. 1979. The Press, Rumor, and Legend Formation. *Midwestern Journal of Language and Folklore* 5.1/2: 1–61.

Myrick, Daniel, and Eduardo Sánchez, dir. 1999. *The Blair Witch Project.* Motion picture. Artisan Entertainment.

Opsasnick, Mark 1994. On the Trail of the Goatman. *Strange Magazine* 14:18–21.

Opsasnick, Mark. 2007. *The Real Story Behind the Exorcist: A Study of the Haunted Boy and Other True-Life Horror Legends from Around the Nation's Capital.* Bloomington: Xlibris.

Parks, Derrick A., dir. 2012. *Return of the Goatman.* Motion picture. Parks Entertainment.

Rozum, John (w), Alexander Saviuk (p), and Rick Magyar (i). 1998. The Face of Extinction. *The X-Files* 1.37. Comic book. Topps.

Smith, Paul. 1992. "Read All About It! Elvis Eaten by Drug-Crazed Giant Alligators": Contemporary Legend and the Popular Press. *Contemporary Legend* 2:41–71.

von Sydow, Carl Wilhelm. 1999 [1934]. "Geography and Folk-Tale Oicotypes." In *International Folkloristics: Classic Contributions from the Founders of Folklore*, ed. Alan Dundes, 137–51. Lanham, MD: Rowman and Littlefield.

Whitney, Annie Weston, and Caroline Canfield Bullock. 1925. *Folk-Lore from Maryland.* Memoirs of the American Folklore Society, Vol. XVIII. New York: G. E. Stechert and Co., 1925.

EDITOR'S SUGGESTIONS FOR FURTHER READING

Couch, J. Nathan. 2014. *Goatman: Flesh or Folklore?* Scotts Valley, CA: Createspace.

Daley, Sean. 1998. "The Legend of the Goatman." *Washington City Paper.* https://www.washingtoncitypaper.com/news/article/13016185/the-legend-of-goatman.

Jenkins, Joseph. 2012 [1998]. "The Goatman of Prince George's County." *Blogger Priest.* https://bloggerpriest.com/2012/10/08/the-goatman-of-prince-georges-county/.

Okonowicz, Ed. 2012. "Prince George's Goatman." In *Monsters of Maryland: Mysterious Creatures in the Old Line State*, 113–22. Mechanicsburg, PA: Stackpole Books.

Opsasnick, Mark. 2007. "Horror on Fletchertown Road." In *The Real Story behind the Exorcist: A Study of the Haunted Boy and Other True-Life Horror Legends from around the Nation's Capital.* Bloomington, IN: Xlibris.

Puglia, David. 2019. "The Goatman and Washington, D.C.: Strange Sightings and the Fear of the Encroaching City." In *Supernatural Cities: Enchantment, Anxiety and Spectrality*, edited by Karl Bell, 145–64. Woodbridge, UK: Boydell & Brewer.

13

Tall, Dark, and Loathsome
The Slender Man and the Emergence of a Legend Cycle in the Digital Age

Andrew Peck

PREFACE

This casebook focuses on monsters in their native environments: from Newfoundland to Haiti, from California's Ojai Valley to New York's Catskill Mountains. Two of the chapters included here hint at *new* possibilities, *new* native habitats. Norine Dresser argued that the American vampire's home, at least in the 1980s, was the television set. Similarly, Andrew Peck contends that Slender Man, a new digital monster for a new millennium, is a native of the World Wide Web. In fact, the Internet will force folklorists to check many of their assumptions about the operation of folklore, legendary monsters included.

In this chapter, Peck, a digital folklore scholar and longtime *Something Awful* "Goon," sets his sights on the *Something Awful* forums, zooming in on a couple weeks when users challenged one another to create visual hoaxes with the verisimilitude of authentic legendry. In the process, a digital monster was born, Slender Man, an Internet fiend so appealing that it took over the forum, enrapturing even those posters who knew the entire venture was an exercise in fakery. Slender Man has since captivated more than its creators. He stars in video games, movie franchises, documentaries, books, special issues of journals, and even as the named instigator of heinous crimes. But in the beginning, before Slender Man's notorious rise to fame, what intrigued Peck most was how digital communities created a new monster while simultaneously following all the old hallmarks of legendry. While one user, Victor Surge, initiated the Slender Man legend cycle, Peck points out that the originator received no special place in the Slender Man canon. Rather, the creation of Slender Man moved forward as a collective effort,

https://doi.org/10.7330/9781646421602.c013

piecemeal, each addition or subtraction carefully monitored and negotiated by the community, maintaining shared expectations and rejecting contributions that would undermine the legend's core.

Digital legends remain a performance, despite cyberspace's asynchronous and disembodied environment, and folklorists can observe the legend process as it develops and unfolds over space and time, instantly self-archived on the World Wide Web. Repetition and variation continue, not due to faulty memory, but because of an urge to create and personalize. Digital monsters blend legendry in intriguing, hybrid ways, combining oral, written, and visual components. While the Internet allows for an open and fluid group membership, collective social expectations delimit who can successfully participate in creation, discussion, and perpetuation of legendary monster characteristics. The research on legendary digital monsters is only just beginning; legendary monster researchers can look forward to exploring a compelling new habitat.

ESSAY

On June 8, 2009, user Gerogerigegege started a thread on the SomethingAwful.com forums dedicated to photoshopping paranormal images with the intent of hoaxing paranormal discussion boards. Two days and several posts later, user Victor Surge replied with a pair of images. The images were black-and-white and featured children playing in the foreground while a faceless, tall, eerily long-limbed humanoid clad in a black suit lurked behind them. Under the second photo, Victor Surge supplied the following "authentic" text: "One of two recovered photographs from the Stirling City Library blaze. Notable for being taken the day which fourteen children vanished and for what is referred to as 'The Slender Man'. Deformities cited as film defects by officials. Fire at library occurred one week later. Actual photograph confiscated as evidence. 1986, photographer: Mary Thomas, missing since June 13th, 1986."

Although details were sparse, the character gained immediate popularity. Soon other users started sharing their own creative interpretations of the Slender Man. Within days, the thread was dedicated almost entirely to performing and discussing "authentic" legends of the creature. But why did users find the creature so appealing? How did users interact with each other to create these performances? And what might this process reveal about the collaborative potential of networked communication?

The Slender Man is a crowd-sourced monster. As users told stories, shared images, and theorized as to the nature of the nascent Lovecraftian horror, they also participated in its creation. Each performance added to and subtracted from how the entity was imagined by the group. Users critiqued these performances, discussing what elements made them most effective. Successive performances built upon existing performances and discussions. Through social interaction, users collaborated in an ongoing process of performance, interpretation, and negotiation that constructed the details, motifs, and shared expectations of the Slender Man legend cycle.

In this article, I argue that the Slender Man is a digital legend cycle that combines the generic conventions and emergent qualities of oral and visual performance with the collaborative potential of networked communication. Digital media affects the emergent nature of performance in four ways: (1) by occurring asynchronously; (2) by encouraging imitation and personalization while also allowing perfect replication; (3) by combining elements of oral, written, and visual communication; and (4) by generating shared expectations for performance that enact group identity despite the lack of a physically present group. By applying these traditional and emergent frameworks to the ways in which individuals perform and discuss the Slender Man, this article ultimately demonstrates how collective performances in digital communication contexts may vary from face-to-face performances while also retaining the latter's sense of vernacularity.

A DIGITAL LEGEND CYCLE

If performing, narrating, and storytelling are things we do regularly in everyday life (Georges 1979:104), and if digital communication is increasingly a part of everyday life (McNeill 2009:84), then it stands to reason that digital communication facilitates everyday performance, narration, and storytelling. As Trevor Blank (2007) has observed, the Internet is fast becoming the premier forum for the study of legends, chain letters, hoaxes, and jokes. In light of this, it is unsurprising that several scholars have explored the folkloric potential of digital communication through analyses of e-mail forwardables (Kibby 2005; Frank 2009), Web-transmitted legends and urban legends (Fernback 2003; Blank 2007), cyber folk art (Foote 2007), occupational lore in online gaming (Gillis 2011), digital newslore (Frank 2011), personal vanity pages (Howard 2005), vernacular religion (Howard 2009), supernatural alternate reality games (Kinsella 2011), digitally altered images (Frank 2004), and digital humor and jokes (Ellis 2001b; Ellis 2002; Kuipers 2005).

This article extends prior scholarship on digital folklore by examining the creation and circulation of one Internet-specific legend cycle. This is important for two reasons. First, most scholarship has not accounted for the early stages of formulation and transmission of e-lore. Since contemporary legends, jokes, and chain e-mails tend to have nebulous origins, this is not surprising. What the case of the Slender Man offers, then, is the opportunity to observe this process of legend creation, negotiation, and circulation from its inception. Second, the Slender Man is an Internet-specific phenomenon. This legend cycle evolved through an ongoing negotiation of performances and discussions that combined the generic conventions of oral and visual storytelling with the practices of networked communication. Hence, this is also a study of how digital communication remediates traditional methods of everyday face-to-face performance.[1]

To that end, in this section, I suggest four ways in which digital communication departs from face-to-face performance, as well as the implications of these departures for those studying performance online.

First, communication on the Internet often occurs asynchronously. Although this is not a constant with the ever-increasing popularity of video chat clients and live blogging, the vast majority of digital expression still occurs in the post-respond style. Neither temporal nor spatial gaps, however, preclude the possibility of digital folk culture or legend performance (Dégh 2001:298; see also Blank 2009; Foote 2007; Howard and Blank 2013).

Bill Ellis discusses legends in terms of their performative and discursive aspects, suggesting that "*legend telling is the communal exploration of social boundaries*" (2001a:11; emphasis in original). Linda Dégh expresses a similarly social view, noting that legends are less about individual texts and more about communication—they are discourses on belief (2001:97, 405). According to Ellis, legend performances typically place events in the group's conception of the real world while also challenging the boundaries of that world (2001a:11). Hence, when I refer to Slender Man legend performance, I am referring to the ways in which individuals, acting as part of a networked group, use the character as a resource for creative expression and discourse that "*challenges accepted definitions of the real world and leaves itself suspended, relying for closure on each individual's response*" (Ellis 2001a:60; emphasis in original).[2] This positions digital legends—like the Slender Man—as an ongoing series of emergent performances.

An emergent performance comes into being through the interaction of performer and audience. Any such interaction begins by drawing on pre-existing social frames (Goffman 1974). According to Bauman, frames act as a shared resource for communication and performance, giving rise to the generic expectations that "make up the structured system of conventionalized performance for the community" ([1977] 1984:37–38). Performances influence and imagine their audiences and, in turn, audiences participate in the creation of the performance (Bauman [1977] 1984:38). This mutually constitutive interaction between performance and audience creates an ongoing feedback loop, affecting not only what is currently being performed but also the nature of successive performances. Each new performance draws upon prior performances—emphasizing and diminishing different aspects based on both the communal negotiation and the individual performer's experiences and perceptions. In this way, each performance is, in and of itself, a statement about what makes for good performance.

In observing digital performance, the largest implication of asynchronicity is that this feedback is not an immediate process. But, while digital feedback lacks social and body language cues, many users have learned to compensate for this with reactions that are more overt than in faceto-face communication, such as posting written feedback. In some cases—like certain memes, reaction animations (.gifs), and emoticons—users actually employ digital expressions that evoke face-to-face reactions. Still, these reactions occur after the fact and between posts. Since digital communication technologies extend the emergent nature of performance temporally, observing this process online means viewing it as an iterative, not concurrent, process.

Second, digital performances endure not only across time but also across networked spaces (Howard 2013:73). Whereas an oral performance disappears into ephemera once delivered, nearly all iterations of the Slender Man legend remain catalogued in their original contexts across the network. Furthermore, digital iterations can be copied perfectly from website to website. This suggests that variation in digital legends occurs more distinctly from a desire to personalize and demonstrate identity than from imperfect attempts at imitation.

Indeed, despite the near-perfect copy fidelity made possible by digital communication, users still actively create legend variants. Although some users certainly just re-post existing Slender Man legends, many more use the character as a resource to create their own performances. As Jeannie Thomas observes, given the ease of copying and pasting images and text online, the generative, mutative, user-driven nature of these performances could be construed as somewhat surprising. Moreover, Thomas writes, it is precisely the unexpected nature of these networked behaviors that make them salient for analysis (2003:159). By imbuing the performance with aspects of social and group identity (Georges 1990), users create and circulate legend variants in a manner not unlike oral performance, but with much greater record and spreadability (Jenkins, Ford, and Green 2013).

Although this seemingly suggests a wide array of available interpretations of the Slender Man legend cycle, it is important to remember that, despite the immense catalogue of performances and variants, the most repeatedly performed elements of the legend (the Slender Man's facelessness, for example) are the most likely to be seen, the most likely to be shared, and, as a result, the most likely to form the basis for new variants. In sum, users approach Slender Man performances with varied expectations based on the prior performances they have observed, while also adhering to a larger set of developing generic expectations based on the most commonly performed forms.

Third, digital technologies allow for a mix of oral, written, and visual elements in everyday communication. Digital legend performances—like the Slender Man—occur through various media modes that are often impractical for face-toface performance (Dégh 2001:298). Since digital communication often bears the signs of both written and spoken language, Nancy Baym suggests that it is best viewed as a mixed modality (2010:63–64). More than just remediation, digital technologies allow performances that blend and extend written, oral, and visual communication in novel ways. The result, as Barbara Kirshenblatt-Gimblett eloquently writes, "is neither speech nor writing as we have known it, but something in between, and, increasingly, with the convergence of technologies, it is multimedia" (1998:284). A Slender Man legend may appear as a written performance of an "authentic" oral interview, or it may be a story performed through a photoshopped image. Therefore, regarding digital communication as a mixed oral/visual/textual modality is fundamental to understanding how the multi- and cross-mediated ways individuals choose to perform the Slender Man legend online depart from non-digital communication.

Fourth, although the nature of group membership online is fluid, far-reaching, and anonymous, specific expectations of behavior emerge around any given network location and guide the emergent nature of performance. Digital communities continue to function because individuals enact social identities that they perceive to be consistent with group expectations and values (Howard 2008:202). These shared expectations are "displayed, reinforced, negotiated, and taught through members' shared behaviors" (Baym 2010:80) and "any newcomer to an Internet chatroom, or a Facebook page, or even a backand-forth mobile phone texting scenario, will know that there exists a certain shared body of knowledge about how to behave in such settings" (McNeill 2009:82). Despite the less cohesive, more fluid nature of digital group membership among individuals, every network location maintains a unique set of shared expectations derived from the product of ongoing group interaction. These shared expectations, in turn, affect how individuals manage and perform within their social and group identities (Ellis 2001a:9). Since audiences and performers imagine each other within the confines of these shared expectations, these shared expectations guide and delimit the emergent possibilities of performance (Dégh 2001:298).

A Crowd-Sourced Cthulhu

On June 8, 2009, SomethingAwful.com forum member Gerogerigegege created a discussion thread called "Create Paranormal Images," inviting other users to create and share mundane images that had been manipulated to appear paranormal. The resulting images, Gerogerigegege hoped, could be used to fool or hoax paranormal investigators and discussion boards. This call for communal play and practical joking befits the often humorous, exaggerated, and irreverent tone of the Something Awful forums and its wide community of users that self-deprecatingly call themselves "goons." Gerogerigegege supplied others with a few photoshopped examples, links to useable photographs, and some tips on creating "authentic-" looking images. Gerogerigegege ended the post by inviting other users to join in.[3]

The thread proved popular, and soon other users began sharing their own images that seemingly captured ghosts, UFOs, wisps, smoke, shadows, and phantasms on film. Users began writing stories to accompany these images and suggested that the images were real by linking them to personal experience. At the same time, users often discussed the process of creating their images, asking for advice or offering tips on photoshopping. User guandi said of his or her photoshopped UFO: "It looks strange in the picture thanks to my crappy camera, but it was actually transparent, just reflecting and diffusing the light of the sunset at the edges and in three moving patches on the bottom of the craft," while adding below that the poor picture quality was actually the calculated result of image manipulation.

Like a game with concealed and mutable rules, users learned what made for good posts by observing the content of others. For example, at no point did users agree to start writing contextual blurbs for images (and, indeed, on the first page of the thread, nearly all images lack accompanying text), yet by the end of the second page, nearly all images were accompanied by text. Most images were either black-and-white, blurry, or grainy. Many contained hazy, translucent shapes that, upon examination, revealed themselves as humanoid or monstrous figures. These qualities made the images reminiscent of spirit photographs, cryptozoological images, and other popular traditions of supernatural photography (Wojcik 1996). In this way, users drew upon a matrix of lived experience with paranormal images in order to create further paranormal images. Put another way, users engaged in performance by referencing existing frameworks which, in turn, gave rise to further shared expectations. It is in this atmosphere that the Slender Man emerged.

On June 10, 2009, user Victor Surge posted two images (see Figs. 13.1 and 13.2) and text to the "Create Paranormal Images" thread. This is the first recorded performance of the Slender Man legend. Users were enamored, and the thread quickly shifted focus to the creature. When asked where the creature had originated (and if it was an original creation), Victor Surge replied:

> The Slender Man as an idea was made-up off the top of my head, although the concept is based on a number of things that scare me. The name I thought up on the fly when I wrote that first bit. The asset I used for a couple of the pictures was the creepy tall guy from Phantasm, which sadly I have not seen, and the others various guys in suits. All of the things that aren't the torso and legs, like the tentacles and Slender Man's face, were painted from scratch however.

As this quote demonstrates, even the earliest performances of the Slender Man legend exhibited a sense of hybridity. Like the paranormal images posted before it, the Slender Man drew upon an existing matrix of belief that included mass media representations of paranormal creatures, the user's personal experiences and fears, and the influence of previous posts to the discussion thread. In other words, the Slender Man was not an entirely new creation and was instead influenced by a vast network of vernacular and institutional performances that had directly and indirectly preceded it. By mixing a pastiche of mass media-influenced horror tropes and imagery with his own vernacular legend performance, Victor Surge's creation emerged to other users as not only familiar but also as a discrete and mysterious entity accessible for vernacular appropriation.

Victor Surge's performance of the Slender Man legend established only a few details about the creature. The Slender Man was a tall human-like figure. It was shadowy, blurry, and ominous, with tentacles reminiscent of the otherworldly abominations penned by horror writer H. P. Lovecraft (best known for creating the eldritch entity Cthulhu). Despite—or perhaps because of—this mysteriousness, Victor Surge's contribution was a hit:

Figure 13.1. "'We didn't want to go, we didn't want to kill them, but its persistent silence and outstretched arms horrified and comforted us at the same time . . .' 1983, photographer unknown, presumed dead." Posted by Victor Surge, June 10, 2009. (Collection of Andrew Peck.)

LEYENDECKER: oh fuck you when i finally saw the guy in the background i lost it this is going to give me nightmares

BEERDEER: As an amateur paranormal investigator, you'd be surprised how much the Slender Man appeared in pictures in times of disaster during that historical period. (AKA I'd like to see more of those)

ZOMBIESCHOLAR: You are an amazing and terrible bastard, sir. Well played. Now to look over my shoulder every couple seconds for the rest of my day . . .

Users asked Victor Surge for more Slender Man images. Victor Surge coyly replied, "Maybe I'll do some more research. I've heard there may be a couple more legit 'Slender Man' photographs out there. I'll post them if I find them." By the next day, Victor Surge posted two more images of the creature. Less than 24 hours later, other users started getting into the act.

On the morning of June 12, 2009, LeechCode5 posted two Slender Man images. To contextualize the first photograph, LeechCode5 recounted a story from his or her uncle about a police investigation into nine teens who vanished from a campsite six years earlier. The second photo (Fig. 13.3) featured a sepiatinged image of a school burning to the ground with

Figure 13.2. "One of two recovered photographs from the Stirling City Library blaze. Notable for being taken the day which fourteen children vanished and for what is referred to as 'The Slender Man.' Deformities cited as film defects by officials. Fire at library occurred one week later. Actual photograph confiscated as evidence. 1986, photographer: Mary Thomas, missing since June 13th, 1986." Posted by Victor Surge, June 10, 2009. (Collection of Andrew Peck.)

the following caption: "The second photo is of an elementary school fire in 1978. No official cause was ever found. Seven students and a teacher became trapped and died before firefighters could respond. Many of the students and teachers from the time have a history of anxiety disorders and panic attacks, even those who weren't at the school on that day. At least one has since committed suicide, and several others legally changed their names once they reached adulthood and have disappeared." These two images represent some of the earliest Slender Man legend variants, and LeechCode5's performance of the Slender Man legend further developed the shared expectations created by Victor Surge's performances. In the second photograph (Fig. 13.3), the Slender Man is implied to be more actively malicious than in prior representations. No longer do individuals just mysteriously disappear; in LeechCode5's telling, the Slender Man is also associated with arson and long-term mental health issues.

Following LeechCode5's example, other users began performing Slender Man legends. The process was slow at first, but as more people began performing their own Slender Man legend variants, participation rose exponentially. This increased participation began to form the character

Figure 13.3. "I've been seriously debating sharing these, but after Victor Surge's posts I feel I have to." Posted by LeechCode5, June 12, 2009. (Collection of Andrew Peck.)

more concretely. Over the next three days, a wide variety of performances emerged. User TrenchMaul contributed an image linking the Slender Man to the 1959 Dyatlov Pass incident. Victor Surge supplied another image that placed the Slender Man in the background of a child's birthday party, with accompanying child-like drawings. VR Native American photoshopped the creature into the background of a sermon delivered by Jim Jones. The character was adapted to appear in sixteenth-century German woodcarvings, old newspaper clippings, and *märchen*-like fairy stories. Each time the character was performed, it added and subtracted a bit from how the group imagined him.

By performing and discussing these legends, users filled in the fine details of the character through a process of negotiation. What's more, users were generally aware that the Slender Man legend had become a collaborative process:

DOOM MATHEMATIC: I'm a big fan of the big organic collaborative creative horror thing that's going on in this thread. Reminds me of the SCP series.

BASH IRONFIST: I'm no good with photoshop, so I'd thought I'd add some text. If anyone is good making some images and wants to collaborate, send me a [private message]!

MR. 47: I'm useless with Photoshop, but the pics here are ripe for some Slender Man work. I'm also putting together a back story for it, and if someone could put some subtle touches on a couple of these, I'd really appreciate it.

TOMBS GRAVE: Think I might hammer out a short story about Slender Man tonight, as words are my area of relative expertise. Should I base it on one of the pictures, or no?

NURSE FANNY: [Replying] Oh! Do your own and try to get somebody to do a picture based off of the story.

As these quotes suggest, imagining the creature collaboratively was highly encouraged. Users would often build on the performances of others or create performative fragments for others to complete. Gerogerigegege, for example, posted an image of a farmhouse that was photoshopped to include the Slender Man. In this post, Gerogerigegege added: "Story tellers, you're more than welcome to write a backstory for this one." A few hours later, BooDoug187 used the photograph as the basis for posting an interview transcript between Ted Henderson, a farmer committed to a mental hospital, and his doctor. Later that day, Leyendecker posted an audio file wherein he and a friend performed a dramatization of BooDoug187's transcript, adding to the previous post that "[a]t the permission of Faye Dauton, the doctor's daughter, the recording of the interview with Mr. Henderson was released." As might be expected, the increase in performances and collaborations also led to a rise in Slender Man legend variants. The rise in variants, consequently, created some strain between individuals who imagined the creature in different ways. It then became necessary for users to negotiate how to deal with these divergent representations.

Users responded to these varied performances with discussion. Faced with a wide variety of performances of the Slender Man legend, users discussed what they liked and disliked at the myriad of circulating variants. Users debated how much backstory the character should have (if any), if the character was a murderer or drove people to madness, what caused the Slender Man to appear, if the creature was more human-like or spider-like, and if the character should be the focus of images or just a part of the background. And, while some users made relatively simple points, remarking on a performance or two they thought was "best," other users gave more pointed criticism:

PUMPKIN SPOON: The only flaw is the conflicting images we get occasionally, I don't know that the more spider-like images work for him, same for when he's out in the open. I was thinking of him seeming fairly human at a glance, with the tentacles and facelessness not apparent until you really look. Although the inhuman height and sort of "stretched" look are pretty consistent. Love it!

TRENCHMAUL: I'm not really digging these folklore backstories though.

NURSE FANNY: I think a more modern thing would be best. You know like kids start disappearing in the 50s. More contemporary with less of a back story or explanation. I dunno it seems creepier if he just shows up out of no where.

BLUEDEANIE: All of the Slender Man stuff is good, though I think these [images] are the best. They seem more plausible. I also like the stories that accompany the first set of pics more-so than the other image 'storytelling' used in the other ones, but that's just me. Either way, keep up the good work.

THOREAU-UP: I think the Slender Man's tentacles need to be a little less obvious. It seems a lot less freakier if you can see them so clearly.

WOODROWSKILLSON: I agree, its better when you don't notice them at first, and only later you realize just how alien the Slender Man is.

MOOSEYFATE: The Slender Man should appear in seemingly innocent pictures (bright colors, happy people, etc.) somewhere in the background for realism.

These discussions not only affected how individuals interacted with performances of the Slender Man but also made clear how individuals judged these performances.

These quotes provide an important glimpse into the standards by which users judged the authenticity of performances of the Slender Man. In the moment, shared expectations developed around such basic questions as "Does it appeal to realism?" and "Is it plausible?" Developing an understanding of these emic criteria for judgment is important because, as Christine Hine notes: "The point for the ethnographer is not to bring some external criterion for judging whether it is safe to believe what informants say, but rather to come to understand how it is that informants judge authenticity" (Hine 2000:49). Despite the knowledge that the creature is fake, users (such as those cited above) tended to prefer performances that were believable, placing the creature in the "real" modern world. This is consistent with Ellis's explanation of the basic social function of legends: they place events in the group's concept of the real world while also challenging the boundaries of that world. Correspondingly, Slender Man legends that seemed more "plausible" tended to receive more praise, while expectations for joking and hoaxing diminished rapidly. Locating authenticity in "reality" reflects one of the earliest shared expectations that emerged around Slender Man legend performances.

The more users who performed these legends, the more fleshed-out these shared expectations became. Although several different aspects of the character emerged from these performances, certain sets and subsets started to become more performed than others. Performances that located themselves in more immediate circumstances remained fairly common, whereas performances that placed the Slender Man in pseudo-*märchen*, woodcarvings, and hieroglyphs became rarer. Choosing motifs when performing Slender Man legends seemed to privilege those elements with closeness to the group's lived experiences. Performances became rooted in "reality," sharing the results of research, contributing an obscure local news story, or—in true contemporary legend fashion—suggesting personal involvement:

> KITH_GROUPIE: All this talk about a slender man from the forest rang a bell with something that happened to me when I was six or so.
>
> VIET TIMH: I find this tall man stuff Fascinating and wanted to learn more. So I checked around and found some really cool stuff. This was the scariest cause it occurred so close to where I live[.]

This shared expectation for plausibility resulted in successive performances playing down some of the more fantastical aspects of the creature. These expectations did not dictate future performances, but they certainly influenced which Slender Man motifs were chosen and how they were performed. Performances began to portray the creature as more human-like, though still with uncanny limb proportions and a featureless face. His black tendrils remained but were often hidden. His shadowed body now resembled a black suit. Performances tended to simply acknowledge his presence, forgoing explanations or backstories. He often lurked in the background, driving those who discovered him slowly insane. If he killed, it was often implied, not explicit.

Nowhere in the thread were these expectations written down. When users did try to create unsolicited lists, charts, or facts detailing the essential nature of the creature, they were met with derision. In response to one such attempt, user BooDoug187 said: "[We know] what he does, don't try to reason the whys and hows. Because there will never be an answer that will make you understand or happy . . . or make you sleep again." User creepy old man shared a similar sentiment, expressing that the mystery was part of the character: "All we know is that anyone who knows how the Slender Man works or why, has never been allowed to share his secrets." In this and several other instances, users were resistant toward standardizing the Slender Man legend cycle because these individual assertions of authority disregarded what made the Slender Man so successful. As user Moto42 noted, the lack of a defined set of characteristics made the character more accessible:

> I'm loving the Slenderman. That's just an awesome name to start with. The minimal backstory to the image was just perfect. Victor, you have a gift for horror it seems. you posted one image and a tiny backstory. Planting a

small seed of an idea into the internet, without even knowing (or planning) for others to run with it, and make it grow.

Then, people saw your idea, and started expanding on it. The Slenderman went from an isolated incident to a full mythos, with woodcuttings, incident reports, coverups and multiple killings to its name in just a few pages of collaborative effort . . .

What I'm trying to say with both of these, is that I am continualy amazed with how a single idea on the internet can sprout and grow into something more incredible than you ever expected, simply through a small amount of creative effort on the part of many individuals. I won't be getting to sleep anytime soon thanks to you all.

The view expressed by Moto42 suggests that the ability of users to tap into the ideas of others while also supplying their own helped inspire the collaborative culture that arose surrounding the Slender Man. Instead of privileging the choices of the original media creator as canonical (as is often the case in commercial media), by refusing to systematize the Slender Man, these users defended their ability to repeat and vary their legend performances, informally locating ownership of the creature across the community.

Standardization would undercut this collaborative and discursive potential, and by resisting a defined set of characteristics for the creature, users kept the Slender Man as an object of legend dialectic (Ellis 2001a; Dégh 2001). By keeping the Slender Man as a shared resource for discussion and performance, users were encouraged to both engage with the group and create individualized forms of expression. In effect, the Slender Man's popularity derives from being seen as a shared public resource.

THE CYCLE CONTINUES

Following these first two weeks on Something Awful, Slender Man performances began to materialize across the Internet. The Slender Man began appearing in blogs, vlogs, drawings, forums, wikis, stories, photoshops, video games, and alternate reality games. In the last few years, the character has become so popular that—in a twist of hybridity—this vernacular creation has begun influencing institutional media producers and offline behaviors. For example, special monsters in the indie video game *Minecraft* were designed as Slender Man homages. A 2014 episode of the television show *Supernatural* saw the main characters on the trail of a malevolent photo-lurking entity known as the Thin Man. The popular Slender Man Web series *Marble Hornets* has over 55 million views on YouTube, and a

Marble Hornets movie entered production in the spring of 2013. And last Halloween, my friends and I snapped photographs of Slender Man costumes in Chicago.

The case of the Slender Man demonstrates how the emergent nature of performance plays out on the Internet. Much like face-to-face communication, each performance emerges from an ongoing interaction between performer and audience. This process of negotiation draws on existing expectations of performance and genre while also establishing new ones. These negotiated expectations emerge not only from perceptions of social and group identity but also from the nature of networked communication. Because digital communication has several fundamental differences from face-to-face communication, performances online emerge uniquely. However, despite differences in feedback, copy-fidelity, media use, and group dynamics, performances still emerge through a process of interpersonal interaction. Therefore, understanding contemporary legends on the Internet relies on understanding the underlying social process of negotiation that circulates them, defines them, and makes them meaningful. It is my hope that this study encourages further scholarship on the unique challenges presented by the convergence of digital media and everyday life.

Author's Note

This article is the product of research conducted throughout 2012 and 2013. During this time, the Slender Man was a well-known figure in many virtual communities, but it lacked a significant non-digital presence. In the conclusion of the article, I argued that because of the creature's growing popularity online, mainstream recognition of the Slender Man seemed inevitable. The article was finalized and accepted for publication in JAF in March 2014. Two months later, I was sadly proven correct.

On May 31, 2014, two 12-year-old girls from Waukesha, Wisconsin, stabbed a friend 19 times and left her to die in the woods. The victim was saved by a passerby, and the two girls who perpetrated the stabbing were apprehended by local authorities. When questioned about their actions, it came to light that the girls committed the crime to win the favor of the Slender Man, whom they had learned about online.

Of all the details of this gruesome story, the involvement of the Slender Man resonated most in subsequent news coverage. The relative obscurity of the character and its de-contextualized association with the stabbing served to kindle a classic moral panic narrative. Headlines and sound bites focused on the dangers of unsupervised tween media use and the corrupting allure of the dark corners of the Internet.

By the end of the summer, nearly a half-dozen cases of violence were linked to the Slender Man by national news outlets. In Florida, a teen "obsessed" with the Slender Man set fire to her family's home. A man accused of killing two police officers in Las Vegas reportedly "often dressed up in costume as Slender Man," according to one of his neighbors. After her daughter donned a white mask and attacked her with a knife, a mother in Ohio attributed the violence to the influence of the Slender Man.

Due to my work on the topic (both popular and academic), I was privileged to provide a counterpoint to many of these sensationalized accounts and mischaracterizations. I spent most of June explaining to news reporters and media personalities that concerns over the Slender Man were largely overblown—akin to scrutinizing children's' mirror use for fear of Bloody Mary—and distracting from many more real dangers young people may face online.

There is surely much more work to be done here. Further study of the Slender Man in the wake of these events could yield valuable insight into ostensive behaviors, media uptake of legend cycles, and the circulation of urban legends among young people in the digital age. As folklorists, we are keenly positioned to explore and weigh in on these issues. I end this addendum with the same sentiment that closed my original article—it is my hope that this study encourages further scholarship on the unique challenges presented by the convergence of digital media and everyday life.

NOTES

1. I use the term "performance" because it captures the wide variety of multimedia possibilities for everyday digital communication. Terms such as "storytelling" or "narration" do not quite capture these events, as they seem to privilege the use of language (written or oral) to convey meaning. Since users often share Slender Man legends in the form of images, it seems inaccurate to use such terms. For the purposes of this article, those who tell stories, draw pictures, manipulate images, and engage in other similar social methods of creative expression are said to "perform" the Slender Man legend. Conversely, I refer to the individuals who receive, discuss, and respond to these performances as the audience.

2. Whether performers or audiences actually believe a legend to be true or not, however, is irrelevant. As Ellis notes, although some scholars have suggested that a belief in the veracity of the narrative is a fundamental aspect of legends, such a criterion is difficult to apply in practice (2001a:5).

3. Unless noted otherwise, all cited quotes come from the "Create Paranormal Images" thread on SomethingAwful.com (http//forums.somethingawful.com/showthread.php?threadid=3150591&userid=0&perpage=40&pagenumber=1).

REFERENCES CITED

Bauman, Richard. [1977] 1984. *Verbal Art as Performance*. Prospect Heights, IL: Waveland Press.

Baym, Nancy K. 2010. *Personal Connections in the Digital Age*. Cambridge: Polity Press.

Blank, Trevor J. 2007. Examining the Transmission of Urban Legends: Making the Case for Folklore Fieldwork on the Internet. *Folklore Forum* 37(1):15–26.

Blank, Trevor J. 2009. Introduction: Toward a Conceptual Framework for the Study of Folklore and the Internet. In *Folklore and the Internet: Vernacular Expression in a Digital World*, ed. Trevor J. Blank, pp. 1–20. Logan: Utah State University Press.

Dégh, Linda. 2001. *Legend and Belief: Dialectics of a Folklore Genre*. Bloomington: Indiana University Press.

Ellis, Bill. 2001a. *Aliens, Ghosts, and Cults: Legends We Live*. Jackson: University Press of Mississippi.

Ellis, Bill. 2001b. A Model for Collecting and Interpreting World Trade Center Disaster Jokes. *New Directions in Folklore* 5. https://scholarworks.iu.edu/dspace/bitstream/handle/2022/7195/NDiF_issue_5_ article_1.pdf?sequence=1.

Ellis, Bill. 2002. Making a Big Apple Crumble: The Role of Humor in Constructing a Global Response to Disaster. *New Directions in Folklore* 6. http://unix.temple.edu/~camille/bigapple/bigapple1.html.

Fernback, Jan. 2003. Legends on the Net: An Examination of Computer-Mediated Communication as a Locus of Oral Culture. *New Media & Society* 5(1):29–45.

Foote, Monica. 2007. Userpicks: Cyber Folk Art in the Early 21st Century. *Folklore Forum* 37(1):27–38.

Frank, Russell. 1990. Communicative Role and Social Identity in Storytelling. *Fabula* 31(1–2):4–57.

Frank, Russell. 2004. When the Going Gets Tough, the Tough Go Photoshopping: September 11 and the Newslore of Vengeance and Victimization. *New Media & Society* 6(5):633–58.

Frank, Russell. 2009. The *Forward* as Folklore: Studying E-Mailed Humor. In *Folklore and the Internet: Vernacular Expression in a Digital World*, ed. Trevor J. Blank, pp. 98–122. Logan: Utah State University Press.

Frank, Russell. 2011. *Newslore: Contemporary Folklore on the Internet*. Jackson: University Press of Mississippi.

Georges, Robert A. 1979. Feedback and Response in Storytelling. *Western Folklore* 38(2):104–10.

Georges, Robert A. 1990. Communicative Role and Social Identity in Storytelling. *Fabula* 31(1–2): 4–57.

Gillis, Ben. 2011. An Unexpected Font of Folklore: Online Gaming as Occupational Lore. *Western Folklore* 70(2):147–70.

Goffman, Irving. 1974. *Frame Analysis: An Essay on the Organization of Experience*. New York: Harper & Row.

Hine, Christine. 2000. *Virtual Ethnography*. London: SAGE Publications.

Howard, Robert Glenn. 2005. Toward a Theory of the World Wide Web Vernacular: The Case for Pet Cloning. *Journal of Folklore Research* 42(3):323–60.

Howard, Robert Glenn. 2008. Electronic Hybridity: The Persistent Processes of the Vernacular Web. *Journal of American Folklore* 121(480):192–218.

Howard, Robert Glenn. 2009. Enacting a Virtual "Ekklesia": Online Christian Fundamentalism as Vernacular Religion. *New Media & Society* 12(5):729–44.

Howard, Robert Glenn. 2013. Vernacular Authority: Critically Engaging "Tradition." In *Tradition in the Twenty-First Century*, ed. Trevor J. Blank and Robert Glenn Howard, pp. 72–99. Logan: Utah State University Press.

Howard, Robert Glenn, and Trevor J. Blank. 2013. Introduction: Living Traditions in a Modern World. In *Tradition in the Twenty-First Century*, ed. Trevor J. Blank and Robert Glenn Howard, pp. 1–21. Logan: Utah State University Press.

Jenkins, Henry, Sam Ford, and Joshua Green. 2013. *Spreadable Media*. New York: New York University Press.

Kibby, Marjorie. 2005. Email Forwardables: Folklore in the Age of the Internet. *New Media & Society* 7(6):770–90.

Kinsella, Michael. 2011. *Legend-Tripping Online: Supernatural Folklore and the Search for Ong's Hat*. Jackson: University Press of Mississippi.

Kirshenblatt-Gimblett, Barbara. 1998. Folklore's Crisis. *Journal of American Folklore* 111(441):281–327.

Kuipers, Giselinde. 2005. "Where Was King Kong When We Needed Him?": Public Discourse, Digital Disaster Jokes, and the Functions of Laughter after 9/11. *Journal of American Culture* 28(1):70–84.

McNeill, Lynne S. 2009. The End of the Internet: A Folk Response to the Provision of Infinite Choice. In *Folklore and the Internet: Vernacular Expression in a Digital World*, ed. Trevor J. Blank, pp. 80–97. Logan: Utah State University Press.

Thomas, Jeannie Banks. 2003. *Naked Barbies, Warrior Joes, & Other Forms of Visible Gender*. Urbana: University of Illinois Press.

Wojcik, Daniel. 1996. "Polaroids from Heaven": Photography, Folk Religion, and the Miraculous Image Tradition at a Marian Apparition Site. *Journal of American Folklore* 109(432):129–48.

EDITOR'S SUGGESTIONS FOR FURTHER READING

Blank, Trevor J., and Lynne S. McNeill, eds. 2018. *Slender Man Is Coming: Creepypasta and Contemporary Legends on the Internet*. Logan: Utah State University Press.

Blank, Trevor J., and Lynne S. McNeill. 2018. "Introduction: Fear Has No Face: Creepypasta as Digital Legendry." In *Slender Man Is Coming: Creepypasta and Contemporary Legends on the Internet*, edited by Trevor J. Blank and Lynne S. McNeill, 3–24. Logan: Utah State University Press.

Evans, Timothy H. 2014. "The Ghost in the Machine." *New York Times*. June 7, 2014. https://www.nytimes.com/2014/06/08/opinion/sunday/the-ghosts-in-the-machine.html.

Evans, Timothy H. 2018. "Slender Man, H. P. Lovecraft, and the Dynamics of Horror Cultures." In *Slender Man Is Coming: Creepypasta and Contemporary Legends on the Internet*, edited by Trevor J. Blank and Lynne S. McNeill, 128–40. Logan: Utah State University Press.

Kitta, Andrea. 2018. "'What Happens When the Pictures Are No Longer Photoshops?': Slender Man, Belief, and the Unacknowledged Common Experience." In *Slender Man Is Coming: Creepypasta and Contemporary Legends on the Internet*, edited by Trevor J. Blank and Lynne S. McNeill, 77–90. Logan: Utah State University Press.

Koven, Mikel J. 2018. "The Emperor's New Lore; or, Who Believes in the Big Bad Slender Man?" In *Slender Man Is Coming: Creepypasta and Contemporary Legends on the Internet*, edited by Trevor J. Blank and Lynne S. McNeill, 113–27. Logan: Utah State University Press.

Manning, Paul. 2018. "Monstrous Media and Media Monsters: From Cottingley to Waukesha." In *Slender Man Is Coming: Creepypasta and Contemporary Legends on the Internet*, edited by Trevor J. Blank and Lynne S. McNeill, 155–82. Logan: Utah State University Press.

Peck, Andrew. 2015. "At the Modems of Madness: The Slender Man, Ostension, and the Digital Age." *Contemporary Legend* 3(5): 14–37.

Peck, Andrew. 2018. "The Cowl of Cthulu: Ostensive Practice in the Digital Age." In *Slender Man Is Coming: Creepypasta and Contemporary Legends on the Internet*, edited by Trevor J. Blank and Lynne S. McNeill, 51–76. Logan: Utah State University Press.

Tolbert, Jeffery A. 2018. "'Dark and Wicked Things': Slender Man, the Folkloresque, and the Implications of Belief." In *Slender Man Is Coming: Creepypasta and Contemporary Legends on the Internet*, edited by Trevor J. Blank and Lynne S. McNeill, 25–50. Logan: Utah State University Press.

Tolbert, Jeffrey A. 2018. "'The Sort of Story That Has Your Covering Your Mirrors': The Case of Slender Man." In *Slender Man Is Coming: Creepypasta and Contemporary Legends on the Internet*, edited by Trevor J. Blank and Lynne S. McNeill, 91–112. Logan: Utah State University Press.

Tucker, Elizabeth. 2018. "Slender Man Is Coming to Get Your Little Brother of Sister: Teenagers' Pranks Posted on YouTube." In *Slender Man Is Coming: Creepypasta and Contemporary Legends on the Internet*, edited by Trevor J. Blank and Lynne S. McNeill, 141–54. Logan: Utah State University Press.

14

Evoking the Shadow Beast
Disability and Chicano Advocacy in San Antonio's Donkey Lady Legend

Mercedes Elaina Torrez

PREFACE

Some folklorists examine contemporary legends to reveal issues of race, class, gender, sexuality, and disability. A critical activist lens uses legend study to expose prejudice and inequity and to advocate for marginalized groups and social justice. In this chapter, inspired by her childhood in South Texas, Torrez confronts San Antonio's Donkey Lady legend, in which she uncovers an embedded history of social injustice and intersectional themes of race, queerness, and disability. Torrez views the Donkey Lady, a spinster who lives alone with a childlike donkey, as a transgressive, queer character, one who prefers donkeys to children and who chooses to live the single life. As an example of the normative bias leveled at the disabled, Torrez points to the emphasis in the legend (and the legend trip) of the Donkey Lady's disfigurement, in addition to her "insanity" following the violence inflicted upon her, arguing that locals desire to transform the Donkey Lady into the "inhuman" monster they already consider her to be. Torrez sees the Donkey Lady legend trips as akin to freak shows, likening them to the history of viewing the deformed as entertainment. In San Antonio, the Donkey Lady's disfigurement itself is understood as terror inducing, making her "monstrous" or a "freak," key terms in disability studies. Students of legendary monsters can ask similar questions about queerness and normativity, using legend texts derived from original fieldwork to back their claims, evidence drawn from text and from teller. Rigorous collection and careful examination of texts in context can reveal community anxieties, social issues, and latent discussions of race, class, gender, sexuality, and disability.

https://doi.org/10.7330/9781646421602.c014

ESSAY

A city ripe with cultural folklore, San Antonio, Texas is a site for many popular tales of the ghostly and otherwise unexplained. From variations of La Llorona, the woman who wails for her lost children, to recitations of The Dancing Devil, a skilled dancer who transforms into the very face of evil, and a tale of ghostly children pushing cars over the famed Ghost Tracks, San Antonio offers a plethora of legends that have been the subject of much research within the ethnographic and folklore community. In general, studies concerned with these folkloric imaginaries have read these legends as either suggestive of sociocultural regulation or ingresses through which the San Antonio community connects to events of the past. In the case of La Llorona, the weeping woman, Barbara Simerka explores how stories of the female specter are meant to regulate children's behavior and warn against cultural improprieties (2000:50). Similarly, José Limón describes how Fordism, and modernity more generally, creates turmoil between generations, coinciding with surges in the dissemination of The Dancing Devil folklore (1994:172). Both Carl Lindahl (2005) and Cathryn Merla-Watson (2011) explore the ostensive, or healing, connection that San Antonians feel while having their cars seemingly pushed over the Ghost Tracks by juvenile specters of the children said to haunt the area. While Lindahl explains the terror and reverence felt by those who visit the Ghost Tracks and take part in the legend (2005:164), Merla-Watson describes how the act of visiting the tracks ostensively connects visitors to the history of labor associated with the area (2011:58).

Although San Antonio's iconic legends have been the subject of much research and debate amongst the ethnographic and folklore community, one exceedingly influential folkloric icon, San Antonio's Donkey Lady, has been virtually unrecognized in the academic discourse concerning San Antonio legends. The tale, itself, recounts the events leading up to a violent attack on a spinster woman and her lone donkey, the incident leaving the woman hideously disfigured with the appearance of the donkey she loved and cared for. The narrative continues to inspire scores from San Antonio's Mexican-American community to seek out the Donkey Lady at the bridge where it is believed she has remained since the attack. The Donkey Lady legend complicates current understandings of Chicana/o, and more specifically San Antonio, folklore as either a means of social control or a form of ostensive healing. Through the lens of spectral studies, it is possible to theorize both the Donkey Lady legend and the act of visiting Donkey Lady Bridge in order to understand how the Donkey Lady narrative engages with questions concerning the intersection of queerness, disability, and race.

Concerned with the politics of haunting, spectral studies seeks to explain the social injustices and traumas associated with the appearance of ghosts and specters. As sociologist and foremost scholar on the ghostly Avery Gordon points out in her formative text *Ghostly Matters*, haunting is "one way in which abusive systems of power make themselves known and their impacts felt in everyday life, especially when they are supposedly over and done with" (2008:xvi). According to Gordon, haunting refers to "those singular and yet repetitive instances when . . . the over and done with comes alive, when what's in your blind field comes into view" (2011:2). Haunting, then, is the ingress of the past into the present, the vehicle that allows social injustices such as trauma, exploitation, or hegemonic oppression to return to the forefront of thought, demanding attention. In contrast to popular views on haunting, these supernatural appearances are not about playful invisibility or an act of ghoulish trickery; instead haunting immerses us in those histories that are hidden just beyond our periphery. For the purposes of this analysis, the peripheral histories illuminated by haunting are those that reveal not just past, but present instances relating to the subjugation of racial, ethnic, or minority groups. Scholar and author Kathleen Brogan highlights the saliency of this point in suggesting that the deep connection between the offenses of the past, namely oppressive acts against marginalized groups, and the current conflicts stemming from similar issues prove to be the decisive factor in recurrent cultural hauntings within literature and folklore (1998:130).[1] Thus, specters and ghosts manifest when "the trouble they represent and symbolize is no longer being contained, repressed, or blocked from view," demanding attention and haunting ceaselessly until the historical tribulations they represent are acknowledged and rectified in the present (Gordon 2011:2).

More than a question of what is simply real or imagined, supernatural specters raise queries regarding the social and historical offenses of the past, challenging master narratives and complicating linear representations of time. When applied to the cultural production of storytelling and folklore, the spectral may take on the shape of cultural imaginaries, folkloric characters that are not necessarily ghosts, but perform the act of haunting just the same. The Donkey Lady presents an idiomatic example of a cultural imaginary as it relates to sociohistorical epistemologies and the politics of haunting. In my analysis of one of San Antonio's most popular legends, I propose that the Donkey Lady narrative engages with issues of queerness to illustrate a broad history of prejudice, injustice, and violence against those who are non-normative. Furthermore, the act of visiting Donkey Lady Bridge exemplifies the complex relationship between disability and race by suggesting that the Donkey Lady's disfigurement reaffirms socio-historical notions of attraction to and exploitation of disability, while also hinting at a possible linkage between the Donkey Lady and the Chicana/o community that persistently transmits her legend.

The Donkey Lady Legend

Though I have grown up knowing and communicating a specific version of the Donkey Lady legend, numerous accounts of the elusive donkey-esque woman exist. These varying accounts, transmitted almost entirely through oral storytelling (with some appearing on online folklore message boards), include descriptions of the Donkey Lady as a seven-foot tall Chinese woman and a grieving widow and mother gone insane. And while each variation of the narrative offers multiple interpretations, I will focus on what is perhaps the most popular and pertinent version of the story entailing:

> A lady whose house, which was near a bridge over a small creek, was burned. She was a recluse and was asleep when the fire began. She herself was severely burned: fingers and toes fused together to appear hoof-like, and face so disfigured and sagging as to appear similar to that of a donkey or horse. She is also said to have fallen while running from the blazing house, the bones of her hands and feet so burnt and brittle that they broke, leaving stumps as limbs. Afterwards, it is said, she went completely insane, lived under the bridge and roamed the woods on the south side of San Antonio. (Range 2011)

Perhaps most important in this account of the narrative is the reason for which her house is set ablaze. As I understand it, the woman now known as the Donkey Lady was a spinster who lived alone save for one donkey. This donkey was not used for labor, nor was he a source of income for the woman; contrariwise, the woman cared for the donkey as though it were her own child, enjoying the donkey's companionship over that of the surrounding community. Legend has it that on an unknown date some of the children from the community that the woman lived in began goading both the woman and her donkey, presumably mocking them for being outsiders within the neighborhood. Provoked by the taunts of the children, the donkey lashes out at the children, biting one of them in a harsh manner. Later that evening, the men of the community learn about the donkey's attack and confront the woman about the incident, rebuking her for caring for the donkey in such a way and allowing it to bite and, presumably, injure a child. When the woman does nothing to rectify the situation, essentially justifying the child's injury as punishment for tormenting both the donkey and herself, the men become angry and subsequently set fire to the woman's home in the dead of night. In escaping the fire the woman suffered the horribly disfiguring injuries that, as described above, caused her appearance to transform from humanistic to animalistic as she became the fabled Donkey Lady.

It is worth noting that in each variation of the legend the woman who later becomes known as the Donkey Lady is never named, but instead remains a mysterious, ambiguous character. Similarly, in nearly all of the narrative variations the woman is not given the distinction of Donkey Lady until she becomes disfigured. What is also interesting about this legend is that much ambiguity surrounds the time at which these events are believed to have taken place. Oral accounts of the story place the Donkey Lady in San Antonio as early as 1900 and as late as the 1950s, yet no definitive conclusion has been reached concerning either the date of the events or the onset of the legend's oral tradition. This ambiguity, however, has not put a damper on the popularity of the legend as scores of San Antonians widely circulate their version of the tale year-round, sparking much debate as to which narrative variation is the most authentic to San Antonio. This fascination with the authenticity of the tale can be seen as a contributing factor in San Antonio's persistent curiosity with the location known as Donkey Lady Bridge.

LEGEND-TRIP TO DONKEY LADY BRIDGE

The legend of the Donkey Lady is not limited to the legend itself as many San Antonians who become familiarized with the tale find themselves making the pilgrimage to Donkey Lady Bridge. Located on the south side of San Antonio, Donkey Lady Bridge lies within a sparsely populated area. Accessible through a small street labeled Jett Road, the bridge is surrounded by lush vegetation, hovering over a diminutive body of water known as Elm Creek. Though the area was originally cut off from visitation and blocked off to prevent unwanted visitors from coming dangerously close to the creek at night, it has since become part of a high use greenway trail, opening the bridge to an increase in visitation and an unprecedented accessibility. However, the previous lack of accessibility to Donkey Lady Bridge was never enough to keep locals from legend-tripping, the act of journeying to the site of a folk narrative or legend, to the infamous bridge. With a sparse few in their forties and fifties only vaguely familiar with the Legend of the Donkey Lady, the majority of those who venture to the bridge are from younger generations. Searching for a quick, late night thrill, or perhaps drawn by sheer curiosity, droves of San Antonians frequent Donkey Lady Bridge, not only around Halloween, but year round seeking out the fabled creature-like woman hoping to catch a glimpse of her glowing yellow eyes. As one local newspaper states:

> According to the legend, if you drive to the one-lane bridge at night . . . turn off your engine and begin honking [to coax the Donkey Lady out of hiding], several things could and sometimes do happen. They include hearing the heehaw of a donkey or a human imitating the sounds, or feeling the back of the vehicle dip suddenly and later finding donkey hoof prints on the vehicle. Over the years, numerous people have taken the Donkey Lady Bridge dare and had scary experiences. (*San Antonio Express-News* 2006)

Reports of confrontations with the Donkey Lady range from shock and terror as to the legitimacy of the tale, to reaffirmations of the narrative's folk status. And although many have attempted what is known as the Donkey Lady Bridge challenge, the curiosity surrounding what is quickly becoming San Antonio's most popular cultural imaginary never seems to diminish. Some may question the cause of San Antonio's utter fascination with this fabled donkey woman, wondering if there could be more to the dissemination of the tale than the thrill of scaring young children or an attempt to quash adolescent boredom. More than a strange tale of a woman turned hideous beast, the Donkey Lady legend holds significance beyond its status as merely a form of frightening entertainment. In theorizing the Donkey Lady folklore, a greater understanding of the intersections of queerness, disability, and race that lie just below the tale's surface can be acquired, thereby exposing a history of social injustice deeply rooted in the cultural haunting of the Donkey Lady.

THEORIZING THE LEGEND

To begin theorizing the Donkey Lady in terms of queerness, disability, and race, it is imperative to understand how the immediate causes for her disfigurement are connected to broader sociopolitical issues of normativity. Concerned with "the politics of representation, focusing on creating knowledge about the histories, activism, and cultures of a people who have been designated as 'other,'" disability studies works to theorize the disabled not in terms of capabilities, but instead brings attention to the ways in which social environments favor those who are "normatively constituted" (James and Wu 2006:3). In their article "Race, Ethnicity, Disability, and Literature:

Intersections and Interventions" Jennifer James and Cynthia Wu explain how "disability as a label . . . generates institutionalized exclusion" for those who are not normatively constituted, whether mentally, physically, or emotionally (2006:4). The distinction of disability essentially becomes a justification for ostracizing anyone who cannot conform to what society deems to be an acceptable way of life. In retelling the tale of the Donkey Lady, many individuals gloss over the fact that the initial cause of the Donkey Lady's disfigurement is a violent outburst from her own community. So much emphasis is placed on the *cucuy* (frightening) aspect of the story that blame is seemingly placed on the Donkey Lady for the violence that has been enacted upon her. A detailed reading of the Donkey Lady legend, however, exposes issues regarding inattentiveness towards unwarranted acts of violence against non-normative women.

Because the Donkey Lady is a spinster caring for a child-like animal, she essentially becomes a transgressive character, deliberately acting against that which is considered to be normal for a woman. Rather than marrying, reproducing, and maintaining normative domestic roles, the Donkey Lady resists these roles, opting for the distinction of spinster and thereby establishing animosity between her and the men of the community. In her book *The Spinster and Her Enemies*, Sheila Jeffreys explains the attitude towards spinsters as that of "contempt for a creature who was chaste and therefore inhuman" (1997:90). This view of spinster women as inhuman due to their unwillingness to submit to normative gender roles resonates exponentially within the Donkey Lady legend as it further suggests that the woman's non-normative status is the main reason why she becomes brutalized. Living as a queer character, queer simply meaning non-normative, and making what Jeffreys refers to as "a positive choice not to marry," the Donkey Lady is automatically viewed as less than human and therefore devalued as the result of her transgressive status (1997:88). The dehumanized perception that the community has of the Donkey Lady is clearly a major contributing factor in her violent disfigurement. It is almost as if the men of the community seek to turn her into the inhuman monster they consider her to be by setting fire to her home and causing her to appear animalistic rather than human.

The relationship between the woman and her donkey represents yet another contributing factor to the hostility and animosity between the woman and her community. Rather than using the donkey for labor, the woman views the donkey as more of a child than a laborious animal. The maternal feelings the woman displays toward the donkey complicate the relationship between woman and beast as this queer, non-normative relationship can be seen as representing failed motherhood. As previously mentioned, the woman is chastised for caring for the donkey as a child, but in allowing the animal to injure an actual child, the woman exhibits a form of failed maternity. Instead of protecting the child from the donkey, an act that would presumably align with a normative woman's maternal instincts, the woman allows her symbolic child, the donkey, to inflict pain on the child. In failing to intervene during the incident and essentially siding with the donkey, the woman establishes herself as a queer mother figure, resisting normative maternal instincts and instead taking part in a queer, non-normative maternal relationship with her donkey. Interestingly, the Donkey Lady's failed maternity aligns with the failed maternity in the La Llorona folklore, but deviates significantly due to the fact that the Donkey Lady represents a queer motherhood. The queer motherhood that the Donkey Lady creates for herself becomes conflated with her transgressive, non-normative identity as she is now not only a spinster woman, but also a non-productive, queer mother caring for a creature that she herself did not birth. For this reason, the Donkey Lady's inaction toward her donkey's retaliation triggers the series of violent events that occur following the children's taunting.

The location of Donkey Lady Bridge is also a contributing factor in the complicated and violent relationship that develops between the Donkey Lady and the community that brutalizes her as the bridge's liminal location works to solidify her non-normative status. The bridge itself is located in a space that is between both urban and rural locations; it is surrounded by rural, undeveloped land, yet it is not free from the urbanization that follows its distinction as a multiuse trail. Skirting the lines of both communities, Donkey Lady Bridge establishes itself as a third space within which the Donkey Lady resides. Philosopher and social theorist Michel Foucault conceives of these third spaces, or liminal locations, as those places "in which individuals whose behavior is deviant in relation to the required mean or norm are placed" (1986:25). The Donkey Lady fits this description through her transgressions against what the community considers to be normative behavior for a woman. Thus Donkey Lady Bridge represents the woman's denied passage into the normative world as it physically separates her from the normative community, thereby solidifying her queer status.

Although her queer status forces the Donkey Lady to live in a liminal space, divorced from the rest of the community, her secluded liminality does not prevent the community from forcefully intruding on her solitude when provoked by the donkey's attack. As Foucault points out, in general, liminal locations such as Donkey Lady Bridge are not "freely accessible like

Figure 14.1. Donkey Lady Bridge, San Antonio, March 2014. (Photo by Mercedes Elaina Torrez.)

a public place," requiring those who wish to enter to "have certain permission and make certain gestures" (1986:26), yet in the case of the Donkey Lady, this permission is never given. What results is the forced entry of the normative world into a queered, deviant third space that the Donkey Lady inhabits. This forced entry, within both the Donkey Lady narrative and the legend-trip to Donkey Lady Bridge, becomes representative of the violent intrusion of normative prejudice into the vulnerable world of the non-normative, leading to the ghastly brutalization of the Donkey Lady.

Each of these immediate causes for the Donkey Lady's disfigurement exposes prejudices that lead to blame being placed on non-normative victims rather than the perpetrators of violence against such individuals, while simultaneously revealing a broad history of social injustice against those who are non-normative. Within the Donkey Lady narrative, it may seem as though the woman's inaction and generally lax attitude toward her donkey's attack on the child invites brutality against her, but blame for these acts should be placed with the party responsible rather than the victim of such a violent act. By ignoring pre-existing prejudices against the Donkey Lady, participants in the legend seek to reinforce predispositions for placing blame on victims rather than focusing attention on the reasons behind such brutalization.

Concerned primarily with the delightfully terrifying thought of a beast-like woman lurking in the woods near a bridge, San Antonians fail to consider the reasons behind the woman's animalistic deformations. In doing so, these individuals are ignorant of the fact that the Donkey Lady is actually the victim of a cruel display of violence, rather than some nameless woman who becomes disfigured in a house fire. The failure of most, if not all, San Antonians to recognize that the cause behind this violence is the Donkey Lady's queer identity leads to the belief that the woman is somehow responsible for her own disfigurement. However, this is not the case. It is integral to the Donkey Lady legend to understand that the woman's disfigurement comes not at her own hands, but at the hands of a violent community seeking to expel her for her non-normative status. Furthermore, in ignoring the fact that the Donkey Lady is a victim within her legend, participants regress into the sociohistorical role of placing blame with victims of violent attacks rather than offenders. What this problematic role translates to is the perpetuation of the idea that the Donkey Lady initially 'had it coming,' a belief that is likely the reason for the Donkey Lady's haunting.

Additionally, suggesting that the Donkey Lady somehow invited this violent event as a result of her inaction raises troubling queries about the woman's agency within the Donkey Lady narrative. By implying that the woman had this event coming to her, participants in the Donkey Lady narrative take away any agency the woman may have had. Rather than her being responsible for the events that happen to her, the woman is no longer in control of the events that happen in her life if those who transmit the tale believe this violence to be inevitable. What this suggests is that the Donkey Lady is only enabled with agency when she acts of her own volition, not when participants in the narrative make dangerous assumptions about the woman's relationship to her community. Also interesting about the Donkey Lady's struggle for agency is the fact that the woman remains nameless in the Donkey Lady narrative until she becomes the victim of unwarranted brutality. According to the accounts of numerous San Antonians, the name of the woman is not known within the Donkey Lady narrative; instead she is simply referred to as a mysterious recluse. Because the woman is not named until after her disfigurement, her identity is entangled in her distinction as a disabled character, granting her partial agency through her disabled status.

In disregarding all notions of violence inflicted against a non-normative woman, readers enact historical views of cruelty and force towards those unwilling or unable to conform. These prejudices against transgressive individuals reaffirm broad sociohistorical views of non-normative women, spinsters, queer mothers, etc., as having no place in society and thus becoming the victims of violence and backlash from the communities that reject them. Such is the case of San Antonio's Donkey Lady. As a result of the act of savage brutality performed against the Donkey Lady she is left horribly disfigured, causing her to descend further from the normative and forcing her to shelter herself within the overgrowth and solitude of Donkey Lady Bridge. Because of the sociopolitical issues surrounding the narrative of the Donkey Lady, her legend continues to haunt minds of San Antonio residents, carrying with it an underlying current of issues regarding both gender based violence and violence towards the non-normative.

READING DISABILITY IN THE LEGEND-TRIP

Beyond the immediate transparency of the Donkey Lady narrative, bodily disfigurement becomes a form of disability as it invites historically pre-scribed attitudes of fear, disgust, and fascination towards that which is non-normative. In her book *Encarnación: Illness and Body Politics in Chicana Feminist Literature*, Suzanne Bost describes bodily disfigurement in terms of corporeal failure, "challeng[ing] . . . how bodies should work, look, and feel" (2010:5). And while the Donkey Lady's disfigurement is not an illness, the failure of her body to work like a normally constituted body causes her to be seen as a disabled character. This rationale is the most logical as it suggests that because the Donkey Lady no longer has the appearance of a regular woman, her body no longer represents what is considered to be a normal physical appearance, rendering her disabled by normative body standards. This form of corporeal disability leads the Donkey Lady's body to become symbolic of "the marks of history" that unite those with "shared [experiences] that create, remedy, or reproduce illness" (2010:5). The marks of history that Bost refers to are those instances when injustices have been enacted upon those with disabilities or illnesses, such as the exploitation of the Donkey Lady's bodily disfigurement for entertainment purposes. With this in mind, it is clear that the Donkey Lady's disability "makes political demands" (2010:5) while creating a link between her suffering and the shared suffering of the community, or collective, of the disabled, their non-normative bodies demanding equal treatment in the face of continued exclusion.

Furthermore, I assert that the act of visiting Donkey Lady Bridge becomes a performance of the spectacle and attraction of disability as it serves as a means of gawking at that which is considered "monstrous" (*Scary for Kids* [n.d.]). The rationale behind many adventurers' visits to

Donkey Lady Bridge involves catching a glimpse of this "thing," a "beastly apparition" said to lurk in the bushes and respond to the taunts of thrill seekers (ibid.). One San Antonio native, who is increasingly familiar with the tale and was willing to share her experiences with the legend-trip, noted how the act of visiting Donkey Lady Bridge was "a way for [our group of friends] to find out if that creature was really out there, if she really did exist and look the way that everyone describes her" (Sanchez 2015). This rationale proves to be problematic in that it asserts the notion that the Donkey Lady is, in fact, a sort of freak show to be taken in for the viewing pleasure of those who visit her bridge. By establishing the Donkey Lady as a source of fetishized fascination, patrons of Donkey Lady Bridge reaffirm the historical point of view that disability should be looked upon as a source of entertainment. Additionally, the need for individuals to seek out the Donkey Lady to fulfill a dare or prove their bravery illustrates a collective history of fear and disgust in the face of disability. As the *San Antonio Express-News* states, many of the individuals searching for Donkey Lady Bridge only do so as a means of thrill seeking, staring fear in the face and looking upon its hideous appearance (2006). The assumption here is that viewing the disabled woman is somehow associated with braving a terrifying and otherworldly specter. Just as the act of visiting the Donkey Lady for entertainment is problematic, the association of fear and repugnance with the Donkey Lady creates a situation in which disability is seen as shameful and fearful existence. Within this assertion of the attraction and fascination associated with the Donkey Lady's corporeal failure and legend-tripping to Donkey Lady Bridge lies a representation of San Antonio's own history of exploitation of disability.

In San Antonio, specifically, the problematic historical viewpoint of disability as entertainment is exhibited through the persistence of San Antonio's Circus Museum collection. Established by prominent San Antonio lawyer and civic leader Harry Hertzberg, the Hertzberg Circus Museum collection is "the oldest public circus collection in the United States and one of the largest [collections] in existence" (O'Connor 2010). Created as part of Hertzberg's emphatic love of the circus, the Hertzberg collection consists of various pieces of circus memorabilia including the wildly popular 'Side-show exhibit,' featuring photographs, cutouts, and diagrams representing popular side-show oddities and performers from the heyday of the freak show (2010). The items in the collection were displayed within the San Antonio Public Library in 1942 and remained with the library through its various moves to new locations, before finally being transferred to San Antonio's Witte Museum in 2003 (Young 2010).[2] Although the collection has changed hands and been relocated numerous times, it remains on display both within the Witte and at the front doors of the museum where a circus elephant statue greets entering guests. The persistence of the Circus Museum has been secured by the Witte Museum as they plan to include "visible storage and publicly accessible research spaces with a special area dedicated to the circus collection" as part of a recent museum renovation (ibid.). The permanence of the Circus Museum, and more specifically the side-show exhibit, exposes San Antonio's long history of viewing disability as a form of attraction and entertainment, a problematic relationship that carries over into the legend-trip to Donkey Lady Bridge. Much like the performers showcased in the side-show exhibit at the Circus Museum, the Donkey Lady is exploited for entertainment's sake as part of San Antonio's complicated history concerning disability. Thus the ongoing fetishized fascination with the attraction of disability becomes the epitome of the Donkey Lady's continuous haunting of San Antonio.

In establishing the Donkey Lady as a source of fetishized fascination, patrons of Donkey Lady Bridge ultimately engage in relieving the Donkey Lady of agency, placing full control in the hands of the normative spectator. The loss of agency can serve as one interpretation for the Donkey Lady's supposed display of violence towards those who venture to disturb her solitude. By damaging car hoods and windshields, the Donkey Lady regains agency by bringing awareness to the sociohistorical and sociopolitical issues concerning disability, heteronormativity, and gender violence that beckon her to remain at the forefront of San Antonio storytelling. Her representation of the anger and hostility of the disabled leaves literal dents with those who come to find her.

Establishing a Collective Narrative

The Donkey Lady folklore is more than a mere source of entertainment and fascination for the Chicana/o community that frequently visits her; the connection between San Antonio's Chicana/o community and the Donkey Lady folklore reveals yet another complex facet to the folklore that cannot be overlooked. Because the legend takes place in San Antonio, a city with a large population of Chicanas/os, it is necessary to explore the meaning associated with the predominance of Chicanas/os both circulating the legend and making the proverbial pilgrimage to Donkey Lady Bridge. In taking part in the legend-trip, Chicanas/os are not divorced from the history of exploitation and fear associated with visiting Donkey Lady Bridge, but instead perform the ritualistic act of coaxing the Donkey Lady from hiding in order to ensure that she continues to illuminate social issues concerning the objectionable treatment of San Antonio's Chicana/o community. In this way, the Donkey Lady's disability can be understood as both connecting the injustices of the past with the present, while also suggesting a repressed, or otherwise unrecognized, identification of San Antonio's Chicana/o community with the folk character.

Disability has previously been exploited to justify discrimination against those who are considered differently abled, with disability often becoming conflated with race to defend inhumane actions towards both the disabled and those of non-hegemonic races (James and Wu 2006:4). As Jennifer James and Cynthia Wu remark, disability is like race in its inherent tradition of alienation and subjugation (2006:5). Being a minority, no matter the racial or ethnic group, an individual is rejected by the hegemony, making it increasingly difficult to create a viable space for a productive life. Much like disability, race and ethnicity become an obstacle that is nearly impossible to overcome in the face of rampant discrimination, thus race becomes a handicap in and of itself. This conflation of race and disability is demonstrated within the Donkey Lady folklore as the site of Donkey Lady Bridge establishes a collective narrative of the marginalization of racial difference.

Though the Donkey Lady folklore is typically viewed as a frightening tale of a woman gone mad with revenge, what many participants in the legend gloss over is the fact that the site of the legend is not merely a location for the folkloric performance of a cultural imaginary. Rather, Donkey Lady Bridge acts as a site of what ethnographer and scholar José Limón refers to as an "emergent collective narrative," calling attention to the causes behind and reactions to disability (1994:174). As the location where a "recurrent belief exists," Donkey Lady Bridge becomes a site for the cultural connection between the Donkey Lady and the San Antonio Chicana/o community that continues to retell and pass on the Donkey Lady's narrative to younger generations (ibid.). In creating an emergent collective narrative, the Donkey Lady folklore becomes an avenue through which the Chicano/a community identifies with the Donkey Lady, the exploitation of her disability becoming conflated with the unfair treatment of Chicanas/os. It would seem as though the predominance of Chicanas/os telling the story suggests that Chicana/o participants in the folklore, whether they are fully cognizant of it or not, are in some way identifying with the marginalization felt by the Donkey Lady. This rationale is certainly plausible if the agitation and exploitation enacted by Chicanas/os at Donkey Lady Bridge is seen as a projection of the Chicana/o community's perpetual feelings of marginalization. If this is the case, the Donkey Lady's cultural haunting becomes representative of the community's identification with her as her haunting becomes a form of advocacy for the marginalized Chicana/o community. By portraying the Donkey Lady as an advocate for the San Antonio Chicana/o community, the Donkey Lady folklore complicates established beliefs of San Antonio folklore as ostensive healing or social control. Instead, the Donkey Lady becomes an extension of the Chicana/o community's fears, anger, marginalization, and disenfranchisement. Thus, the Donkey Lady's suggested advocacy opens a new avenue of thought in which a folk character transcends the boundaries of folk status, coming alive in a very real way for the community that both receives and transmits her legend.

To this point I would like to propose that the Donkey Lady, specifically in her violent behavior towards those who dare to conjure her, can be seen as an extension of what Gloria Anzaldúa dubs the Shadow-Beast. Described as the rebel inside of her, Anzaldúa's Shadow-Beast is the representation of that which will not accept the constraints of normativity, "kick[ing] out with both feet" in protest of limitations and prejudices. In a literal kicking out of feet (hooves), the Donkey Lady strikes back against the collective history of subjugation brought upon her by those frequenting her bridge (2010:38). Furthermore, I contend that the Donkey Lady represents the Shadow-Beast in all Chicanas/os; she is that force that will not be tamed and will not be silenced. She lingers on the tongues and in the minds of San Antonio's Chicana/o community because her haunting represents the need for social change, the need to strike back against the constraints and limitations brought on by identifying as a Chicana/o. In becoming the Shadow-Beast, the Donkey Lady, and the Chicana/o community that she represents, carry on what the donkey started, striking back at those who taunt the marginalized and exploited. This act of striking back at the hegemony leaves marks that illustrate an inability to accept the subjugation and exploitation of Chicanas/os by the hegemonic classes and races, and solidifies the Donkey Lady as a cultural projection of the Chicana/o community.

CONCLUSION

More than a terrifying tale of a disfigured donkey-woman seeking revenge against those who caused her ill-fated transformation, the legend of San Antonio's Donkey Lady exposes a collective history of violence, fear, fascination, and misunderstanding of disability. Research on the Donkey Lady provides insight into the complex intersections of ethnicity and ability that are reflective of broad histories of marginalization. Her representation of the non-normative allows for multiple interpretations of how the transgressive have been and continue to be looked down upon, chastised, and degraded by hegemonic structures while also insisting that the Donkey Lady be viewed as an advocate for social change. Rather than simply explaining the Donkey Lady legend as a means of social control used by the Chicana/o community or a form of participation in ostensive healing, this research complicates demonstrated epistemologies regarding the relationship between folklore, legend-trips, and the communities or groups that keep these stories alive. This development in the body of folkloric and ethnographic research opens up alternate avenues for creating cultural meaning and establishing the overall significance of folk narratives, and in doing so, gives a voice to one of San Antonio, Texas's most popular and iconic folk characters.

NOTES

1. For a more in-depth reading of cultural haunting see Brogan (1998) and Holland (2000).

2. Harry Hertzberg indicated in his will that the Witte Museum be given sole ownership of the collection should the city of San Antonio no longer be able to care for the collection.

REFERENCES

Anzaldúa, Gloria E. 2010. Movimientos De Rebeldía Y Las Culturas Que Traicionan. *Borderlands/La Frontera: The New Mestiza*, 3rd ed., 37–45. San Francisco, CA: Aunt Lute Books.

Bost, Suzanne. 2010. Introduction. *Encarnación: Illness and Body Politics in Chicana Feminist Literature*, 1–33. Bronx, NY: Fordham University Press.

Brogan, Kathleen. 1998. *Cultural Haunting: Ghosts and Ethnicity in Recent American Literature*. Charlottesville, VA: University of Virginia Press.

Foucault, Michel. 1986. Of Other Spaces. *Diacritics* 42.2: 22–27. doi:10.2307/464648.

Gordon, Avery F. 2008. Introduction. *Ghostly Matters: Haunting and the Sociological Imagination*, xv–xx. Minneapolis, MN: University of Minnesota Press.

Gordon, Avery F. 2011. Some Thoughts on Haunting and Futility. *Borderlands* 10.2: 1–5.

Holland, Sharon Patricia. 2000. *Raising the Dead: Readings of Death and (Black) Subjectivity*. Durham, NC: Duke University Press.

James, Jennifer C. and Cynthia Wu. 2006. Editors' Introduction: Race, Ethnicity, Disability, and Literature: Intersections and Interventions. *MELUS* 31.3: 3–13.

Jeffreys, Sheila. 1997. *The Spinster and Her Enemies: Feminism and Sexuality, 1880–1930*. North Melbourne, Vic: Spinifex Press.

Limón, José E. 1994. *Dancing with the Devil: Society and Cultural Poetics in Mexican-American South Texas*. Madison: University of Wisconsin Press.

Lindahl, Carl. 2005. Ostensive Healing: Pilgrimage to the San Antonio Ghost Tracks. *Journal of American Folklore* 118.468: 164–185.

Merla-Watson, Cathryn. 2011. Spectral Materialisms: Colonial Complexes and the Insurgent Acts of Chicana/o Cultural Production. Doctoral dissertation. University of Minnesota.

O'Connor, Robert F. 2010. Hertzberg Circus Collection and Museum. *Handbook of Texas Online.* https://tshaonline.org/handbook/online/articles/lbh04.

Range, Katherine. 2011. San Antonio's Donkey Lady Bridge Is Chilling, Whether Truth or Tale. *Examiner.* 4 Aug. 2011. Accessed 9 May 2014. Examiner.com.

San Antonio Express-News. 2006. Donkey Lady Tales Travel around Area. 25 Oct. Reprinted at *MySanantonio.com.* 25 Oct. 2012. http://www.mysanantonio.com/entertainment /halloween/article/Donkey-Lady-tales-travel-around-area-3979768.php. Accessed 15 Dec. 2016.

Sanchez, Sabrina. 2015. Personal Interview, 21 Sept.

Scary for Kids. [n.d.]. Donkey Lady Bridge in San Antonio. http://www.scaryforkids.com /donkey-lady/. Accessed 9 May 2014.

Simerka, Barbara. 2000. Woman Hollering: Contemporary Chicana Reinscriptions of a Llorona Mythography. *Confluencia* 16.1: 49–58.

Young, Ken. 2010. Some Notes on the Hertzberg Circus Collection. *Ken Young's Page of Circus Links.* 12 July. http://www.kenyoung.net/hcc.html. Accessed 15 Dec. 2016.

EDITOR'S SUGGESTIONS FOR FURTHER READING

Arora, Shirley L. 1994. "'Look, Daddy. I Have Teeth!' A Devil Legend in Contemporary Hispanic Tradition." *Contemporary Legend* 4: 5–29.

Campbell, Claire. 2012. "Hidfolk of Texas." In *First Timers and Old Timers: The Texas Folklore Society Fire Burns On,* edited by Kenneth L. Untiedt, 265–72. Denton: University of North Texas Press.

Glazer, Mark. 1994. "'El Diablo En El Baile': Cultural Change, Tradition, and Continuity in a Chicago Legend." *Contemporary Legend* 4: 31–44.

Lindahl, Carl. 2005. "Ostensive Healing: Pilgrimage to the San Antonio Ghost Tracks." *Journal of American Folklore* 118 (468): 164–85.

Rushing, J. Rhett. 2012. "Monsters in Texas." In *First Timers and Old Timers: The Texas Folklore Society Fire Burns On,* edited by Kenneth L. Untiedt, 285–92. Denton: University of North Texas Press.

15

Going Van Helsing in Puerto Rico
Hunting the Chupacabra Legend

Benjamin Radford

PREFACE

Researcher and skeptic Benjamin Radford has sought on-the-ground empirical evidence of numerous North American monsters, including the Lizard Man of Scape Ore Swamp, Champ of Lake Champlain, and Ogopogo of Okanagan Lake. A New Mexico resident, Radford began his investigation shortly after chupacabra reports surfaced near his hometown. Five years of extensive research followed, taking him across the Caribbean to Hispaniola, where he riffled through dingy archives and questioned local witnesses in search of the truth of the chupacabra. His efforts led to the definitive book on the goat-sucking monster, *Tracking the Chupacabra: The Vampire Beast in Fact, Fiction, and Folklore* (2011).

What Radford found was a modern-day vampire legend dressed in the guise of an alienlike creature symbolic of U.S. relations with Latin America—a strange, foreign entity leeching the lifeblood of natives. As legends are wont to do, the chupacabra deftly attached itself to larger legend complexes of government conspiracies, extraterrestrials, and indigenous origins. Radford also notes how the chupacabra blended neatly with the contemporary media, both in content—he sees the movie *Species* (1995) as the original chupacabra inspiration–and in diffusion—he credits the mass media as the main chupacabra disseminator. Radford ultimately concluded that a memorate, a legendary personal experience narrative told by Madelyne Tolentino and inspired by *Species*, was the match that lit the chupacabra blaze, the flames kindled in a receptive legend environment and then fanned by an intrigued public. While monster study has yet to achieve high prestige in the academy, Radford's extensive travel, fieldwork, interviewing,

https://doi.org/10.7330/9781646421602.c015

and archival research do credit to the professionalism and diligence of legend researchers today. New researchers would do well to model such enthusiasm and dedication, even if on a much smaller scale.

ESSAY

The chupacabra stands out as an unusual North American monster in a continent populated by strange creatures. Its cryptozoological brethren include Bigfoot, the Loch Ness Monster, Mothman, Lizard Man, and various other legendary oddities.

Rooted in conspiracy theory and anti-American sentiment, the chupacabra is a bizarre amalgamation of vampiric monster and legend. Bigfoot is of course named for what it leaves behind: big footprints. The chupacabra is also known for what it leaves behind: exsanguinated animals. Though goats are said to be its favorite prey (*chupacabra* means *goat sucker* in Spanish), it has been blamed for attacks on sheep, rabbits, chickens, and other animals. It is, in other words, a vampire, and this realization informed my research. Vampires are of course the stuff of legend, though far less so of cryptozoology.[1] But vampirism is the chupacabra's signature characteristic, and thus my research began with examining vampire legends.

While some mistakenly believe that chupacabra sightings date back to the 1970s or earlier, the creature first appeared in 1995 in Puerto Rico. The mythology of the chupacabra's origin has two distinct and intertwined themes. The first is that the beast is a Frankenstein's monster–type creation birthed in top-secret government genetics experiments conducted in secret laboratories hidden deep in the island's El Yunque rainforest. When a hurricane damaged the facility, the chupacabra escaped into the surrounding jungle where it lived for years, preying on small animals. The second theory is that the chupacabra was originally an extraterrestrial creature, a sort of alien pet that escaped from a visiting spacecraft during one of many alleged UFO visitations (more on that later). The two origin stories are neatly combined into one science fiction/conspiracy narrative with the assumption that the U.S. government had used alien genetics in its unholy science experiments, which were then accidentally loosed upon the world. Since then, the creatures are said to have spread to other parts of the globe—including as far away as Russia—though most reports remain close to its (adopted) Latin American home. The chupacabra had a heyday of about five years, when it was widely reported in Mexico, Chile, Nicaragua, Argentina, Brazil, and Florida, among other places. Tracing its folkloric journey became a central part of my five-year investigation into the monster, eventually resulting in my 2011 book *Tracking the Chupacabra*.

The chupacabra appears in three different physical forms: the "original" is that of a three- to five-foot-tall bipedal creature with long claws, red eyes, and a distinctive row of spikes down its back, first reported in August 1995 by Puerto Rican eyewitness Madelyne Tolentino; the second is a canid mammal (e.g., dogs, coyotes, and foxes) first reported in 2000; and the third is a catchall category that includes any unusual animal, alive or dead, that anyone reports seeing or thinks—for whatever reason—might be the dreaded chupacabra. Whatever form it takes, in twenty-five years it has become a global phenomenon—the world's third best-known cryptozoological monster after Bigfoot and the Loch Ness Monster.

I became interested in researching this creature because it combined several of my passions. I'd always had an interest in monsters, and had previously researched and written about Bigfoot, lake monsters (including British Columbia's Ogopogo and its folklore; see Radford and Nickell 2006), and other beasties; plus the legend angle fascinated me. Furthermore, the chupacabra had been reported in my home state—in fact only a few miles from my residence outside of Albuquerque, New Mexico. Speaking passable Spanish helped, and I soon identified vampirism as being not only the key to understanding the creature but also to proving (or disproving) its existence. This cryptozoological mystery leaves behind hard evidence of its supposed presence in the form of dead bodies. Those bodies, if subjected to scientific forensic examination, should yield conclusive evidence one way or the other. My goal was, if possible, to solve the mystery as definitively as I could, adopting a multidisciplinary approach including legend, cryptozoology, forensics, and field investigation.

Vampiric Roots of the Chupacabra

Vampires are a worldwide phenomenon (Bullard 2000; Beresford 2008; Dundes 1998). The vampires most Westerners are familiar with are revenants—human corpses said to return from the grave to harm the living. Other, older versions of the vampire were not thought to be human at all but instead supernatural entities and therefore did not take human form when they stalked their prey. The chupacabra is just this sort of vampire.

Paul Barber, author of *Vampires, Burial, and Death*, notes that the idea of some people returning from the dead and sucking blood or bodily sustenance is universal. Stories from nearly every continent and every culture have some localized version of the vampire, and "bear a surprising resemblance to the European vampire" (1988, 2). Vampire mythology is broad, so in relation to the chupacabra, I focused on two distinctive elements of vampirism: (1) vampires draining blood, energy, or other bodily substance through physical contact; and (2) vampires being blamed for unexpected deaths or unexplained misfortune (in this case, the death of livestock).

The location of the legend's emergence was of course important. Puerto Rico's status as a colony of the United States was relevant as well, and to better appreciate the nuances, I examined how vampire legends arose in Africa during and after colonialism. Luise White, in her book *Speaking with Vampires: Rumor and History in Colonial Africa* (2000), investigated stories of vampires throughout East Africa and found commonalities among people across many cultures (primarily in Uganda, Zambia, and Kenya) who told similar stories (with localized variants) of vampires that sucked the blood and other forms of metaphorical livelihood out of ordinary Africans.

Given its cultural and historical context, it was inevitable that the vampire would appear in Latin America. Historian Robert Jordan notes that "Latin American society is already one known for its propensity for religious superstition and the prevalence of supernatural events such as miracles, spiritual visions, sightings of the Virgin Mary, Satan, etc." (2008, 3). Indeed, folklorist Thomas Bullard adds, "Folk traditions in [Latin America] indicate that the chupacabra stories flourished not by accident but by a long acceptance of vampire-like activity—that this latest monster simply thrived in soil already fertilized by expectation" (2000, 9).

The perception and resentment of native resources being taken by outsiders are very much a part of the Latin American cultural fabric. Legend scholar Veronique Campion-Vincent, in discussing stories and legends of organ theft in Latin America, notes that "the theme of the white ogre—of the malevolent white man endowed with somewhat supernatural attributes who needs blood or organs from the colored people whom he dominates—has been noted by many anthropologists in several third world regions" (1990, 19).

While the chupacabra is not necessarily interchangeable with the American "white ogre" metaphor in this respect, one of the most widespread theories about the monster's origin is that the U.S. government specifically created the chupacabra in an evil, clandestine genetics experiment gone wrong. Thus, in the minds of many Hispanics and Latin Americans, the chupacabra very much represents the United States. Jordan argues that the chupacabra as a symbol is "a form of cultural resistance which many people of Puerto Rico, Mexico, and the greater part of Latin America use to maintain social bonds and gain control over growing fears surrounding the perceived destructive effects of 'toxic' U.S. political and economic imperialism" (2008, 2). Historian Lauren Derby, writing in the journal *Past and Present*, argues that "the chupacabras belief was an urban legend, a popular commentary on modernity and its risks as they are perceived in Puerto Rico" (2008, 292). Thus we find that the chupacabra is not only born in legends, but vampire legends specifically.

THE LEGEND SPREADS

By following the legend's threads, we can see how one woman's sighting of something odd outside her home in rural Puerto Rico spawned one of the most famous cryptozoological monsters in history. The chupacabra is the first cryptozoological monster of the Internet age; had it been sighted a few years earlier, it's likely that few outside of Puerto Rico would have heard of this particular Hispanic vampire. The rumors spread through traditional routes and ripened in the late 1990s, just as the island was being increasingly wired to the Internet, allowing legends to more easily spread beyond its shores.[2]

In the days and weeks following the first sighting of what would later be named as (and assumed to be) the chupacabra, most of the early reports were spread through traditional rumor routes: over back fences and among neighbors and friends. But soon local tabloids smelled a sensational news story and propelled it throughout the island. Among the four newspapers that served Puerto Rico in 1995, *El Vocero* was among the most popular, the *National Enquirer* of Puerto Rico. This sensationalist coverage shaped the information and legends that most Puerto Ricans encountered about the monster. Because mainstream newspapers largely ignored the lurid chupacabra stories, *El Vocero* happily filled the news void. As a result, few Puerto Ricans were exposed to whatever few folkloric, skeptical, and scientific analyses were available.[3] The majority of chupacabra stories circulated in Puerto Rico at the time were written by only a handful of *El Vocero* reporters; one in particular, Ruben Dario Rodriguez, accounted for nearly half of the stories.

As legend scholars Gillian Bennett and Paul Smith note, "one of the things that helps to define a legend is *uncertainty* about whether it is true" (2007, xx) and, as with any legend, there was no consensus about the chupacabra's reality or meaning. Some Puerto Ricans made fun of it, while many seized the opportunity to cash in on it with merchandise and music. There were occasional panics over the chupacabra, with concerned citizens forming patrols and armed vigilante mobs hoping to find the chupacabra. Some individuals, particularly ranchers and farmers, feared the creature—or at least its presumed threat to their livelihood—while most urban Puerto Ricans were unconcerned by the rumors.

The folklore of the chupacabra was widely shared on talk radio and tabloids but was propelled onto the international stage in large part due to a local UFO researcher group and its leader, Jorge Martín. Martín (a fervent conspiracy theorist who claimed Puerto Rico was being used as a base for extraterrestrials) contacted Tolentino, resulting in a widely shared illustration by Martín based on her description. (She would later note some inaccuracies in his depiction, which I later corrected in my own illustration.)

Martín and his group played an important (and largely unrecognized) role in shaping the chupacabra legend, adding an assumed backstory to the creature's biography that became canon. Tolentino had a strange sighting without a context, while Martín had a ready-made context, one he'd spent years looking into: animal mutilations and UFOs. Tolentino never claimed, assumed, or suggested that the curious creature she saw had attacked any animals or sucked any blood, nor that it was extraterrestrial (see Radford 2021).[4]

Martín, on the other hand, saw her sighting as a piece of a puzzle he'd been looking for. The chupacabra could fit, or "explain," two of his pet theories at once, and he soon added his preferred backstories to the beast when reporting and publicizing it in a "folkloresque" process. As Michael Dylan Foster and Jeffrey A. Tolbert explain, "A folkloresque product is rarely based on any single vernacular item or tradition; usually it has been consciously cobbled together from a range of folkloric elements, often mixed with newly created elements, to appear as if it emerged organically from a specific source . . . it is imbued with a sense of 'authenticity' (as perceived by the consumer and/or creator) derived from an association with 'real' folklore" (2016, 5). The chupacabra became a new popular culture product, drawn from—and given believability by—familiar motifs, including rumors of vampires, extraterrestrial contacts, government conspiracies, and monsters.

Though Martín's audience of the UFO community was relatively small, the chupacabra made another leap onto the international stage in March 1996, when the popular daytime Univision talk show *El show de Cristina* tackled the topic and broadcast it into Spanish-speaking households throughout Latin America and North America (particularly Florida and Texas). Almost immediately the chupacabra began being reported (mostly online and in some local newspapers) in cities where the broadcast was seen. The chupacabra nevertheless was confined mostly to the Spanish-speaking world for another nine months until January 12, 1997, when the goat sucker got its big break on American television in an episode of *The X-Files* ("El Mundo Gira," season 4, episode 11) in which Mulder and Scully investigate the death of a young migrant worker. Given the production schedule for the television show, the writer likely began working on the story in early 1996, just as the chupacabra scare was waning in Puerto Rico but spreading to Mexico and Nicaragua. From 1997 on, the chupacabra was widely discussed across North America and elsewhere, though it remained mostly reported (as a cryptozoological entity attacking animals) in Spanish-speaking areas.

The chupacabra found fertile ground in Puerto Rico and elsewhere in Latin America at least in part due to its status as a vampire and symbol of colonialism. This was especially true in Puerto Rico, as we have seen, but chupacabra reports elsewhere featured the anti-American conspiracy motif as well (in Chile, for example, rumors circulated that the chupacabra had escaped a top-secret NASA facility where the U.S. agency was trying to create hybrid beings that could survive on Mars). The chupacabra was particularly resonant in Mexico, the only Spanish-speaking country to share a border with the United States; in fact, it's common for the public to assume that the chupacabra is of Mexican, not American (i.e., Puerto Rican), origin. In Mexico the chupacabra was often conceptualized more in terms of intra-country socioeconomic inequality than international inequality. The then president of Mexico, Carlos Salinas, for example, was often satirically described as a chupacabra, draining the riches from the common citizens for his own benefit.

What began as a single, simple sighting of something strange took on legendary form through rumor, tabloid stories, Internet chatrooms, and television, amplified and altered at each turn in classic folkloresque fashion. The original chupacabra likely would have merited little more than a footnote in Forteana had it not been fortified by vampire legends and conspiracy rumors.

BLENDING FORENSICS WITH FOLKLORE

Now that I had a handle on the chupacabra's background in vampire lore, the next phase of my research focused on reputed forensic evidence of alleged chupacabra bodies and their victims. I researched animal predation, medical pathology, and claims of mysterious animal mutilations that in other contexts had previously been attributed to Satanists or extraterrestrials. Concluding that there was no evidence that the dozen or so claimed "chupacabra" carcasses were anything other than misidentified ordinary animals (often in the advanced stages of sarcoptic mange)—and that the routine rumors that their victims had "been drained of every drop of blood" were wholly unverified—I turned my attention back to trying to establish the monster's folkloric origin as a memorate, Tolentino's oral narrative relating her personal encounter with the monster.

The genesis of some legendary figures, such as the Jersey Devil, have been roughly established and the topic of considerable research (see, for example, Regal and Esposito 2018). On the other end of the spectrum there is Slender Man, whose date and circumstances of first creation have been conclusively established (Kitta 2015; Blank and McNeill 2018) because of its recency. In the case of the chupacabra, we had a specific origin dating back to a specific identifiable single eyewitness who, in the second week of August 1995, outside her home in a suburb of San Juan, first saw what would later become known as the chupacabra.

I traveled for the research, including to Cuero, Texas, for the television show *MonsterQuest*; to the jungle border between Costa Rica and Nicaragua to investigate the possibility of an extant population of the creatures; and most importantly to Puerto Rico, to interview the original eyewitness firsthand. In the process I was able to get a better look at where the creature was sighted and under what conditions.

Tracking the Teller

Madelyne Tolentino, the original teller, had been the focus of little or no skeptical investigation or folkloric research since she had initially reported her sighting to Jorge Martín, the conspiracy theorist mentioned earlier. After the chupacabra legend took on a life of its own, Tolentino's report had been largely forgotten, the attention moving from a baffling and unique sighting in Puerto Rico to mangy coyotes in Texas.

I was able to contact Tolentino through her ex-husband, whom I found on Facebook, and she agreed to be interviewed. A colleague and I flew to Puerto Rico, and we met Tolentino at a coffee shop outside of San Juan. I recorded the interview and worked with her to create an updated, more accurate depiction of what she saw. We then went to the home where she lived at the time of the sighting, and she described her memorate in greater detail. We continued the interview at her nearby new home. During the interview Tolentino mentioned that the creature she saw strongly resembled the alien monster Sil in the 1995 horror/science fiction film *Species*. Her description closely matched the monster, from the alien wraparound eyes to the humanoid form and especially the distinctive row of spikes down its spine.

This was a small detail that I had seen mentioned only once in passing, in an interview she gave in 1996 to a Puerto Rican UFO investigation group, published in a 1997 book by Scott Corrales titled *Chupacabras and*

Figure 15.1. Madelyne Tolentino and her ex-husband standing at the site of her original chupacabra sighting. (Photograph courtesy of Benjamin Radford.)

Figure 15.2. Benjamin Radford's hand-drawn rendering of the chupacabra based on Madelyne Tolentino's recollection. (Courtesy of Benjamin Radford.)

Other Mysteries. In it Tolentino states that she saw "a movie called *Species*. It would be a very good idea if you saw it. The movie begins here in Puerto Rico, at the Arecibo observatory . . . It was a creature that looked like the chupacabra, with spines on its back and all . . . The resemblance to the chupacabra was really impressive" (Corrales 1997, 45).

Though clearly fictional, the film *Species* was specifically intended to be realistic and plausible, not only in its special effects but also in its setting of (then) present-day Puerto Rico. The use of real locations, including the Arecibo Radio Observatory, lent the film further credibility—especially to Puerto Ricans. The significance dawned on me that the monster in *Species* being identical to the chupacabra Tolentino later claimed to see was a cause-and-effect relationship instead of a remarkable coincidence. Tolentino regarded *Species* as a fictionalized account of obviously real events that were going on in Puerto Rico at the time, informed by rumors then circulating (spread in part by Jorge Martín and his UFO group). The original and most influential chupacabra eyewitness in history, it turned out, described an H. R. Giger–inspired alien she'd seen in a movie as the monster she encountered in real life.

The Sil alien and the creature that Tolentino described are indeed remarkably similar. Both have large, red or black wraparound eyes; an elongated head; a tiny or nonexistent nose; five long fingers; a series of spikes along the spine; long, thin arms; long, thin legs; no ears; a small, almost nonexistent mouth, and so on. The folkloric parallels were even more striking: Sil and the chupacabra have identical origin stories; as noted, the two main explanations for the chupacabra are that it is either an extraterrestrial alien life-form or the result of top-secret U.S. government genetics experiments gone wrong. These happen to be *exactly* the two origin explanations of the *Species* creature: Sil is *both* an extraterrestrial alien life-form *and* the result of top-secret U.S. government genetics experiments gone wrong. The similarity of the Sil creature from the *Species* film to the Puerto Rican chupacabra is clear, direct, and unmistakable. We need not assume that the teller was lying—merely that she could have been, and upon closer inspection almost certainly was, mistaken in her memorate.

During my visit to Puerto Rico, I also visited other areas with links to chupacabra lore, including the El Yunque rainforest (said to be an early home of the beast); the Arecibo Radio Observatory; and the town of Moca (said to have been the site of mysterious vampire attacks in 1975, though they had no real connection to the monster). Interviewing the original teller was crucial to understanding the specific form this vampire took, though others provided its legendary context.

Chupacabra Fakelore

In the wake of worldwide fame, chupacabra fakelore soon surfaced. Though both vampire legends and "mysterious" animal predation date back many centuries, I've uncovered no evidence of any blood-sucking *chupacabra*, in Puerto Rico or anywhere else, before the 1990s. Its recent vintage and lack of provenance pose problems for those who claim it exists, because real animals don't simply appear out of nowhere; all animals are subject to the same evolutionary pressures and must have descended from earlier, equally known animals. The tree of life simply doesn't have a branch for the chupacabras, any more than it does for Bigfoot, Nessie, or the Jersey Devil.

When forced to account for this conspicuous lack of historical record, some resort to fakelore to provide a background (for more on this, see Loxton and Prothero 2015; Meurger and Gagnon 1989; Radford and Nickell 2006). It's not surprising that Latin America would serve as a plausible setting for chupacabra origin stories. In his book *Enchanted Legends and Lore of New Mexico*, Ray John De Aragon includes a fanciful tale titled "The Sheepherder and the Chupacabra," in which a shepherd named Francisco recounts a story presented as a memorate by an old *curandera* [medicine woman] who "said that many, many years ago, people were finding dead cattle, dead chickens, dead *cibolos* (bison), dead sheep, and goats and even a person who seemed like the blood had been drained out." She herself claimed to have seen the beast, which she kept at bay using a Roman Catholic detente (embroidered picture): "I just held my detente out with my hand toward him. I don't go anywhere without my detente. You never know when you're going to see a chupacabra." Heeding the old woman's lessons, Francisco, too, carries a detente, which—along with the Lord's Prayer—later saves his life when confronted by the beast (2012, 90–91). In classic contemporary legend style De Aragon presents the story as true, though it appears to have been fabricated by De Aragon, with no recorded teller or historical provenance. As Jeffrey Tolbert (2015, 39) notes, "This playful (or cynical) manipulation of the boundaries of fiction and reality—akin to what historian Michael Saler . . . has called the 'ironic imagination'—is discursively powerful, and seems particularly easy to effect when the creators of popular media invoke the conventions of folklore."

Another fakeloric claim to a natural history of the chupacabra comes from Bob Curran (2005) in his book *Vampires: A Field Guide to the Creatures That Stalk the Night*. He describes early explorer Francisco Vázquez de Coronado's encounter with the goat sucker. In a chapter titled "El Chupacabra," Curran writes: "A legend says that as he camped during the night, Coronado's livestock were attacked. It is told that some of his men drove off the attackers—described as small, dark, horny-skinned men—with torches and spears." These "horny-skinned men" with spears were said to have been chupacabras.

In the archives of the Universidad Interamericana at Bayamon, Puerto Rico, I discovered a Spanish-language booklet published in 1996 boldly titled *La verdadera historia del chupacabras* (*The True History of Chupacabras*) which, as the title suggests, purports to reveal the true history of the beast. The ninety-six-page book—written under the name Redaccion Noticiosa—suggests that the Taino Indians (an Arawak-related group who inhabited many Caribbean islands when Columbus reached the Americas) hunted the chupacabra for food. Another fakeloric origin story for the chupacabra relates a memorate from a Chilean man who said his forefathers knew of the beast and its Satanic origins (Corrales 2004, 127). For monster enthusiasts and cryptozoology buffs (who, unlike folklorists, typically engage with the chupacabra as an extant monster instead of a legend) the lack of a pre-1995 history poses a problem and creates a vacuum filled by fakelore.

CHUPACABRA CONCLUSIONS

I adopted a blend of approaches in researching the chupacabra. A classical folkloric approach privileges study of the legend's transmission over establishing any objectively verifiable "truth" behind the legends. Whether a legend is "true" or not is typically beside the point. This position is sometimes at odds with, for example, an investigative approach; a journalist cannot be content to record and examine rumor motifs and variants but wants to, ideally, prove or disprove, verify or debunk those rumors. In my research I combined both approaches, adopting a respectful, instead of adversarial, skeptical approach, especially with the tellers and other eyewitnesses. A mocking or hostile approach is not only unnecessary but counterproductive, and many "skeptics" could learn much from a folkloristic approach to investigating mysteries. Legend scholars, in turn, could also benefit from a more skeptical approach at times. Though establishing the etic "reality" of monsters such as the chupacabra falls outside the purview of typical legend research, sometimes it can indeed be uncovered through polite but pointed questions.

I began with a literature search, and once I realized how recently the creature had appeared, I grew more confident in my ability not only to trace the folklore but perhaps to actually solve the global mystery. While Bigfoot and Nessie reports, sightings, and evidence date back a half century or more and involve mountains of evidence (tracks, eyewitness sightings, photographs, hoaxes, and so on), the chupacabra had only been around for about a decade by the time I began researching it. The quantity of material to analyze was a fraction of that of many other high-profile monsters, about whom writing a truly comprehensive and authoritative book would be an unachievable task.

Most of the material on the chupacabra appeared in poorly sourced references; there was very little folkloric or scholarly research on the topic, with the bulk of the references to online blogs or tabloids, and occasionally to a book chapter. In addition, there were a handful of popular culture depictions, such as a Marvel comics single issue of *The Fantastic Four* and a booklet published by a Christian ministry suggesting a Satanic origin.

Persistence was also key; I didn't solve the chupacabra mystery out of any innate brilliance but instead because I was willing to do the demanding archival research and fieldwork necessary to follow wherever the legend led. My investigation took about five years, from dingy Puerto Rican library archives to the muggy Central American jungle to dusty Texas towns. It was through adopting a scientific, empirical, evidence-based approach that the investigation was completed. Folklorists and monster researchers just getting started should not be deterred by an apparent abundance of previous research, especially if the literature is primarily confined to the popular and tabloid press, as was the case here. Often the answers to mysteries are right there—if you know where to look and take the time to dig for them.

NOTES

1. Although as Linda Dégh and Andrew Vázsonyi note, "Dracula, the most popular among all monsters, has no real folklore. There is only the single, brief, trivialized story, taken in many cases directly from Bram Stoker's novel and its multifarious media adaptations, containing not much more than the fact that the Transylvanian count was a vampire. The public seems convinced, nonetheless, of the existence of a lush legend realm. The term *fictitious legend* best describes the case of Dracula. Fictitious, not because the story is untrue and the hero of the legend nonexistent, but because the legend itself does not exist" (1983, 25).

2. Some Puerto Ricans, borrowing from werewolf mythology, believed that only silver bullets would stop the chupacabra, and several Puerto Rican UFO groups claimed that the creature was the source of the AIDS epidemic. One group put forth the theory that the chupacabra "was one of twenty or more beings that had descended to Earth to conduct experiments with human blood in order to produce blood viruses aimed at eliminating humanity" (Corrales 2004). An interesting folkloric take on the chupacabra legend can be found in the book *Caribbean Mythology and Modern Life: Five One-Act Plays for Young People*, by Paloma Mohamed (2003). The first play in the book, "Chupacabra," deals with HIV/AIDS in the context of Caribbean culture, and draws its characters from various Latin

American mythologies (for example, the Ole Higue—a variation of the Old Hag/succubus archetype—of Guyana folklore, and the bloodsucker Obayifo from African myths; see Hufford 1982). Some say the chupacabra appears accompanied by the stench of sulfur, referencing a common folkloric motif demonstrating its supposed demonic origin.

3. This would later become a minor impediment to researching the early rumors; while large newspapers of record such as *El Nuevo Dia* were fully archived in libraries, there was far less available for daily tabloids such as *El Vocero*. I visited the tabloid's office in downtown San Juan searching for back issues from late 1995 but was told none were available; I eventually found a few in university libraries.

4. A similar process happened in the evolution of the most famous sighting and photograph of the Champ lake monster in 1977 by Sandra Mansi. Though she also was the original eyewitness, she did not attach a specific meaning or label to her initial sighting; the interpretation of the experience as confirming a preexisting narrative came from others (see Radford and Nickell 2006).

REFERENCES CITED

Barber, Paul. 1988. *Vampires, Burial, and Death: Folklore and Reality.* New Haven: Yale University Press.
Bennett, Gillian, and Paul Smith. 2007. *Urban Legends: A Collection of International Tall Tales and Terrors.* Westport, CT: Greenwood.
Beresford, Matthew. 2008. *From Demons to Dracula: The Creation of the Modern Vampire Myth.* London: Reaktion Books.
Blank, Trevor J., and Lynne S. McNeill, eds. 2018. *Slender Man Is Coming: Creepypasta and Contemporary Legends on the Internet.* Boulder: University Press of Colorado.
Bullard, Thomas E. 2000. "Chupacabras in Perspective." *International UFO Reporter* 25(4): 1–30.
Campion-Vincent, Veronique. 1990. "The Baby-Parts Story: A New Latin American Legend." *Western Folklore* 49: 9–25.
Corrales, Scott. 1997. *Chupacabras and Other Mysteries.* Murfreesboro, TN: Greenleaf.
Corrales, Scott. 2004. "Chupacabras: A Study in Darkness." In *The New Conspiracy Reader: From Planet X to the War on Terrorism—What You Really Don't Know,* edited by Al Hidell and Joan D'Arc, 118–28. New York: Citadel.
Curran, Bob. 2005. *Vampires: A Field Guide to the Creatures That Stalk the Night* Pompton Plains, NJ: Career.
De Aragon, Ray John. 2012. *Enchanted Legends and Lore of New Mexico: Witches, Ghosts, and Spirits.* Charleston, SC: History Press.
Dégh, Linda, and Andrew Vázsonyi. 1983. "Does the Word 'Dog' Bite? Ostensive Action: A Means of Legend-Telling." *Journal of Folklore Research,* 20 (1): 5–34.
Derby, Lauren. 2008. "Imperial Secrets: Vampires and Nationhood in Puerto Rico." *Past and Present* 199 (supplement 3): 290–312.
Dundes, Alan, ed. 1998. *The Vampire: A Casebook.* Madison: University of Wisconsin Press.
Foster, Michael Dylan, and Jeffrey A. Tolbert, eds. 2016. *The Folkloresque: Reframing Folklore in a Popular Culture World.* Boulder: University Press of Colorado.
Hufford, David. 1982. *The Terror That Comes in the Night: An Experience-Centered Study of Supernatural Assault Traditions.* Philadelphia: University of Pennsylvania Press.
Jordan, Robert Michael. 2008. "El Chupacabra: Icon of Resistance to U.S. Imperialism." MA thesis, University of Texas at Dallas.

Kitta, Andrea. 2015. "What Happens When the Pictures Are No Longer Photoshops? Slender Man, Belief, and the Unacknowledged Common Experience." *Contemporary Legend* 3 (5): 62–76.

Loxton, Daniel, and Donald Prothero. 2015. *Abominable Science! Origins of the Yeti, Nessie, and Other Famous Cryptids.* Vancouver: Columbia University Press.

Meurger, Michel, and Claude Gagnon. 1989. *Lake Monster Traditions: A Cross-Cultural Analysis.* London: Fortean Tomes.

Mohamed, Paloma. 2003. *Caribbean Mythology and Modern Life: Five One-Act Plays for Young People.* Dover, MA: Majority Press.

Radford, Benjamin. 2011. *Tracking the Chupacabra: The Vampire Beast in Fact, Fiction, and Folklore.* Albuquerque: University of New Mexico Press.

Radford, Benjamin. 2021. "Chupacabra @25: Revisiting the First Sighting." *Fortean Times* 398: 46–48.

Radford, Benjamin, and Joe Nickell. 2006. *Lake Monster Mysteries: Investigating the World's Most Elusive Creatures.* Lexington: University Press of Kentucky.

Redaccion Noticiosa. 1996. *La Verdadera Historia del Chupacabras.* San Juan, Puerto Rico: Redaccion Noticiosa.

Regal, Brian, and Frank J. Esposito. 2018. *The Secret History of the Jersey Devil: How Quakers, Hucksters, and Benjamin Franklin Created a Monster.* Baltimore: Johns Hopkins University Press.

Tolbert, Jeffrey A. 2015. "'Dark and Wicked Things' Slender Man, the Folkloresque, and the Implications of Belief." *Contemporary Legend* 3 (5): 38–61.

White, Luise. 2000. *Speaking with Vampires: Rumor and History in Colonial Africa.* Berkeley: University of California Press.

EDITOR'S SUGGESTIONS FOR FURTHER READING

Calvo-Quirós, William A. 2014. "Sucking Vulnerability: Neoliberalism, the Chupacabras, and the Post–Cold War Years." In *The Un/Making of Latina/o Citizenship: Culture, Politics, and Aesthetics,* edited by Ellie D. Hernández and Eliza Rodriguez y Gibson, 211–33. London: Palgrave Macmillan.

Nickell, Joe. 2000. "The Flatwoods UFO Monster." *Skeptical Inquirer* 224 (6): 15–19.

Radford, Benjamin. 2010. *Scientific Paranormal Investigation: How to Solve Unexplained Mysteries.* Corrales, NM: Rhombus.

Radford, Benjamin. 2011. *Tracking the Chupacabra: The Vampire Beast in Fact, Fiction, and Folklore.* Albuquerque: University of New Mexico Press.

Radford, Benjamin. 2014. *Mysterious New Mexico: Miracles, Magic, and Monsters in the Land of Enchantment.* Albuquerque: University of New Mexico Press.

Radford, Benjamin. 2016. "Mistaken Memories of Vampires: Pseudohistories of the Chupacabra." *Skeptical Inquirer* 40 (1): 50–54.

16

Daniel Boone, Yahoos, and Yeahohs
Mirroring Monsters of the Appalachians

Carl Lindahl

PREFACE

Daniel Boone (1734–1820), American pioneer, frontiersman, and hunter, is himself a legend, his deeds as legendary as they are historical, and the Yeahohs, Bigfoot-like creatures purported to haunt the Appalachian wilderness since the days of Boone, provide an instructive opportunity for unraveling interwoven folk narrative/belief genres. This chapter touches on five such folk narrative genres that evoke varying degrees of truth claims: sightings, legends, anti-legends, tall tales, and unreasonable lies. Lindahl notes the importance of performance and audience interpretation throughout the monster storytelling process. What one hears as a tall tale or an unreasonable lie, another might hear as a legend. This process continues with every subsequent rendition, invoking the "frisson" of legend—a sudden strong feeling of excitement or fear—the visceral "What if?" factor that emerges regardless of sincere belief.

Irish author and satirist Jonathan Swift plays a surprising central role in the story of Bigfoot in the Appalachians. Boone and his companions carried Swift's *Gulliver's Travels* while pioneering, the novel a source of campfire entertainment and possible inspiration for tales of their own exploits, Swift's Brobdingnag resembling the wonders and terrors of their own Appalachian wilderness. Cryptozoologists and monster hunters have been drawn to a Swiftian-influenced passage in historian John Mack Faragher's biography *Daniel Boone: The Life and Legend of an American Pioneer.* Faragher writes of a tale Boone told about killing a ten-foot hairy giant, one Boone supposedly referred to as a "Yahoo," hominid-like creatures featured in *Gulliver's Travels.* Boone's account gave cryptozoologists reason to believe Boone had an early encounter with Bigfoot in the Appalachian Mountains;

https://doi.org/10.7330/9781646421602.c016

Lindahl, though, diagnoses Boone's performance as a tall tale, one that the innkeeper's son reported as a legend and that Faragher unintentionally misrepresented, the passage then taking on a second life through secondhand accounts. Today, Boone's name operates as a sort of guarantor, as a venerable man whose honor is beyond repute, a historical friend of a friend, his legendary reputation as a jokester and raconteur seemingly overlooked.

What resulted was an intertextual monster legend: *Gulliver's Travels* merging with the life of Daniel Boone, the life of Daniel Boone intermeshed with the legend of Daniel Boone, the legend of Daniel Boone (with Faragher's accidental encouragement) interbreeding with the legend of Bigfoot, creating the legendary Appalachian Yahoos or Yeahohs or Yahoes (or Woodboogers). Lindahl's study is an excellent example of how legendary traditions can join forces, reconstitute, sustain themselves through symbiotic relationships, and even birth something new out of the union.

ESSAY

In *Daniel Boone: The Life and Legend of an American Pioneer,* John Mack Faragher argues that a hero's legend is as important as his life:

> Folkloric evidence offers more than simply an opportunity to reconstruct the facts of [Boone's] life. The record of Daniel Boone consists largely of the stories of humble American men and women [that] not only document the life of an American frontier hero but reveal the thoughts and feelings of the diverse peoples of the frontier . . . The things people choose to say about Boone provide clues to their own concerns. (Faragher 1992, xvi)

Any folklorist would subscribe to Faragher's statement and welcome his project of exploring Boone legendry as mirroring the minds of those who have retold, reshaped, and reacted to one hero's "story." One significant recent turn in that ever-evolving story is a focus on his relationship with Yahoos and Bigfoot-like beings that have inhabited the imagination of European-American mountaineers from the time they first entered the Kentucky wilderness. One passage from Faragher's book seems to have spurred a new spate of Yahoo tales, and may now serve as a spur for assessing a body of traditional Appalachian monster legends.

SIGHTINGS, LEGENDS, TALL TALES, AND UNREASONABLE LIES

Something lurking in the southern mountains during the Civil War possessed the power to terrify three generations. In 1951, third-generation

granddaughter Buna Hicks (1888–1984) told of the horror her mother had
experienced in Watauga County, North Carolina, nearly a century before:

> That Yape. . . . Well, back in them war times you know, way back years ago,
> my mother had to help get the work done and get out, and get in wood.
> And she went one evening to get her load . . . of wood, and . . . she's just
> picking up little old pieces of wood, here and yonder, and she come to an
> old brush fence that they had cut and made, and there stood . . . she didn't
> really know what it was, a-standing up against the fence . . . she called it
> a Yape. She really didn't know the name of it. . . . [I]t's hairy all over, just
> staring there, and its big eyes rolled around and looking around right at
> her. And . . . she was scared so till it shocked her near to death, said she
> dropped her wood and she run for life. . . .
>
> And she got her in a-home, and my grandma . . . , her mother, said,
> "Don't tell me what it is." She couldn't stand to hear it, says, "Wait till in
> the morning, because I can't stand for you to tell it tonight." And [my
> mother] said she hated it so bad that she couldn't tell her about what she
> had seed. She said it scared her so that when she got there she just fell in
> the door. . . . It was awful. (Lindahl 2004, 1:129–31, 344n27)

In the Southern Appalachians, sightings and stories of Bigfoot-like
beings stretch back into the eighteenth century. Buna's Yape account is
more a sighting than a story. She says little about the Yape, and the Yape
itself is not an actor but a prop: it simply stands and stares at Buna's
mother. In Buna's telling we learn more about a mountain girl's life in Civil
War times than we do about the monster. The story teaches that females
lived in isolation while men were off fighting, that young girls performed
considerable work in the woods alone, and that fear was a daily part of
female lives. Otherwise, this sliver from Buna's family saga is no more
than a pin stuck in a cryptozoologist's map, marking one more claim for
the existence of one of North America's most often seen, and eternally
uncaptured, creatures.

In Appalachia, family legends of terrors that stalked the mountain
woods have overwhelmingly centered on Indians or on fearsome animals,
as in the following tale recorded by folklorist Leonard Roberts in 1955.
Hallie Allen is the narrator, and her tale is told as true. Roberts had heard
many similar versions since first encountering it as a child. The villain
was a *painter*, or panther, often heard, seldom seen, and almost never captured or killed. The survivor of that storied night was a nameless woman
who inhabited Hallie Allen's stretch of eastern Kentucky long before she
was born.

Back in the olden times they was houses far apart, and neighbors didn't live close like they do now. And they was a woman. She had a little baby.

And so she went over to her neighbor's house one day, and so she had to go across a *big* hill, and around a big ridge. And they was painters and bears, wild deers, out then. And painters: when a mother'd have her little baby, why they could smell that breast milk and they would want to catch the little [ones]. They could smell them—and find that they had babies.

So the woman, she started back home one evening and she got on the top of the hill and she heared a painter coming a-hollering, screaming. And so she knew that it would sure get her. And she commenced pulling her clothes off. You could throw anything down to em and they'd just tear it all into thread before they'd go on. And so she pulled her apron off. She heared it coming, and she pulled her apron off, and she throw it down. And *it* tore it all into threads. And then she had her skirt off next. And she pulled her skirt off. And she throwed it down, and she went just as far as she could, and it tore it up. Well, about that time, she had her blouse ready to throw off, to throw to it. She throwed it down. It tore it in threads. And then she commenced on the little baby's clothes. She heard it a-coming, and she had its wrap ready to throw to it, and she throwed it down. It took it a right smart while for him to tear that baby's wrap up.

And by the time she heard it coming again a-screaming, why she had the little dress ready to throw to it. She throwed it to it, and it tore it up. By the time then that she heared it coming again, why she had the little baby's slip. She was getting near home then. And she throwed this little baby's slip to it, and by [that time], why she was into the yard. And she just fell up, she was so nigh gone. She just fell up. And her husband was there at the house, and he run out with the dogs, big hound dogs, and chased it and shot it. (Roberts 1945–1983a)

Buna's Yape tale and Hallie's painter tale run parallel in notable ways. Both depict an isolated world where wilderness rules. Both star a female forced to fend for herself in that wilderness. Both females encounter a monstrous animal and flee toward home. Both barely make it to safety, having reached home so terrified and exhausted that they "fell up" or "fell in" the door.

There are four types of Appalachian narratives that purport to describe what happens when people run into monsters: sightings, legends, tall tales, and "unreasonable lies." Sightings are narrative sketches in which a person sees a monster, but little else happens. Legends are fuller accounts of human-monster interactions; they are told as true, but their truth is debatable and often questioned by hearers. Tall tales are told as true by narrators playfully intent on deceiving their listeners. The narrator typically wears an earnest expression and speaks with seeming sincerity, setting the story in a natural environment familiar to the audience and describing in detail everyday actions to add a realistic touch. But gradually the teller introduces improbabilities that grow increasingly unlikely as the story progresses. A seasoned narrator never admits that anything about the story is false, and seasoned audiences typically respond with similarly feigned sincerity. Such tall tales may be said to function at times as jokes on gullible believers. The fourth category, the "unreasonable lie," is a term used by some mountain families to label tall tales that stretch far beyond the realm of the implausible (consider, for example, stories about the giant lumberjack Paul Bunyan) and though told as true are openly recognized as fantasy by teller and audience alike.

The numerous traits shared by Buna's and Hallie's tales serve only to enhance a signal difference. "The Painter" is a legend but "The Yape" merely a sighting. Unlike Buna's Yape, Hallie's painter possesses agency, and its pursuit of mother and child sparks a plot. Hallie's tale is one of numberless versions told as true throughout the twentieth century in the Appalachians, each presented as a horror experienced by an ancestor or a person of note in a mountain community. The tale, though set in the past, unfolds in the local landscape, and records events that evoke for teller and listener a sense of the terror that the mountain woods still hold.

Among the many tales that share a basic plot with "The Painter," narrative details break down along gender lines. The pursued male is typically a hunter or a fisherman who appeases the beast with his kill or his catch. But when a female is pursued, she nearly always performs a high-stakes striptease, dropping pieces of her personal packaging that the panther stops to sniff and claw and lick. The pursuing beast is typically portrayed as male, with at least a hint of sexual predator in his stalking motions. The female is down to her last garment when she finally reaches safety.

As a sighting, Buna's Yape account yields some details of her mountain world, as we have seen, but the various versions of the painter legend give us much more. For example, they articulate gender roles. The men are in the woods by choice and surrender to the beast only the flesh they have captured that day. The women are there because they have to pass from one place to another; they are forced to throw away their civilizing garments and physical modesty in fleeing the beast. Men walk away coolly, but women desperately throw themselves into the shelter of their homes. In all versions, if anyone shoots the painter, it is a man. The legends teach men and women different lessons about how to behave in the wilds, and even whether they should be there in the first place.

Legends tell not only the story of the beast but, more important, the story of the people who face the beast. The monster is their mirror. It may seem inapt to compare a Bigfoot to a big cat, but I contend, and hope to illustrate, that in Appalachia legendry, monsters do not stray so far in appearance or action from the people who tell their stories or the animals often seen in the surrounding mountains.

Swiftian Monsters and Daniel Boone: Tall Tales and Unreasonable Lies

Daniel Boone (1734–1820) is the source of what seems to be the earliest surviving monster account told by Europeans in the Kentucky mountains. In 1770, years before Kentucky's first permanent European settlement, six newcomers worked their way through its wilderness. As Boone recalled, "We had with us for our amusement the *History of Lemuel Gulliver's Travels*," Boone's favorite book after the Bible. Boone and his fellow hunters read *Gulliver's Travels* aloud to each other whenever opportunity afforded (Boone 1796).[1] These men, surrounded by uncharted land, amused themselves with the fictional story of a man adrift in an uncharted world.

One memorable *Gulliver's Travels* passage describes the giant folk of Brobdingnag; Boone mentions Gulliver's "account of his young *Mistress Glumdalclitch* carrying him on a market day for a show to a town called Lulbregrud." Glumdalclitch, Swift's "Little nurse," would be an outlandishly tall being anywhere other than Brobdingnag, where she stood "not above forty foot high, being small for her age" (Swift 1980: 84–89).

This account stuck with its listeners. Some days after it was first read aloud, one of Boone's companions returned from a hunting foray and launched Swift's book into mountain lore. Boone states, "Alexander Neeley came to camp one night and told us he had been that Day to Lulbegrud and had killed two Brobdernags in their Capital." Neeley's words provoked a tall tale guessing game. "Only with some effort were his companions able to figure out that Neeley had been hunting at a salt lick by a creek and had killed two buffalo" (Boone 1796; Brown 2008, 49, 299n45; Lofaro 2003, 163). Through Neeley's little narrative, Kentucky was transformed into Swift's land of giants. The jest became a reality, a place on the map. The men called the creek Lulbegrud, and so it is known today. The beasts and waters of the new land took their names from an oversized world dreamed up by the era's most wildly imaginative author.

This testimony is remarkable in showing both a comic tall tale and a place-name in the act of creation—a landscape christened to fit the contours of fantasy. Boone's account is also remarkably anti-legendary: it portrays him and his companions as playful in a way that rarely emerges in accounts of the Kentucky wilderness. Unlike the Yape and the panther,

Boone's Brobdingnagians generate no terror. Yet as his party played their tall tale game, they were camped in a place that most Europeans found terrifying. Dangers were everywhere: Boone and a companion had recently *twice* been captured nearby by Indians. The two had been abandoned by other hunters who, finding the trip "too disastrous," had broken camp and fled for safety in the east (Daniel Boone Bryan, quoted in Faragher 1992, 82). Nearly every other traveler through that wilderness reported constant intense danger. Boone's life was a catalog of such perils: he was captured by Indians numerous times, endured the violent wilderness deaths of one brother and two sons, engaged in fights fatal to innumerable allies and enemies, yet never expressed a hint of fear. In one account, deep in the woods, his unnerving joy provoked apprehension in others: Casper Mansker and his team of hunters

> were moving quietly through the forest when they heard a most unusual noise. Mansker signaled to the others to take cover, and slowly he crept forward toward the sound, his gun loaded and primed. There on a deerskin spread on the ground of a clearing was a man flat on his back and "singing at the top of his voice!" It was Daniel Boone. (Faragher 1992, 85)

Boone's fearlessness and his delight in the wilderness were often remarked upon and sometimes described as so intense he unsettled others (Brown 2008, 274; Lofaro 2003, 163).

The Brobdingnag-buffalo game also evokes the traveler's age-old right to "lie with authority" (Shakespeare 2006, 223n139): to return to civilization with tales of monsters. Swift's *Travels*, known today as biting satire, was also the inheritor of a long line of published travel narratives depicting worlds of wonder lying beyond beaten paths. More than two millennia before Swift, Herodotus wrote of savage lands populated by the cannibalistic Anthropophagi, headless anthropoids with eyes in their chests, and flying snakes (see Herodotus 1910, especially the descriptions of the Androphagi and the Libyan lands west of the Maxyans). Such wonders became a trope for subsequent traveling storytellers, most famously Shakespeare's Othello, who invokes them to impress Desdemona's father—and in the process seduce Desdemona. Desdemona's father, says Othello,

> questioned me the story of my life. . . .
> I ran it through,
> . . . my [travels'] history: . . .
> And of the Cannibals that each other eat,
> The Anthropophagi and men whose heads
> Do grow beneath their shoulders. This to hear
> Would Desdemona seriously incline: . . .
> She gave me for my pains a world of sighs. . . .

She wished she had not heard it, yet she wished
That heaven had made her such a man . . .
And bade me, if I had a friend that loved her,
I should but teach him how to tell my story. . . .

(Shakespeare 2006: I.3.129–65; see note 139)

The wanderer, explorer, frontiersman is regarded not merely as a reporter on that unseen world, but also as its emissary. As Desdemona more than suggests, just to tell the story of that world is somehow to become part of it. In retelling the story of Gulliver, Boone's party merged their world with Gulliver's.

Some assert that Boone retold the tales from *Gulliver's Travels* as if they were personal experiences (Brown 2008, 2). Yet Boone's surviving tales, like Hallie Allen's painter tale, stop short of the out-and-out fantasy of Swift and Othello. Forty-foot-tall girls, or beings whose heads grow beneath their shoulders, take us beyond the forms that surround us daily. Fantasy monsters did find a limited role in the Appalachians, where the Garland family of Kentucky told what they called "unreasonable lies" about "the Land of Yeahoe" (a name that evokes "Yahoo," soon to be introduced), inhabited by headless women and flying snakes. "The Land of Yeahoe" could almost be Libya as described 2,400 years ago by Herodotus (1998); no one in the Appalachians considered these stories to be true (Lindahl 2004, 2:391–92, 666–67n104). But Boone's monsters and the monsters of those who shared Boone's world were much closer to the size and shape of the known people and predators of the southern mountains. Swift's fantasies gave birth to the Brobdingnagians, at least eight times taller than humans. But Boone's Brobdingnagians were no bigger than buffalo, and Boone's other Swift-inspired tales centered on the Yahoos of *Gulliver's Travels*, creatures so similar to humans in form and size that all the inhabitants of their island mistake Gulliver for a Yahoo, and Gulliver himself acknowledges his near identity to the creature: "The beast and I were brought close together; and our countenances diligently compared . . . My horror and astonishment are not to be described, when I discovered in this Abominable animal, a perfect human Figure" (Swift 1980, 220). In this scene man and beast mirror each other with disturbing precision, just as is often found in legends that later emerged in Appalachia.

FARAGHER'S YAHOOS AND BOONE'S GIANT

Faragher's *Daniel Boone* contains a passage that ignited the interest of cryptozoologists and their critics. There is a very suspect tradition that at age eighty-two Boone traveled to Limestone, Kentucky,

Figure 16.1. "The Servants Drive a Herd of Yahoos into the Field" by Louis John Rhead in an illustrated edition of *Gulliver's Travels*.

and was honored by a gala dinner that included all of the distinguished local citizenry. After the meal one of the men asks Boone for a story, and he begins a tale but is interrupted by a man who claims that his story is "impossible." With this remark Boone shuts up, and . . . refuses to speak further. Later that evening. . . . the son of the tavern keeper . . . presses the old man to tell the story. "You shall have it, honey," says Boone, . . . and proceeds to tell of killing a ten-foot, hairy giant he called a "Yahoo." The Yahoos were giant beasts in human shape from Boone's favorite book, *Gulliver's Travels*. It was a tall tale that Boone repeated during his last year, one such as he would have told in a winter camp. (Faragher 1992, 308–9)

This passage contains two notable misrepresentations. First, Jonathan Swift does not describe his Yahoos as "giant beasts": rather, they appear to be of human size.[2] Second, there is only one surviving account from the son of the tavern keeper that relates Boone's private performance, and it never mentions the word *Yahoo* but rather identifies the monster as a "giant," using that word nineteen times. Unintentionally, through these two errors, Faragher equated Swift's Yahoos with Boone's giant and gave cryptozoologists reason to believe they had discovered one of the earliest recorded accounts of Bigfoot.

Faragher's misconnection eventually set Boone and the Yahoos into the midst of the Bigfoot debate. Within two years of the book's appearance,

Bigfoot denier Hugh H. Trotti published a piece in the *Skeptical Inquirer* titled "Did Fiction Give Birth to Bigfoot?" presenting the thesis that Boone's Yahoo tales, borrowed from Swift, were the original inspiration for the Bigfoot legend. Trotti, a careful reader of both Faragher and Swift (he finds more references to *Gulliver's Travels* than appear in Faragher's index, and he accurately disputes Faragher's claim that Swift's Yahoos are "giant beasts"), concludes, "There is no real reason why Bigfoot cannot have come to life from the pages of Jonathan Swift's book and made the rounds of the camps of deer hunters and trappers of the frontier. The creature tales based on a literary Yahoo would have to last only a few decades, such a legend could easily survive until today" (Trotti 1994, 542).

In 1997, also writing in *Skeptical Inquirer*, David Zuefle expressed doubt that Boone's readings from Swift could have accounted for all North American Bigfoot traditions, but he offered evidence to bolster Trotti's view that Boone had influenced local Appalachian tales. Zuefle noted that Leonard Roberts had recorded oral narratives centered on a manimal—a beast so nearly human in appearance that, like Swift's Yahoo, it could be mistaken for a brutish, feral person—known in mountain lore as a "Yeahoh." Zuefle reasonably inferred that this name could have been derived from Swift's "Yahoo." So the researchers had armed themselves with much information connecting "Yahoo" to "Yeahoh," even though neither mentioned (or seemed to be aware) that the Boone tale did not mention the word *Yahoo* in the first place, nor did either researcher have any idea of the plot or nature of the Boone tale beyond Faragher's ten-word plot summary: "killing a ten-foot hairy giant he called a 'Yahoo.'"

This short phrase appears repeatedly on the Internet, but because the story itself does not appear there, it is long past time to retell it. I have not been able to find a published version, so I resorted to microfilm copies of the handwritten text (Payne 1875–1876). Boone had been dead for more than half a century when Buckner Payne wrote the letters containing the story of the hairy giant. In 1875 and 1876, Payne wrote historian Lyman Copeland Draper to claim that an aged Boone had visited Payne's father's tavern in Limestone, Kentucky, around 1816 (seventeen years after Boone is known to have last set foot in the state). Payne stated that he, as a young boy, was the only one present for Boone's performance.

In the following summary, words in italics quote directly from the letters. Payne most often refers to Boone in the third person, but in some dramatic passages—for example, "I had to shoot"—he renders Boone's narrative in the first person, presumably exactly as Payne remembered it from his childhood:

Boone and his son are in the woods searching to recover stolen horses. While the two men are separated, Boone hears gunfire. The shots' timing and sounds lead him to believe that his son is under attack from a wounded bear or panther. He rushes toward the sounds to see *the largest man that he had ever seen . . . walking very fast* toward his son, who is aiming at the giant from behind a tree. *The giant got up to* [Boone's] *son & caught him by his buckskin dress with one hand while with the other he jerked his gun from him, threw it, and broke it. [T]hen, catching his son by the knap of the neck & the seat of his britches . . .* [the giant] *raised him up over his head just as easy, honey, as I would raise up a child & slammed him on the ground; he raised him the second time & slammed him the same way . . . I had to shoot: a third slam would be sure to kill my son if it had not already done it. While the giant was stopping to raise him the third time I fired & the giant fell over on my son. I immediately ran up & jerked him off to find my son senseless & not breathing. I immediately made every effort for his restoration to life. It seemed to me more than an hour before he breathed . . .*

[The rest of the story is devoted to a description of the dead giant and its wounds:] Boone's son *said he had aimed to hit* [the giant] *in the heart both shots. The giant was naked. I* [that is, Boone] *turned him over on his back & found both of the bullet holes near the left nipple . . . but neither of them had entered the body but had passed round & came out at the back. I then passed my finger into each of the holes & found the giant had . . . solid bone about ¾ of an inch thick which I found out by cutting through the bone with my tomahawk. The giant was not an Indian, for he was a pale yellow with long yellowish hair & not black as is common among Indians. His body was likewise covered with short hair; not very thick. His teeth were all . . . grown together in his head with rather small eyes & nose with very large feet & hands. We then stretched him out . . . & in measuring it with my hands I found that he was at least 10 ½ feet high.* (Payne 1875–1876; spelling standardized)

Boone's diction is understated, but the giant's thrice-repeated act of lifting a man high into the air and then dashing him to the ground pushes the narrative toward tall tale territory. The provisional autopsy ultimately crosses into the tall tale world by describing a bullet that breaks the giant's skin but then, unable to penetrate the thick breastbone, travels around it and exits through the giant's back. As a clincher, Boone measures the giant at more than ten feet in height. The story has begun in the normative style common to both "true" hunting tales and tall tales, as both are narrated with careful attention to detail and process. But as Boone's account, like a typical tall tale, introduces improbabilities gradually transforming into impossibilities, I agree with Faragher that this giant-killing narrative, the previously unexamined story behind the Yahoo-Yeahoh controversy, is indeed a tall tale.

CRYPTOZOOLOGISTS, BELIEVERS, AND BOONE

The Boone giant-killing story could easily be considered the forerunner of a Bigfoot tale. But again, the skeptical scholars who considered the possibility that Boone's reading of Swift had given rise to Bigfoot stories (Trotti 1994; Zuefle 1997) did not know this tale. Rather, when Zuefle introduced Kentucky Yeahoh folktales to support the Yahoo-Bigfoot connections, he served up Yeahohs that were quite unlike Bigfoot. Although hairy and humanoid, the folktale Yeahoh was not a giant, not male, and it did not attack human beings. But these details did not keep respondents from using the name "Yeahoh" and its association with Daniel Boone as evidence to assert the reality of current-day giant hairy monsters.

An Internet poster named Dave Tabler drew together all of the strands I have presented thus far (2015). In a piece titled "Yeahoh, Yahoo or Bigfoot?" on the website *Appalachian History: Stories, Quotes and Anecdotes*, Tabler begins by citing Faragher's "giant" phrase, proceeds to Boone's tall tale guessing game based on *Gulliver's Travels*, invokes Trotti's thesis that Boone's stories about Swift's Yahoos gave birth to the Bigfoot legend, and ends by reprinting a Yeahoh tale recorded from a Kentucky mountain woman in the mid-twentieth century (Roberts 1955, 162). Tabler seems to accept the notion that Swift is behind the term "Yeahoh," but he ends by asking if Swift's Yahoos gave rise to Bigfoot tales or if, conversely, Swift based his Yahoos on yarns he had heard from travelers to distant places.

Appalachian respondents to Tabler were much less interested in the hairy women of the folktales than in a hairy giant like Bigfoot, and far less interested in tales than in real-life cryptids. Buck R. wrote, "People have shot at big foot and wood boogers. Yes Yes it is a fact they exist." And Kevin Jones responded: "If you don't think Bigfoot exist, try spending a few nights in the southern part of Jefferson National Forest on the Virginia/Kentucky border. You will get visited. The people of Bristol, Va. have known about them for centuries. They're known as woodboogers. They'll rip you to pieces" (Tabler 2015). No mention here of Boone or of Yeahohs: "woodbooger" seems to be preferred name. But, for what it's worth, the Virginia/Kentucky line marks the region where all of the Yeahoh folktales recorded by Leonard Roberts were told.

As Faragher's quote about the "hairy giant" became widespread on the Internet, Appalachian correspondents focused increasingly on Daniel Boone. Rejecting the idea that Boone could have stretched the truth, they used his name as proof that Yeahohs indeed exist. In one Internet string from the site *Sasquatch Chronicles*, "David" posts Faragher's paragraph in full and an "Editorial" response to that paragraph states, "The 'Yahoo' killing may be true and the [*sic*] Boone's 'tall tale' account may be based on an actual event." The editorial author finds correspondences between Faragher's paragraph and certain purported Bigfoot sightings. "I find it interesting Boone related the Yahoo killing to 'a number of people during his last year.' . . . Even today many old timers seem to make death bed encounter confessions after holding their tongue their whole life long for fear of ridicule. I also find it interesting certain areas of Kentucky and West Virginia still refer to night howlers as Yahoos" (*Sasquatch Chronicles* 2016).

David's post spurred considerable interest from Kentuckians, some indicating that they had heard hints of a tale concerning Boone and a monster. One poster responded, "I knew that there was a story somewhere about Boone shooting something way back when." Others wrote that they'd heard stories more detailed than Faragher's but also different from Payne's: "The version I heard was that he carted the body into Boonsboro and showed it off to the townsfolk there, about 100 people at the time." And others simply emphasized the importance of Daniel Boone as a witness: "I lived in Maysville Kentucky for two years 1984–86 & I can tell you, down there Boones [*sic*] stories are highly regarded and believed." For many, it seems, the real attraction of the Boone accounts is the convergence of two legendary figures: the Yahoo and Boone himself. Just to mention Boone in connection with the Yahoo makes both more real, more important.

THE SIGNATURE YEAHOH TALE OF THE KENTUCKY MOUNTAINS

True, all of the earliest evidence for the Swift-Boone-Yahoo connection is based on a constellation of narratives either written by Swift or attributed to Boone between 1735 and 1876, and reported from Ireland, Kentucky, and Missouri. But the supporting narrative evidence offered by Zuefle, Tabler, and others comes from much later oral performances: four tales recorded near the Kentucky/Virginia line in the 1950s. To the four that Roberts recorded, I can add a fifth from the same region (Adams 1993). This is a highly localized tradition of substantial importance for the region's people.[3]

All five are clearly stories; they cannot be mistaken for sightings. But their genre is fluid. One is told in the first person, and is unmistakably a tall tale; another is garbed in biblical language as if were an ancient myth of "The Origin of Man"—the title that Roberts bestows on two versions (1955, 1945–1983b).

The plot is simple, its skeleton readily apparent in the shortest version, told by Nancy McDaniel:

Once upon a time they's a man layin' out, and he went to a cave. And he was layin' out in there and the Yeahoh come and throwed a deer in to him, and leave out. One time that Yeahoh come and got down in there with him and not long after that she had a kid. Then one time he took a notion to leave her and he would go to leave and she wouldn't let him go. She'd make him come back. A-finally he got out and made her think she was going with him. And they went and he got on a ship going to cross the waters. And he got started and rode on off and left her. And she stood there and hollered and screamed after him. And when she seen he'd got away from her and she couldn't go, why she tore the baby in two and throwed one half in after him. (Roberts 1955, 162)

The longer versions of Lee Maggard and Joe Couch, as well as the fifth told by James Taylor Adams of Letcher County, Kentucky, and Wise County, Virginia, narrate an extensive buildup in which the human male and the hairy woman watch each other apprehensively. These tales trace the conflict, conjoining, and eventual irrevocable parting of nature and culture. In the Couch and Maggard tellings, the human is alone, lost, and hungry. He has sought shelter in a cave when the Yeahoh comes upon him. In Joe Couch's first-person, tall tale version, the starving man fears the Yeahoh but she offers him raw meat: he was "afraid to eat it raw, and afraid not to eat it being she give it to me . . . She was goin' to see I didn't starve" (Roberts 1957, 50).

Three tellings highlight a fundamental distinction between nature and culture: the raw meat of the animal and the cooked meat of humankind. The manimal offers the man raw meat; he offers her cooked meat. In two versions the beast likes or learns to like cooked food. In the third the two never reconcile their eating habits. In all three the Yeahoh never speaks like a human: she utters only the sound "Yeahoh" (Maggard, in Roberts 1957, 49) or "a-growlin' noise kindly like a dog makes when he's a-gnawin' on a bone with another dog a-standin' there lookin' at him" (Adams 1993, 24–25). Adams's man tries to teach his Yeahoh human speech, but she "never got so she could say airy word. So, they just had to get along by makin' signs to one another" (29).

"You know, a body'll get use to anything!" (Adams 1993, 29). In all versions man and manimal lie together and have one or more children. The children display their dual parentage in dramatic ways: they are simply "half-ape and half-man" (Bill McDaniel, in Roberts 1945–1983b), "half man and half Yeahoh" (Maggard, in Roberts 1957, 49), "one side . . . hairy and the other side slick" (Couch, in Roberts 1957, 50), "hairy, like her, from its waist up. But its waist down, hit was smooth, like him" (Adams 1993, 29–30).

The children are breathing evidence that nature and culture cannot fully blend: human and animal coexist but do not commingle; neither half fully absorbs the other. In the end, the children cannot live. It is nature's role to do the killing and reestablish the stark division between human and animal. True, the human makes the first move—he must leave the Yeahoh. But it is the Yeahoh who destroys the child and divides it up in a special way: "She just grabbed the little young'un and tore it right open with her nails. Throwed me the hairy part and she kept the slick side" (Couch, in Roberts 1957). Or "She took her [half-ape] part of the kid . . . and fell into the water" and drowned (Bill McDaniel, in Roberts 1945–1983b); or "She throwed the part that looked like him out towards the boat an' she hugged the part that looked like her up to her breast an' went a-runnin' . . . till she was out a-sight in the woods" (Adams 1993, 32). The severed halves of the child mark a bloody boundary that must never be crossed again.

Conclusion: Monsters as Mirrors

A sighting, a legend, a tall tale, an unreasonable lie: each is, in its own way, a truth claim. The teller tells the tale as true. Of the four, only the unreasonable lie departs so outrageously from daily life that we identify it immediately as a falsehood and recognize the narrator as a jokester.

In Kentucky folklore, a Yeahoh can be many things. In the "unreasonable lies" told by the Garland family, the Yeahoe are, apparently, headless women sharing a fantasy world with flying snakes, far beyond the pale of legend. For some the Yeahoh could also be a ten-foot-tall monster like the giant that, according to Buckner Payne, Boone shot. Boone's narrative, like many in the Appalachians, begins as a sighting but grows into a legend-like narrative; only at the end, in my judgment, does it reveal itself as a tall tale. Yet one person's tall tale can become another's legend. Passages from Payne's letters suggest that Boone's giant story was a tall tale to some and a legend to others. Before Boone told the story to young Payne, the tavern keeper's son, a group of men had gathered in the tavern to welcome the old frontiersman, and one of them, a Captain Ward, asked, "Col Boon I would like for you to recite your encounter that you had with a giant which you killed. I would like to have my own memory refreshed." Then, writes Payne, "My Father (Rev William Payne) remarked at this moment that he (the giant) was over 10 feet high," to which a man named Campbell responded, "inadvertently and with out thought, 'impossible that any man could be so high.'" The captain asks Campbell to leave immediately and explains that Boone will not speak "in the presence of any one that had thrown a shade of doubt over what he had said or might say." But Campbell doesn't leave, and Boone remains silent. Later that day, Buckner Payne is alone with Boone: "I said to him that I longed to hear the story about the giant." Boone replies, "You shall have it, honey, but I would not have opened my lips to this time if that man had remained." Boone's giant tale was run by two audiences that day, and at least one member of the first seems to have expected a tall tale or an unreasonable lie, thus cutting off the performance (in normative Appalachian tall tale performances, a typical audience response is to express no disbelief or surprise). But it appears that young Buckner Payne was a believer: he heard a legend. For some, but not all, Boone's giant was apparently too big to invite belief. For many in the mountains, a true legend requires a relatively plausible monster.

Nevertheless, there is much more to a mountain legend than passing a plausibility test. Among the older Kentucky mountain narrators near the Virginia line, the Yeahoh is most often a "Hairy Woman" (Adams 1993), a female beast that mates with a human man. This creature and her amorous dealings with men are no more plausible than Boone's giant, and as we've seen, some narrators tell her story as a tall tale shading toward an unreasonable lie. Yet even when told as a myth or tall tale, the "Hairy Woman" Yeahoh story inspires the frisson of legend among those who have shared it with me. Even if listeners view the tale, rationally, as impossible, they still register the fate of the torn-up child in an immediate way. They feel it viscerally, and powerfully enough to awaken that emotional, "What if?" reaction that living legends tend to provoke. Jacob Grimm, arguably the earliest legend scholar, distinguished the real-life effect of legend from the fantasy world of fairytales: "The Fairy-tale lacks that local habitation" that make the legend "more home-like. The Fairy-tale flies, [but] the legend walks, knocks at your door" (Grimm 1883, xv). The episode of the torn-up child of the Yeahoh tales continues to knock at the doors of Kentucky mountain homes.

None of the five mountain tales mentions Daniel Boone, and three don't even drop the name Yeahoh, but all plumb a question deeply embedded in many Yahoo narratives as well as many legends about or attributed to Boone: how close to nature can a person come before being transformed by it and rendered a monster himself? Daniel Boone inspired wonder at his fearlessness: was he too comfortable in the wilderness to be fully human? He was so close to nature that he confounded others. He stands on the fuzzy line dividing humans from animals. He may seem to have dwelt on the slick, hairless side of the divide, but to some who tell his stories he was as close as a man could come to being a manimal. The Yeahoh encapsulates the terror of the Appalachian wilderness, and Boone the monstrous, impossible courage required to dispel that terror. Did Boone, like Gulliver in his favorite book, stare at the beasts of a wild land only to see a "perfect human Figure" (Swift 1980, 220)? Boone, the man who is nearly a monster, reflects the Yeahoh, a monster all the more fearsome for being nearly human. Boone and the Yeahoh are each other's mirror. The size of the monster is not that important. In the mountains it is the mirror, not magnification, that takes the truest measure of legendary terror.[4]

NOTES

1. Boone's account is recorded in a legal deposition that he gave in 1796; in this and the two following paragraphs, I have standardized the spelling of the transcriber, who gives Boone's last name as "Boon" and renders Swift's title *The History of Samuel Gulever's Travels*. I have kept the 1796 spellings only for the "Brobdernags" and "Lulgegrud" Creek; Swift's names are "Brobdernagians" and "Lorbrulgrud" (Swift 1980, 97).

2. Swift never specifically mentions the size of the Yahoos, but he makes it clear that they closely resemble Gulliver. Before he sees one, Gulliver mistakes the Yahoos' tracks for human footprints. Both the Houyhnhnms and the Yahoos believe Gulliver is a Yahoo; only the clothes he wears make him look different. The Houyhnhnms stand Gulliver next to a Yahoo and find them almost identical; a Yahoo who sees Gulliver naked makes sexual advances at him; and Gulliver himself comes to recognize Yahoos as members of his own species (Swift 1980, 211, 213, 213n17, 220, 228, 254–55).

3. This Appalachian Yeahoh tale is extremely rare elsewhere. There is a similar story from Maine, but it features a male, not a female, monster; there is also one related Canadian oral tale and a number of printed European sources featuring male apes that tear their hybrid offspring in half when the human mothers escape. The five Appalachian versions summarized here account for all of the ape-mother stories yet reported from North America. In a note introducing two of the tales collected by Leonard Roberts, Archer Taylor characterizes the Appalachian Yeahoh tale as a "long-sought parallel" to a centuries-old travelers' tale that researchers, including "the best students of the folktale," had sought "vainly" before Roberts recorded it (Roberts 1957, 48; see also Dorson 1975, 485–87; Altrocchi 1944, 96–99).

4. I thank Special Collections, Hutchins Library, Berea College, and sound archivist Harry Rice for invaluable help in accessing the Leonard Roberts Collection and its audio recordings.

REFERENCES CITED

Adams, James Taylor. 1993. *Grandpap Told Me Tales: Memories of an Appalachian Childhood.* Big Stone Gap, VA: Fletcher Dean.

Altrocchi, Rudolph. 1944. *Sleuthing in the Stacks.* Cambridge, MA: Harvard University Press.

Boone, Daniel. 1796. Deposition concerning Lulbegrud Creek, September 15. Draper Manuscripts, State Historical Society of Wisconsin, Madison. DM 4C93.

Brown, Meredith Mason. 2008. *Frontiersman: Daniel Boone and the Making of America.* Baton Rouge: Louisiana State University Press.

Dorson, Richard M. 1975. *Folktales Told around the World*. Chicago: University of Chicago Press.

Faragher, John Mack. 1992. *Daniel Boone: The Life and Legend of an American Pioneer*. New York: Henry Holt.

Grimm, Jacob. 1883. *Teutonic Mythology*, vol. 3. Translation of *Deutsche Mythologie*, 3rd ed. (1854) by James Steven Stallybrass. London: George Bell & Son.

Herodotus. 1910 [c. 430 BCE]. "The Fourth Book, Entitled Melpomene." In *The History of Herodotus*. Translated by George Rawlinson. Wikisource online edition. https://en.wikisource.org/wiki/The_History_of_Herodotus_(Rawlinson)/Book_4.

Lindahl, Carl. 2004. *American Folktales from the Collections of the Library of Congress*. 2 vols. Armonk, NY: M. E. Sharpe.

Lofaro, Michael A. 2003. *Daniel Boone: An American Life*. Lexington: University Press of Kentucky.

Payne, Buckner. 1875–1876. Letters to Lyman Copeland Draper, November 6, December 8, December 11, 1875, and January 1876. Draper Manuscripts, State Historical Society of Wisconsin, Madison. DM 16C23–26.

Roberts, Leonard W. 1945–1983a. Leonard Roberts Papers. Special Collections, Berea College, Berea, KY. Sound recording LR-49a. Transcribed Carl Lindahl.

Roberts, Leonard W. 1945–1983b. Leonard Roberts Papers. Special Collections, Berea College, Berea, KY. Sound recording LR-8. Transcribed Carl Lindahl.

Roberts, Leonard W. 1955. *South from Hell-fer-Sartin: Kentucky Mountain Folk Tales*. Lexington: University Press of Kentucky.

Roberts, Leonard W. 1957. "Curious Legend of the Kentucky Mountains." *Western Folklore* 16 (1): 48–51.

Sasquatch Chronicles. 2016. "Killing a Yahoo." Blog by "David," with "Editorial" and 14 responses. September 9. https://sasquatchchronicles.com/killing-a-Yahoo/.

Shakespeare, William. 2006 [ca. 1604]. *Othello*. Edited by Michael Neill. Oxford: Oxford University Press.

Swift, Jonathan. 1980 [1726]. *The Annotated Gulliver's Travels*. Edited by Isaac Asimov. New York: Random House.

Tabler, Dave. 2015. "Yeahoh, Yahoo or Bigfoot?" *Appalachian History: Stories, Quotes and Anecdotes*. May 20. http://www.appalachianhistory.net/2015/05/yeahoh-yahoo-or-bigfoot.html.

Trotti, Hugh H. 1994. "Did Fiction Give Birth to Bigfoot?" *Skeptical Inquirer* 18 (5): 541–42.

Zuefle, David. 1997. "Swift, Boone, and Bigfoot: New Evidence for a Literary Connection." *Skeptical Inquirer* 21(1) 57–58.

EDITOR'S SUGGESTIONS FOR FURTHER READING

Carden, Gary. 2012. "Appalachian Bestiary: Wondrous and Fearsome Creatures of the Southern Wild." *North Carolina Folklore Journal* 59 (2): 60–92.

Neralich, Jon. 1996. "'They're Gonna Come After You': Snake Stories from the Ozarks." *Mid-America Folklore* 24 (2): 55–64.

Puglia, David J. 2014. "Daniel Boone." In *Encyclopedia of American Studies*. Baltimore: Johns Hopkins University Press. https://eas-ref.press.jhu.edu/view?aid=866.

Rayburn, Otto Ernest. 1960. "Some Fabulous Monsters and Other Folk Beliefs from the Ozarks." *Midwest Folklore* 10 (1): 27–32.

Roberts, Leonard W. 1988 [1955]. *South from Hell-fer-Sartin: Kentucky Mountain Folk Tales*. Lexington: University Press of Kentucky.

17

The Mothman of West Virginia
A Case Study in Legendary Storytelling

David Clarke

PREFACE

The notorious American cryptid Mothman's fame may be due more to its prevalence in American popular culture than its very real origins in honestly reported sightings. These origins can be traced to four teenagers who told police that while driving in Point Pleasant, West Virginia, a strange flying creature, a six-foot tall winged man with red eyes, chased and harassed their car for miles, sometimes at speeds of over a hundred miles per hour. Additional town sightings followed.

In subsequent media attention, however, it was one man in particular, John Keel, who fostered the Mothman legend, first by covering it as a journalist and then later, following the collapse of the Silver Bridge, by penning *The Mothman Prophecies*, a firsthand New Journalism account of his Mothman investigation. The book is a classic of "Fortean" research, that is, investigation into anomalous phenomena first systematically referenced by Charles Fort, the man most responsible for shaping modern views of the paranormal and the supernatural.

In the present chapter, journalist and legend scholar David Clarke provides intimate access to Keel through firsthand correspondence and interviews, focusing on Keel's role in developing and perpetuating the Mothman legend. Keel and his book have become inextricable elements of the larger Mothman legend. Some of the legend's motifs that Keel reported, particularly the infamous "men in black," have spread and taken root globally. But Mothman remains firmly planted in Point Pleasant, West Virginia: internationally known but local to the core, a perfect meeting of local sightings and international intrigue.

https://doi.org/10.7330/9781646421602.c017

ESSAY

What stands six feet tall, has wings, two big red eyes six inches apart and glides along behind an auto at 100 miles an hour? Don't know? Well neither do four Point Pleasant residents who were chased by a weird "man-like thing" on Tuesday night.

—Mary Hyre, *Athens (OH) Messenger*, November 17, 1966.

In November 1966, a syndicated dispatch from West Virginia reported that police were investigating reports of a mysterious "birdlike" monster five miles north of the city of Point Pleasant. The story was published across North America and a version appeared on the front page of *Pacific Stars and Stripes*, read by American troops in Vietnam. It described how two young married couples saw the creature as they cruised around the thirty-five-acre McClintic Wildlife Management Area near midnight on November 15. The four teenagers were driving near a wartime munitions dump, known locally as the TNT area, when a tall grayish figure appeared near the entrance to an abandoned power station. They said it was "shaped like a man, but bigger" but its most striking features were a pair of glowing red eyes and "big wings folded against its back." The wings unfolded and it took off vertically. Understandably terrified, they turned their car around and sped toward Route 62. As they drove toward the city limits, the creature appeared again and followed them at uncanny speed (Sergent and Wamsley 2002, 81).

The four witnesses, Roger and Linda Scarberry and Steve and Mary Mallette, stopped at the Mason County Sheriff's Office and reported their experience to Deputy Millard Halstead. The officer returned to the TNT area with the teenagers but nothing unusual was found. The next morning the Sheriff's Office called a press conference that resulted in mass media coverage. Most of the newspaper stories referred to the unidentified creature as "birdlike" but one headline, read: "Bird, Plane or Batman? Mason Countians Hunt 'Moth Man'" (Sergent and Wamsley 2002, 92). The Mothman moniker was a direct reference to the live-action television series *Bat-Man*, based on the DC comic superhero, showing on the ABC network. The label stuck, and by December *Mothman* was used by most of the media reports of further sightings.

In the months that followed, numerous other individuals came forward to report extraordinary experiences with Mothman in and around Point Pleasant and other locations along the Ohio River Valley. The TNT area quickly became established as an area for legend trips. According to the police, more than a thousand people traveled to the area in cars, many carrying guns, in search of the Mothman. One account describes the area as "ablaze from the lights of cars and flashlights as the curious traveled up and down the maze of dirt roads ... every intersection was jammed with parked cars and small clumps of laughing, jostling young adults"; abandoned buildings "rang with the shrieks of youngsters, scaring themselves" (Sergent and Wamsley 2002, 78).

The typical American legend trip is defined as "an organized (although sometimes spontaneous) journey to an isolated area to test the bravery of a group when faced with supernatural phenomena" (de Vos 1996, 56). People who participate in legend trips react in different ways. Some may believe in the literal truth of the legend and others will suspend their disbelief or take an intermediate position between belief and disbelief. Even those who dismiss the narrative as false play a role by taking part in the trip for a thrill, to test their own courage, to defy authority, or simply because it seems to be instinctively the correct thing to do (de Vos 1996, 55).

The legend trip often involves the telling of legends, with believers acting out the content to make the story come alive. This is known as ostension, the process by which people act out themes or events found within folk narratives. Linda Dégh and Andrew Vázsonyi proposed three subcategories of ostension: *pseudo-ostension* involves the intentional acting out of a well-known story or legend to fool others or inspire them to believe. An example of this is the creation of "fake" crop circles to persuade others that flying saucers have landed. Another sub-category is *proto-ostension*, where someone presents a version of an existing legend in the form of a personal experience that they claim happened to them. Finally, there is *quasi-ostension*, where an ambiguous event, natural or man-made, is misinterpreted in terms of an existing legend, such as an unfamiliar bird or animal reported as a monster (Dégh and Vázsonyi 1983, 18–20; Ellis 2003, 162–63). All three types of ostension are found in the Mothman legend as the narrative has grown and evolved from the initial sightings in 1966.

THE MOTHMAN PROPHECIES

All effective legends require a storyteller, and in the case of Mothman this role was played by a New York journalist and UFOlogist, John A. Keel (1930–2009). His writings transformed a local legend into an international phenomenon that included a Hollywood film adaptation of the basic story.

Keel's interest in strange phenomena began in the 1940s when he read the books of Charles Fort (Fort 1919; Steinmeyer 2008). Born in Albany, New York, in 1874, Fort spent many years researching scientific literature in the New York Public Library and the British Museum Library in search of evidence for a range of strange phenomena and experiences.

His unconventional theories about visitors from other worlds led Keel to the writings of Ray Palmer, editor of the pulp magazine *Amazing Stories*, which promoted the flying saucer mystery from 1947. In June of that year pilot Kenneth Arnold reported seeing nine mysterious flying objects moving at supersonic speed above the Cascade Mountains in Washington State, and news media coverage of his experience effectively launched the modern UFO phenomenon. In 1952, while serving with the American Forces Network in Europe, Keel observed his first UFO, in daylight, above the Aswan Dam in Egypt. After leaving the army in search of adventure, he spent three years traveling through the Middle East and Asia. It was on this trip, while crossing into the Himalayan state of Sikkim, that he followed and briefly glimpsed a mysterious creature that local people identified as the "abominable snowman" or Yeti. This experience and Keel's idiosyncratic accounts of other cryptozoological and Fortean mysteries were published in his autobiography, *Jadoo: Mysteries of the Orient* (1957). Because of the journalistic and investigative work of John Keel, the Mothman proto-legend became an international media phenomenon. In turn this fed back into the larger corpus of UFO-related "mysteries" and other strange experiences, often through ostensive acts.

Keel returned to cryptozoology and UFOlogy during the mid-1960s as result of his friendship with the British-born biologist and Fortean writer Ivan Sanderson. A collection of North American monster legends form the central text of Keel's *Strange Creatures from Time and Space* (1970). Chapter 16 traces reports of what he calls "Winged Weirdoes" to ancient Babylonian winged deities, the Garuda of the Orient and the Thunderbird legends of the Native Americans. Another chapter collects accounts of alleged personal experiences with "Man Birds" from nineteenth-century newspaper archives. He also includes a contemporary story from Kent, England, where a group of teenagers reported seeing a huge black headless figure with batlike wings one night in November 1963 (Underwood 1971, 198). These disparate stories and legends segue into the chapter dedicated to "West Virginia's Mothman" (Keel 1970). This includes a list of what Keel describes as the twenty-six "most responsible" sightings of the creature by residents of West Virginia, Ohio, and Kentucky from September 1966 to November 1967. Keel claims that more than one hundred people reported seeing this "winged impossibility" and he summarizes their accounts as follows: "Those who got a close look at it all agreed . . . it was grey, apparently featherless, as large—or larger—than a big man, had a wingspread of about ten feet, took off straight up like a helicopter, and did not flap its wings in flight. Its face was a puzzle, no one could describe it. The two red eyes dominated it" (Keel 2002, 88).

John Keel's book *The Mothman Prophecies*, published in 1975, is the most accomplished account of the legend. It was republished twice, in 1991 and 2002, with a new afterword contributed by the author in both editions. The most recent reprint coincided with the release of a movie based upon the legend. Cryptozoologist Loren Coleman, West Virginia authors Donnie Sergent Jr. and Jeff Wamsley, and a number of documentary filmmakers have since collected and published additional personal experience narratives that were not included in Keel's books (Coleman 2002; Sergent and Wamsley 2002; Grabias 2002; Breedlove 2017).

In his own account, Keel says he felt drawn to the community of Point Pleasant. His first field trip was in December 1966, when he employed his credentials as a journalist to make contact with local law enforcement officials. Checking into a motel on the Ohio side of the river, he visited the Mason County courthouse, where he met Deputy Halstead. The officer assured him the young witnesses "saw something. I don't know what. Some say it's just a crane" (Keel 2002, 97). A sketch of the Mothman by "one of the original eyewitnesses" (Roger Scarberry) a transcript of an interview given by Linda Scarberry in 2001, and letters from Keel to Linda and her parents are reproduced in a later collection subtitled *The Facts Behind the Legend* (Sergent and Wamsley 2002, 16). These sources explain how Keel was introduced to the extended families of the original Mothman witnesses and others who had reported personal experiences with the creature. On this first visit Keel met Mary Hyre, a journalist at the *Athens (OH) Messenger,* who covered the Mothman phenomena in her weekly column "Where the Waters Mingle" (Sergent and Wamsley 2002). Keel quickly gained the trust of Hyre and the other witnesses, and within hours of his arrival joined them on a legend trip to the ruins of the abandoned power plant in the TNT area. On entering the ruined building the group experienced a feeling of terror and one Mothman witness, Connie Carpenter, briefly reported glimpsing the striking red eyes of the monster (Keel 2002, 99).

Keel's book describing how he found the Mothman phenomenon was accompanied by reports of UFOs and other strange phenomena in West Virginia and the Ohio Valley. Accounts of sightings begin to appear in local newspapers from April 1967 (Sergent and Wamsley 2002, 102–24). During his field investigations Keel also collected stories of unexplained animal mutilations and disappearances, poltergeists, and electromagnetic anomalies that disrupted radios and telephone systems. One UFO contact narrative that coincided with the arrival of Mothman was provided by traveling salesman Woodrow Derenberger. He claimed a UFO shaped like "an old fashioned kerosene lamp chimney" landed on the road in front of his truck on a road near Parkersburg, West Virginia, at 7 p.m. on November 2, 1966. A tall, tanned humanoid emerged from the object and approached him. A conversation ensued in which the man said his name was Cold and he came from a country much less powerful than the United States. Cold promised to return and then disappeared in the UFO. Derenberger's farm in Mineral Wells later became a magnet for legend trippers in search of a UFO experience. He went on to write a book about his experiences in which he claimed to have taken trips with his mysterious visitor, Indrid Cold, to a planet called Lanulos (Derenberger and Hubbard 1971). Keel provided a foreword and promoted this and other UFO contactee stories in his own books and syndicated writings.

During his visits to the Ohio Valley, Keel discovered that some Mothman and UFO witnesses had also reported surreal visitations from foreign-looking strangers wearing black clothes who arrived in large, apparently brand-new black cars. They asked questions about Keel's movements and tried to persuade witnesses not to talk about their unusual experiences. These sinister men in black (MIB) play a major role in the book that was written eight years after the events it describes. Although Keel did not invent the MIB, he coined the acronym and was responsible for elevating an obscure UFOlogical legend to the pop culture status it currently enjoys (Rojcewicz 1987). Folklorist Peter Rojcewicz compares MIB stories with older traditions that associate blackness with the devil. In folklore, the evil one is a shape-shifter who can appear as a "man in black" (155). Whereas some of the Mothman and UFO witnesses believed the MIB were government agents or members of the Mafia, Keel suspected they were part of a wider "ultra-terrestrial" phenomenon (Keel 1971). In his books he presents the ultra-terrestrials as shape-shifting intelligences that inhabit a parallel universe. Their demonic presence may explain the advice he gave to Linda Scarberry to keep a crucifix in her home as a deterrent to the MIB (Sergent and Wamsley 2002, 29–30). Deborah Dixon notes that Keel's book is heavily coded in terms of insider-outsider references and "it is unclear how much of the anxiety [he] expresses . . . stems from his own projection of racial conflict in the US, or simply reiterates the concerned views expressed to him" (Dixon 2007, 201).

In *The Mothman Prophecies* Keel explains how the more he became immersed in the mysteries he discovered in West Virginia, the more he found it difficult to detach himself from the events he reported on. Instead, as he put it, "the phenomenon" appeared to play with his own thoughts and beliefs (Keel, personal communication 1992). In chapters 10 and 11 he describes his sightings of unexplained moving lights in the Ohio River

Valley. These experiences occurred in the presence of other journalists and police officers. On several occasions Keel and Hyre attempted to communicate with the lights using a handheld torch. He also claimed to have participated in telephone conversations with mysterious nonhuman intelligences, including Indrid Cold, who featured in the Derenberger narrative. Keel used his "ultra-terrestrial" theory to separate these entities from the more popular concept of extra-terrestrials that he had rejected in 1967 when his inquiries "disclosed an astonishing overlap between psychic phenomena and UFOs" (Keel 1971). According to his account, during his field investigations, anomalous voices contacted him by telephone, day and night, to relay ominous messages and warnings about impending earthquakes, assassination attempts, and assorted other disasters. A cluster of these prophecies related to an unspecified catastrophe on the Ohio River that was the center of the Mothman and UFO "flap."

In the later stages of his investigation Keel returned to his apartment in New York for the Christmas holiday. On December 15, 1967, soon after President Lyndon Johnson switched on the festive lights at the White House, the television broadcast was interrupted by breaking news that the Silver Bridge that spanned the river at Point Pleasant, linking West Virginia with Ohio, had collapsed at rush hour. The falling structure sent forty-six drivers and pedestrians, including some Mothman witnesses, to their deaths. The collapse of the bridge occurred thirteen months after the Mothman legend began. Some of Keel's informants believed the Mothman/UFO phenomena were a premonition of the tragedy or part of its cause. It was certainly true that the number of anomalous experiences reported in the local media decreased after the disaster (Keel 2002; Sergent and Wamsley 2002).

A number of later sources link the collapse of the bridge to the "Curse of Chief Cornstalk," a Shawnee chief who is commemorated in the state park by a monument. in one version of the story, Chief Cornstalk traveled to Fort Randolph to negotiate a truce and avoid bloodshed between settlers and Native American tribes in 1777. He was taken hostage and later killed, together with his son, in reprisal for the death of a soldier who was part of a group caught in an ambush. As he died the chief is said to have laid a curse on Point Pleasant (Colvin 2014; Sherwood 2013, 26).

In his book Keel refers to the events of 1966–1967 as "the year of the Garuda," making a direct link between the Mothman and the legend of a giant humanoid birdlike creature that appears in Hindu and Buddhist mythology. In these traditions the Garuda bird is the mount of the Hindu god Vishnu and is sometimes depicted in anthropomorphic form as a man with wings and other birdlike features. Loren Coleman detected what he believes is a hint of European banshee traditions in "the strong sense of the foreboding dread of gloom [that] underlies Keel's chronicling of all the events leading up to the collapse of the Silver Bridge" (Coleman 2002, 199). The banshee, or *bean-sidhe*, is a female spirit in Irish fairy-lore who heralds the death of a family member by wailing or shrieking. The banshee is "invariably attached to a family, and it must be to one of the old families." It can even follow a family abroad, with documented examples from Canada and elsewhere (Briggs 1967, 25). In West Virginia the Mothman legend was associated with a small group of Point Pleasant families who reported frequent experiences with the creature before the bridge collapsed. One of the original witnesses, Linda Scarberry, claims she saw the creature on several later occasions and noted its distinctive red eyes (Sergent and Wamsley 2002, 22). There are many and varied descriptions of the banshee's size, color, and dress but some describe her as having red eyes from continual weeping.

Beliefs about luck or ill luck brought by the appearance of specific animals are common in folklore. Birds are widely regarded as an omen, or even a cause, of death, particularly if a wild bird enters a house or beats against a window. In English folklore moths are also regarded as omens of death when they appear in the homes of a dying person (Opie and Tatum 1990, 266–67).

The next section will explore how the story changed and evolved after the publication of Keel's seminal account in 1975.

The Mothman in Television and Film

Almost three decades after the original publication of *The Mothman Prophecies*, a new version of the legend appeared in the form of a movie in 2002. The movie's writers and director Mark Pellington adapted the story for an international audience, working with John Keel, who said, "They have managed to squeeze the basic truths into their film. Not an easy task" (Keel 2002, 336). The writers chose to depict the Mothman as a shape-shifting supernatural omen of death. The MIB that feature prominently in Keel's book were omitted from the screenplay, but the ultra-terrestrial, Indrid Cold, does make an appearance. He passes on predictions about earthquakes and plane crashes to Gordon Smallwood, a fictional character played by actor Will Patton. Cold also uses the telephone to communicate with the lead character, an investigative journalist based on Keel. The promo trailers claim the film is "based on true events" and the credits underscore this message, informing viewers that the film is "based upon the book by John A. Keel."

Producer Gary Lucchesi said he and actor Richard Gere rejected earlier scripts "that took the idea of a monstrous figure all too literally" (Dixon 2007, 202). Instead they chose to create "a psychological mystery with surreal overtones" and to address the question of "what happens when sane, reasonable people are faced with the unbelievable . . . in this case it was the harbinger of death" (Pellington 2002a).

Gere plays a New York journalist, John Klein, whose wife dies from a brain tumor shortly after an encounter with Mothman. He later discovers drawings of a winged creature, or angel of death, produced by his wife before her demise. Two years later Klein inexplicably becomes lost while driving to a reporting assignment and finds himself hundreds of miles away in West Virginia. There he discovers the residents of Point Pleasant are under siege from a range of baffling phenomena. Klein becomes obsessed with solving the mystery and understanding its apparent link with the death of his wife. He joins a police officer, Connie Mills, played by Laura Linney, to investigate a series of strange experiences, including sightings of a giant winged creature with red eyes. Mothman is occasionally glimpsed but never fully revealed. The film poster plays on its elusive nature, posing the question: "What do you see?" above the image of a Rorschach inkblot.

Actor Alan Bates plays Dr. Alexander Leek, an expert on ultra-terrestrial phenomena, to whom a grief-stricken Klein turns in his quest for answers. When they meet in Chicago, Leek draws directly on the theories developed in Keel's books, warning the journalist: "There has never been a shred of evidence to show these things exist materially . . . [but] all sorts of things exist around us that don't 'exist' . . . electricity, microwaves, infrared waves, these things have been around us forever. They show up in cave paintings . . . they are a normal condition of the planet. They are just not part of our concept of what constitutes physical reality" (Pellington 2002b).

When Klein demands to know if "they" are responsible for the death of his wife, Leek says their motivations are "not human." All that matters is that "you noticed them and they noticed that you noticed them." In the film, the two characters portray opposing aspects of Keel's personality: the skeptic and the believer/experiencer (Leek is Keel spelled backward). A similar dualism was explored in the long-running television series *The X-Files*, where the opposing dialectics are articulated by two characters of different genders. In his review, John Shirley described *The Mothman Prophecies* as the first truly Fortean film: "It is sceptical while being relentlessly open-minded about the anomalous; it refuses to come to easy answers, easy filings-away; it carries with it an atmosphere in which anything can happen, and reality itself is always suspect" (Shirley 2002).

One result of the dissemination of the legend via the ostensive mass medium of film was the appearance of fresh Mothman narratives in online forums (Coleman 2002). Some of these were accounts of personal experiences with winged creatures. Others referred to sightings of Mothman before other natural and man-made disasters in recent history. These include accounts of "a winged creature" just before the leak of nuclear materials at the Chernobyl reactor in 1986 and the September 11 attacks by terrorists on New York and Washington, DC (Colvin 2014). The source of these stories can be traced to a scene in the film when Klein visits Leek in Chicago and is provided with a list of other occasions in which the Mothman creature has appeared, across the world, as a "prediction of disaster." A factual link between Mothman, Chernobyl, and other disasters is repeated, without qualification, in the nonfiction documentary *Search for the Mothman* (Grabias 2002), which was included in the DVD release of *The Mothman Prophecies* feature film. Another incorrect claim made in the end credits of the film is that "the ultimate cause of the collapse of the Silver Bridge was never determined." In fact, an investigation by the National Bureau of Standards traced the collapse to the failure of one of the eyebars on the bridge supports (Sherwood 2013, 31).

Loren Coleman writes that he and Keel "did our best to straighten out the record regarding that mythos that became the Chernobyl 'Mothman' accounts," confirming that the Chernobyl story and other examples given in the 2002 movie "were pure fiction . . . It is a bit of movie fiction that has, unfortunately, moved into pseudo-factoid cryptozoology" (Hanks 2012). The Chernobyl Mothman is just one example of ostension arising from the dissemination of the Mothman legend.

The section that follows will examine how the Mothman revival in the first decade of the twenty-first century led to further ostensive action, including the creation of a museum and an annual festival in Point Pleasant that has established the West Virginia community as a permanent focus for Mothman-themed legend trips.

THE MOTHMAN REVIVAL

In the past two decades the Mothman has been adopted by the West Virginia community as a permanent attraction, with a museum, statue, and annual festival. The recent revival of interest in the legend has led to debates about the truth of the original accounts documented by John Keel and others. Folklore scholars understand that most legends emerge from the complex and often lengthy exchange of opinions that involve "believers, skeptics, and others in between," and although believers help to keep legends alive, "skeptics do too" (McNeill and Tucker 2018, 10).

The release of the Mothman movie led to a revival of interest in the legend in West Virginia, although key scenes, including the collapse of the Silver Bridge, were actually filmed in Pennsylvania. In 2003, a twelve-foot-tall metal sculpture depicting the Mothman by artist Bob Roach was placed on the corner of Fourth Street and Main Street in Point Pleasant. Based on a painting by Frank Fazetta that appears on the dust jacket of the 1991 reprint of *The Mothman Prophecies*, it was unveiled by John Keel at the second Mothman Festival. The event is held annually on the third weekend of September, and visitors have grown from 500 in 2002 to 4,000 in 2014 (mothmanfestival.com). It features guest speakers, live bands, Mothman and MIB costumes, a pancake-eating contest, a 5K run, and hayride tours. In 2005, a local entrepreneur, Jeff Wamsley, opened the Mothman Museum, dedicated to the legend, offering minibus tours of the TNT area and other places linked with the events in 1966–1967 (Sergent and Wamsley, 2002; Sherwood 2013).

The revival of the legend also led to skeptical reappraisals of the eyewitness accounts documented by Keel, Coleman, and others. Nonextraordinary explanations have been proposed, including the activities of pranksters and misperceptions arising from media coverage of the phenomenon. Some skeptics have reexamined claims reported in 1966 that the original Mothman scare was caused by the presence in West Virginia of a large, rare bird such as a sandhill crane or a large owl (Sergent and Wamsley 2002). In his book Keel said he carried photographs of these animals during his investigations, and none were recognized by Mothman witnesses. However, when skeptic Joe Nickell visited the TNT area, he noted it is surrounded by the McClintic Wildlife Management Area, "then, as now, a bird sanctuary" (Nickell 2002). He traced the grandson of a man who shot a snowy owl during the Mothman sightings in 1966. Although only two feet tall, this "giant owl," as a newspaper called it, has a wingspan of nearly five feet. Nickell noted that eyewitness accounts of the creature's glowing red eyes could be explained by the owl theory. It is well known to ornithologists that owl retinas can appear as bright circles at night when, like mirrors, they reflect artificial light such as from cars or flash lamps.

Others have linked the Mothman and MIB with rumors about psychological operations by the Defense Logistics Agency, which maintained a facility in the Ohio Valley area during the 1960s. In 2014, a writer in *Soldier of Fortune*, a mercenary magazine, claimed the original Mothman sighting was caused by the activities of Green Berets, who were at the time

Figure 17.1. Just off Main Street, the twelve-foot chrome Mothman statue, erected in 2003, haunts Mothman Park, Point Pleasant, West Virginia. (Photograph courtesy of Simon Sherwood.)

experimenting with new techniques to insert special forces into enemy-held territory in Vietnam. One method covertly tested in the Point Pleasant area, he claimed, was "the high-altitude, low-opening (HALO) freefall parachuting technique." Luminous paint was used during the exercise to keep track of soldiers, but "what the Green Berets making those jumps hadn't figured on was the fact that people on the ground could see it as well" (Hutchison 2014).

Further examples of pseudo-ostension can be found in the form of the UFO contactee stories reported in Keel's books. Some of these have since been revealed as fictional narratives inspired by the original legend. These include a narrative told by a psychology student, Tom Monteleone, who claimed he had met Indrid Cold and traveled to Lanulos shortly after Woodrow Derenberger's UFO encounter received media coverage in 1966–1967 (Keel 2002, 240–46). Monteleone later confessed his claims were

invented as part of a college experiment (Clark 1998, 701). In an afterword
to the 1991 edition of his book, Keel writes that he was aware that "Tom's
whole tale [was] a hilarious put-on and that all contactee stories were highly
suspect" (1991, 271). In addition, there is some evidence that some of the
anomalous phone calls received by Keel in 1966–1967 were pranks played
by Gray Barker (1925–1984), a fellow UFOlogist who joined the New York
journalist on some of his field investigations. Barker was a West Virginia
resident and author of a 1970 novel based upon the Mothman legend and
the collapse of the Silver Bridge (Barker 1970; Sherwood 2002). Barker's
1956 book *They Knew Too Much about Flying Saucers* launched the legend of
the "three men in black." He later confessed to a number of UFO-related
hoaxes and is suspected of having placed at least one of the bizarre phone
calls described in Keel's 1975 book (Sherwood 2002).

CONCLUSION: "BASED ON TRUE EVENTS"?

Hollywood interpreted the Mothman legend as a psychological horror story.
Others have interpreted the events described in John Keel's book as being
factually reported, or at least "based on true events," as the film poster
implied. Keel began his writing career as a reporter and, as a journalist
myself, my concluding remarks will examine his literary contribution to the
legend in the context of its strength as a "good story" (see Hobbs 1987).

The *Mothman Prophecies* was written in the "New Journalism" style that
was popular when Keel was at his most prolific (Wolfe and Johnson 1975).
This was a departure from the traditional model for news reporting because
it did not place emphasis upon the importance of neutrality and factual
accuracy. New Journalism immersed the writer within the story, "channel-
ling a character's thoughts, using non-standard punctuation and exploding
traditional narrative forms" (Boynton 2005). This style often involved a
mixture of personal observation, overheard dialogue, and extracts from
documents or original notes, "frequently focusing as much on the quest
for information as on the information itself" (Harcup 2014, 116). In her
discussion of *The Mothman Prophecies*, Deborah Dixon makes this explicit,
noting that Keel "adopts a pulp fiction style of writing that simultaneously
undercuts the eyewitness veracity the original testimonies strived for and
buttresses his own authoritative position as the purveyor and interpreter"
(2007, 201).

In 1992, Keel explained to me how he struggled to find a publisher for
the book until he revised the introductory chapter, "Beelzebub Visits West
Virginia," to include "a strong opening . . . based on a true story" (personal

communication). His storytelling slowly builds a feeling of dread and fore-boding as he describes the events of a stormy night in November 1967, just weeks before the collapse of the Silver Bridge. A stranger approaches a farmhouse in the hills of rural West Virginia and raps upon the door until a young woman answers.

> She opened the door a crack and her sleep-swollen face winced with fear as she stared at the apparition on her doorstep. He was over six feet tall and dressed entirely in black. He wore a black suit, black tie, black hat, and black overcoat, with impractical black dress shoes covered with mud. His face, barely visible in the darkness, sported a neatly trimmed moustache and goatee. The flashes of lightning behind him added an eerie effect. (Keel 1975, 1)

The Man in Black asks, "May I use your phone?" in a deep, unfamiliar accent. The woman and her partner refuse to help and the MIB is left to repeat his request at another dwelling nearby. Keel explained the origins of this story in an extended interview:

> I had been out in the hills with another journalist following up stories about lights in the sky. Our car had run off the road on a very rainy night and I was dressed in a necktie and a full suit . . . you didn't see that very often on back roads in West Virginia, a black suit . . . and I went around pounding on doors to get somebody to call a truck for me. It turned out that the people who finally made the call were among the people that were on the bridge that later collapsed. The day after I knocked on their door, they told every-body they knew that a strange man in a black suit and a beard had called and he must have been the devil. (Roberts and Clarke 1992, 19)

In the version that appears in his book, Keel reveals how he learned that accounts of his visit to this rural area had subsequently entered folklore as a premonition of the collapse of the Silver Bridge: "It had, indeed been a sinister omen. One that confirmed their [area residents'] religious beliefs and superstitions. So a new legend was born" (Keel 2002, 2). This narra-tive was so striking that it was reinterpreted for a scene in the movie, when John Klein arrives at Gordon Smallwood's farm after he finds himself in West Virginia following a missing time experience. In both the book and the film, the scene functions as a plot twist of the type commonly found in contemporary legends with a supernatural theme. Keel invokes film noir in his account of it, comparing the West Virginia setting with "an opening scene of a Grade B horror film from the 1930s" (Keel 1975, 1). Similarly, contemporary legends with a supernatural theme "often depend on their twisted endings and ambiguous characters and situations for effect" (de Vos 1996, 7). Keel goes on to invoke dark landscapes and ordinary characters that face macabre, unexpected twists and turns as the story unfolds.

John Keel's role as the storyteller who interprets the disparate stories in the form of an overarching narrative was pivotal in what Linda Dégh and Andrew Vázsonyi call the dialectics of the legend (1973), providing the story its latent power and longevity. The subsequent sharing of these stories in literature, film, and online has encouraged others to confront and examine their view of the world, of what is possible and impossible, via the medium of the story. In a letter to the Mothman witnesses dated March 15, 1970, Keel recognized that West Virginia's Mothman "is now part of history . . . in time it will become a folk legend" (Sergent and Walmsley 2002, 135). This reinvigorated legend has been embraced by members of the community in Point Pleasant, which played a part, alongside the movie, in its recent revival.

REFERENCES CITED

Barker, Gray. 1970. *The Silver Bridge*. Clarksburg, WV: Saucerian Books.
Boynton, Robert. 2005. "The Roots of the New New Journalism." *Chronicle of Higher Education*, March 4. https://www.robertboynton.com/articleDisplay.php?article_id=1515.
Breedlove, Seth, dir. 2017. *The Mothman of Point Pleasant*. Wadsworth, OH: Small Town Monsters.
Briggs, K. M. 1967. *The Fairies in Tradition and Literature*. London: Routledge & Kegan Paul.
Clark, Jerome. 1998. *The UFO Encyclopedia*, 2nd ed. Detroit: Omnigraphics.
Coleman, Loren. 2002. *Mothman and Other Curious Encounters*. New York: Paraview.
Colvin, Andrew, ed. 2014. *Searching for the String: Selected Writings of John A. Keel*. Seattle: Metadisc Productions.
Dégh, Linda, and Andrew Vázsonyi. 1973. "The Dialectics of the Legend." *Folklore Preprint Series* 1:6 (December): 1–65.
Dégh, Linda, and Andrew Vázsonyi. 1983. "Does the Word 'Dog' Bite? Ostensive Action: A Means of Legend-Telling." *Journal of Folklore Research* 20 (1): 5–34.
Derenberger, Woodrow W., with Harold W. Hubbard. 1971. *Visitors from Lanulos*. New York: Vintage.
de Vos, Gail. 1996. *Tales, Rumors, and Gossip*. Westport, CT: Libraries Unlimited.
Dixon, Deborah. 2007. "A Benevolent and Sceptical Inquiry: Exploring 'Fortean Geographies' with the Mothman." *Cultural Geographies* 14:189–210.
Ellis, Bill. 2003. *Aliens, Ghosts and Cults: Legends We Live*. Jackson: University of Mississippi Press.
Fort, Charles. 1919. *The Book of the Damned*. New York: Boni & Liveright.
Grabias, David, dir. 2002. *Search for the Mothman*. Screen Gems.
Hanks, Micah. 2012. "Mothy Misconceptions: Clearing the Air about the Mothman Mythos." *Mysterious Universe*, January 25. https://mysteriousuniverse.org/2012/01/mothy-misconceptions-clearing-the-air-about-the-mothman-mythos/.
Harcup, Tony. 2014. *Dictionary of Journalism*. Oxford: Oxford University Press.

Hobbs, Sandy. 1987. "The Social Psychology of a 'Good' Story." *Perspectives on Contemporary Legend* 2:133–48.

Hutchison, Harold. 2014. "UFO Mystery Solved." *Soldier of Fortune* 39 (2): 3.

Keel, John A. 1957. *Jadoo: Mysteries of the Orient*. New York: Julian Messner.

Keel, John A. 1970. *Strange Creatures from Time and Space*. Greenwich, CT: Fawcett.

Keel, John A. 1971. *Our Haunted Planet*. Greenwich, CT: Fawcett.

Keel, John A. 1975. *The Mothman Prophecies*. New York: Saturday Review Press.

Keel, John A. 1991 [1975]. *The Mothman Prophecies*. London: New English Library.

Keel, John A. 2002. "Afterword." In *The Mothman Prophecies*, 333–36. London: New English Library.

McNeill, Lynne, and Elizabeth Tucker, eds. 2018. *Legend Tripping: A Contemporary Legend Casebook*. Logan: Utah State University Press.

Nickell, Joe. 2002. "Mothman Revisited: Investigating on Site." *Skeptical Inquirer* 12 (4). https://www.csicop.org/sb/show/mothman_revisitedinvestigating_on_site.

Opie, Iona, and Moira Tatum, ed. 1990. *A Dictionary of Superstitions*. Oxford: Oxford University Press.

Pellington, Mark, dir. 2002a. "Cast and Crew Interviews." *The Mothman Prophecies*. Lakeshore Entertainment Corporation.

Pellington, Mark, dir. 2002b. *The Mothman Prophecies*. Lakeshore Entertainment Corporation.

Roberts, Andy, and David Clarke. 1992. "The John Keel Interview." *UFO Brigantia* 34:15–21.

Rojcewicz, Peter M. 1987. "The 'Men in Black' Experience and Tradition." *Journal of American Folklore* 100:148–60.

Sergent, Donnie Jr., and Jeff Wamsley. 2002. *Mothman: The Facts behind the Legend*. Point Pleasant, WV: Mothman Lives.

Sherwood, John C. 2002. "Gray Barker's Book of Bunk: Mothman, Saucers and MIB." *Skeptical Inquirer* 26 (3). https://www.csicop.org/si/show/gray_barkers_book_of_bunk_mothman_saucers_and_mib.

Sherwood, Simon J. 2013. "A Visit to Point Pleasant: Home of the Mothman." *Paranthropology* 4 (1): 25–35.

Shirley, John. 2002. "The Mothman Prophecies." *Locus Online*, February 9. http://www.locusmag.com/2002/Reviews/Shirley_Mothman.html.

Steinmeyer, Jim. 2008. *Charles Fort: The Man Who Invented the Supernatural*. London: Heinemann.

Underwood, Peter. 1971. *A Gazetteer of British Ghosts*. London: Souvenir.

Wolfe, Tom, and E. W. Johnson, eds. 1975. *The New Journalism*. London: Pan.

EDITOR'S SUGGESTIONS FOR FURTHER READING

Clarke, David. 2016. "A New Demonology: John Keel and *The Mothman Prophecies*." In *Damned Facts: Fortean Essays on Religion, Folklore and the Paranormal*, edited by Jack Hunter, 54–68. Cyprus: Aporetic.

Coleman, Loren. 2017. *Mothman: Evil Incarnate*. New York: Cosimo Books.

Hasken, Eleanor, and Jesse Fivecoate. 2017. "Episode Ten: The One about Mothman (feat. Ashley Wamsley-Watts)." *Encounters*. Podcast. https://www.stitcher.com/podcast/eleanor-hasken/encounters/e/49555894.

Keel, John A. 2002 [1975]. *The Mothman Prophecies*. New York: Saturday Review Press.

Laycock, Joseph P. 2008. "Mothman: Monster, Disaster and Community." *Fieldwork in Religion* 3 (1): 70–86.

18

The Windigo as Monster
Indigenous Belief, Cultural Appropriation, and Popular Horror

Gail de Vos

PREFACE

Some North American monster legends have indigenous origins, and many that don't are ascribed them anyway. The windigo, an important North American entity, is difficult to define. Many readers will immediately recognize it—a tall, slender, often hungry, near-skeletal being of the north that preys on humans and brings the cold—perhaps not by name but by popular media's depiction (or, some might say, appropriation), in the White Walkers of *Game of Thrones*, the giant Wendigos of *Final Fantasy*, or the lurking Tuunbaq of *The Terror*. As with any oral tradition, many iterations of the windigo exist. In this chapter, Gail de Vos, legend scholar and instructor in the Aboriginal Teachers Education Program at the University of Alberta, compares the older Algonquin folk windigo variants to the contemporary popular versions prevalent in mass media today. A pure comparison between the "original" text and the "popular" text is not sufficient—by definition, there is never a single "original" text, and subsequent tellers and artists have the same artistic license to make subtle changes for reasons of audience and environment as do all folk performers. Instead, researchers scrutinize how the monster legend is used, examining its changing function as it migrates through differing audiences, historical eras, and social contexts.

This variety of legend research must be partially descriptive, defining the phenomenon before it can be assessed. De Vos spends a significant portion of her essay describing, through variants and recurring motifs, exactly what the windigo is (or was). She pays special attention to notions of ownership and appropriation. While the white man has transformed the windigo into a stock horror monster (an almost irresistible urge fed by lurid details

https://doi.org/10.7330/9781646421602.c018

in the original folk texts), natives too have transformed the windigo: from a starving, stalking beast (perhaps a commentary on hunger) to a metaphor for modern concerns about politics, technology, and society.

The windigo provides a prime example of legend creolization. The Algonquin legend seems to have hybridized early on with the French and French Canadian loup-garou (werewolf) and later with American horror legends such as the Slender Man. Folklorists, dedicated to the collection and analysis of legend in situ, can also appreciate the analysis of monster legends as they evolve, emically and etically, and how mass media adopts, co-opts, and adapts macabre legends for their own benefit.

ESSAY

The majority of non-Indigenous authors writing on the windigo deliver representations of a fearsome mythological monster in films, novels, television series, cartoons, and comic books, without any contextual background, seldom respecting its indigenous roots and focusing instead on horror and the supernatural.[1] This chapter compares the past indigenous windigo to more recent conceptions of the windigo as it appears in current non-indigenous mass media and in contemporary indigenous thought and creative works and provides concise social and historical context for a better appreciation of this often misunderstood and frequently misrepresented legendary creature. Because of the dearth of awareness about indigenous beliefs, the general population does not see the windigo as a sacred entity, viewing it instead as a "monster" figure, incessantly reimagined and re-formed in successive "borrowings" until there is very little remaining of the traditional legend. Cultural appropriation is defined as the taking and adapting, without permission, of unique aspects of a people's culture, including their traditional dress, music, and knowledge, by people of another culture, settler or indigenous. In Canada, for Indigenous nations, cultural appropriation is entrenched in colonization and the ongoing subjugation of their traditions and beliefs (Pitt 2018).

One of the most exasperating issues with mainstream media adapting, adopting, and appropriating elements of Indigenous cultures is the resulting pan-Indian composite, which denies the unique cultural attributes of each autonomous Indigenous nation, and the irreverent use of cultural figures that are considered private and revered. This cultural appropriation is not done maliciously but in ignorance, without respect for or acknowledgment of the windigo's indigenous cultural foundations. Adding to this disconnect, it must be noted that to many contemporary Indigenous people, the windigo no longer refers to an individual spirit or monster but rather to anxiety-inducing organizations, systems, or technologies.

THE HISTORICAL INDIGENOUS WINDIGO

Oral and written stories of the windigo were told and collected as early as the 1630s in Algonquian communities but, although the idea of the windigo is old, it has evolved and varied over time. As an example of the historical indigenous conception of the windigo, I begin with Ojibwe[2] scholar and storyteller Basil Johnston's frequently repeated account of the traditional Algonquian windigo:

> The Weendigo was a giant Manitou in the form of a man or a woman, who towered five to eight times above the height of a tall man. But the Weendigo was a giant in height only; in girth and strength, it was not. Because it was afflicted with never-ending hunger and could never get enough to eat, it was always on the verge of starvation. The Weendigo was gaunt to the point of emaciation, its desiccated skin pulling tautly over its bones. With its bones pushing out against its skin, its complexion the ash gray of death, and its eyes pushed back deep into their sockets, the Weendigo looked like a gaunt skeleton recently disinterred from the grave. What lips it had were tattered and bloody from its constant chewing with jagged teeth. (1995, 221)

The windigo is a relatively recent popular selection for the mainstream entertainment industry, employed as a stock villain equivalent to other monstrous creatures like zombies, werewolves, and vampires. Unlike these other stock monsters, however, the windigo remains a viable constituent of the belief systems of many Native American and First Nation peoples, particularly those belonging to Algonquian tribal nations. This cultural group extends from California to Virginia but is principally located on the northern plains and boreal forests of North America and includes the Anishinaabe/Ojibwe people in the Great Lakes and upper Midwest and the Cree, a diverse group of northern Algonquian people (Smallman 2014, 11). For these people, the windigo (also known as wendigo, wee-tee-ko, wihtikow, and witiko, among other names) is a cannibalistic spirit being that can transform a man, woman, child, or animal into an asocial and murderous being or a giant cannibal itself (Smallman 2014, 13). According to historical legend, there have been at least two distinct visions of the windigo: a giant that hunted Indigenous people and an evil spirit that could transform others into cannibals. This duality within windigo traditions has been extant among Ojibwa-speaking groups at least as early as the mid-1700s (Smallman 2014, 54). According to Shawn Smallman, the windigo could also be a clown-like figure in ritual dances in the narratives of the Plains Cree while at the same time remaining a threatening figure. The Mi'kmaw believed the windigo, or chenoo, was a giant that maintained an association with spirit transformation, and the Anishinaabe/Ojibwe maintained that some of the giant windigos had begun as transformed humans (Smallman 2014, 65). In all these communities, windigo narratives were told for a wide variety of reasons, including entertainment. For the entire community, they provided a means to discuss the issues of hunger and starvation in a nonthreatening manner, and for children, they were practical cautionary tales that kept them away from the dangers of the forest.[3]

Steve Pitt (2018) describes the windigo as a powerful cannibalistic monster from the spiritual traditions of Algonquian-speaking First Nations that has been transformed from its human form because of greed or weakness. Pitt writes, "Various Indigenous traditions consider windigos dangerous because of their thirst for blood and their ability to infect otherwise healthy people or communities with evil. Windigo legends are essentially cautionary tales about isolation and selfishness, and the importance of community." The windigo is frequently considered a supernatural being, strongly associated with the coldness of a northern winter, or it may appear as a monster or a spirit who can possess humans and make them monstrous. Prevalent descriptors throughout the literature encompass a formidable and towering man-beast as tall as a tree, a demonic and malevolent spirit, a flesh-eating demon, a carnivorous beast, a relative of Bigfoot, an albino Sasquatch, a Yeti that resembles a werewolf, or an antlered zombie. The one thing these accounts have in common is a distinct murkiness in relating the windigo's physical and behavioral attributes. Many accounts embrace the image of an icy-gray, human-like, balding figure with a malnourished and skeletal body that is deformed, missing its lips and its toes. Others consider the windigo a large hairy Bigfoot-like creature with glowing eyes and long sharp claws, a giant that has a heart of ice or is made entirely of ice (Dillon 2014b). Some describe the windigo as smelling of decay, hissing while breathing, with a mouth full of jagged teeth or long yellowed fangs and an overly long tongue.

The windigo is always depicted as hungry no matter how much human flesh it consumes; its body and its hunger grow in portion to the amount of flesh ingested. Several narratives declare that windigos, using dark magic, can control the weather and summon predators, ordering them to attack on command. Although many of the accounts and reworkings of the windigo claim it is a mute creature, others maintain that it baits its prey with shrieks or growls, sometimes mimicking human voices calling for aid (Dove n.d.). Traditionally, the windigo was a master of creating confusion, distraction, and fear, utilizing its brute strength, power, and intimidation tactics to lure its victims close enough to be consumed (Friedland 2018, 53). It is often credited with extraordinary eyesight, hearing, and a sense of smell, making it an exceptional hunter.

Carol Warrior, in her dissertation on the windigo, provides an overview of an analysis undertaken by Anthony Wayne Wonderly in 2009 of fifty oral windigo stories told by a variety of Cree, Ojibwe, and other Algonquian peoples in which he classifies the overall story types into three categories. Category 1, "Windigos in Narrative Space," offers accounts of conflicts of mythical heroes or godlike protagonists against powerful mythical giants. Category 2, "Windigos in a World of Spiritual Power," contains narratives of a human with spiritual power assuming windigo form to battle a malicious windigo antagonist. Category 3 stories, "Windigos in a Human World," feature cannibalistic monsters as humanlike predators in the human world. "Whether or not they are giants," Warrior observes, "these windigos are capable of living among, being mistaken for, and even intermarrying with Algonquian folk. In their icy hearts, however, their sole interest is to secure human prey" (2015, 27). Warrior also examined Howard A. Norman's 1970s collection of 150 Swampy Cree windigo narratives. A prime descriptor of the windigo in these narratives is "a wandering giant with a heart made of ice who preys on Indian people" and is considered so frightful that a person encountering the spirit "would be so overtaken by fear and disorientation that their heart would stop" (28). Windigos in these narratives could be cured or killed through a variety of means, including melting their icy hearts. Killing a windigo could be accomplished with a conventional weapon such as a club or a firearm. Numerous narratives indicate that only a shaman can dispatch a windigo with specialized rituals and ceremonies or that the icy heart must be removed from the windigo and melted in a roaring fire (Pitt 2018). Others claim that, as with werewolves or vampires, silver bullets or a pure silver blade staked through the heart are the only methods that will kill the windigo. According to one source, the heart must then be shattered into pieces and the pieces locked in a silver box and buried in a church cemetery. The rest of the body must be dismembered with a silver-plated axe, salted, and burned. The ashes are then to be scattered to the winds (Dove n.d.).

In traditional Algonquian views there were five distinct stages of windigo transformation. The stages include the public identification of a windigo; the local community's effort to treat the individual; the local community's caring for the individual when treatment is ineffective; and, if that failed, the recruitment of a leading shaman (when possible) to treat the individual through drumming sessions and lengthy rituals. The fifth stage, implemented only when everything else failed, was the public killing of an individual considered. The aftermath of the killing of the windigo would include the destruction of the body and community discussion. Local communities operated by consensus, including during the final stage, which was the point at which missionaries became involved (Smallman 2014, 133). None of these accounts ever mentioned the necessity of silver bullets or tools to dispatch the windigo. Fire was the constant element for destroying a windigo since the windigo, associated with winter, iciness, and bitter cold, was ultimately susceptible to fire, which not only provided warmth to defuse the windigo but was a purifying agent and ultimately the epitome of extreme consumption itself. Fire could kill both a physical windigo and a windigo infection of the spirit because it was the only force with a hunger greater than the windigo's (Lietz 2016, 52). The vast majority of the traditional stories, however, illuminated that the most conventional response to a windigo was not killing it but attempting to heal it. Only when that failed was killing the windigo to protect others standard protocol (Friedland 2018, 86). Execution, always the last resort, was never a vengeful act but considered a valid and legitimate preventative action to ensure group safety, reflecting the obligation of the community and the shamans to firmly and finally incapacitate the windigo. Such perceptions of legitimate responsibility in legal and cultural systems gave rise to conflicts between Indigenous communities and the Canadian government. This dichotomy resulted in several documented cases in the early 1900s in which Canadian legal authorities imprisoned and executed Indigenous legal authorities who were carrying out traditional decisions to destroy a windigo. Since that time, the only methods of incapacitation that do not carry the risk of criminal charges are reporting behavior to the police and intervention by mental health services to attend to the afflicted (Friedland 2018, 92).

The local legends varied by area and changed over time and through cultural exchange. After contact in Canada, voyageurs and Indigenous people made connections to European traditions. French voyageurs arrived primed with their own traditional myths and legends about supernatural monsters, particularly the *loup-garou*, or werewolf. The similarities between werewolves and windigos aided the voyageurs' understanding of both windigo stories and the potential for additional cross-cultural exchanges with the First Nations communities. Both types of creatures, fabricated by external conditions that replace their humanity with monstrous attributes, are ostracized by their former communities and feared for their terrorized attacks and feasting on people who are isolated and vulnerable (DeSanti 2015, 191).

European folklore, religious beliefs, and political interests have long been important aspects of the evolving windigo. One constant in these diverse variants was the focus on cannibalism. The overriding character-istic of the windigo is that it is a predator and a cannibal—it consumes other human beings, though the actual forms of cannibalism and motiva-tions for the act may fluctuate. The varied landscapes and North American Indigenous beliefs surrounding the windigo are exemplified by the diverse variety of descriptors, actions, and sensations that have been collected and catalogued. Because of these wide-ranging variants, difficulties arise in attempting to describe and clarify the intrinsic nature of the traditional windigo, opening an assorted cache of possibilities and complications for adaptions, adoptions, and cultural appropriations of the creature by purvey-ors of mainstream entertainment.

The Windigo in Mass Media

Indigenous creatures became a staple of North American horror literature as the genre developed in the early eighteenth and nineteen centuries, with a plethora of Native American ghosts and the ubiquitous trope of haunted burial grounds. The horror genre is well suited to absorbing and adapting elements of horror from other cultures. Author and literary scholar Joe Nazare, in his exploration of the appropriation and reclamation of Native American mythology in the horror genre, states that "the positing of the Native American as brooding boogeyman and howling, inarticulate fiend of the wilderness clearly served as a pretext and justification for cultural domination" (2000, 25). Bluntly stated, what may be sacred in one culture is often considered nightmarish horror material for another (Warrior 2015, 15). The mass media windigo is a stock horror figure in stories where inno-cent people are trapped, stalked, and dispatched in grisly fashion (DeSanti 2015, 198). In fact, the windigo proved an easy fit. Note, for example, the similarity of the imagery from this traditional windigo legend to modern depictions of mass media monsters: "The approach of a Wendigo is pre-ceded by shrieking winds and a cold so fierce that it would cause the trees to crack. It was said that the Wendigo's upper body would be hidden by dark snow clouds as it hunted down its prey, and when it finally caught a man, it would drink its blood and eat its flesh" (Lietz 2016, 21).

Fictional windigos in all arenas of popular culture have boomed, and the Internet provides extensive lists of windigo-inspired media. It is evident that the tall, slender monster that preys on humankind from the shadows intrigues mainstream consumers (Hast n.d.). Enthusiasts of Slender Man have pointed to similarities between it and the windigo: both are tall, lanky, and bony, with pale skin and terrible claws.[4] Both are portrayed as silent, tormenting others by their mere presence. These portrayals of the windigo in popular culture, however, misrepresent both the windigo and Indigenous people. In both older oral accounts and contemporary ones, depictions of First Nation windigos challenge the mass media depiction of a mindless, perilous, vengeful, male antagonist who is amoral, destructive, and unresponsive to societal mores. There is also an implication of savageness and primitiveness associated with these representations of the modified monster, frequently mirrored in the portrayal of the Indigenous people who form its background foundations. This windigo cannot be salvaged but only feared and ultimately destroyed.

The most significant and influential windigo in non-indigenous fiction appears in Algernon Blackwood's novella *The Wendigo* (1910). Blackwood based this novel on stories he had heard in northern Ontario. Indigenous studies scholar Grace Dillon observes, "Despite its painful racism, the story became a horror classic that has been redone on CBC Radio and perhaps inspired Tolkien's description of the Nazgul's cry" (2014b, 590). Joe Nazare agrees, stating that Blackwood's "subtly-demonizing rhetoric transforms the Wendigo from a native myth into a descriptive template for the Indian savage" (2000, 30). Windigo print narratives have continually appeared on bookshelves since Blackwood's novel, including a wide variety of titles and treatments from Stephen King's *Pet Sematary* (1983)[5] to *Wendigo Wood: A Folk Horror Comic* (2018), a British comic book series described as a six-issue arc about a search that reveals "the forest home of the urban legend of the Wendigo."[6] As of the writing of this chapter, Goodreads lists over fifty adult novels that have been identified as windigo tales. A substantial increase in the number of children's picture books and young adult novels about the windigo cannot be overlooked. The monstrous windigo continues to be exploited because of the terror it evokes but, as mentioned earlier, it has become increasingly disconnected from its indigenous roots while being blended with other traditions.

The White Walkers in *Game of Thrones* may have been influenced by the contemporary portrayal of the windigo: tall, slender beings of the north that bring the cold with them and can transform the dead into murderous beings (Smallman 2014, 73). Windigos populate role-playing games such as

Dungeons & Dragons and multiple video games, including *Final Fantasy*, *The Legend of Dragoon*, *The Secret World*, *Until Dawn*, and *Fallout 76*. They maintain some of the traditional elements of the indigenous windigo. The Dungeons & Dragons windigo, for example, is defined as a force of nature and an insubstantial savage fey spirit that travels invisibly with the winter winds, manifesting itself only to feed its constant hunger or to transform others into flesh-eating windigos. It is a master in spells of illusion, defense, cold, and force magic.[7]

The windigo in *Fallout 76*, acknowledged to be outside of its traditional territory, is included because it is now considered a recognizable and fearsome monster from American folk and popular culture. *Fallout 76* creatively but dubiously adapts the windigo to a new locality, in postapocalyptic West Virginia. They are described as cannibals, the most vicious monsters in the game: slouching, slender, tall figures with razor-sharp claws that tear enemies apart with alarming speed. They are mutants descended from the banished heads of a cannibal raider tribe who were twisted by the radiation in the Wendigo Cave in which they first hid in the Appalachian Mountains.[8]

The windigo has long been a mainstay villain in Marvel Comics, with over 300 appearances to date. DeSanti states that although Marvel stories accurately depict the cannibalistic dispositions and consumption of human flesh as the triggers for becoming a windigo, the creature's physical appearance would not be all that recognizable to a traditional Algonquian community (2015, 190). DeSanti points to a slight exception illustrated by one of my favorite illustrators and supporters of traditional folklore, Charles Vess, who departs from previous Marvel depictions of the Windigo in both physical appearance and the incorporation of some of the uncommon features that parallel Ojibwe traditions. In his 1986 short comic story at the end of an issue of *The Amazing Spider-Man*, Vess's "Cry of the Wendigo" depicts the windigo as a thin, wraithlike force that stalks its prey.[9] This, DeSanti maintains, is closer to traditional Ojibwe understandings, with Vess's characterization touching on lesser-known correlations between the windigo and the fear of being lost, confused, and alone (2015, 190).

Positive appreciation of non-indigenous windigo interpretation from Indigenous scholars is rare. Grace Dillon, in her foreword to Shawn Smallwood's *Dangerous Spirits* (2014a), decries the lack of authentic research or acknowledgment in adoptions of the windigo in much of contemporary popular culture with an examination of Johnny Depp's character Tonto in the film *The Lone Ranger*. His Tonto is a windigo hunter. Tonto is Cheyenne, however, and the windigo is part of the Algonquin belief system. Two frequently mentioned films offering evidence that their film-makers researched the cultures and traditions are Larry Fessenden's *Wendigo* (2001) and Antonia Bird's *Ravenous* (1999). In *Wendigo*, the depiction of the remote, frozen setting matches the traditional association with being lost and vulnerable, along with the motif of shape-shifting, which is an aspect of all manitous. The film does not, however, address the cannibalistic nature of the monster. *Ravenous* is more successful in handling the windigo complex: cannibalism is a metaphor for the colonization of Indigenous people and individuals becoming windigos while retaining their normal appearance (DeSanti 2018, 17). More recently, and in keeping with the contemporary Indigenous development of the windigo, in Armand Ruffo's (Ojibwe)[10] *A Windigo Tale* (2010), the windigo is employed in telling a story about the intergenerational trauma of residential schools.

Television serials such as *Supernatural, Grimm, Hannibal, X-Files, Charmed*, and *My Little Pony: Friendship Is Magic*, among others, have also incorporated the windigo. *Supernatural* offers some rudimentary understanding of the indigenous windigo at the same time as it melds the windigo with the werewolf. Dean Winchester, one of the protagonists in *Supernatural*, states: "More than anything, a Wendigo knows how to last long winters without food. It hibernates for years at a time. When it's awake, it keeps its victims alive. It stores them so it can feed whenever it wants" (Radford 2019). *Charmed*, on the other hand, made no acknowledgment of the tradition or association with indigenous culture. The name of the windigo is taken without any attempt to understand where it came from, underlying the force of cultural appropriation. There is the idea of melting the windigo's frozen heart and an allusion to cannibalism is made, with this windigo consuming the hearts of its victims, but most of the characteristics are borrowed from the werewolf of popular culture (DeSanti 2015, 192).

Canadian historical records demonstrate a strong connection between the indigenous windigo and the French werewolf, one that continues in contemporary media. The two are often combined into one fearsome, dangerous, and often victorious monster. In many instances, this conflation accompanies a reluctance or inability to demonstrate the fluidity, complexity, and adaptability of Indigenous people and their culture. The image and role of the windigo evolves, but people remain tethered to the imagined and stereotypical past fabricated for them by generations of media portrayals. This is a major contention of contemporary Indigenous people: many of their interpretations and understandings of the windigo have undergone change. Instead of the worn and tired monster, it is this contemporary windigo that should be at the helm as we move forward.

The Windigo in Contemporary Indigenous Thought

The windigo legend provides a prime example of the dangers of cultural appropriation and the habitual dismissal of "Others'" beliefs that seem to permeate Euro-American popular culture and the folk horror genre. There is wide agreement that there is a distinct oversimplification of the windigo among non-Indigenous people, who equate it to a monster who has been corrupted by an evil spirit or force (Banias 2018). In the mass media the idea and image of the windigo remain largely separate from indigenous culture.

Shawn Smallman found that the narrative tradition of the windigo faded throughout the twentieth century in some Indigenous communities at the same time as it was adopted by non-Indigenous groups as a symbol in literature and film. He writes, "Over the last twenty years, Indigenous authors and directors have reclaimed the windigo as a symbol to understand and critique colonialism" (2014, 29). Cultural appropriation and the habitual association of Indigenous people with the historical past pervade these non-indigenous endeavors. Indigenous works, on the other hand, equate the windigo spirit with traumas associated with residential schools, sexual abuse, cultural loss, environmental destruction, and other elements of colonialism. Basil Johnston, quoted by Smallman, describes the contemporary windigo as the spirit of selfishness: "These new Weendigoes are no different from their forebears. In fact, they are even more omnivorous than their old ancestors. The only difference is that the modern Weendigoes wear elegant clothes and comport themselves with an air of cultured and dignified respectability" (2014, 67).

Jack D. Forbes, Indigenous scholar and political activist, in his treatise on the *wetiko* as a contemporary disease of selfishness and greed that spreads through discourse and socialization, maintained that a person can become a windigo when he or she is subsumed or brutalized and that the disease is highly contagious. Warrior quotes Forbes as saying that the disease "is spread by history books, television, military training programs, police training programs, comic books, pornographic magazines, films, right-wing movements, fanatics of various kinds, high-pressure missionary groups, and numerous governments," and also scholarly writing (or writing that puts on academic or authoritative airs) (2015, 34). Warrior suggests that, once colonialism is understood as wetiko disease, the stories offer listeners suggestions and examples of how to trick, evade, or defeat an aggressive contemporary windigo. This also explains "how and why, in contemporary Native American fiction, villainy is not made of what a fearsome figure is, but instead, on what it does. Windigos disrupt interdependency, skew reciprocity, and destroy relationships, especially the relationships needed for life to reproduce itself without human mediation or technological intervention" (215). Warrior maintains that Indigenous storytellers like Forbes teach people how to recognize and avoid windigos and, more important, teach people how to live a balanced, nurturing, and sustaining lifestyle rather than a destructive one (222). The windigo is an enduring and contemporary symbol because it speaks to universal human fears far beyond the frozen subarctic. Smallman suggests that "in contemporary Indigenous traditions, the windigo has become associated with the danger of greed, capitalism, and Western excess, while in European and Canadian imagery, it is the symbol of evil, wilderness, and madness—two diametrically opposed visions of the same phenomenon" (2014, 67).

Most of my Indigenous colleagues are offended by the application of the terms "myth," "legend," and "folklore" to their belief systems and object to the plundering of their cultural traditions, which are considered sacred and private. Algonquian people firmly believe in the ongoing evolution of the windigo complex, but as it evolves within their community, not as it is imposed on their community for outsiders' entertainment. Often, contemporary indigenous allusions to the windigo are understated, with only those who are already aware of the modern windigo tradition recognizing them. Author Waubgeshig Rice (Anishinaabe), in his recent post-apocalyptic novel, *Moon of the Crusted Snow*, for example, uses the futuristic setting to introduce the windigo as a murderous white man who snowmobiles into the First Nation community and proceeds to corrupt it. "I never explicitly say that this is a Wendigo story," he explains. "It is inspired by them. Throughout my writing career I have tried to walk as respectfully as I could within and without my background in terms of the stories and the ceremonies that are involved with it" (Robb 2018).

Similarly, Jack Forbes's compilation of the psychological traits of this contemporary windigo includes greed, lust, inordinate ambition, materialism, untrustworthiness and, above all, arrogance (Forbes 1992, 52). There is wide-scale agreement with Forbes among Indigenous authors and scholars. Contemporary indigenous art, stories, ceremony, humor, and relationships are battling against the new forces of the windigo.[11] Danielle Boissoneau (Anishnaabe kwe), for example, states, "Mirroring Windigo society's malevolent and gruesome truths with our art, our stories, and relationships is one way to expose Canada for what it is: a gruesome, cannibalistic design that, when coupled with capitalism, becomes the latest manifestation of the Windigo" (2017, 6). This windigo, which in the old legends transformed only in the winter, is now a peril throughout the year. The essence of the contemporary Indigenous windigo is not easy to categorize or illustrate and is not the one that mainstream media capture and cannibalize in their ruthless search for horrific monsters, motifs, and plots. As Brady DeSanti (Ojibwe) explains:

> To best understand the windigo, to see it as more than a talking-head vil-
> lain or, alternatively, a hodgepodge assemblage of random features resem-
> bling something like the construction of the Frankenstein monster, it must
> be properly positioned and evaluated . . . He is at once a giant man-eating
> monster, a transmitter of cannibalistic urges to humans, and a warning
> against overindulging in personal gratifications to the neglect of the com-
> munal whole. (2015, 198)

For many contemporary Indigenous people, the windigo of main-stream popular culture is another example of the theft of their culture and identity. This disregard for authenticity and respect is, for these individuals, exemplified today in the aftermath of residential schools, broken treaties, racist policies and attitudes, and destructive environmental practices. Contemporary indigenous art, stories, ceremony, laughter, and relationships are battling this latest manifestation of the windigo (DeSanti 2015, 192). Certain individuals, groups of individuals, corporate bodies, and governments can be identified as windigos, or aspects of wetiko disease (Levy 2013, 227). Danielle Boissoneau emphasizes, "Where once Windigo was hideously terrifying, now it smiles, showing off its perfect teeth and glowing skin, which indicates the evolution and sophistication of the Windigo spirit" (2017, 5).

The windigo as monster is a popular trope that is here to stay, both in the mainstream horror genre and in Indigenous contemplation and worldview. Rather than unconditionally condemning the appropriation of this figure from the Algonquian peoples, I advocate understanding and acknowledging the backgrounds, the conflicts, the underlying meanings, and the context that the windigo has held for centuries before it became a horror mainstay. Perhaps then we, outside of the Algonquian societies, will pay more attention to how we adopt, adapt, and transform traditional beliefs for entertainment and remediate how the windigo is portrayed in future endeavors. I hope, too, as we contemplate the context, our understanding and acceptance of the people themselves will expand and solidify. It is crucial that we acknowledge the evolving nature of other beliefs and legends and stop fossilizing them as we have done with the windigo. My overall aspiration is for the mainstream to cease mindlessly pilfering other cultures and traditions and respectfully request permission to adopt aspects of them, with full understanding and appreciation, in storytelling in all media and formats.

In all practicality, unfortunately, the horrific windigo is a too strong, well-known, and financially feasible scare factor to be easily put aside. Perhaps we can do better in the future?

NOTES

1. Several examples out of a myriad of them include the film *The Manitou* (1978), in which a psychic's girlfriend finds out that a lump on her back is a growing reincarnation of a 400-year-old demonic Native American spirit; Marvel Comics' recurring character Wendigo (first appearing in 1973 in the *Hulk*), the product of a mystical curse that causes anyone that ingests the flesh of another human, while within the wilderness, to transform into the beast; and, in prose, *The Curse of the Wendigo* (2006), by Scott R. Welvaert, in which his two protagonists, Agate and Buck, tracking down their missing parents in the haunted Canadian woods are hunted by a shape-shifting creature called the Wendigo when an ancient curse is set in motion.

2. The spelling of this term is not fixed. I have used the spelling each author prefers rather than making them consistent.

3. In a recent discussion with my Indigenous university students from northern Alberta, they reiterated present-day indigenous use of these stories as cautionary tales for children, meant to keep them from wandering off. One student, Wanda Nanooch, added that the name of the windigo was never to be mentioned to avoid it coming to life: if the windigo hears its name, it begins to roam again.

4. See https://theslenderarchives.weebly.com/canada.html.

5. Several reviews of the 2019 film *Pet Sematary* remark that the windigo has a much larger, and more frightening, presence than in the original film. See Navarro 2019 for more details.

6. See https://www.kickstarter.com/projects/ghostislandcomic/wendigo-wood-1-a-folk-horror-comic.

7. See https://dungeonsdragons.fandom.com/wiki/Wendigo.

8. See https://fallout.gamepedia.com/Wendigo.

9. Unfortunately, Marvel holds the copyright to this image and neither Charles Vess nor I could obtain permission to include it in this chapter.

10. From the *Style Guide for Reporting on Indigenous People*: "Whenever possible, identify which First Nation an individual is affiliated with. As more than half of First Nations people do not live on-reserve, it is best to state such affiliation and where they currently reside. Not all individuals who are a member of a First Nation have resided in that community" (Journalists for Human Rights 2017, 4).

11. See, for example: Louise Erdrich's (Chippewa) novel *Tracks* (1988), her poem "Windigo" in *Jacklight* (1984), which she prefaces by saying that in some Chippewa stories, a young girl destroys the windigo by forcing boiling lard down its throat, resulting in the release of the human at the core of ice; Tomson Highway's (Cree) *Kiss of the Fur Queen* (1998), in which a pedophile priest plays the part of the windigo; Drew Hayden Taylor's (Ojibway) novel *The Night Wanderer: A Gothic Novel* (2007) and the graphic novel adaptation (2013); Jay Odjick (Algonquin) and Patrick Tenascon's (Algonquin) graphic novel *Kagagi: The Raven* (2011); Neal McLeod's (Cree) collection of poetry *Songs to Kill a Witikow*; and the picture book *The Spirit Trackers* by Jan Bourdeau Waboose (Anishinaabe), illustrated by Francois Thisdale (2017).

REFERENCES CITED

Banias, M. J. 2018. "Why the Wendigo Is Not My Monster." https://mysteriousuniverse
.org/2018/10/why-the-wendigo-is-not-my-monster/.

Blackwood, Algernon. 1917 [1910]. *The Wendigo.* In *The Lost Valley and Other Stories,* 71–132. New York: Knopf.

Boissoneau, Danielle. 2017. "Cannibal 150." *Briarpatch Magazine,* July 30, 4–6. https://briar
patchmagazine.com/articles/view/cannibal-150.

DeSanti, Brady. 2015. "The Cannibal Talking Head: The Portrayal of the Windigo 'Monster' in Popular Culture and Ojibwe Traditions." *Journal of Religion and Popular Culture* 27 (3): 186–201.

DeSanti, Brady. 2018. "Classroom Cannibal: A Guide on How to Teach Ojibwa Spirituality Using the Windigo and Film." *Journal of Religion and Film* 22 (1): 1–30. http://digital
commons.unomaha.edu/jrf/vol22/iss1/36.

Dillon, G. L. 2014a. Foreword to *Dangerous Spirits: The Windigo in Myth and History,* by Shawn Smallman, 15–19. Victoria, BC: Heritage House.

Dillon, G. L. 2014b. "Windigo." In *The Ashgate Encyclopedia of Literary and Cinematic Monsters,* edited by Jeffrey Andrew Weinstock, 589–93. Burlington, VT.: Ashgate.

Dove, Laurie L. n.d. "How Wendigoes Work." *howstuffworks.* https://science.howstuffworks
.com/science-vs-myth/strange-creatures/wendigoes.htm.

Forbes, Jack D. 1992. *Columbus and Other Cannibals: The Wetiko Disease of Exploitation, Imperialism, and Terrorism.* Los Angeles: Autonomedia.

Friedland, Hadley Louise. 2018. *The Wetiko Legal Principles: Cree and Anishabek Responses to Violence and Victimization.* Toronto: University of Toronto Press.

Hast, Jess. n.d. "Meet the Wendigo." *Horror.* https://horror.media/meet-the-wendigo.

Johnston, Basil. 1995. *The Manitous: The Spiritual World of the Ojibway.* New York: Harper Collins.

Journalists for Human Rights. 2017. *Style Guide for Reporting on Indigenous People.* http://www
.jhr.ca/en/wp-content/uploads/2017/12/JHR2017-Style-Book-Indigenous-People
.pdf.

Levy, Paul. 2013. *Dispelling Wetiko: Breaking the Curse of Evil.* Berkeley, CA.: North Atlantic Books.

Lietz, Michelle. 2016. "Cannibalism in Contact Narratives and the Evolution of the Wendigo." Master's thesis, Eastern Michigan University. http://commons.emich
.edu/theses/671.

Navarro, Megan. 2019. "The Creature in the Woods: The Role of the Wendigo in Stephen King's *Pet Sematary*." *BloodyDisgusting.* https://bloody-disgusting.com/editorials/
3545561/ground-sour-wendigo-evil-personified-stephen-kings-pet-sematary/?fbclid
=IwAR37arpr4pyEIILJCZs0nA1xbY0SZHb0fcGM7r_lk8y-ohCuZDiVp8bDpBo.

Nazare, Joe. 2000. "The Horror! The Horror? The Appropriation, and Reclamation of Native American Mythology." *Journal of the Fantastic in the Arts* 11 (1): 24–51.

Pitt, Steve. 2018. "Windigo." In *The Canadian Encyclopedia.* https://www.thecanadianencyclo
pedia.ca/en/article/windigo.

Radford, Lyra. 2019. "12 Terrifying Facts about the Wendigo and Its Dark History." *Graveyard Shift.* https://www.ranker.com/list/wendigo-facts/lyra-radford.

Robb, Peter. 2018. "Ottawa Writer's Festival: Into the Uncanny Valley with Waubgeshig Rice." *artsfile.* https://artsfile.ca/ottawa-writers-festival-into-the-uncanny-valley-with
-waubgeshig-rice/.

Smallman, Shawn. 2014. *Dangerous Spirits: The Windigo in Myth and History.* Victoria, BC: Heritage House.

Warrior, Carol Edelman. 2015. "Baring the Windigo's Teeth: The Fearsome Figure in Native American Narratives." PhD diss., University of Washington.

EDITOR'S SUGGESTIONS FOR FURTHER READING

Blackwood, Algernon. 1917 [1910]. *The Wendigo*. In *The Lost Valley and Other Stories*, 71–132. New York: Knopf.

Brightman, Robert A. 1988. "The Windigo in the Material World." *Ethnohistory* 35 (4): 337–79.

Brightman, Robert A. 2015. "The Return of the Windigo, Again." *Semiotic Review* 2. https://www.semioticreview.com/ojs/index.php/sr/artice/view/22.

Carlson, Nathan D. 2009. "Reviving Witiko (Windigo): An Ethnohistory of 'Cannibal Monsters' in the Athabasca District of Northern Alberta, 1878–1910." *Ethnohistory* 56 (3): 355–94.

Fogelson, Raymond D. 1980. "Windigo Goes South: Stoneclad among the Cherokees." In *Manlike Monsters on Trial: Early Records and Modern Evidence*, edited by Marjorie M. Halpin and Michael M. Ames, 132–51. Vancouver: University of British Columbia Press.

Podruchny, Carolyn. 2004. "Werewolves and Windigos: Narratives of Cannibal Monsters in French-Canadian Voyageur Oral Tradition." *Ethnohistory* 51 (4): 677–700.

Preston, Richard J. 1980. "The Witiko: Algonkian Knowledge and Whiteman Knowledge." In *Manlike Monsters on Trial: Early Records and Modern Evidence*, edited by Marjorie M. Halpin and Michael M. Ames, 111–31. Vancouver: University of British Columbia Press.

Swenson, Kirk R. 2018. "The Hunters and the Haunted: Blackwood's Transformation of the Wendigo." *Supernatural Studies* 5 (1): 33–49.

Thiess, Derek J. 2018. "Dan Simmon's *The Terror*, Inuit 'Legend,' and the Embodied Horrors of History." *Journalist of Fantastic in the Arts* 29 (2): 222–41.

19

Monsters, Legends, and Festivals
Sharlie, Winter Carnival, and Other Isomorphic Relationships

Lisa Gabbert

PREFACE

Lisa Gabbert observes that Americans most often meet legendary monsters firsthand not in the field but at festivals—an overlooked venue for monster performance and performance of the monstrous. Monsters are fêted in their own festivities throughout the continent, from Fouke, Arkansas's Boggy Creek Monster Festival to Asbury Park, New Jersey's Jersey Devil & Fable Festival to Manitowoc, Wisconsin's Windigo Fest. Using the example of Sharlie, Idaho's resident Payette Lake Monster, and the McCall Winter Carnival, Gabbert attempts to account for the fast friendship between monsters and festivals. Sharlie is not the official mascot of McCall, but rather an unofficial one—an eponymous menu item here, a trinket in a gift shop there. But Sharlie sightings are voluminous during Winter Carnival, a festival that doesn't celebrate the lake monster per se, but incorporates Sharlie throughout, especially in snow sculpting and the annual parade.

John A. Gutowksi and Richard M. Dorson laid the groundwork for the exploration of legend and festival—that is, Americans playing with their monsters—and here Gabbert pushes this line of inquiry further, clearly delineating the genres' interrelationships. While Gabbert addresses boosterism, she emphasizes, as previous scholars have not, the isomorphic dimensions, that is, the corresponding relationships between monsters, legends, and festivals: "the expansion of ontological possibilities, the porousness of boundaries, ambivalence, and the mediation of insiders and outsiders." Monsters and festivals both fall in the interstices of cultural categories, betwixt and between—monsters not human nor animal, festivals not

https://doi.org/10.7330/9781646421602.c019

everyday life nor completely outside of it—a liminality that makes for a natural pairing between genres.

Gabbert's essay should serve as a starting point for the study of monsters and festivals, with the interested folklorist having no shortage of venues: from Rhinelander, Wisconsin's Hodag County Festival to Braxton County, West Virginia's Flatwoods Monster Fest to Beeville, Texas's Chupacabra BBQ Throwdown, research opportunities abound. Monsters, legends, and festivals share folkloristic features, providing a traceable trajectory for future monster research.

ESSAY

A question: Where are Americans most likely to encounter monsters? An obvious answer might be the mass media. We see monsters in films and on television, and we might read about them in books or in tabloid newspapers. We also encounter them on the Internet, especially participatory media, Slender Man being the current example par excellence (Blank and McNeill 2018). Certainly most Americans have not had some kind of direct, firsthand encounter with the preternatural, and those who have might only catch a glimpse of something mysterious, somewhere, and likely only once in their lives. People who claim full-fledged, interactive monster encounters are much rarer (alien abductions and "I-had-Bigfoot's-baby" claims come to mind) and in most cases, we are likely to doubt their sanity.

I suggest that the primary and perhaps only place that Americans regularly encounter monsters immediately and firsthand is within festival contexts. Alessandro Falassi notably defined festival as "a periodic celebration composed of a multiplicity of ritual forms and events directly or indirectly affecting all members of the community, and explicitly or implicitly showing the basic values, the ideology, and the worldview that are shared by community members and are the basis of their social identity" (1987, 296). These periodic celebrations, with their multiplicity of forms and events, are essential but overlooked contexts for the performance of monstrosity. Halloween, for example, is technically a holiday, but it also is a festival (Santino 1984), and it is the traditional time of year when monsters roam the streets and possibilities of encounters with the supernatural open up. Comicon is another example, a kind of commodified festival where fans encounter and enact not only their favorite heroes but also their favorite villains and monsters. Not all American monsters are "festivalized," that is, incorporated into festival, but many are: the Mothman Festival in Point Pleasant, West Virginia; Bigfoot Daze in Willow Creek, California; the Lizardman

Festival of Bishopville, South Carolina; and the UFO Festival of Roswell, New Mexico are a few examples of this phenomenon. This fact, that festival seems to be a natural context for the presentation of monsters in the United States, begs the question: Why? What is the relationship between monsters and festival and why are monsters so easily incorporated? I begin with the example I know best, which is that of Sharlie, the lake monster of Idaho's Payette Lake and his/her relation to the McCall Winter Carnival.[1]

Sharlie is the name of the lake monster that supposedly lives in Payette Lake, a large, glacial lake that borders the remote mountain resort town of McCall, Idaho. Sharlie is referred to by both male and female pronouns, as evidenced by its given name, which is somewhat ambiguous in terms of gender. The idea that Payette Lake contains some kind of watery creature is based on a long history of mysterious sightings which, according to newspaper records, date back to at least the 1930s and likely even earlier. Sightings of something strange in the lake have been reported dozens of times in the local newspaper over the past eighty years, the most recent of which was in August 2019. The details found in newspaper reports, archival materials, and interviews I have conducted range from more mundane, personal experience narratives of "slightly dramatic" instances (Goldstein, Grider, and Thomas 2007, 29), such as sightings of a strange wake, ripple, or wave in the lake on an otherwise calm and clear day, to full-fledged legends describing thirdhand events to highly dramatic memorates of sightings such as the one I recorded in 1997 in which a narrator described a creature with bulging eyes and three humps rising from the water (Gabbert 2011, 202). In the summer of 2000 I saw something myself that I have never been able to rationally explain: I would describe it as being like a very large sea lion, since it looked like it had fur, and this is a motif in lake monster sightings (see Fife 1948, 101).

Mysterious qualities are commonly attributed to bodies of water in which monsters are presumed to reside: lake monsters don't just live anywhere, you know. These environmental qualities are an important part of the legend complex, though they are not necessarily articulated in sightings or more formal legends (Meurger 1988). Payette Lake, for example, has a history of mysteriousness that dates back even further than Sharlie sightings. Rumors that it is "bottomless," for example, have existed practically since the area was settled, when the territorial controller announced that the depth of the lake was unknown. Such rumors existed throughout the twentieth century and occasionally resurface (*pa-bum!*) today. Additionally, the lakes in which monsters reside often are said to contain underground tunnels that connect to other lakes in the region, to the ocean, or even across the ocean to lakes in Europe, making a tangible narrative link between

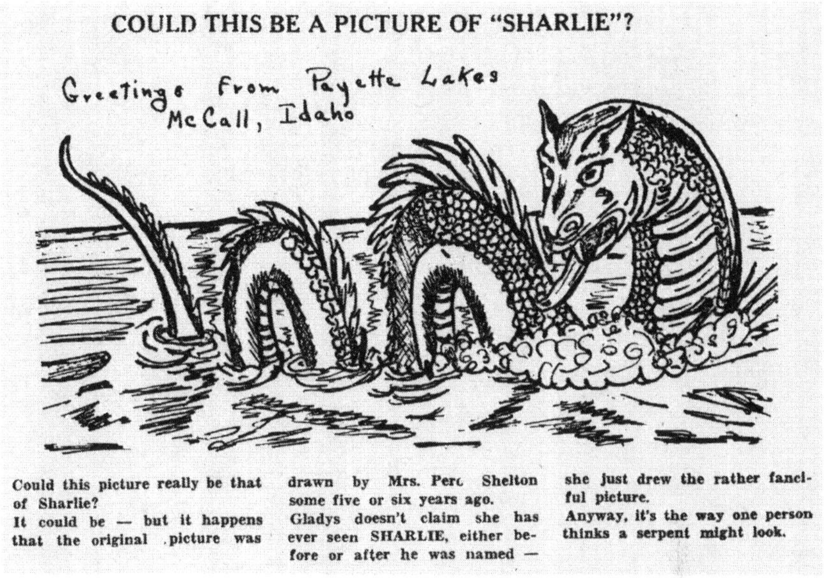

COULD THIS BE A PICTURE OF "SHARLIE"?

Greetings from Payette Lakes McCall, Idaho

Could this picture really be that of Sharlie? It could be — but it happens that the original picture was drawn by Mrs. Perc Shelton some five or six years ago. Gladys doesn't claim she has ever seen SHARLIE, either before or after he was named — she just drew the rather fanciful picture. Anyway, it's the way one person thinks a serpent might look.

Figure 19.1. An early drawing of Sharlie, originally published in a local newspaper.

North American lake monster traditions and European ones. Payette Lake, for example, is rumored to have underground tunnels that connect it to lakes in Oregon, as well as underwater caves where Sharlie hides, serving as explanations for why s/he can't be found (see Douglass 1956). Finally, the actual water of lake monster lakes is considered somewhat dangerous. The water sometimes is described as being unusually cold, or dark, or as having underwater currents or pockets of perilous water that might claim lives. Payette Lake is thought to have strange pockets of hot water since the region is volcanic, and there exist historical legends about airplanes, horses, and people allegedly disappearing into the lake, never to be found, as illustrations of its dangerous qualities. It is no surprise then, given these monster-friendly environmental characteristics, that Sharlie took up residence there. Besides, the area also is quite beautiful, and there is a nice view.

Sharlie never became an official mascot of McCall, though s/he is loosely connected to various forms of boosterism. If one visits McCall, one can see a children's statue of a lake monster in Rotary Park, and there is (or used to be) a restaurant called Sharlie's. A local hamburger joint offers Sharlie burgers on the menu, and one might find lake monster imagery for sale in the local shops. But Sharlie is much more of a folk or unofficial village mascot than an official one. McCall was founded as a lumber town and now bills itself as a year-round recreational and sporting area. During much of the mid-twentieth century, for example, the town's official motto was "Ski Town USA" as it sought to promote winter downhill skiing. Today, images of winter and summer sports and recreation, not lake monsters, are used in advertising and branding.

The easiest and most reliable way to see Sharlie, if you are not lucky enough to see him/her swimming in the lake during the summer, is during the McCall Winter Carnival. Winter Carnival is a festival held by the McCall Chamber of Commerce celebrating winter sports and winter outdoor activities. It begins at the end of January, lasts ten days, and attracts thousands of people. Winter Carnival originated in 1924 as an annual event featuring dog-sledding and ski-jumping competitions, and it lasted until 1939, when it was disbanded due to World War II and other reasons. It was revived in 1965 as a way of boosting winter tourism by attracting tourists to the area during an economically slow part of the winter season. The main attraction of the revived Winter Carnival is the construction of large snow sculptures, which transform the town into an outdoor museum. The other main attraction is a colorful Mardi Gras parade, held on the first Saturday, in which anyone can participate if they fill out an entry form. Other attractions include, depending on the year, a children's Mardi Gras parade, a beard-and-hairy-leg contest, snowshoe competitions, dog-sledding races, downhill and Nordic ski competitions, and a polar dive.

Winter Carnival is not a Sharlie festival, meaning that Sharlie is not an official mascot. Locals, however, consistently choose to include Sharlie in the activities. Images of Sharlie or dragon-like creatures that reference Sharlie inevitably are found in the local snow-sculpture competition, in which teams compete against each other for cash prizes in various categories. The sculptures are supposed to adhere to an overall given theme, but local people adapt their sculptures to include Sharlie no matter what. Sharlie has been sculpted chasing water-skiers; lounging in a martini glass; driving a fire truck; and facing off with Bigfoot in a western-style shootout, to name just a few of the dozens of lake monster images I have seen sculpted or documented in archival photographs. Sharlie also always makes a grand appearance in the main Mardi Gras parade in the form of an undulating Chinese dragon, and the dragon has been incorporated into the children's parade as well. Locals also will sometimes create their own Sharlie parade entries in addition to the annually occurring dragon: one year, for example, someone covered a digger in heavy green plastic and constructed a long lake monster head and neck using the shovel for the mouth. The operator, hidden inside the cab, had Sharlie interact with the crowds by speaking into a loudspeaker, mostly asking for candy.

Figure 19.2. Sharlie as a snow sculpture at McCall's Winter Carnival. (Photograph courtesy of Lisa Gabbert.)

So why is Sharlie so easily and regularly included in a festival that is not even about him/her? One answer certainly is that Sharlie is used for promotional and boosterism purposes. Winter Carnival is a festival designed to attract tourists, and what might be more attractive to outsiders and tourists than a monster? But there also are more meaningful generic and isomorphic relationships at play, as the qualities attributed to monsters, legends, and festivals overlap in a number of ways. These qualities include the expansion of ontological possibilities, the porousness of boundaries, ambivalence, and the mediation of insiders and outsiders. The rest of this essay explores these qualities in order to uncover more deeply these symbiotic relations.

Lake monsters are a species of cryptids, creatures whose existence is unproven by science but that are postulated possibly to exist based on folklore. Cryptids fall into the realm of legend, a folklore genre commonly defined as a type of narrative and/or folk belief. Tim Tangherlini, for example, defines legend as "a monoepisodic, localized and historicized traditional narrative told as believable in a conversational mode" (1996, 437), while Elliott Oring variously has defined legends as "narratives which focus on a single episode . . . which is presented as miraculous, uncanny, bizarre, or sometimes embarrassing" (1986, 125) and as stories that involve a rhetoric of truth (2008). Yet, as scholars have illustrated, legends are not merely narratives but also often involve elements of personal experience (Hufford 1982). My own working definition, which follows the critiques of Robert Georges (1971), is that legends are an extraordinary event or proposition purported to be true (Gabbert 2015). I use this definition because legends are not just narratives but events that frequently reach out from the past to impinge on the present. Stories about Sharlie sightings can be traced back through the twentieth century and are frequently told in third person, but they are compelling to an audience because they posit an unusual possibility that continues to exist in the present. They offer a remote possibility of an encounter with the monster for the audience at hand.

A key component of legends is that they are told "as if" the extraordinary proposition or event being purported were true, or at least possibly true; that is, they are told in the subjunctive tense. The subjunctive tense in English is a mood tense, a tense used to describe things that are not known actual facts. Yet the tricky thing is that grammatically the subjunctive tense can look identical to the indicative form, the tense that is used to describe actual facts. Legends make use of this grammatical slippage between the subjunctive and the indicative, making them powerful rhetorical devices that cause the audience to temporarily question given contours of reality and compel them to ask: Could this possibly be true? Could this possibly have happened? When someone tells me that they thought they saw Sharlie in Payette Lake, or I tell you, my readers, that I thought I saw Sharlie during the summer of 2000, those narratives mediate boundaries, existing at the margins between fiction and nonfiction, truth and fantasy, and narrative and reality. This subjunctive qua indicative usage allows for an in-betweenness that also is enhanced stylistically depending on whether the legend is told seriously, in a jesting manner, or a combination of both. Legends ultimately play with reality, and this is why they are closely related to the lying genres, such as tall tales and pranks, which also play with reality (Marsh 2015). Legends bring basic ontological categories into conscious awareness and cause us to question them, or at least to recognize the arbitrariness of how the world is organized and categorized.

Festivals, which are a complex umbrella category containing many different genres, events, and activities within them, also make claims on and play with reality, and they do so by enacting the subjunctive behaviorally. Victor Turner famously described festival as "society in its subjunctive mood . . . its mood of feeling, willing, and desiring, its mood of fantasizing, its playful mood" (1987, 76). Festivals are a play genre, meaning that they invoke an alternative reality and are considered by participants to be "not real." The purpose of festivals is to temporarily transform everyday life into "something else," and possibility—the potential transformation of onto-logical categories—is a key characteristic as participants act "as if" life were on different terms for the festive period. Some of the claims on reality that festivals make reinforce the status quo: rituals, for example, which often exist within festival contexts, produce a transformation of social status, the purpose of which is to uphold social norms. Heritage festivals also often reify given categories (Garlough 2011). Other aspects of festival, however, particularly those associated with the carnivalesque (Bakhtin 1968), seek to temporarily upend given social categories and expand possibilities of given reality. Carnivalesque aspects of festivals invert social roles through symbolic inversion, for example, and given categories and rules of everyday life are suspended, mixed up, or crossed, using an array of devices such as costume and masking, alcohol consumption, dance, sleep deprivation, and an excess of food, visuals, and music to accomplish this transformation. Festival is one of the great means by which social life is transformed, crys-tallized, rearranged, and enacted in alternate ways (see Gabbert 2019 for an overview). Like legends, festivals offer possibility, the purpose of which is to both reify and rearrange given categories.

As monsters are a species of legend, their qualities also lend themselves to festival purpose. The first definition in the *Oxford English Dictionary* (*OED*) offers a definition of monsters as "a mythical creature which is part animal and part human, or combines elements of two or more animal forms, and is frequently of great size and ferocious appearance." The emphasis in this definition is on combinations of disparate elements: animal and human, or various pieces of animal forms. A monster by definition is a combina-tion of things that don't normally go together, and so the monstrous form itself is a rearrangement of given categories. By bringing together disparate natural/given elements as part of their being, monsters visually perform what festivals do at an experiential level and what legends do narratively: they cross boundaries. Sharlie is not a creature made up of disparate parts (a more concrete example would be Dorson's tripodero, unfortunately likely extinct [1982:8]), but as a cryptid s/he defies natural history categories and the proposition of her/his existence challenges the boundaries of common sense. In this sense, Sharlie and other cryptids bring together categories that are normally separate.

Another definition of monster (definition #4 in the *OED*) that extends the ideas above is that a monster is a creature of huge size. Sharlie is described as quite large, although exactly how large remains in the realm of speculation. The creature I saw seemed approximately the size of a sea lion or walrus, but in other narratives Sharlie's length is estimated as being twenty-five feet or longer. This emphasis of the monstrous as a large and thus unnatural body easily lends itself to festival contexts, as gigantism is an important festive trope. Unlike miniaturism, which seeks to control and contain (Stewart 1992), gigantism touches on chaos and lack of order, a primary quality of the carnivalesque. Inherent in the idea of the carnivalesque is the grotesque, which features twisted, unnatural, or diseased bodies, and parts/processes of bodies normally kept hidden, such as the sexual organs and those associated with digestion and elimination. Indeed, Bakhtin's ideas regarding the carnivalesque were taken from the writings of the early modern writer Rabelais, whose novels featured giants named Gargantua and Pantagruel and whose subversive actions, frequently based on their giant bodies, bodily functions, and things done to the bodies of others, consistently upended and resisted conventional social norms. Effigies of giants commonly are featured in traditional festivals in Spain and France, and so the nature of the monstrous as a large and unnatural body fits the festive tropes of gigantism and the grotesque.

Gigantism also is used in display. Festivals often put important symbols and ideas up for display, usually increasing their size so that they can be seen, touched, worshipped, and so on (Abrahams 1987). Sharlie is not worshipped, but s/he is an important idea or symbol for the community. In Winter Carnival, Sharlie is often sculpted in snow, and the general unspoken aesthetic rule is "The bigger the better." Larger sculptures please audiences and often win prizes. I worked on a Sharlie snow sculpture that won the Grand Prize in 2001, and that particular sculpture was as long as the side of a large furniture store, perhaps seventy-five feet. Sharlie entries in the parades are also quite large. That festivals enlarge and display community symbols represents a well-established relationship between festival and a body politic, and so there seem to be relations between the monstrous body, festival, and the social body more broadly that warrant further exploration.

Another relationship between monsters and festival can be found in the idea of strangers and the ways in which monsters and festivals mediate insiders and outsiders. Michael Dylan Foster notes in his study of the Namahage festival in northern Japan that the Namahage are associated with the concept of the "marebito," which means something like an outsider welcomed temporarily into the community (2013, 308). Monsters have an essential strangeness, and they can be said to represent an outsider, a stranger, or something foreign to the community. The Namahage, representing a foreign element, temporarily breach the boundaries of the community or the household to be treated as respected guests.

Festivals, particularly local tourist festivals such as Winter Carnival, also mediate between insiders and outsiders. As Foster notes, "Namahage ritualizes transgression and the breaching of boundaries by outside forces. This theme, of course, resonates powerfully with tourism, structured as it often is around the incursion of outsiders into a community" (2013, 303). Winter Carnival is supposed to be good for the community and it accomplishes this purpose by bringing outsiders/tourists "in" for overall communal economic health. The idea is that tourists bring in and spend outside money, which then circulates within the community for the presumed betterment of all, although whether that actually occurs is a topic of debate. If Winter Carnival were a provincial festival by and for the community only, it would not, presumably, accomplish its purpose, which is to rejuvenate and refresh the community economically by bringing in outside money. On the other hand, too many outsiders and strangers also can be damaging. Winter Carnival remains a community festival despite being oriented toward tourists. If it becomes too "outward-facing," too oriented toward strangers and/or tourists and not oriented enough toward the community, it is no longer a community festival but simply a commodified event attended by people with few local connections. Festival organizers therefore constantly adjust Winter Carnival events as they attempt to seek a balance between these two dimensions.

Sharlie embodies this insider/outsider and familiar/strange dynamic. Sharlie is essentially strange, and narratives of Sharlie sightings indicate a strangeness in the world that is not fully comprehensible. On the other hand, Sharlie also is a member of the community, something I strongly suspect is true for other North American monsters connected to specific locales. Sharlie is famous: having been featured in innumerable local newspaper and magazine articles, Sharlie brings attention to the town. Sharlie is not considered particularly threatening and is associated with playfulness and fun. Sharlie also has lived in the area a long time and therefore is an old-timer. Sharlie thus mediates categories of strangeness/stranger and familiarity/community member. A monster is attractive to tourists because it is a member of the community, but because it is also strange it warrants attention. As Foster suggests, it is a stand-in for the process of tourism, and it is no surprise that Sharlie is constantly incorporated into a festival for tourists, despite the fact that Winter Carnival is not a Sharlie festival.

Yet another quality of monsters that overlaps with festival are the related themes of ambivalence and play. Ambivalence means to have contradictory ideas or feelings. On the one hand, as liminal entities that cross boundaries, monsters are viewed with apprehension and awe. To some local people, Sharlie represents the remote possibility of a mysterious creature that lives in the lake, and stories of Sharlie sightings are fundamentally mysterious. On the other hand, Richard Dorson noted long ago that Americans (at least in the dominant culture) tend to play with their monsters. "Belief and dread are not wholly absent," Dorson wrote, "but in contrast to the rest of the world we engage in hoaxes, pranks, tall tales and tomfoolery with our legendary creatures" (Dorson 1982, 4).

This playful, joking attitude toward lake monsters and other legendary creatures is well documented and dates at least to the middle of the nineteenth century, a period known for the circulation of tall tales and hoaxes, those of Mark Twain being the most famous examples. The sea serpent of Silver Lake, Wyoming County, for example, was a hoax dating from 1855 (Hawley 1946; Douglass 1956), the Utah Bear Lake Monster of 1868 also proved a hoax (Morrell 2011; see chapter 11 in this volume), and Dorson offers numerous humorous nineteenth-century examples of monsters and hoaxing in his book *Man and Beast in American Comic Legend* (1982). This playful, joking attitude continues into the modern era. Elizabeth Tucker (2004; see chapter 10 in this volume) traced the history of the Lake Lieberman lake monster as a kind of college joke, noting that it didn't matter that the monster was a known fabrication—students participated in a host of traditions surrounding the lake creature anyway. Certainly local people in McCall traditionally play with the idea that the lake contains a cryptid. Sharlie is the subject of cartoons and illustrations in the newspaper, and has been associated with practical jokes, tall tales, oral jokes, and other playful forms of behavior. Sharlie is associated with children, themselves figures of play. People also dismiss reports of Sharlie sightings as drunken hallucinations, or they offer more rational explanations for the unexplainable, such as the idea that Sharlie sightings are really only sightings of ducks, sturgeon, or half-submerged logs. Such contradictory attitudes illustrate a stance of ambivalence.

The names of lake monsters also reflect this playful attitude, along with a strong degree of affection. Lake monster names tend to be diminutive, perhaps to linguistically offset the monster's presumed gigantism. Like many other lake monster names, Sharlie ends with an /ee/ sound, a common ending for female names (e.g., Amy, Tracy, Shelly, Christie, Keri), making the monster slightly feminine and therefore symbolically smaller in size. Other examples include Old Greeny, a monster that lives in Cayuga Lake, New York; Tessie of Lake Tahoe, California; Peppie of Lake Pepin, Minnesota; and even Lieby for the campus-created monster of Lake Lieberman, New York (Tucker 2004). Champ of Lake Champlain, Vermont, does not follow the /ee/ sound but is diminutive nonetheless.

The history of how Sharlie was named implicates these playful contexts of jokes, tall tales, and lying. Sharlie was not always called Sharlie. Prior to his/her formal naming, the creature had no real name, although s/he was referred to in print in at least one instance as "Slimy Slim" and in another as "Serpy Sam," indicating early attributions of maleness. At other times s/he was simply referred to as "the sea creature." "Sharlie" was chosen as the result of a naming contest held by Boone McCallum, the editor of the *Payette Lakes Star* newspaper in 1953. The contest was advertised nationally, and the newspaper offered a cash prize to the person who submitted the winning suggestion. Sharlie was submitted by Le Isle Hennefer Tury of Virginia. The referent was widely known at the time, but today it is quite obscure. It refers to a stock phrase—"Vas you dere, Sharlie?"—from a well-known routine by the famous comedian Jack Pearl, a vaudeville and Broadway performer and early radio personality. Over the course of his career, Pearl played a character called the Baron Munchausen, which, as all good folklorists know, is a reference to the tall tales of the fictional Baron Munchausen, loosely based on a real Prussian military figure, whose exploits were first published in 1785. Pearl introduced his Munchausen character to radio in 1930, telling outrageous tales in the fake German accent for which he was known. Pearl's straight man's name was Charlie. Charlie's job was to question the truth of the baron's tales and Pearl's standard retort was: "Vas you dere, Sharlie?" Pearl's show was so popular that "Vas you dere, Sharlie?" was still a nationally known phrase at the time of the naming contest, and so it is that the name of a local lake monster emerged out of a complex of legends, belief, tall tales, memorates, the mass media, vaudeville comedy, local boosterism, and competition for a cash prize.

Themes of ambivalence and play also are core characteristics of festivals. The carnivalesque expands possibilities and rearranges social categories and therefore is a period of creativity, but such an opening up is a dangerous move since no one can predict what will happen. Bakhtin (1968) characterized carnivalesque laughter, which tears down and destroys at the same time that it renews, as inherently ambivalent. Winter Carnival in McCall contains only a few carnivalesque elements, but the real ambivalence inheres in local people's attitudes toward the festival and toward tourism as an economic option. As noted above, the festival is supposed to bring money to local businesses during a slow part of the year and so on the one hand, local people support Winter Carnival and think it is good for the community. On the other hand, tourists cause problems such as traffic jams, making it difficult to get around town. They also sometimes damage or ruin the snow sculptures by climbing on them to take photographs.

Further, Winter Carnival is run entirely by volunteer effort and requires a lot of work, and people may feel pressured to contribute or participate for the good of a larger whole. So while people generally think that Winter Carnival is good for the community, many people also have mixed feelings about it, including those who support it. The inclusion of Sharlie in Winter Carnival does not necessarily translate to a one-to-one representation of ambivalence about tourism or Winter Carnival per se, but as an inherently ambivalent and somewhat carnivalesque figure, Sharlie articulates attitudes that inhere in both monsters and the nature of festivals at broad levels.

Finally, as noted above, festivals themselves are a play genre (Abrahams 1972). By definition festivals constitute a pause from the workaday world; they utilize play categories to transform reality, and they are considered a "time out of time," meaning that they invoke an alternative reality or trans-form ordinary reality into something else for a short period.[2] The thought that play is somehow "not real" permeates ideas about play and is of utmost importance. Play is considered "not real" or "not serious," and actions done within the play frame do not count in the same way as they do in everyday life. On the other hand and paradoxically, participants act as if the play is real, which allows the play to occur.

This framing of "not real" or "not serious" does not mean, however, that play cannot be a serious affair. The transformations of ordinary reality that occur during festival and other forms of play involve fewer conse-quences than would be the case outside of festival time, making festival an important realm for social experimentation. Participants interpret the trans-formation from the ordinary world to the festive one as "not real," or "not serious," but play theorists have shown that the boundaries between the play frame and ordinary reality are quite permeable, allowing for the distinct possibility that the transformations, inversions, and exchanges occurring in festival might bleed out into ordinary reality, affect society and, in effect, become "real."[3] This possibility of elements spilling over from the play frame into reality leads us directly back to both the theme of ambivalence and to legend, that slippery genre that exists between reality and fiction with which this essay began.

One of the earliest works on monsters and festival in the United States was John Gutowski's (1998) study of "Turtle Days," a festival that grew out of the hunt for a giant turtle named Oscar in Indiana after World War II. In that study, Gutowski noted that the flurry of activities generated by the hunt for Oscar, which included hunting expeditions, experiments with technol-ogy, media attention, and local entrepreneurship, were all "proto-festival" activities that he felt articulated broad American themes. Gutowski did not identify the isomorphism laid out here between legends, festivals, and monsters, but his study, along with Dorson's ideas, upon which he relied, laid the groundwork for this framework. Americans do play with their monsters, and one way they do so is to incorporate them into festivals because festivals embody and perform the qualities of monsters and legends. Unfortunately, monsters, festivals, and monster festivals remain understudied, largely, I think, because many (most?) American examples are connected to tourism and boosterism, and thus are easily dismissed as unimportant and even crass examples of commodification. But there are reasons that Americans play with their monsters and reasons why people use monsters—as opposed to other traditional folkloric forms—in festive contexts. Legends, monsters, and festivals play with reality and invoke all of the ambivalence associated with doing so. This framework makes the legend/monster/festival complex a rich potential for the exploration of human behavior.

NOTES

1. Additional information about Sharlie and the McCall Winter Carnival can be found in my book *Winter Carnival in a Western Town: Identity, Change, and the Good of the Community* (2011). Preliminary ideas for this essay were outlined in that work's chapter 5.

2. Roger Callois's play categories (2001) are *Agon*, which means "competition"; *alea*, which means "chance"; *mimicry*, which is role-playing; and *ilinx*, which is "vertigo."

3. This potential, of course, is partially the basis for Jack Santino's (2017) idea of the "ritualesque," when groups attempt to use temporary public festive/symbolic behavior for instrumental purposes—that is, to affect society outside the temporary event.

REFERENCES CITED

Abrahams, Roger D. 1972. "Folk Drama." In *Folklore and Folklife: An Introduction*, edited by Richard M. Dorson, 351–62. Chicago: University of Chicago Press.

Abrahams, Roger D. 1987. "An American Vocabulary of Celebrations." In *Time out of Time: Essays on the Festival*, edited by Alessandro Falassi, 173–83. Albuquerque: University of New Mexico Press.

Bakhtin, Mikhail. 1968. *Rabalais and His World*. Translated by Hélène Iswolsky. Bloomington: Indiana University Press.

Blank, Trevor J., and Lynne S. McNeill, eds. 2018. *Slender Man Is Coming: Creepypasta and Contemporary Legends on the Internet*. Logan: Utah State University Press.

Callois, Roger. 2001 [1961]. *Man, Play, and Games*. Urbana: University of Illinois Press.

Dorson, Richard A. 1982. *Man and Beast in American Comic Legend*. Bloomington: Indiana University Press.

Douglass, Harry S. 1956. "The Legend of the Serpent." *New York Folklore Quarterly* 12 (1): 37–42.

Falassi, Alessandro. 1987. "Festival: Definition and Morphology." In *Time out of Time: Essays on the Festival*, edited by Alessandro Falassi, 1–10. Albuquerque: University of New Mexico Press.

Fife, Austin E. 1948. "The Bear Lake Monsters." *Utah Humanities Review* 2:99–106.

Foster, Michael Dylan. 2013. "Inviting the Uninvited Guest: Ritual, Festival, Tourism and the Namahage of Japan." *Journal of American Folklore* 126 (501): 302–34.

Gabbert, Lisa. 2011. *Winter Carnival in a Western Town: Identity, Change, and the Good of the Community.* Logan: Utah State University Press.

Gabbert, Lisa. 2015. "Legend Quests and the Curious Case of St. Anne's Retreat: The Performative Landscape." In *Putting the Supernatural in Its Place: Folklore, the Hypermodern, and the Ethereal,* edited by Jeanie Thomas, 146-69. Logan: University of Utah Press.

Gabbert, Lisa. 2019. "American Festival and Folk Drama." In *The Oxford Handbook of American Folklore and Folklife Studies,* edited by Simon J. Bronner, 277–97. Oxford: Oxford University Press.

Garlough, Christine. 2011. "Festival and the Potential of Acknowledgement: Representing 'India' at the Minnesota Festival of Nations." *Western Folklore* 70:69–98.

Georges, Robert. 1971. "The General Concept of Legend: Some Assumptions to Be Reexamined and Reassessed." In *American Folk Legend: A Symposium,* edited by Wayland D. Hand, 1–19. Berkeley: University of California Press.

Goldstein, Diane, Sylvia Grider, and Jeannie Banks Thomas. 2007. *Haunting Experiences: Ghosts in Contemporary Folklore.* Logan: Utah State University Press.

Gutowski, John. A. 1998. "The Beast of 'Busco: An American Tradition." Special issue, *Midwestern Folklore* 24 (1–2).

Hawley, Herbert J. 1946. "The Sea Serpent of Silver Lake." *New York Folklore Quarterly* 2:191–96.

Hufford, David. 1982. *The Terror That Comes in the Night: An Experience-Centered Study of Supernatural Sleep Traditions.* Philadelphia: University of Pennsylvania Press.

Marsh, Moira. 2015. *Practically Joking.* Logan: Utah State University Press.

Meurger, Michel. 1988. *Lake Monster Traditions: A Cross-Cultural Analysis.* London: Fortean Tomes.

Morrell, Alan L. 2011. "A Nessie in Mormon Country." In *Between Pulpit and Pew: The Supernatural World in Mormon History and Folklore,* edited by W. Paul Reeve and Michael Scott Van Wagenen, 159–67. Logan: Utah State University Press.

Oring, Elliott. 1986. "Folk Narratives." In *Folklore Groups and Folklore Genres: An Introduction,* edited by Elliott Oring, 121–45. Logan: Utah State University Press.

Oring, Elliott. 2008. "Legendry and the Rhetoric of Truth." *Journal of American Folklore* 121 (480): 127–66.

Santino, Jack, ed. 1994. *Halloween and Other Festivals of Death and Life.* Knoxville: University of Tennessee Press.

Santino, Jack, ed. 2017. *Public Performances: Studies in the Carnivalesque and the Ritualesque.* Logan: Utah State University Press.

Steward, Susan. 1992. *On Longing: Narratives of the Miniature, the Gigantic, the Souvenir, and the Collection.* Durham, NC: Duke University Press.

Tangherlini, Timothy R. 1996. "Legend." In *American Folklore: An Encyclopedia,* edited by Jan Brunvand, 437–39. New York: Garland.

Tucker, Elizabeth. 2004. "The Lake Lieberman Monster." *Midwestern Folklore* 30 (1): 36–45.

Turner, Victor. 1987. "Carnival, Ritual and Play in Rio de Janeiro." In *Time out of Time: Essays on the Festival,* edited by Alessandro Falassi, 76–90. Albuquerque: University of New Mexico Press.

EDITOR'S SUGGESTIONS FOR FURTHER READING

Dorson, Richard M. 1982. *Man and Beast in American Comic Legend*. Bloomington: Indiana University Press.

Gabbert, Lisa. 2011. "Laughter, Ambivalence, and the Carnivalesque: Lake Monsters and Festive Culture." In *Winter Carnival in a Western Town: Identity, Change, and the Good of the Community*. Logan: Utah State University Press.

Goldstein, Diane. 2007. "Commodification of Belief." In *Haunting Experiences: Ghosts in Contemporary Folklore*, by Diane Goldstein, Sylvia Grider, and Jeannie Banks Thomas, 171–205. Logan: Utah State University Press.

Gutowski, John A. 1978. "The Protofestival: Local Guide to American Folk Behavior." *Journal of the Folklore Institute* 15 (2): 112–32.

Gutowski, John A. 1998. "The Beast of 'Busco: An American Tradition." Special issue, *Midwestern Folklore* 24 (1–2).

Harris, Jason. 2015. "Shadows of the Past in the Sunshine State: St. Augustine Ghost Lore and Tourism." *Western Folklore* 74 (3–4): 309–42.

Hasken, Eleanor, and Jesse Fivecoate. 2017. "Episode 29: The One about the Mothman Festival." *Encounters*. Podcast. https://www.stitcher.com/podcast/eleanor-hasken/encounters/e/52243234.

Tucker, Elizabeth. 2015. "Messages from the Dead: Lilly Dale, New York." In *Putting the Supernatural in Its Place: Folklore, the Hypermodern, and the Ethereal*, edited by Jeannie Banks Thomas, 170–91. Logan: University of Utah Press.

Discussion Questions and Projects

Chapter 3: "Alligators-in-the-Sewers: A Journalistic Origin"

- Is the author's kernel of truth persuasive? Do you think this little incident inspired New York City's alligators-in-the-sewers legend? Why or why not?
- Legends of alligators are just the beginning. What other legendary plants, animals, and creatures purportedly live under the streets of New York?
- Take a look at author Loren Coleman's International Cryptozoology Museum website. What interests might folklorists and cryptozoologists share? How are the two occupations different?

Chapter 4: "Sasquatch-Like Creatures in Newfoundland: A Study in the Problems of Belief, Perception, and Reportage"

- When it comes to monsters, why is it important to distinguish between sightings and the *perceptions* of sightings?
- What do you know about Sasquatch? Bigfoot? The Abominable Snowman? How did you learn about these monsters?
- In your area, which local fauna are most likely to be mistaken as monsters? Alternatively, can you identify any potential monsters that might be mistaken as local fauna?

Chapter 5: "The 'Char-Man': A Local Legend of the Ojai Valley"

- Are there any legend trips popular with teenagers in your area? Do any involve monsters or the supernatural?
- It seems that Char-Man's disfigurement is central to his legend. Why might a disfigured person be associated with a monster? Should this knee-jerk reaction be of broader societal concern?
- If legend climate is as important as Seemann suggests, which local changes in your region can you identify that might transform the legend environment?

Chapter 6: "The Jersey Devil"

- What's the appeal of a Jersey Devil cocktail? A Jersey Devil mascot? A Jersey Devil stuffed animal? Can you attempt to account for the popularity of such legendary monster novelty items?
- Does your state promote or sell any commodified folklore or traditions? How about any commodified legendary experiences, such as a haunted house or ghost tour?

- Watch Angus Gillespie's 2009 *MonsterQuest* episode "Devils in New Jersey." Do monster legends transfer in a satisfying way to mysterious phenomenon television investigations?

CHAPTER 7: "AMERICAN VAMPIRES: LEGEND, THE MEDIA, AND TUBAL TRANSMISSION"

- Can you identify a monster that you learned more about from television or media than from friends or word of mouth?
- Do you remember how you first learned about vampires?
- How would you describe vampires? What is your understanding of their key characteristics?

CHAPTER 8: "THE WAYS AND NATURE OF THE ZOMBI"

- Ackermann and Gauthier present a very different idea of the zombie than mainstream American popular media. How does their presentation of the zombie differ from the idea of the zombie that exists in your mind?
- Where did you first learn about zombies? Was it word of mouth, popular media, or a combination of the two?
- These authors stand out in this casebook for not being folklorists or even in folklore-adjacent specialties. Which elements of their approach do you find more or less compelling compared to those of other authors in this casebook?

CHAPTER 9: "ECOTYPES, ETIOLOGY, AND CONTEMPORARY LEGEND: THE 'WEBBER' CYCLE IN WESTERN NEWFOUNDLAND"

- How is the Webber monster an example of ecotypification? What does studying the Webber teach us about Stephenville?
- What might monsters tell us about local cultural values and local cultural ecology generally?
- Can you identify any "small-town" monsters like the Webber? How do they differ from nationally known monsters such as Bigfoot, the Jersey Devil, and the Mothman?

CHAPTER 10: "THE LAKE LIEBERMAN MONSTER"

- Do you know of any other lake monsters? Why do you think lakes are such an attractive place for monsters to hide?
- Does your campus have any monsters, ghosts, or other supernatural creatures associated with it?

- While monsters are often thought of as something to be feared, is it possible that some people take pride in their monsters? Why?

CHAPTER 11: "A NESSIE IN MORMON COUNTRY: THE BEAR LAKE MONSTER"

- Legend hoaxers will often use a variety of appeals to authority. What rhetorical appeals did Joseph Rich bring to his monster hoax to increase his claim's plausibility?
- Why do you think Americans so often ascribe Native American origins to legendary monsters?
- Local histories are surprising repositories of monsters and supernatural lore. Find a public domain local history for a town that interests you on Google Books. Search key terms such as *monster, ghost,* or *demon.* What do you find?

CHAPTER 12: "GETTING MARYLAND'S GOAT: DIFFUSION AND CANONIZATIONS OF PRINCE GEORGE'S COUNTY'S GOATMAN LEGEND"

- Does your state boast an unofficial state monster or other supernatural creature? Who is it? What is known about it?
- Do a monster search in your local newspaper. What comes up? What's been reported? Are you familiar with any of these monster legends? Do they circulate in oral tradition as well?
- Where's your nearest folklore archive? Does it include any monster legends?

CHAPTER 13: "TALL, DARK, AND LOATHSOME: THE SLENDER MAN AND THE EMERGENCE OF A LEGEND CYCLE IN THE DIGITAL AGE"

- Do you think Slender Man is a proper monster, or would he be better categorized as something else?
- Do you think it is possible for a monster's native habitat to be cyberspace?
- Do an Internet search for digital monsters. What other monsters might a folklorist gainfully research?

CHAPTER 14: "EVOKING THE SHADOW BEAST: DISABILITY AND CHICANO ADVOCACY IN SAN ANTONIO'S DONKEY LADY LEGEND"

- What's your sociocultural reading of the Donkey Lady legend? Does it correspond with Torrez's?

- The "monstrous" is a key term in disability studies. Are there other monsters, in this casebook or elsewhere, that would benefit from a disability-focused interpretation?
- Race, gender, and sexuality are three interpretive lenses at the forefront of contemporary scholarship. What might legendary monsters be able to add to these discussions?

CHAPTER 15: "GOING VAN HELSING IN PUERTO RICO: HUNTING THE CHUPACABRA LEGEND"

- Radford sees the chupacabra legend as an apt metaphor for U.S. relations with Latin America. What history is Radford referring to?
- Watch *Species* and then examine Radford's sketch. Do you see a resemblance? Do you find Radford's theory persuasive?
- How might a monster hunter, a folklorist, and a skeptic approach the chupacabra legend differently? What do the three have in common?

CHAPTER 16: "DANIEL BOONE, YAHOOS, AND YEAHOHS: MIRRORING MONSTERS OF THE APPALACHIANS"

- What's the difference between a sighting, a legend, an anti-legend, a tall tale, and an unreasonable lie?
- Take a look through an online monster discussion board such as *The Bigfoot Forums*. How are sightings and beliefs conveyed? What are the evidentiary expectations?
- Look up reported Bigfoot sightings near you. When was Bigfoot last seen? What was the context of the sighting?

CHAPTER 17: "THE MOTHMAN OF WEST VIRGINIA: A CASE STUDY IN LEGENDARY STORYTELLING"

- How did journalist John Keel transform the Mothman legend?
- Read Keel's *The Mothman Prophecies*. Do monster legends blend well with the narrative nonfiction genre?
- Listen to Eleanor Hasken and Jesse Fivecoat's *Encounters* podcast "Episode 10: The One about 'The Mothman of Point Pleasant.'" How does this presentation of Mothman differ from Keel's (and Clarke's)?

CHAPTER 18: "THE WINDIGO AS MONSTER: INDIGENOUS BELIEF, CULTURAL APPROPRIATION, AND POPULAR HORROR"

- Who properly owns native belief? When is it acceptable for cultures to share stories, and when does this amount to cultural pilfering?
- Have you encountered windigo-inspired creatures in works of fiction by another name?
- Read Algernon Blackwood's horror novella *The Wendigo*. What do you think of Blackwood's interpretation of the windigo legend?

CHAPTER 19: "MONSTERS, LEGENDS, AND FESTIVALS: SHARLIE, WINTER CARNIVAL, AND OTHER ISOMORPHIC RELATIONSHIPS"

- How are legends, festivals, and monsters much the same?
- What is "boosterism," and how can monsters help in promotional endeavors?
- Monster festivals appear to be more ubiquitous than first meets the eye. Does your favorite monster have a celebration? How is it fêted?

Glossary of Key Terms

THIS GLOSSARY ADDRESSES TERMINOLOGY USED IN LEGEND STUDIES, particularly in legendary monster studies, and especially as used in the essays presented in this casebook. For a more in-depth examination of these and other key legend terms, I recommend that readers consult the several excellent folkloristic encyclopedias and dictionaries available in the discipline and then proceed to peruse the corresponding original scholarship.

active tradition-bearer. Someone who self-consciously participates in and transmits a tradition. Compare with *passive tradition-bearer.* The classic work on the topic is von Sydow's "On the Spread of Tradition."

artistic license. The right of a creator to deviate from established fact for the purposes of imaginative invention; can be controversial in legend as the line between fact and fiction is ambiguous.

authenticity. The quality of being told, performed, or made in the traditional or accepted fashion; in folklore, authenticity is often less important than the perception of authenticity.

community re-creation. In folkloristics, the concept that groups update and modify circulating folklore to meet present local needs.

conspiracy theory. A tangled, interconnected web of contemporary legends that perpetuate a theory of elite, underhanded, clandestine control of the world, ranging from secretive cabals to audacious false flag operations. Usually speaks to a group's already ingrained worldview.

contagious magic. The concept that objects once in contact remain influential on one another, even when no longer in contact: for example, a witch stealing a strand of hair to use in casting a spell on the hair's original owner.

contemporary legend (also urban legend, occasionally belief legend). A plausible but unverifiable narrative repeatedly retold; the "contemporary" refers not to any requirement of novelty, but rather to the legend, in any era, speaking to contemporaneous needs and anxieties. Differentiated from a "historical legend" set in the distant past, usually about extraordinary heroes and events.

copylore (also xeroxlore). Folklore transmitted through non-oral, visual means, such as the Xerox machine. Relevant today to memes and image macros. See Dundes and Pagter for the classic works.

cosmology. The study of the origins of the universe and the people within it.

creepypasta. Horror-themed digital text legends so named because they are spread through the World Wide Web in variable forms as copypasta (i.e., copying and pasting); intriguing to folklorists because of their similarity to analog contemporary legend.

creolization. In folkloristics, the mixing or blending of disparate ethnic cultural elements, the unique combination of which ultimately generates something novel.

cryptid. A creature purported but not proven to exist.

cryptozoology. The study of unverified creatures purported to exist.

diachronic (also longitudinal). In legend studies, the study of a legend as it evolves, transforms, and changes over time. Compare with *synchronic*.

diffusion. In folklore, the study of how and where a particular piece of folklore spreads. Assumes that folklore spreads by social contact rather than polygenesis.

ecotype (also oicotype). A migratory tradition that takes on local cultural characteristics. See von Sydow's "Geography and Folk-Tale Oicotypes" for the classic work.

emic. As observed, categorized, or interpreted from a native (e.g., folk group) perspective, as opposed to an analytic perspective. A scholar may classify a given narrative as a "legend," for example, while the community categorizes it as local history. Forms the root of "phonemic"—speech sounds made by a language group. Compare with *etic*.

ethics. In folkloristics, the proper treatment and protection of tradition-bearers, their personal safety, their belief systems, and their ways of life.

etic. As observed, categorized, or interpreted from an analytic (e.g., scholarly) perspective, as opposed to a group's own cognitive categories. Often used by folklorists in defining folklore genres, such as legend, myth, and folktale. Forms the root of "phonetic"—speech sounds classified by an analyst. Compare with *emic*.

euhemerism. The theory that myths, and by extension legends, originally derive from factual and historical characters or events, which are then transformed and modified through *migration* and *community re-creation*. Term inspired by Greek mythologist Euhemerus. Compare with *kernel of truth* and *origins*.

experience-centered study of belief. David Hufford's theory, highly influential among folklorists, stating that traditional beliefs, including those decried as irrational, are at root reasonable and rationally derived from observation and inference. See Hufford's works in "Recommended Reading List" below.

festival. A period set aside for stylized community celebration.

fieldwork. Ethnographic, survey, and interview research conducted out in the community, as opposed to in libraries or archives.

FOAF. A friend of a friend, or the person to whom the events or experiences of a contemporary legend are most often attributed. A FOAF is near enough to the teller to lend credibility and immediacy, but too distant from the audience to provide confirmation or corroboration. First coined by English author Rodney Dale in his book *The Tumour in the Whale* (1978); later inspired the title of the International Society for Contemporary Legend Research's newsletter *FOAFTale News*.

folklore archive. Repositories for folklore records organized into databases according to classification systems.

folktale. A traditional fictional narrative told for entertainment.

function. What a particular piece of folklore *does* within an integrated social system.

informant. The once-predominant term in folkloristics and anthropology for a person from a community or tradition who provides information about the tradition in question. Some have objected to the term because of its stool-pigeon connotation. Alternatives include collaborator, interviewee, interlocutor, consultant, participant, tradition-bearer, or traditional practitioner.

intertextuality. In legend studies, the connection between two (or more) legend texts that influences the meaning of one of those texts.

interviewing. The folklorist's foremost fieldwork tool: the typically audio-recorded, dually transcribed consultation of a willing participant who holds valuable information about a community or practice.

invented tradition. The idea that traditions do not spring naturally from the earth but rather are created by humans, often for political ends and subject to constant updating to meet present needs, despite an aura of timeless traditionality. See Hobsbawm and Ranger's *Invention of Tradition* for the classic work.

kernel of truth. A tidbit in a legend that proves factual. Legends can grow out of kernels of truth, and/or legend tellers can use kernels of truth as evidence of a legend's veracity.

local legend. A legend intrinsically bound to a particular geographic area. Compare with *migratory legend*.

legend climate. The physical context surrounding a legend setting or the telling of a legend.

legend trip (also legend quest). One form of ostension, an intentional journey to a location associated with a legend. See McNeill and Tucker's *Legend Tripping* for the definitive collected works.

liminality. A magical time, place, or state betwixt and between two other times, places, or states: for example, midnight as an enchanted hour that's both yesterday and tomorrow or college as a time between childhood and adulthood.

memorate. A traditional narrative of a personal experience.

migration. In legend studies, the idea that legends travel with and alongside the movement of people.

migratory legend. A legend dispersed widely across space in which the plot remains consistent but the characters and locations are updated to make local sense. "The Boyfriend's Death" is a quintessential example. Closely related to concepts of *migration, diffusion, ecotype,* and *community re-creation.* Compare with *local legend.* See Reidar Th. Christiansen's *The Migratory Legends* for the classic work.

monster. In legend studies, a strange, frightening, or unusual human or creature, real or imaginary, believed or not believed, that is, at the time of the telling, purported but not scientifically verified to exist in our world.

motif. A building block of a legend that draws attention to itself. May include a character, object, action, or event.

myth. In folkloristics, a sacred narrative. See also *urban myth.*

origins. In folkloristics, the birthplace of a tradition, often not discernable as traditions usually do not spring fully fledged from any one person or place, but are gradually created and re-created over time and space.

ostension. In folkloristics, behavior that relies on legend as a guide to action, for example, a prankster placing razor blades in Halloween candy and then reporting it to the media, a parent X-raying Halloween candy to check for razor blades, or a father poisoning his child and blaming the death on tainted Halloween candy.

participant-observation. One of the hallmarks of ethnographic research; the idea that, to fully understand a subject, a researcher should go beyond observing a phenomenon and seek to actively participate in it. Assumes reflexivity—the concept that a researcher affects the scene or outcome rather than being a neutral observer.

participatory media. Media in which the audience also plays an active role in the media's construction, for example, web forums, social media, and wikis. Contrasted with passive media, such as traditional television, film, and print newspapers.

passive tradition-bearer. Someone who is aware of a tradition, understanding its confines, perhaps even supporting or appreciating it in other ways, but who does not actively participate in or transmit the tradition. Compare with *active tradition-bearer.* See von Sydow's "On the Spread of Tradition" for the classic work.

performance. In legend studies, the telling of the legend, with attention not only to the text but to all present behavioral and contextual dynamics, including gesture, tone of voice, and setting.

rapport. A warm, trusting, and respectful relationship with a consultant or a community, the establishment of which is a goal for folklorists in their research endeavors.

sympathetic magic. The concept that like produces like, such as a ritual that uses a similar or associated object to cause an effect on something else, for example, sticking a pin in a voodoo doll to cause a person pain.

synchronic (also latitudinal). In legend studies, the study of a legend as it exists in multiple locations at one point in time. Compare with *diachronic*.

transcription. The written verbatim text, often first captured in an audio interview.

transmission. The process by which folklore is passed from one person to another.

type. Narratives seen as holding common characteristics, despite existing in multiple variants. Connected in folkloristics to the idea that types compromise bundles of motifs that tend to hold together in sequence.

urban legend. See *contemporary legend*. While both are accepted terms, most folklorists prefer contemporary legend as "urban" constitutes a potential misnomer because such legends can be heard in suburban, rural, and cyberspace settings. The urban label arose to indicate commentaries on urban change associated with modernization.

urban myth. A term used by the popular media to mean a "falsehood"; spurned by folklorists, who prefer either "contemporary legend," "urban legend," or "belief legend."

variant. A variation within a type.

vernacular. The language spoken by the ordinary folks of a region, but often used analogously to refer to the folk level of a particular region or practice.

version. A single instance of a legend performance or a particular transcript of a text.

worldview. A group's underlying outlook or attitude that can sometimes be discerned, or at least compared to another group's, through an accumulation of folk ideas evident in beliefs, stories, and speech.

Recommended Reading List

THIS LIST IS NOT MEANT TO BE COMPREHENSIVE; rather, it is an idiosyncratic overview of the readings I consulted in putting together this casebook. The books, articles, and chapters found here are not necessarily North American-, legend-, or monster-centric, but they helped me in thinking about North American monster legends.

Alford, Peggy E. 1992. "Anglo-American Perceptions of Navajo Skinwalker Legends." *Contemporary Legend*, 1st ser., 2: 119–36.

Ames, Michael M., and Marjorie Halpin, eds. 1980. *Manlike Monsters on Trial: Early Records and Modern Evidence.* Vancouver: University of British Columbia Press.

Asma, Stephen T. 2009. *On Monsters: An Unnatural History of Our Worst Fears.* Oxford: Oxford University Press.

Baker, Ronald L. 1972. "Monsterville: A Traditional Place-name and Its Legends." *Names* 20 (3): 186–91.

Barber, Paul. 1988. *Vampires, Burial, and Death: Folklore and Reality.* New Haven: Yale University Press.

Bassett, Fletcher S. 1885. *Legends and Superstitions of the Sea and of Sailors in All Lands and at All Times.* Chicago and New York: Belford, Clarke, and Co.

Beck, Henry Charlton. 1947. "Jersey Devil and Other Legends of the Jersey Shore." *New York Folklore Quarterly* 3:102–6.

Beck, Horace Charlton. 1973. *Folklore of the Sea.* Middletown, CT: Wesleyan University Press.

Bell, Karl. 2012. *Spring-Heeled Jack: Victorian Urban Folklore and Popular Cultures.* Woodbridge, UK: Boydell.

Bell, Karl, ed. 2019. *Supernatural Cities: Enchantment, Anxiety, Spectrality.* Woodbridge, UK: Boydell.

Bennett, Gillian. 1999. *"Alas, Poor Ghost!" Traditions of Belief in Story and Discourse.* Logan: Utah State University Press.

Bishop, Norma. 1984. "The Ingleby Monster and the Penns Valley Legend Complex." *Keystone Folklore* 3 (1): 24–31.

Blank, Trevor J., and Lynne S. McNeill, eds. 2018. *Slender Man Is Coming: Creepypasta and Contemporary Legends on the Internet.* Logan: Utah State University Press.

Blank, Trevor J., and David J. Puglia. 2014. *Maryland Legends: Folklore from the Old Line State.* Charleston, SC: History Press.

Brewster, Paul G. 1949. "The Piasa Bird: A Legend of the Illini." *Hoosier Folklore* 8 (4): 83–86.

Brightman, Robert A. 1988. "The Windigo in the Material World." *Ethnohistory* 35 (4): 337–79.

Brightman, Robert A. 2015. "The Return of the Windigo, Again." *Semiotic Review* 2. https://www.semioticreview.com/ojs/index.php/sr/artice/view/22.

Bronner, Simon J. 2006. "'And Then He Heard These Footsteps': Tales and Legends." In *American Children's Folklore*, 143–59. Atlanta: August House.

Bronner, Simon J. 2012. "Legendary Locations, Laughs, and Horrors." In *Campus Traditions: Folklore from the Old-Time College to the Modern Mega-University*, 277–342. Jackson: University Press of Mississippi.

Bronner, Simon J. 2014. "'The Shooter Has Asperger's': Autism, Belief, and 'Wild Child' Narratives." *Children's Folklore* 36: 35–53.

Brunvand, Jan Harold. 1981. *The Vanishing Hitchhiker: American Urban Legends and Their Meanings.* New York: Norton.

Buhs, Joshua Blu. 2009. *Bigfoot: The Life and Times of a Legend.* Chicago: University of Chicago Press.

Buhs, Joshua Blu. 2011. "Tracking Bigfoot through 1970s North American Children's Culture: How Mass Media, Consumerism, and the Culture of Preadolescence Shaped Wildman Lore." *Western Folklore* 70 (2): 195–218.

Butler, Gary R. 1997. "The *Lutin* Tradition in French-Newfoundland Culture: Discourse and Belief." In *The Good People: New Fairylore Essays*, edited by Peter Narváez, 5–21. Lexington: University Press of Kentucky.

Bynum, C. W. 1997. "Wonder." *American Historical Review* 102 (1): 1–26.

Campbell, Claire. 2012. "Hidfolk of Texas." In *First Timers and Old Timers: The Texas Folklore Society Fire Burns On*, edited by Kenneth L. Untiedt, 265–72. Denton: University of North Texas Press.

Campion-Vincent, Véronique. 1992. "Appearances of Beasts and Mystery-Cats in France." *Folklore* 103 (2): 160–83.

Carden, Gary. 2012. "Appalachian Bestiary: Wondrous and Fearsome Creatures of the Southern Wild." *North Carolina Folklore Journal* 59 (2): 60–92.

Carpenter, Carole H. 1980. "The Cultural Role of Monsters in Canada." In *Manlike Monsters on Trial: Early Records and Modern Evidence*, edited by Michael M. Ames and Marjorie M. Halpin, 97–108. Vancouver: University of British Columbia Press.

Chinery, David. 1987. "Snooping for Snipes: America's Favorite Wild Goose Chase." *Children's Folklore Newsletter* 10 (Spring): 2–4 and 10 (Fall): 3–4.

Christiansen, Reidar Th. 1958. *The Migratory Legends: A Proposed List of Types with a Systematic Catalogue of the Norwegian Variants.* Folklore Fellows Communications no. 175. Helsinki: Suomalainen Tiedeakatemia.

Clark, Jerome, and Loren Coleman. 2006. *The Unidentified/Creatures of the Outer Edge: The Early Works of Jerome Clark and Loren Coleman.* Charlottesville, VA: Anomalist Books.

Clark, Robert T. 1946. "The Literary Growth of the Louisiana Bullfrog." *Publications of the Texas Folklore Society* 21: 105–11.

Clarke, David. 2003. "Phantom Helicopters: A Rumor-Generated Visual Epidemic." *Contemporary Legend*, new ser., 5: 67–91.

Clarke, David. 2004. *The Angel of Mons: Phantom Soldiers and Ghostly Guardians.* Chichester, UK: Wiley.

Clarke, David. 2006. "Unmasking Spring-Heeled Jack: A Caste Study of a 19th Century Ghost Panic." *Contemporary Legend*, new ser., 9: 28–52.

Clarke, David. 2016. "A New Demonology: John Keel and *The Mothman Prophecies*." In *Damned Facts: Fortean Essays on Religion, Folklore and the Paranormal*, edited by Jack Hunter, 54–68. Cyprus: Aporetic.

Clarke, David, and Andy Roberts. 1990. *Phantoms of the Sky: UFOs—A Modern Myth?* London: Robert Hale.

Clarke, David, and Andy Roberts. 2007. *Flying Saucerers: Social History of UFOlogy.* Loughborough, UK: Alternative Albion.

Cohen, Jeffrey Jerome. 1996. "Monster Culture (Seven Theses)." In *Monster Theory: Reading Culture*, edited by Jeffrey Jerome Cohen, 3–25. Minneapolis: University of Minnesota Press.

Coleman, Loren. 2006. *Mysterious America: The Ultimate Guide to the Nation's Weirdest Wonders, Strangest Spots, and Creepiest Creatures.* New York: Paraview Pocket Books.

Compora, Daniel. 2013. "Undead America: The Emergence of the Modern Zombie in American Culture." *Supernatural Studies* 1 (1): 31–38.

Compora, Daniel. 2014. "Michigan's Monstrous Trio." *FOAFTale News* 82: 2–4.

Costello, Peter. 1975. *In Search of Lake Monsters.* St. Albans, UK: Granada.

Cox, William T. 1910. *Fearsome Creatures of the Lumberwoods.* Washington, DC: Judd & Detweiler.

Cray, Ed. 1964. "Loch Ness Monster Again." *Western Folklore* 23 (1): 57.

Daston, Lorraine J., and Katharine Park. 2001. *Wonders and the Order of Nature, 1150–1750.* Cambridge, MA: Zone Books.

Dégh, Linda. 1969. "The Haunted Bridges Near Avon and Danville and Their Role in Legend Formation." *Indiana Folklore* 2: 77–78.

Dendle, Peter. 2006. "Cryptozoology in the Medieval and Modern Worlds." *Folklore* 117 (2): 190–206.

Dendle, Peter. 2007. "The Zombie as Barometer of Cultural Anxiety." In *Monsters and the Monstrous: Myths and Metaphors of Enduring Evil*, edited by Niall Scott, 45–57. Amsterdam: Rodopi.

De Vos, Gail. 2012. *What Happens Next? Contemporary Urban Legend and Popular Culture.* Westport, CT: Libraries Unlimited.

Dorson, Richard M. 1973. *America in Legend: Folklore from the Colonial Period to the Present.* New York: Pantheon Books.

Dorson, Richard M. 1982. *Man and Beast in American Comic Legend.* Bloomington: Indiana University Press.

Dresser, Norine. 1989. *American Vampires: Fans, Victims, Practitioners.* New York: Norton.

Dundes, Alan, ed. 1998. *The Vampire: A Casebook.* Madison: University of Wisconsin Press.

Dundes, Alan, and Carl R. Pagter. 1978. *Work Hard and You Shall Be Rewarded: Urban Folklore from the Paperwork Empire.* Bloomington: Indiana University Press.

Ellis, Bill. 1981. "The Camp Mock-Ordeal Theater as Life." *Journal of American Folklore* 94 (374): 486–505.

Ellis, Bill. 1982. " 'Ralph and Rudy': The Audience's Role in Recreating a Camp Legend." *Western Folklore* 41 (3): 169–91.

Ellis, Bill. 2003. *Aliens, Ghosts and Cults: Legends We Live.* Jackson: University of Mississippi Press.

Evans, Timothy H. 2014. "The Ghost in the Machine." *New York Times*, June 2014. https://www.nytimes.com/2014/06/08/opinion/sunday/the-ghosts-in-the-machine .html.

Fife, Austin E. 1948. "The Bear Lake Monsters." *Utah Humanities Review* 2: 99–106.

Fine, Gary Alan. 1982. "Legendary Creatures and Small Group Culture: Medieval Lore in a Contemporary Role-Playing Game." *Keystone Folklore*, new ser., 1 (1): 11–27.

Fort, Charles. 1919. *The Book of the Damned.* New York: Boni & Liveright.

Forth, Gregory. 2007. "Images of the Wildman inside and outside Europe." *Folklore* 118 (3): 261–81.

Foster, Michael Dylan. 2008. *Pandemonium and Parade: Japanese Monsters and the Culture of Yokai.* Logan: Utah State University Press.

Foster, Michael Dylan. 2012. "Haunting Modernity: Tanuki, Trains, and Transformation in Japan." *Asian Ethnology* 71 (1): 3–29.

Foster, Michael Dylan. 2013. "Early Modern Past to Postmodern Future: Changing Discourses on Japanese Monsters." In *The Ashgate Research Companion to Monsters and the Monstrous*, edited by Asa Simon Mittman and Peter J. Dendle, 133–50. Aldershot, UK: Ashgate.

Foster, Michael Dylan. 2013. "Licking the Ceiling: Semantic Staining and Monstrous Diversity." *Semiotic Review* 2. https://semioticreview.com/ojs/index.php/sr/article /view/24.

Foster, Michael Dylan. 2015. *The Book of Yokai: Mysterious Creatures of Japanese Folklore.* Berkeley: University of California Press.

Foster, Michael Dylan. 2020. "Afterword: Scenes from the Monsterbiome." In *Monster Anthropology: Ethnographic Explorations of Transforming Social Worlds through Monsters*, edited by Yasmine Musharbash and Geir Henning Presterudstuen, 213–28. London: Bloomsbury Academic.

Friedman, John Block. 2000. *The Monstrous Races in Medieval Art and Thought.* Syracuse: Syracuse University Press.

Friedman, John Block. 2013. Foreword to *The Ashgate Research Companion to Monsters and the Monstrous*, edited by Asa Simon Mittman and Peter J. Dendle, xxv–xxxix. Aldershot, UK: Ashgate.

Fry, Gladys-Marie. 1975. *Night Riders in Black Folk History.* Knoxville: University of Tennessee Press.

Gabbert, Lisa. 2011. "Laughter, Ambivalence, and the Carnivalesque: Lake Monsters and Festive Culture." In *Winter Carnival in a Western Town: Identity, Change, and the Good of the Community*, 191–222. Logan: Utah State University Press.

Gallehugh, Joseph F. Jr. 1976. "The Vampire Beast of Bladenboro." *North Carolina Folklore Journal* 24 (2): 53–58.

Gatschet, Albert S. 1899. "Water-Monsters of American Aborigines." *Journal of American Folklore* 12 (47): 255–60.

Gillespie, Angus Kress, comp. 1977. "The Jersey Devil." *New Jersey Folklore: A Statewide Journal* 1 (2): 24–29.

Gillespie, Angus K. 1987. *American Wildlife in Symbol and Story.* Knoxville: University of Tennessee Press.

Gillespie, Angus Kress. 1993. "The (Jersey) Devil in the Details." *New Jersey Outdoors* (Fall 1993): 40–43.

Gilmore, David D. 2003. *Monsters: Evil Beings, Mythical Beasts, and All Manner of Imaginary Terrors.* Philadelphia: University of Pennsylvania Press.

Goldstein, Diane. 2007. "Commodification of Belief." In *Haunting Experiences: Ghosts in Contemporary Folklore*, edited by Diane Goldstein, Sylvia Grider, and Jeannie Banks Thomas, 171–205. Logan: Utah State University Press.

Goldstein, Diane. 2007. "Scientific Rationalism and Supernatural Experience Narratives." In *Haunting Experiences: Ghosts in Contemporary Folklore*, edited by Diane Goldstein, Sylvia Grider, and Jeannie Banks Thomas, 60–78. Logan: Utah State University Press.

Goldstein, Diane, Sylvia Grider, and Jeannie Banks Thomas, eds. 2007. *Haunting Experiences: Ghosts in Contemporary Folklore.* Logan: Utah State University Press.

Goss, Michael. "Alien Big Cat Sightings in Britain: A Possible Rumour Legend?" *Folklore* 103 (2): 184–202.

Gutowski, John A. 1978. "The Protofestival: Local Guide to American Folk Behavior." *Journal of the Folklore Institute* 15 (2): 112–32.

Gutowski, John A. 1998. "The Beast of 'Busco: An American Tradition." *Midwestern Folklore* 24: 3–148.

Halpert, Herbert Norman. 1947. "Folktales and Legends from the New Jersey Pines: A Collection and a Study." PhD diss., Indiana University.

Halpin, Marjorie M. 1980. "Investigating the Goblin Universe." In *Manlike Monsters on Trial: Early Records and Modern Evidence*, edited by Michael M. Ames and Marjorie M. Halpin, 3–26. Vancouver: University of British Columbia Press.

Hammel, Eugene. 1951. "The Side Hill Guanos." *Western Folklore* 10: 322.

Harling, Kristie. 1971. "The Grunch: An Example of New Orleans Teen-age Folklore." *Louisiana Miscellany* 3 (2): 15–20.

Harris, Jason. 2015. "Shadows of the Past in the Sunshine State: St. Augustine Ghost Lore and Tourism." *Western Folklore* 74 (3–4): 309–42.

Harris, William. 1977. "The White River Monster of Jackson County, Arkansas: A Historical Summary of Oral and Popular Growth and Change in a Legend." *Mid-South Folklore* 5: 3–23.

Hawes, Bess Lomax. 1968. "La Llorona in Juvenile Hall." *Western Folklore* 27 (3): 153–70.

Hawley, Herbert J. 1946. "The Sea Serpent of Silver Lake." *New York Folklore Quarterly* 2: 191–96.

Henderson, M. Carole. 1976. "Monsters of the West: The Sasquatch and the Ogopogo." In *Folklore of Canada*, edited by Edith Fowke, 251–61. Toronto: McClelland & Stewart.

Heuvelmans, Bernard. 1965. *On the Track of Unknown Animals*. Translated by Richard Garnett. New York: Hill & Wang.

Hill, Douglas, and Pat Williams. 1965. *The Supernatural*. New York: Hawthorn Books.

Hobsbawm, Eric. 1983. "Introduction: Inventing Traditions." In *The Invention of Tradition*, edited by Eric Hobsbawm and Terence Ranger, 1–14. Cambridge, UK: Cambridge University Press.

Hobsbawm, Eric, and Terrence Ranger, eds. 1983. *The Invention of Tradition*. Cambridge, UK: Cambridge University Press.

Hudson, Arthur Palmer, and Peter Kyle McCarter. 1934. "The Bell Witch of Tennessee and Mississippi: A Folk Legend." *Journal of American Folklore* 47 (183): 45–63.

Hufford, David J. 1976. "Ambiguity and the Rhetoric of Belief." *Keystone Folklore* 21: 11–24.

Hufford, David. 1977. "Humanoids and Anomalous Lights: Taxonomic and Epistemological Problems." *Fabula* 18 (1): 234–41.

Hufford, David J. 1982. *The Terror That Comes in the Night: An Experience-Centered Study of Supernatural Assault Traditions*. Philadelphia: University of Pennsylvania Press.

Hufford, David J. 1982. "Traditions of Disbelief." *New York Folklore* 8 (3): 3–4, 47–55.

Hufford, David J. 1995. "Beings without Bodies: An Experience-Centered Theory of the Belief in Spirits." In *Out of the Ordinary*, edited by Barbara Walker, 11–45. Logan: Utah State University Press.

Hufford, David J. 1995. "The Experience-Centered Analysis of Belief Stories: A Haunting Example in Honor of Kenny Goldstein." In *Fields of Folklore: Essays in Honor of Kenneth S. Goldstein*, edited by R. D. Abrahams, 55–89. Bloomington, IN: Trickster.

Hufford, David J. 2001. "An Experience Centered Approach to Hauntings." In *Hauntings and Poltergeists: Multidisciplinary Perspectives*, edited by J. Houran and R. Lange, 18–40. Jefferson, NC: McFarland.

Hunter, Don, and Rene Dahinden. 1993. *Sasquatch/Bigfoot: The Search for North America's Incredible Creature*. Rev. ed. Richmond Hill, ON: Firefly Books.

Hurston, Zora Neale. 1938. "Zombies." In *Tell My Horse: Voodoo and Life in Haiti and Jamaica*. Philadelphia: J. B. Lippincott.

Ingemark, Camilla Asplund. 2008. "The Octopus in the Sewers: An Ancient Legend Analogue." *Journal of Folklore Research* 45 (2): 145–70.

James, Ronald M. 1992. "Knockers, Knackers, and Ghosts: Immigrant Folklore in the Western Mines." *Western Folklore* 51 (2): 153–77.

Jones, Louis C. 1944. "The Ghosts of New York: An Analytical Study." *Journal of America Folklore* 57 (226): 237–54.

Jung, Carl G. 1959. *Flying Saucers: A Modern Myth of Things Seen in the Skies*. New York: New American Library.

Keel, John A. 1970. *Strange Creatures from Time and Space*. Greenwich, CT: Fawcett.

Kimiecik, Kathy. 1998. "The Strange Case of the Silver Lake Sea Serpent." *New York Folklore* 9 (2): 10–11.

Kirtley, Bacil F. 1964. "Unknown Hominids and New World Legends." *Western Folklore* 23 (2): 77–90.

Koven, Mikel J. 2000. " 'Have I Got a Monster for You!' Some Thoughts on the Golem, the X-Files and the Jewish Horror Movie." *Folklore* 111: 217–30.

Koven, Mikel J. 2003. "The Terror Tale: Urban Legends and the Slasher Film." *Scope: An Online Journal of Film Studies*. https://www.nottingham.ac.uk/scope/documents/2003/may-2003/koven.pdf.

Koven, Mikel J. 2007. "Studying the Urban Legend Film." In *Film, Folklore, and Urban Legends*, 99–111. Lanham, MD: Scarecrow.

Koven, Mikel. 2008. "The Folklore of the Zombie Film." In *Zombie Culture: Autopsies of the Living Dead*, edited by Shawn McIntosh and Marc Leverette, 19–34. Lanham, MD: Scarecrow.

Koven, Mikel. 2015. "Tradition and the International Zombie Film: The Movies." In *Putting the Supernatural in Its Place: Folklore, the Hypermodern, and the Ethereal*, edited by Jeannie Banks Thomas, 90–125. Logan: University of Utah Press.

Langlois, Janet L. 1978. "Belle Gunness, the Lady Bluebeard: Community Legend as Metaphor." *Journal of the Folklore Institute* 15 (2): 147–60.

Laycock, Joseph P. 2008. "Mothman: Monster, Disaster and Community." *Fieldwork in Religion* 3 (1): 70–86.

Leach, MacEdward. 1961. "Jamaican Duppy Lore." *Journal of American Folklore* 74 (293): 207–15.

Levina, Marina, and Diem-My T. Bui 2013. *Monster Culture in the 21st Century: A Reader*. New York: Bloomsbury Academic.

Lindahl, Carl. 2005. "Ostensive Healing: Pilgrimage to the San Antonio Ghost Tracks." *Journal of American Folklore* 118 (468): 164–85.

Manning, Paul. 2005. "Jewish Ghosts, Knackers, Tommyknockers, and Other Sprites of Capitalism in the Cornish Mines." *Cornish Studies* 13 (1): 216–55.

Manning, Paul. 2017. "No Ruins. No Ghosts." *Preternature: Critical and Historical Studies on the Preternatural* 6 (1): 63–92.

McCloy, James F., and Ray Miller Jr. 1976. *The Jersey Devil*. Moorestown, NJ: Middle Atlantic.

McCloy, James F., and Ray Miller Jr. 1998. *Phantom of the Pines: More Tales of the Jersey Devil*. Moorestown, NJ: Middle Atlantic.

McLeod, Michael. 2009. *Anatomy of a Beast: Obsession and Myth on the Trail of Bigfoot*. Berkeley: University of California Press.

McNeil, Lynne. 2015. "Twihards, Buffistas, and Vampire Fanlore: The Internet." In *Putting the Supernatural in Its Place: Folklore, the Hypermodern, and the Ethereal*, edited by Jeannie Banks Thomas, 126–45. Logan: University of Utah Press.

McNeill, Lynne, and Elizabeth Tucker, eds. 2018. *Legend Tripping: A Contemporary Legend Casebook*. Logan: Utah State University Press.

Meder, Theo. 2007. "The Hunt for Winnie the Puma: Wild Animals in a Civilized Dutch Environment." *Contemporary Legend*, new ser., 10: 94–127.

Meurger, Michel, and Claude Gagnon. 1989. *Lake Monster Traditions: A Cross-Cultural Analysis*. London: Fortean Tomes.

Milligan, Linda. 1990. "The 'Truth' about the Bigfoot Legend." *Western Folklore* 49 (1): 83–98.

Milspaw, Yvonne J., and Wesley K. Evans. 2010. "Variations on Vampires: Live Action Role Playing, Fantasy and the Revival of Traditional Beliefs." *Western Folklore* 69 (2): 211–50.

Mitchell, Pat. 1989. "Of Sea Serpents and Sinkhole Sam." *Kanhistique* 15 (3): 2–3.

Mittman, Asa Simon, and Peter J. Dendle, eds. 2012. *The Ashgate Research Companion to Monsters and the Monstrous.* Aldershot, UK: Ashgate.

Monger, George. 1992. "Dragons and Big Cats." *Folklore* 103 (2): 203–6.

Moran, Mark, and Mark Sceurman. 2004. *Weird U.S.: Your Travel Guide to America's Local Legends and Best Kept Secrets.* New York: Sterling.

Murad, Turhon A. 1988. "Teaching Anthropology and Critical Thinking with the Question 'Is There Something Big Afoot?'" *Current Anthropology* 29 (5): 787–89.

Musharbash, Yasmine, and Geir Henning Presterudstuen, eds. 2014. *Monster Anthropology in Australasia and Beyond.* New York: Palgrave Macmillan.

Musharbash, Yasmine, and Geir Henning Presterudstuen, eds. 2020. *Monster Anthropology: Ethnographic Explorations of Transforming Social Worlds through Monsters.* London: Bloomsbury Academic.

Narváez, Peter. 1997. "Newfoundland Berry Pickers 'In the Fairies': Maintaining Spatial, Temporal, and Moral Boundaries through Legendry." In *The Good People: New Fairylore Essays*, edited by Peter Narváez, 336–68. Lexington: University Press of Kentucky.

Neralich, Jon. 1996. "'They're Gonna Come After You': Snake Stories from the Ozarks." *Mid-America Folklore* 24 (2): 55–64.

Newall, Venetia. 1981. "West Indian Ghosts." In *The Folklore of Ghosts*, edited by Hilda R. Ellis Davidson and W.M.S. Russell, 73–93. Cambridge: D. S. Brewer.

Nickell, Joe. 2000. "The Flatwoods UFO Monster." *Skeptical Inquirer* 24 (6): 15–19.

Opsasnick, Mark. 2007. *The Real Story behind the Exorcist: A Study of the Haunted Boy and Other True-Life Horror Legends from around the Nation's Capital.* Bloomington, IL: Xlibris.

Osbone, August Knapp. 1955. "The Green Fly Monster." *New York Folklore Quarterly* 2: 214–15.

Owens, Trevor. 2015. "Lego, Handcraft, and Costumed Zombies: What Zombies Do on Flickr." *New Directions in Folklore* 13 (1–2): 71–92.

Park, Katharine, and Lorraine J. Daston. 1981. "Unnatural Conceptions: The Study of Monsters in Sixteenth- and Seventeenth Century France and England." *Past & Present* 92 (1): 20–54.

Parsons, Elsie Clews. 1928. "Spirit Cult in Hayti." *Journal de la Société des Américanistes de Paris* 20: 157–79.

Peck, Andrew. 2015. "At the Modems of Madness: The Slender Man, Ostension, and the Digital Age." *Contemporary Legend*, ser. 3, 5: 14–37.

Peck, Andrew. 2017. "Capturing the Slender Man: Online and Offline Vernacular Practice in the Digital Age." *Cultural Analysis* 16 (1): 30–48.

Poole, W. Scott. 2011. *Monsters in America: Our Historical Obsession with the Hideous and the Haunting.* Waco: Baylor University Press.

Puglia, David J. 2019. "The Goatman and Washington, D.C.: Strange Sightings and the Fear of the Encroaching City." In *Supernatural Cities*, edited by Karl Bell, 145–64. Woodbridge, UK: Boydell & Brewer.

Radford, Benjamin. 2010. *Scientific Paranormal Investigation: How to Solve Unexplained Mysteries.* Corrales, NM: Rhombus.

Radford, Benjamin. 2011. *Tracking the Chupacabra: The Vampire Beast in Fact, Fiction, and Folklore*. Albuquerque: University of New Mexico Press.

Radford, Benjamin. 2016. *Creepy Clowns*. Albuquerque: University of New Mexico Press.

Radford, Benjamin, and Joe Nickell. 2006. *Lake Monster Mysteries: Investigating the World's Most Elusive Creatures*. Lexington: University Press of Kentucky.

Rayburn, Otto Ernest. 1960. "Some Fabulous Monsters and Other Folk Beliefs from the Ozarks." *Midwest Folklore* 10 (1): 27–32.

Regal, Brian. 2015. "The Jersey Devil: A Political Animal." *NJS: An Interdisciplinary Journal* 1 (1): 79–103.

Rhone, George E. 1963. "The Giwoggle." *Keystone Folklore Quarterly* 8 (1): 44–48.

Rieti, Barbara. 1997. "'The Blast' in Newfoundland Fairy Tradition." In *The Good People: New Fairylore Essays*, edited by Peter Narváez, 284–98. Lexington: University Press of Kentucky.

Rojcewicz, Peter M. 1987. "The 'Men in Black' Experience and Tradition." *Journal of American Folklore* 100: 148–60.

Rudinger, Joel D. 1976. "Folk Ogres of the Firelands: Narrative Variations of a North Central Ohio Community." *Indiana Folklore* 9: 41–93.

Rudy, Jill Terry, and Jarom Lyle McDonald. 2016. "Baba Yaga, Monsters of the Week, and Pop Culture's Formation of Wonder and Families through Monstrosity." *Humanities* 5 (2): 40–57.

Rushing, J. Rhett. 2012. "Monsters in Texas." In *First Timers and Old Timers: The Texas Folklore Society Fire Burns On*, edited by Kenneth L. Untiedt, 285–92. Denton: University of North Texas Press.

Sanderson, Ivan T. 2006 [1961]. *Abominable Snowmen*. Kempton, IL: Adventures Unlimited.

Scott, Niall, ed. 2007. *Monsters and the Monstrous: Myths and Metaphors of Enduring Evil*. Amsterdam: Rodolpi.

Senior, W. A. 2003. "Where Have All the Monsters Gone?" *Journal of the Fantastic in the Arts* 14 (2): 214–16.

Sergent, Donnie Jr., and Jeff Wamsley. 2002. *Mothman: The Facts behind the Legend*. Point Pleasant, WV: Mothman Lives.

Shoalts, Adam. 2019. "The Evolution of 'Monsters' in North American Exploration and Travel Literature, 1607–1930." PhD. diss., McMaster University.

Shoemaker, Henry W. 1951. "The Werewolf in Pennsylvania." *New York Folklore Quarterly* 7 (2): 145–55.

Shoemaker, Henry W. 1957. "Werewolves in the Pennsylvania Wilds Once More." *Keystone Folklore Quarterly* 2 (1): 6–7.

Simpson, George Gaylord. 1984. "Mammals and Cryptozoology." *Proceedings of the American Philosophical Society* 128 (1): 1–19.

Smith, Paul. 1992. "'Read All about It! Elvis Eaten by Drug-Crazed Giant Alligators': Contemporary Legend and the Popular Press." *Contemporary Legend* 2: 41–71.

Stecker, John K. 1965 [1926]. "Reptiles of the South and Southwest in Folk-lore." In *Rainbow in the Morning*, edited by J. Frank Dobie, 56–69. Dallas: Southern Methodist University Press.

Steese, Charles M. 1956. "Hoop Snakes and Huckleberries." *Keystone Folklore Quarterly* 1 (3): 33–35.

Stewart, Susan. 1982. "The Epistemology of the Horror Story." *Journal of American Folklore* 95 (375): 33–50.

Sullivan, Jeremiah J., and James F. McCloy. 1974. "The Jersey Devil's Finest Hour." *New York Folklore Quarterly* 30: 231–38.

Suttles, Wayne P. 1972. "On the Cultural Trail of the Sasquatch." *Northwest Anthropological Research Notes* 6 (1): 65–90.

Thomas, Jeannie Banks. 2007. "The Usefulness of Ghost Stories." In *Haunting Experiences: Ghosts in Contemporary Folklore*, edited by Diane Goldstein, Sylvia Grider, and Jeannie Banks Thomas, 25–59. Logan: Utah State University Press.

Thomas, Jeannie Banks, ed. 2015. *Putting the Supernatural in Its Place: Folklore, the Hypermodern, and the Ethereal*. Logan: University of Utah Press.

Tolbert, Jeffrey A. 2013. "'The Sort of Story That Has You Covering Your Mirrors': The Case of Slender Man." *Semiotic Review* 2 https://semioticreview.com/ojs/index.php/sr/article/view/19.

Tryon, Henry H. 1939. *Fearsome Critters*. Cornwall, NY: Idlewild.

Tucker, Elizabeth. 2006. "Cropsey at Camp." *Voices: The Journal of New York Folklore* 32 (3–4): 42.

Tucker, Elizabeth. 2007. *Haunted Halls: Ghostlore of American College Campuses*. Jackson: University Press of Mississippi.

Van Duzer, Chet. 2013. "Hic Sunt Dracones: The Geography and Cartography of Monsters." In *The Ashgate Research Companion to Monsters and the Monstrous*, edited by Asa Simon Mittman and Peter J. Dendle, 387–436. Aldershot, UK: Ashgate.

Van Duzer, Chet A. 2013. *Sea Monsters on Medieval and Renaissance Maps*. London: British Library.

von Sydow, Carl Wilhelm. 1948 [1932]. "On the Spread of Tradition." *Selected Papers on Folklore*, 11–43. Copenhagen: Rosenkilde and Bagger.

von Sydow, Carl Wilhelm. 1948 [1934]. "Geography and Folk-Tale Oicotypes." *Selected Papers on Folklore*, 44–59. Copenhagen: Rosenkilde and Bagger.

Walker, Barbara, ed. 1995. *Out of the Ordinary: Folklore and the Supernatural*. Logan: Utah State University Press.

Ward, Donald. 1977. "The Little Man Who Wasn't There: Encounters with the Supranormal." *Fabula* 18: 212–25.

Weinstock, Jeffrey Andrew, ed. 2020. *The Monster Theory Reader*. Minneapolis: University of Minnesota Press.

Wells, Rosemary. 1997. "The Making of an Icon: The Tooth Fairy in North American Folklore and Popular Culture." In *The Good People: New Fairylore Essays*, edited by Peter Narváez, 426–54. Lexington: University Press of Kentucky.

Woodyard, Chris, and Simon Young. 2019. "Three Notes and a Handlist of North American Fairies." *Supernatural Studies* 6 (1): 56–85.

Permissions

Ackermann, Hans-W., and Jeanine Gauthier. "The Ways and Nature of the Zombi." *Journal of American Folklore* vol. 104, no. 414 (1991): 466–494. Reprinted with the permission of the American Folklore Society.

Ashton, John. "Ecotypes, Etiology, and Contemporary Legend: The 'Webber' Cycle in Western Newfoundland." *Contemporary Legend* n.s. 4 (2001): 48–60. Reprinted with permission of the International Society for Contemporary Legend Research and Mrs. Sheila Ashton.

Coleman, Loren. "Alligators-in-the-Sewers: A Journalistic Origin." *Journal of American Folklore* vol. 92, no. 365 (1979): 335–338. Reprinted with the permission of the American Folklore Society and the author.

Dresser, Norine. "American Vampires: Legend, the Media, and Tubal Transmission." From *American Vampires: Fans, Victims, Practitioners* (1989). Excerpted with permission of the author.

Gillespie, Angus Kress. "The Jersey Devil." *Journal of Regional Cultures* vol. 5 (1985): 59–73. Reprinted with permission of the University of Wisconsin Press and the author.

Haring, Lee, and Mark Breslerman, "The Cropsey Maniac." *New York Folklore* vol. 3 (1977): 15–27. Reprinted with permission of the New York Folklore Society and the authors.

Leary, James P. "The Boondocks Monster of Camp Wapehani." *Indiana Folklore* vol. 6, no. 2 (1973): 174-190. Reprinted with permission of the Hoosier Folklore Society and the author.

Morrell, Alan L. "A Nessie in Mormon Country." In *Between Pulpit and Pew: The Supernatural World in Mormon History and Folklore* (2011), ed. W. Paul Reeve and Michael Scott Van Wagenen, 159–167. Logan: Utah State University Press. Reprinted with permission of Utah State University Press and the author.

Peck, Andrew. "Tall, Dark, and Loathsome: The Emergence of a Legend Cycle in the Digital Age." *Journal of American Folklore* (2015) vol. 128, no. 509: 333–348. Reprinted with permission of the University of Illinois Press and the author.

Puglia, David J. "Getting Maryland's Goat: Diffusion and Canonization of Prince George's County's Goatman Legend." *Contemporary Legend* series 3, vol. 3 (2013): 63–77. Reprinted with permission of the International Society for Contemporary Legend Research and the author.

Seemann, Charlie. "The 'Char-Man': A Local Legend of the Ojai Valley." *Western Folklore* vol. 40, no. 3 (1981): 252–260. Reprinted with permission of the Western States Folklore Society and the author.

Taft, Michael. "Sasquatch-Like Creatures in Newfoundland: A Study in the Problems of Belief, Perception, and Reportage." In *Manlike Monsters on Trial: Early Records and Modern Evidence* (1980), ed. Marjorie Halpin and Michael Ames, 83–96. Vancouver: University of British Columbia Press. Reprinted with permission of the University of British Columbia Press and the author.

Torrez, Mercedes Elaina. "Evoking the Shadow Beast: Disability and Chicano Advocacy in San Antonio's Donkey Lady Folktale." *Contemporary Legend* series 3, vol. 6 (2016):

1–16. Reprinted with permission of the International Society for Contemporary Legend Research and the author.

Tucker, Elizabeth. "The Lake Lieberman Monster." *Midwestern Folklore* vol. 30, no. 1 (2004): 36–45. Reprinted with permission of the Hoosier Folklore Society and the author.

Index

About the Editor

David J. Puglia is Associate Professor and Deputy Chairperson in the English Department at Bronx Community College of the City University of New York, where he teaches courses in folklore and children's literature. He has been a member of the International Society for Contemporary Legend Research since 2010 and of ISCLR's Executive Council since 2013. In 2011, he won the Dr. David Buchan Student Essay Prize for his Goatman research (featured in this casebook). He is the author of three books on state and regional legend and lore: *South Central Pennsylvania Legends & Lore* (2012), *Maryland Legends: Folklore from the Old Line State* (2014; co-author Trevor J. Blank), and *Tradition, Urban Identity, and the Baltimore "Hon": The Folk in the City*. He has edited several other scholarly projects, including the journal *New Directions in Folklore* (2014–2018) and ISCLR's newsletter *FOAFTale News* (2015–16), and serves on the editorial boards of *Voices: The Journal of New York Folklore*, *Supernatural Studies*, and *New Directions in Folklore*. He lives in New York with his wife Mira, who is also a folklorist.

About the Authors

Hans-W. Ackermann is Professor Emeritus in the Department of Microbiology at Laval University.

John Ashton was Principal of Sir Winfred Grenfell College in Corner Brook, Newfoundland and Labrador.

Mark Breslerman was Lee Haring's student at Brooklyn College.

David Clarke is Reader and Principal Lecturer in Journalism and co-founder of the Centre for Contemporary Legend at Sheffield Hallam University in the United Kingdom.

Loren Coleman is a cryptozoologist and Director of the International Cryptozoology Museum in Portland, Maine.

Gail de Vos is an author, storyteller, librarian, and Adjunct Associate Professor at the University of Alberta.

Norine Dresser is a folklorist who taught for twenty years at California State University, Los Angeles.

Lisa Gabbert is Associate Professor in the English Department at Utah State University and served as Director of the Folklore Program from 2013 to 2019.

Jeanine Gauthier was a senior nurse in the Douglas Hospital Center for Mental Diseases in Verdun, Quebec.

Angus Kress Gillespie is Professor of American Studies at Rutgers University, where he founded the New Jersey Folk Festival and served as its director for forty-five years.

Lee Haring is Professor Emeritus of English at Brooklyn College of the City University of New York.

James P. Leary is Professor Emeritus of Folklore and Scandinavian Studies at the University of Wisconsin, where he co-founded the Center for the Study of Upper Midwestern Cultures.

Carl Lindahl is Martha Gano Houstoun Research Professor in the Department of English at the University of Houston.

Alan L. Morrell is the Artifacts Curator of the Church History Museum in Salt Lake City, Utah.

Andrew Peck is Assistant Professor of Strategic Communication at Miami University.

Benjamin Radford is Deputy Editor of *Skeptical Inquirer* science magazine and a Research Fellow with the non-profit educational organization the Committee for Skeptical Inquiry.

Charlie Seemann is the former Executive Director of the Western Folklife Center in Elko, Nevada.

Michael Taft, now retired, was the head of the Archive of Folk Culture at the American Folklife Center, Library of Congress.

Mercedes Elaina Torrez is the Coordinator of the Academic Learning Center at Texas A&M University, San Antonio.

Elizabeth Tucker is Distinguished Service Professor of English at Binghamton University.